New Museum Theory and Practice

To Mark

New Museum Theory and Practice

An Introduction

Edited by Janet Marstine

Blackwell
Publishing

Editorial material and organization © 2006 by Blackwell Publishing

BLACKWELL PUBLISHING
350 Main Street, Malden, MA 02148-5020, USA
9600 Garsington Road, Oxford OX4 2DQ, UK
550 Swanston Street, Carlton, Victoria 3053, Australia

The right of Janet Marstine to be identified as the Author of the Editorial Material in this Work
has been asserted in accordance with the UK Copyright, Designs, and Patents Act 1988.

First published 2006 by Blackwell Publishing Ltd

8   2011

Library of Congress Cataloging-in-Publication Data

New museum theory and practice : an introduction / edited by Janet Marstine.
    p. cm.
    Includes bibliographical references and index.
    ISBN: 978-1-4051-0558-3 (hard cover : alk. paper)
    ISBN: 978-1-4051-0559-0 (pbk. : alk. paper)   1. Museum exhibits.   2. Museum
exhibits—Political aspects.   3. Museum techniques.   4. Museums—Philosophy.   I.
Marstine, Janet.

    AM151.N49 2005
    069'.5—dc22

                                                                              2005013098

A catalogue record for this title is available from the British Library.

Set in 10.5/13pt Dante
by Graphicraft Limited, Hong Kong
Printed and bound in Singapore
by C.O.S. Printers Pte Ltd

The publisher's policy is to use permanent paper from mills that operate a sustainable forestry
policy, and which has been manufactured from pulp processed using acid-free and elementary
chlorine-free practices. Furthermore, the publisher ensures that the text paper and cover board
used have met acceptable environmental accreditation standards.

For further information on
Blackwell Publishing, visit our website:
www.blackwellpublishing.com

CONTENTS

FIGURES

PREFACE:
HOW TO USE THIS BOOK

This book is organized to meet the needs of readers without prior knowledge of new museum theory. It appeals to students in diverse areas of culture studies, including history, literary criticism, anthropology, gender studies, sociology, art history, studio art, American studies, and museum studies. In 12 newly commissioned chapters and an extensive introduction, it combines theory and practice so that students both gain familiarity with a conceptual framework and devise strategies to apply this framework. As a unity, the essays call for the transformation of the museum from a site of worship and awe to one of critical inquiry; they look to a museum that is transparent in its decision-making, willing to share power, and activist in promoting human rights. The larger goal of the project is to empower the reader to become an advocate for change.

The introduction makes abstract concepts of museum theory accessible to undergraduate and beginning graduate students. It defines museum theory by deconstructing the notion of authenticity and discussing issues of framing. It notes the crucial role that artists, from pop art to cyberfeminism, have played in the development of new museum theory. It identifies four archetypes of the museum: shrine; market-driven industry; colonizing space; and post-museum – an institution that declares itself an active player in the making of meaning. It presents the Foucauldian and alternative views of museum history. Finally, it introduces the debate on whether museums can or cannot change.

Part I presents theory through historical overviews and vivid examples. Section A, "Surveys and Groundwork," traces the development of the museum and of museum theory with histories of architecture, feminist curation, and conservation. Section B, "Case Studies in Contemporary Practice," explores the museum as a contested site through four examples: shrine

(Monticello); spectacle (Experience Music Project); indigenous cultural center (Djomi Museum); and vestige of colonial authority (South African National Gallery).

Part II offers guidance on how to put theory into practice. It "walks" the reader through a museum exhibit, diverse museum websites, and a museum archives, explaining how to become a critical thinker in each of these venues. It also identifies opportunities for students to explore new museum theory in their studio art education and in the university gallery.

All chapters include mini-introductions that synopsize the theoretical concerns of the authors. Questions for discussion follow each chapter; they make connections among chapters and foster independent thinking.

ACKNOWLEDGMENTS

Many thanks are due to the colleagues, friends, and family members who helped keep me confident, focused, and sane. At Blackwell, Jayne Fargnoli, executive editor, culture studies, saw the potential for this project even before I did. I will be forever grateful for her unswerving faith in my efforts and her keen understanding of my vision for the book. Ken Provencher, senior development editor, walked me through the process with patience and generosity. At Central Washington University (CWU), Art Department chair Michael Chinn provided the flexible teaching environment I needed to get this project done. CWU dean of the College of Arts and Humanities Liahna Armstrong was a gifted mentor and a dear friend throughout. At Bowdoin College, Department of Art History colleagues Linda Docherty, Clifton Olds, and Susan Wegner inspired in me a lifelong commitment to undergraduate teaching, a commitment that is at the very heart of this book. And online, my contributors – half of whom I've never even met – created with me a virtual community of museum theory that mitigated my feelings of isolation, both in my small town of Ellensburg in the shadow of the Cascade Mountains and in my home away from home, Aarhus, Denmark. The contributors' collaborative efforts are what gives this textbook its organic quality. A special note of appreciation goes to reviewers Bettina Carbonell, Helen Rees Leahy, and Christopher Steiner; their insightful analysis of the manuscript gave perspective to the project.

I relish time shared with the friends who are my safety net: taking walks with Barbara Pickett; having conversations at the playground with Alison Carpenter and Denise Horton; observing Shabbat with Elise Herman; accepting the many small kindnesses of Joan Wood; doing errands with Sherry Hainsworth; eating sushi lunches with Dae-ae Kim; taking trips to the Danish countryside with Cecilia Brynskov; discovering Dutch humor from Petra

Sjouwerman; making interdisciplinary connections with Virginia Mack and Viola Burau; experiencing life as an adoptive mother with Mary Chris Bulger; sharing life's little ironies with Janet Strahosky.

My parents, Connie and Sheldon Marstine, showed me, as always, unconditional support. My paternal grandmother, Helen Marstine, who is now 101 years old, has been a model of determination. My late maternal grandmother, Ellie Goodman, instilled in me my museum-going appetite. My late brother, Clay, led me to prioritize gender theory in my work. My in-laws, too, were part of the process. Debbie Polishook sketched out for me the world of publishing and Rob Polishook showed me the importance of taking risks. Janis Polishook was always willing to listen. Sy Polishook restrained himself from asking when I would be done. My children, Jeanie and Jakey, trudged enthusiastically (at least most of the time) through countless museums and checked my capacity to become too self-absorbed. My husband, Mark Polishook, coached me through too many hand-wringing sessions with kindness and humor. I dedicate this book to him, the love of my life.

INTRODUCTION
Janet Marstine

What is New Museum Theory?

We live today in a profoundly museological world – a world that in no small
measure is itself a product and effect of some two centuries of museological
meditations. Museums are one of the central sites at which our modernity
has been generated, (en)gendered, and sustained over that time. They are so
natural, ubiquitous, and indispensable to us today that it takes considerable
effort to think ourselves back to a world without them, and to think through
the shadows cast by the massive and dazzling familiarity of this truly un-
canny social technology. Our world is unthinkable without this extraordinary
invention.[1]

As museum theorist Donald Preziosi asserts, museums are such a dominant
feature of our cultural landscape that they frame our most basic assumptions about the past and about ourselves. People who might not ordinarily
think much about museums may find themselves engaged in debate if an
institution's decisions challenge their value systems. Even if you've never
been to the Smithsonian, your conception of the bombing of Hiroshima
may be colored by the heated discourse on the exhibition of the Enola Gay,
the B-29 that dropped the bomb, which opened in 1995 at the National Air
and Space Museum. Poor planning, insensitivities to closely held beliefs,
and grandstanding by flag-waving congressmen pitted veterans and their
families against historians with new theories, and led to the rejection of
critical inquiry in favor of a celebratory tale. How does the Enola Gay represent the heroic use of technology in a fight of good over evil and how
does it mark the beginning of the end, the direction of technology for mass
destruction? The museum was prevented from posing this difficult but important question.[2]

1

Though you may not have set foot in the British Museum, your perceptions of the UK as a democracy and as a former colonial power are likely mediated by the "Elgin Marbles" controversy, in which the British Museum refuses to return those famous Parthenon sculptures to Greece, their country of origin. The museum justifies its claims through a rhetoric of "salvage:" Lord Elgin "rescued" the sculptures through legitimate means some 200 years ago from the politically turbulent Ottoman Empire, and the British are keeping them still to guard against damage from the neglect, earthquakes, and pollution they might face in Greece. The fact is the "Elgin Marbles" have become as much a part of British heritage as they have of Greek culture. As Timothy Webb has shown, they came to represent Britain as the inheritor of democracy from ancient Athens, thus justifying political decisions including the colonization and domination of other peoples.[3] For Greeks, the British Museum's position is a human rights issue that is denying the nation the jewel of its cultural patrimony. The Greek government charges that Lord Elgin acquired the sculptures through illicit means. Particularly given the recent building campaigns – including a new Acropolis Museum – and the conservation efforts that were part of Greece's 2004 Olympics preparations, Britain's denial of the request for repatriation seems like a slap in the face. In the museum, things are more than just things; museum narratives construct national identity and legitimize groups.

When we look at a museum object we might think that we see something pure and "authentic" – untouched since its creation. We have a tendency to see museum objects as unmediated anchors to the past. Some of our teachers reinforce this notion by characterizing the museum visit as reifying or making "real" the abstract ideas of the classroom with "concrete" artifacts. But, as Fogg Art Museum curator Ivan Gaskell explains, objects have an "afterlife" which must be acknowledged if we are to be critical thinkers.[4] Decisions that museum workers make – about mission statement, architecture, financial matters, acquisitions, cataloguing, exhibition display, wall texts, educational programming, repatriation requests, community relations, conservation, web design, security and reproduction – all impact on the way we understand objects. Museums are not neutral spaces that speak with one institutional, authoritative voice. Museums are about individuals making subjective choices.

In fact, "authenticity" is an illusive construct, an idea that was conceived in the late eighteenth century, around the same time as the museum. At what moment is an object at its "most authentic"? When an artist finishes the last brushstroke? When a monument is first unveiled to the public?

When a garment is worn over and over again in a religious ceremony? Authenticity supposedly evokes an aura, a transcendent experience. But all objects are organic and change over time, despite a conservator's work. And conservators, in consultation with curators, make subjective choices, as the dark varnishes of paintings at the Louvre and the pristine cleaning of canvases at the National Gallery in London attest. In addition, though most museum attributions are reliable, connoisseurship is an art that entails some risk of error; the Rembrandt Research Project has, since 1968, been painstakingly sorting through some 600 purported Rembrandts to identify misattributions. Moreover, our contemporary context shapes our notions of what we think is authentic. For many people, open-air museums such as Colonial Williamsburg in the US, Beamish in the UK, and Skansen in Sweden seem like "authentic" restorations or reconstructions of life in the past. Yet these museums are constantly redefining themselves to both shape and reflect cultural values. As anthropologists Richard Handler and Eric Gable have shown, Williamsburg projected several distinct paradigmatic images over the course of the twentieth century, from colonial revival nostalgia in the 1930s, to Cold War patriotism in the 1950s, to populist social history in the 1980s.[5] Some cultures admire the copy. In Chinese tradition, copying work by the masters is a sign of self-cultivation and of intellectual and moral strength. The cult of authenticity in western culture today is a protective gesture against the relativism of postmodernism and the commodification of culture. It reflects a desire to find our own authentic selves. It is also a distraction from and validation of the "othering" in which museums engage. Claiming "authenticity" is a way for museums to deny the imperialist and patriarchal structures that have informed their institutions.

In the last few decades, museums have grown exponentially in number, size, and variety, and now more people go to museums than ever before. Art museums in the US alone attract approximately a hundred million visitors annually and have been spending some $3 billion on expansion over the last few years.[6] Legoland amusement park in Denmark contains a museum on the history of toys, culminating, of course, in the invention of Lego bricks. San Quentin Prison in California has a museum with a miniature gas chamber and sells the inmate-written *Cooking with Conviction* in its museum store. The feminist collaborative WomEnhouse hosts a virtual museum in which users enter through what's designated "the hymen" to explore projects on the politics of the body, at www.cmp.ucr.edu/womenhouse. The Louvre in Paris has bolstered its image as a sacred yet tourist-oriented space through a glass pyramid addition by architect I. M. Pei that leads to a shopping mall. As professor of comparative literature Andreas Huyssen has shown, museums are a mass medium, "a hybrid space somewhere between public fair and department store." They are a response to the quest for authenticity fueled by the cultural amnesia of our times; the information overload and fast pace of the digital revolution evoke a desire for stability and timelessness. According to Huyssen, this "museal sensibility" also pervades the restorations of city centers, the employment of museum architects for flagship stores of fashion houses like Prada, and the making of our own personal "museums" through video recordings, websites, memoirs, and collectibles.[7]

Within this "museal sensibility," there exists an assumption that museums are neutral, uncontested spaces. When people in Britain are asked to characterize a museum, most conjure up images of kings and queens, armor and weapons. In the US, museums are seen as the most trustworthy and objective of all the institutions that educate American children. According to a recent American Association of Museums survey, 87 percent of respondents deem museums trustworthy while 67 percent trust books and only 50 percent trust television news.[8] Yet, to achieve cultural literacy, it is crucial to understand that museums don't just represent cultural identity, they produce it through framing. To grasp the concept of framing, it is helpful to think about how the meanings of the object shift when it is moved from one institutional context to another. For example, a Maori pendant might be valued for its aesthetic qualities in the art museum and for its link to ancestors in a Maori cultural center.[9]

As Preziosi explains, a frame is not just a piece of wood that assigns the work inside it the signification of art. Framing is a metaphorical process that creates a vision of the past and future based on contemporary needs. Philosopher Jacques Derrida first appropriated the concept of framing for cultural theory in his 1987 essay *"Parergon,"* which critiques Immanuel Kant's "Analytic of the Beautiful." Derrida challenges Kant's assumption that picture frames, drapery on sculpture, and other devices that distinguish what is part of a work from what is outside it are merely ornaments, *"parerga"* or "by-work" to the objects they enhance. Frames not only set boundaries; they provide an ideologically based narrative context that colors our understanding of what's included. In fact, rather than isolating a work from the wider world, framing links the two. Architectural features, lighting design, audio-tour headsets, the museum café, and the larger museum itself are all framing devices. Administrative processes such as registration and cataloguing are at least as important as curation and design, those elements visible to the public. Framelessness, such as is common at museums of modern art, is a framing device as well.[10]

Traditionally, museums frame objects and audiences to control the viewing process, to suggest a tightly woven narrative of progress, an "authentic" mirror of history, without conflict or contradiction. With its pure white walls, minimalist aesthetics, and lack of contextual material, the Van Gogh Museum in Amsterdam, for instance, presents a chronological display that maintains a romanticized image of the artist as a genius and a martyr. Authenticity is posited through Van Gogh's brushstroke, which is upheld as the quintessential marker of creativity. The postmodern museum is sometimes more self-reflexive. Frames are challenged, fragmented, and made transparent as the museum declares itself an active player in the making of meaning. What's typically marginalized or beyond the frame is brought inside of it to dissolve the frame itself. The "Buddenbrooks" House, the ancestral home of writer Thomas Mann in Lübeck, Germany, embraces this approach; faced with the problem that only a few household objects survive, curators in 2000 chose to create a bold, artistic, clearly fictive evocation of period atmosphere, complete with ambient noise such as sounds of the nineteenth-century street. In so doing, they identified the display as a framing device, rather than trying to mimic period style and present it as fact, a formula that disguises framing and that many historic houses cling to in their attempt to evoke nostalgia.

New museum theory, sometimes called critical museum theory or the new museology, holds that, though museum workers commonly naturalize their policies and procedures as professional practice, the decisions these workers make reflect underlying value systems that are encoded in institutional narratives. As Preziosi argues in the quote at the beginning of this introduction, museums are a "social technology," an "invention" that packages culture for our consumption; it's our job to deconstruct this packaging so that we can become critical consumers and lobby for change. In our analysis, we need to look at what museums don't say – what is implicit – as well as what they do state – what is explicit. Theorists call for the transformation of the museum from a site of worship and awe to one of discourse and critical reflection that is committed to examining unsettling histories with sensitivity to all parties; they look to a museum that is transparent in its decision-making and willing to share power. New museum theory is about decolonizing, giving those represented control of their own cultural heritage. It's about real cross-cultural exchange. New museum theory is not, however, monolithic; it embraces many viewpoints. Most contested is the question of change in the museum. Are museums changing or are they merely voicing the rhetoric of change? Are museums capable of change? Are they stuck in time, limited by elitist roots? Or have they always been in the process of change?

New museum theory is an emerging field, formally interjected into academic discourse with Peter Vergo's 1989 anthology *The New Museology*.[11] Vergo and the generation of museum theorists that followed were influenced by artists who, beginning in the 1960s, proclaimed that all representation is political and who articulated through their work a critique of the museum. Fueled by the distrust of institutional control that marked the 1960s, artists began to demand a voice in determining how their works were displayed, interpreted, and conserved. Inspired by the Civil Rights movement, they challenged the museum to be more inclusive, to solicit work by women and artists of color. They looked to Dada and Surrealist exhibitions, which showed that, to transform art, artists also needed to transform spaces of display. And they read the essays of Marxist philosopher Walter Benjamin, who argued that aura and authenticity are social constructions inappropriate and irrelevant to twentieth-century culture.[12]

For example, Marcel Broodthaers, from 1968 to his early death in 1976, created his own subversive museum spaces in which he self-consciously performed museum roles from director to registrar to curator. His infamous "Musée d'Art Moderne, Départment des Aigles" (Museum of Modern Art, Department of Eagles) toured northern Europe for several years in a variety of permutations. For this project, Broodthaers collected over 300 objects that depicted eagles as a heraldic device, and made his own eagles as well. To him, eagles were a powerful symbol of authority and imperialism. He may also have used the eagle as a word pun to convey his bitterness with the museum system; in French, the word for eagle – *aigle* – is close to the word *aigre* – meaning bitter, as in vinegar (or *vinaigre* in French). By appropriating eagle iconography and recontextualizing it in his own museum space, Broodthaers parodied the control that both museums and governmental authorities try to impose. In its new surroundings, the eagle becomes a symbol of wisdom and artistic freedom.

Many other artists have had similarly subversive goals. Daniel Buren in 1965 decided to work exclusively with 8.7-centimeter-wide vertical stripes, color alternating with white or clear bands, and he works this way still. He situates these stripes in strategic places in the museum, such as the grand staircase or the walls surrounding what's considered the "masterpieces" of the collection. The stripes poke fun at the museum's fetishistic insistence that painting is the "highest" art and the brushstroke the marker of genius. They also critique the rituals of display that evoke the notion of "aura." Robert Smithson took a different approach. He rejected the museum altogether, instead creating earthworks that could not be commodified and that changed over time. He saw the gallery as a dead space. He explained, "A work of art when placed in a gallery loses its charge, and becomes a portable object or surface disengaged from the outside world. A vacant white room with lights is still a submission to the neutral. Works of art seen in such spaces seem to be going through a kind of aesthetic convalescence."[13] (Ironically, Smithson's 1970 *Spiral Jetty* at Great Salt Lake was "acquired" in 1999 by Dia Art Foundation as a gift from the estate of the artist.) Louise Lawler critiques the museum through photographing elements of display. Devoid of visitors and other distracting elements, Lawler's photographs present revealing juxtapositions that help the viewer to scrutinize the subjective nature of exhibition practices. Details of art objects and their framing devices, such as wall texts, wall coverings, period furniture, and architectural flourishes, show how the museum makes meaning.

Fred Wilson, Andrea Fraser, and Mark Dion critique the museum from within. During guest residencies in the museum, they examine what is hidden from view as well as what is on display. They curate exhibitions that disrupt the carefully crafted institutional narratives that they find. They perform the diverse roles of museum workers to show how such ritualized behavior constructs meaning. And they create collaborative opportunities to effect change in museum staff and visitors.

Cyberfeminists use the net to undermine the museum as a patriarchal structure and build new modes of communication in which artist, curator, and user not only share power but also become one another. Old Boys' Network (OBN), a real and virtual coalition founded in Berlin in 1997 and active through 2002, was the first international cyberfeminist alliance (www.obn.org). Through its functions and its ironic title, it appropriates the patriarchal systems of support of the museum and of cyberspace to forge new feminist communities. The OBN website provides the utility of a conventional museum website, including a databank of artists' work, a library, and a calendar of events. But it differs dramatically from the museum through its equalizing, self-reflexive tone, its facilitating of collaboration, and its contextualizing of subversive projects in which gender figures prominently. Members explain their goals clearly through FAQs and theoretical writings. A forum, a listserve, and real-time conferences encourage the sharing of ideas and generate new members. Members' projects challenge patriarchal systems. Cornelia Sollfrank, a founding member of OBN, engages in hacking. In "Female Extension" (1997), she hacked into the first net.art competition held by a museum, flooding Hamburg's Galerie der Gegenwart with more than 200 entries by virtual women net artists. This action was her way of resisting for net.art the commodification, hierarchal classification, and shutting down of communication that the modern museum imposes. Such projects create a challenge for "real-time" museum curators who are trying to figure out what it means to "collect" internet art.[14]

The object of this book is to introduce readers to key strands of the discourse in new museum theory and to empower them to take part in determining the future of museums by drawing on theory. The 12 original chapters make significant contributions to the field while creating an organic whole that makes an effective textbook for undergraduate and graduate courses in museum studies. Using language accessible to diverse audiences, it presents theory through vivid examples and historical overviews in part I, and shows how to put this theory into practice in part II. Both parts are equally important in preparing the reader to become a voice for change. Chapters cover a range of museums around the world – from art to history, anthropology to music, along with historic houses, cultural centers, Keeping Places, virtual sites, and commercial display institutions that appropriate the conventions of the museum. The text considers large encyclopedic museums, steeped in history, noting their ability to influence; it explores smaller and newer museums as well, some of which have more freedom to take risks. Authors come from the UK, Canada, the US, and Australia, and from a variety of fields that inform culture studies. Some are academics, others are curators, and several are both. On the potential for change in the museum, several authors are optimistic and others more cautious. The wide scope and multiplicity of viewpoints together generate a vision of museums that is multi-dimensional and that avoids the trap of overgeneralization.

What is a Museum?

In contemporary culture, the notion of the museum holds diverse and contradictory meanings. Theorists, who come from many disciplines including sociology, psychology, anthropology, art history, history, philosophy, linguistics, literary criticism, and gender studies, typically see the museum in multiple guises but disagree on what these guises are. Most commonly heard are the metaphors of museum as shrine, market-driven industry, colonizing space, and post-museum. These categories are not mutually exclusive and clearly overlap. Moreover, no one museum represents exactly one of these paradigms. For example, a museum may profess to be a shrine but financial issues are still central – they're just hidden from public view; an institution may aim to be a center for critical inquiry but there will always be groups who see it as a colonized space where they don't have a voice.

Shrine

One of the longest-standing and most traditional ways to envision the museum is as a sacred space. This is an iconic image to which many museums still aspire. In the paradigm of the shrine, the museum has therapeutic potential. It is a place of sanctuary removed from the outside world. Museum collections are fetishized; the museum as shrine declares that its objects possess an aura that offers spiritual enlightenment as it inspires Platonic values of beauty and morality. Sir Kenneth Clark, formerly director of the National Gallery in London and host of the popular 1970s BBC television series *Civilization*, championed this ideal. He waxed lyrical: "The only reason for bringing together works of art in a public place is that . . . they produce in us a kind of exalted happiness. For a moment there is a clearing in the jungle; we pass on refreshed, with our capacity for life increased and with some memory of the sky."[15] The museum as shrine leads viewers to assign meanings to objects totally unrelated to their original function or intention. Wall texts providing context and other educational materials are eschewed to promote a one-on-one relationship between viewer and object. Clark maintained, "We do not value pictures as documents. We do not want to know about them; we want to know them, and explanations may too often interfere with our direct responses."[16] With the rise of the Cold War such beliefs crystallized. As vice-president Richard Nixon suggested in his 1955 keynote speech at an American Association of Museums conference, having a meditative and individual experience before an object was a symbol of democracy; the social history of an object was associated with Soviet-style propaganda.[17]

The paradigm of museum as shrine depends on the institution's declaration of authority. Visitors believe they have a transformative experience because the director/curator is a connoisseur. The expertise of the "museum man" (the expert is always a patriarchal figure) gives an assurance that museum objects are "authentic" masterpieces that express universal truths in an established canon or standard of excellence. The current director of the

Metropolitan Museum of Art, Philippe de Montebello, recently asserted, "it is the judicious exercise of the museum's authority that makes possible that state of pure reverie that an unencumbered aesthetic experience can inspire."[18] Implicit in the argument is that the art museum is more significant than other kinds of museums; the notion of the aura gives it special status. Nonetheless, the paradigm of museum as shrine is relevant to diverse institutions. Anthropologist James Clifford noted, "Ethnographic contextualizations are as problematic as aesthetic ones, as susceptible to purified, ahistorical treatments."[19]

As a shrine, the museum protects its treasures. This idea is preserved in English nomenclature. The word "curator" comes from the Latin *curare*, "to care." Some museums in the UK use a more possessive term, "keeper," reflecting a colonialist history. In any case, the museum as shrine dedicates itself to acquisitions, connoisseurship, and conservation of its permanent collection. Objects are prioritized over ideas. Temporary exhibitions are dismissed as crass marketing that panders to the "masses." Education is based on "trickle-down" theories and there is little interest in defining the audience or opening two-way communication with communities. To maintain myths of authenticity, conservation is secreted or presented as an objective science that brings the work back to its "original" condition. Objects are not repatriated unless the law demands it. Collections are thought to be reborn in the museum, where they are better guarded and more appreciated.

The museum as shrine is a ritual site influenced by church, palace, and ancient temple architecture. Processional pathways, which may include monumental staircases, dramatic lighting, picturesque views, and ornamental niches, create a performative experience. Art historian Carol Duncan explains, "I see the totality of the museum as a stage setting that prompts visitors to enact a performance of some kind, whether or not actual visitors would describe it as such."[20] Preziosi adds, "all museums *stage* their collected and preserved relics . . . Museums . . . use theatrical effects to enhance a belief in the historicity of the objects they collect."[21]

Most museum theorists believe the museum as shrine is an elitist paradigm that does not meet the needs of contemporary culture.[22] Directors and curators who embrace the paradigm counter by suggesting the only other alternative is to become market-driven, to "give in" to the impulse to become part of an "industry" that caters to its "clients." But being sensitive to the audience is a gesture of respect, not pandering. Becoming more democratic does not mean a museum has to abandon scholarship, but instead that it engages in research that has resonance for the communities it serves.

Market-driven industry

In the past, museums commonly positioned their institutions as "pure" environments for their collections, unsullied by commercial concerns. But, of course, all museums need to raise funds to operate. The work of museum directors, trustees, development officers, and even curators involves key financial decision-making. There are four basic funding sources available for museums: government (municipal, state/regional, and national); corporation; charitable foundation; and private benefactor. Museums outside the US used to be able to count on government funding to meet their needs, but recent budget cuts have forced many to adopt the American model of self-support. All funding sources demand something in return. Government agencies might want to see the museum revitalizing an urban center, marking a historical event, or reaching out to an underserved community. Corporations usually demand their logo be placed conspicuously on museum advertising, banners, and placards. Charitable foundations require that the mission of the museum projects they fund complements their own goals. Private benefactors may request that a wing be named after them, that the museum hold a vanity exhibition of their collections, that they obtain positions on elite boards, that the objects they donate be exhibited in a certain way, or that the museum bend to tax laws. Financial policy is a secretive area in which the rules are often unspoken and negotiated in mutually exploitative relationships. There is little scholarship on the museum's economic workings, however, because documentation is often scanty, confidential, and/or hard to obtain in the museum archives.[23]

Museums tend to hide the fact that the objects in their collections have value as commodities. An important part of a curator's job is to keep an eye on the market – to consider potential acquisitions, to establish insurance values, and to advise donors. Yet the public is rarely told what an object costs and what the institution had to do to obtain it. When such information is revealed – for instance, when Thomas Hoving published his confessional *Making the Mummies Dance*, detailing the unsavory practices that took place under his directorship at the Metropolitan Museum from 1966 to 1977 – readers were shocked.[24] The fetishization of objects makes viewers aware that museum collections are valuable, but traditionally curators have insisted that economic worth has no impact on interpretation. As Ivan Gaskell

11

explains, this is a fallacy. It is true that, while an object is in a museum collection, it is an "ex-commodity;" nevertheless, that object helps determine the value of other similar objects on the market. And if it is in an institution that allows deaccessioning – selling works in its collection – the object is a "dormant commodity." Accreditation agencies discourage deaccessioning (even censuring institutions that use the proceeds from it for anything other than acquisitions) not only because museums are supposed to hold their collections in perpetuity for succeeding generations, but also because this act acknowledges the commodity status of objects.[25]

In today's economy, many museums have become more open about their economic realities and have adopted business models to generate adequate revenues. Not all museums are as declarative about their market orientation as the Victoria and Albert, which promoted its café with the highly criticized advertisement "An ace caff with rather a nice museum attached." More commonly, museums position themselves as tourist attractions. Some even find themselves more dependent on out-of-towners than on local visitors. Performance studies scholar Barbara Kirschenblatt-Gimblett explains, "heritage and tourism are collaborative industries, heritage converting locations into destinations and tourism making them economically viable as exhibits in themselves."[26] To attract tourists, museums hold temporary exhibitions, also known as "blockbusters" for the crowds they can generate. Some present daring shows but many recycle topics of proven popularity, what art historian Andrew McClellan calls a "steady diet of Impressionism, mummies, and anything with 'gold' in the title."[27] Wall texts, also known as "scripts," are usually limited to 75 words so as not to overly tax the visitor; controversial theories, so as not to offend, are saved for the accompanying catalogue, which has a limited readership. Crowds move quickly through the galleries and the objects become mere advertisements to sell reproductions on cards, coffee mugs, posters, and umbrellas. Temporary exhibitions bring in a significant portion of a museum's income, not only through ticket and souvenir sales but also because grant money is usually tied to attendance level – traditionally considered the measure of success. Some museums partner with airlines and hotels to offer package deals.

To provide the facilities that tourists need and to generate additional income, museums have undergone extensive building campaigns. New facilities may include reception and orientation areas, restaurants, cafés, shops, bookstores, ATM machines, cloakrooms, rest rooms, school group areas, children's wings, education centers, and theaters. And though these areas are sited in basements, lobbies, or hallways, apart from exhibit galleries, they can be an attraction in themselves, a "playpen of consumption," as sociologist Nick Prior put it.[28] To create and maintain expensive exhibits and facilities, museums often rely on corporate sponsorship. Corporations in need of good public relations, such those involved in the tobacco, petroleum, and weapons industries, often seek out such sponsorships. Corporate sponsorship usually elicits self-censorship from the museum; in an effort to attract large and affluent audiences to the shows and spaces they support, companies commonly avoid funding heated or obscure topics. Sometimes museums tolerate conflicts of interest to host major exhibitions. In 1999, the Brooklyn Museum allowed Charles Saatchi, well known for aggressively selling off the contemporary art that he amassed, to stage a provocative exhibition there, entitled "Sensation," representing his collections; the show was funded in part by an auction house, dealers, and Saatchi himself, all of whom stood to benefit financially from the Brooklyn's endorsement of the collection.[29]

The discourse on the museum as a market-driven industry has been shaped by Marxist theory, which looks critically at the economic and social foundations of culture. Historian Neil Harris and sociologist Tony Bennett have shown the links between the museum, the amusement park, the international exposition, and the department store in the nineteenth century. With their thousands of objects hierarchically arranged, these spaces borrowed from each other to instill capitalist values of innovation, consumption, and display.[30] Most museum theorists agree that today the museum has borrowed from the cinema and the theme park to become a spectacle that engages all the senses, whether staged to evoke an aesthetic experience, a historical context, or an interactive learning environment. Some, like Kirschenblatt-Gimblett, say that such spectacle is complex but has the potential to create a powerful learning experience. Others, such as philosopher Jean Baudrillard and art historian Rosalind Krauss, claim that such sensory stimulus collapses into meaninglessness.[31] Marxist Guy Debord formulated spectacle theory in a seminal study of 1967. He argues that the high production quality of the spectacle obscures the values encoded by the system that fabricates it. The spectacle floods viewers with imagery, distracting them from identifying an agenda and seeking change. Debord states, "The spectacle is not a collection of images; rather, it is a social relationship between people that is mediated by images . . . In form as in content the spectacle serves as a total justification for the conditions and aims of the existing system."[32] From this perspective, the spectacle of mystery that pervades the

13

Trammel and Margaret Crowe Collection of Asian Art in Dallas, a private museum, reinforces stereotypes of Asia as "other" as it compels visitors to marvel at objects it positions as exotic.

Colonizing space

Many commentators see the museum as a colonizing space engaged in classification processes that define people. They look to postcolonial theory, which examines how imperialist and patriarchal structures have shaped and continue to shape culture, and which identifies strategies for change. "Exhibitions are privileged arenas for presenting images of self and 'other,'" museum theorist Ivan Karp explains. Museums construct the "other" to construct and justify the "self."[33] In forming collections by appropriating – making one's own – objects from non-western cultures, museums reveal more about the value systems of the colonizer than about the colonized. As museums impose evolutionary hierarchies of race, ethnicity, and gender, they encode an agenda that effectively unifies white (male) citizens of imperial powers (the self) against conquered peoples (the other). As colonizing spaces, museums naturalize the category of "primitive," in which non-western cultures are in arrested development and frozen in time – metaphorically dead. Such museums offer no acknowledgment of the imperialist histories that inform their institutions.

From their beginnings, museums and their benefactors have plundered to create their collections and have interpreted objects from a Eurocentric perspective. Though they may claim to have had benevolent motivations – to have salvaged objects that could not be protected by their source communities – the potential growth in the wealth and status of the collector, the museum, and the state was usually the primary motivating force. In the memoirs of his directorship at the Met, Hoving bragged about making illicit deals in a high-stakes game to procure non-western objects.[34] When artifacts from non-western cultures entered museum collections, their original context and function were little considered. Masks, primarily from West Africa, were favored over other objects from diverse geographical regions because these masks were thought to possess a "sculptural quality," because similar objects inspired Picasso and other modern European artists, and because masks were made by men, as opposed to what were considered "decorative" arts, such as textiles, produced by women. Historical timelines were seldom offered, suggesting that indigenous cultures never changed. Individual skill was rarely recognized; curators described non-western makers as simply following convention, as opposed to western artists whose original-ity distinguished them as creative and intellectual.[35]

Museums commonly showed disrespect for important indigenous spir-itual beliefs. In some traditions, photography is thought to capture the sub-ject's soul. Yet museums used such photographs of indigenous peoples as data, as illustrations, or even as part of their picture libraries, literally selling the subject's image without his or her permission. Also, museums have a long tradition of exhibiting human remains. Skulls and bones were often displayed alongside wax models in dioramas to suggest Darwinian racial typologies. Physiognomy was interpreted as evidence of moral character, and that of native peoples was judged to be inferior. Sometimes even living people were put on display as ethnographic specimens. Even today, insens-itive viewpoints and policies persist. James Wood, director of the Art Insti-tute of Chicago, wrote recently, "The collections of our great museums provide a unique opportunity to demonstrate that curiosity about others is the greatest form of knowledge." But making "others" into "curiosities" perpetuates colonialist positions. Wood disparages what he calls "local, tribal memory" in favor of a "cosmopolitan one" that "encourages the visitor to be an aesthetic citizen of the world rather than of a mere place."[36] Yet separating an object from its source community and recontextualizing it can make the museum a dead space. Remarking on the passivity that museums evoke, the modernist museum architect Louis Kahn noted that the visitor's first urge, upon entering the institution, is to go get a cup of coffee in the café.[37]

As early as the beginning of the nineteenth century, when Napoleon's troops plundered the treasures of France's new empire, politician and art critic Antoine-Chrysostome Quatremère de Quincy lamented the tearing of objects from their original context. In the 1960s, Marxist philosopher Theodor Adorno used the German word "museal," meaning museum-like, to de-scribe objects that are no longer connected to the culture that produced them or to the present. He declared in a now-famous essay of 1967, "Mu-seum and mausoleum are connected by more than a phonetic association. Museums are like the family sepulchres of works of art. They testify to the neutralization of culture."[38] Adorno believed that the museum contributed to a contemporary culture of amnesia, a particular phenomenon of capitalist society. Postmodern theorists hold that intended significance or experience is irretrievable; the meanings of objects shift with every reframing. As David Phillips explains, even if a Renaissance altarpiece is hung in the museum at the same level as it was in a church, under similar dim lighting, even if a full ceremonial costume is pieced together and displayed before a video show-ing such dress in use, the museum remains an "assertive environment" that impacts on the viewing experience.[39]

For all of these reasons, Alpha Konare, former president of the Interna-tional Council of Museums (ICOM) and now president of the Republic of Mali, remarked in a 1983 essay, "The traditional museum is no longer in tune with our concerns; it has ossified our culture, deadened many of our cultural objects, and allowed the essence, imbued with the spirit of the people, to be lost."[40] These sentiments express why Eurocentric museums established by colonizing powers in non-western cultures are often neglected. Some indigenous peoples believe that collecting destroys, rather than pre-serves, their traditions. When objects are not being used, they lose their value. As Malcolm McLeod, former keeper of ethnography at the British Museum, reports, in West Africa, the storage areas of colonial-era museums are often neglected, decaying, looted, and unused. Such institutions have no collections policies and no acquisition funds. Museum employees are trou-bled by what's already been accumulated. Temporary exhibitions of local heirlooms that are soon returned to their owners, or on topical themes valued by the community, are more successful. The needs of the commun-ity must be prioritized over the desires of tourists if such institutions are to have resonance.[41]

Recent laws and agreements around the world have called for the repat-riation of cultural property. UNESCO has declared that repatriation is a basic human right; all communities are equal and when any group loses part of its cultural patrimony, all of humankind suffers. UNESCO asserts that, even when objects were sold or given away to western collectors, individual members of a culture did not have the right to deny these objects to future generations, thus canceling out a museum's claims. UNESCO also recog-nizes that subjugated cultures do not have the means to buy back their cultural property, and helps to negotiate between opposing parties. Some western museums continue to resist repatriation, however, fearful that com-pliance will challenge their authority and empty their institutions. Of course, it is usually only the most symbolically representative objects that are re-quested.[42] Moreover, museums that collaborate with source communities often find that, together, they can identify solutions that meet both parties' needs. Sometimes, indigenous communities agree that objects should re-main in the museum for safekeeping, but they want to determine how these objects are treated. They may wish to specify how objects from their com-munities should be stored, displayed, and conserved; they may also seek the right to perform religious ceremonies in the museum and/or to borrow objects for particular celebrations. Other times, indigenous communities request repatriation but offer the gift of other objects and/or their expertise in activities such as translating, interpreting, and providing oral histories.

Western museums that fight repatriation often justify their position on the basis of access. But many source communities hold that only elders or initiates should have access to objects endowed with special powers or that reveal privileged information. Some anthropologists add that access should be the privilege of the source community, whose members often have little or no means to travel to museums. Furthermore, the viewer gets fuller intellectual and/or spiritual access to the object when it is with its source community. Elders provide interpretation to appropriate viewers, and the repatriated object helps traditional cultural activities to thrive. Western museums do not provide full access themselves. Most display only a small portion of the materials they have collected.

Western museums sometimes also protest that source communities do not offer adequate protective and conservation measures. Yet indigenous communities have developed ingenious methods to safeguard their cultural treasures. Often a culture's most precious assets are protected by taboos that restrict the objects to elders. Such objects are typically kept in shrines, meeting houses, or granaries that shelter them from the elements and limit access to them. Objects are frequently hung above a fire to get rid of pests and molds. Some are preserved with oil or bark cloth. Sometimes, communities do not want their material culture to be preserved but to follow the life cycle. For most source communities, what's important is that their culture – not the object – is transmitted through time. When an object becomes too fragile to be useful, a replacement is made; the culture is not static or frozen but continues to maintain its identity by creating new objects, each with its own personality.[43]

The resistant museum commonly responds by using buzzwords like "consulting" and "partnering" but doesn't really try to alter power relationships. It will repatriate, if required by law. And it will bring in advisers from source communities for special projects. But to decolonize the museum, institutions need to develop long-term relationships with source communities, built on trust. This has been most successful in North America and Australia where source communities live near museums. Fewer inroads have been made in Europe.[44]

Feminist theory has shown that museums are also a gendered space, where women's production and history are under-represented and oversimplified

17

and where the masculine gaze has colonized the female body. Feminists look at how stereotypical notions of masculinity and femininity have been naturalized, and create strategies and actions that subvert these binary positions. They have shown that the western canon of achievement equates masculinity with intellect and innovation and femininity with emotion and passivity. Masculine domination (self) is dependent on feminine submission (other) for its identity. Although feminist voices have been raised for change in the museum since the mid-nineteenth century, most museum narratives continue to convey gender stereotypes. Gay and lesbian identity is rarely acknowledged.[45]

The masculine gendering of the museum space has a profound impact on the way we construct meaning. As Evelyn Hankins has demonstrated, when Juliana Force and Gertrude Vanderbilt Whitney established the permanent home of the Whitney Museum in four New York townhouses in 1931, creating a decorative environment intended to welcome rather than intimidate, critics and scholars dismissed the site as a feminized space not containing serious art. Hankins attributes the lack of appreciation of American modernism today to this legacy. She contrasts the Whitney with the Museum of Modern Art (MoMA), which also had several female founders who influenced policy and which was sited in 1939 in a former townhouse. Commentators regarded MoMA as the institution that set the canon for modern art – a canon of European artists who are still seen as the stars. Hankins credits the difference to MoMA director Alfred H. Barr, Jr, who constructed a masculine space. Barr characterized MoMA's female founders as philanthropists, rather than policy makers, and discouraged them from taking on a public role. He flaunted his own credentials from Princeton and Harvard to prove that he was the expert. And he removed all the decorative flourishes from the townhouse, transforming it into a functionalist "white cube" that conveyed purity and restraint.[46]

Carol Duncan has shown how MoMA imposed a masculine gaze within the galleries. Identifying patterns she saw throughout the museum, she described a modernism in which male artists objectify the female body as a vehicle to reach abstraction. Women artists were not admitted to the canon but existed only as muse and model. And no context was provided to explain why this was so. The ideal visitor was imagined to be a heterosexual male whose desire activated the modernism of the work. Duncan's article was an impetus for feminists to show that the personal is political – that they can channel their own experiences to disrupt the masculinity of the museum space.[47]

18

Professor of English and history Barbara Melosh has described how history museums are giving new visibility to women's lives, yet are still measuring women's achievements on the basis of a canon of great men. Melosh calls this compensatory history. Museums like the National Women's Hall of Fame in Seneca Falls, New York, show that women are not just victims, but these institutions still value public over private life and make no conceptual inroads. Such displays are oversimplifying and celebratory, repressing conflict and contradiction. Melosh calls for museums to revise the way they represent history to take into account women's full experience – private and public – and to explore how women both reject and participate in the dominant culture.[48]

Post-museum

The fourth paradigm, post-museum, is the most hopeful. Museum theorist Eilean Hooper-Greenhill uses this term to suggest an institution that has completely reinvented itself, that is no longer a "museum" but something new, yet related to the "museum." The post-museum clearly articulates its agendas, strategies, and decision-making processes and continually re-evaluates them in a way that acknowledges the politics of representation; the work of museum staff is never naturalized but seen as contributing to these agendas. The post-museum actively seeks to share power with the communities it serves, including source communities. It recognizes that visitors are not passive consumers and gets to know its constituencies. Instead of transmitting knowledge to an essentialized mass audience, the post-museum listens and responds sensitively as it encourages diverse groups to become active participants in museum discourse. Nonetheless, in the post-museum, the curator is not a mere facilitator but takes responsibility for representation as she or he engages in critical inquiry. The post-museum does not shy away from difficult issues but exposes conflict and contradiction. It asserts that the institution must show ambiguity and acknowledge multiple, ever-shifting identities. Most importantly, the post-museum is a site from which to redress social inequalities. Proponents of the post-museum recognize that an isolated museum visit will not spark change, and they don't want the platform of equality to become just another means for the museum to assert social control. Still, they imagine that the post-museum can promote social understanding. Huyssen hopes for the museum to become "a space for the cultures of this world to collide and to display their heterogeneity, even irreconcilability, to network, to hybridize and to live together in the gaze and the memory of the spectator."[49]

Champions of the post-museum agree that it is just emerging. In the US, many cite the Native American Graves Protection and Repatriation Act (NAGPRA), passed by Congress in 1990, as a psychological and cultural impetus. NAGPRA protects burial sites. It also required all museums to inventory their Native American and Hawaiian human remains and ceremonial artifacts by 1995, and to present a list of relevant objects to federally recognized tribes. NAGPRA states that tribes have a legal right to request the return of these objects. The Act has helped Native American communities found and/or expand museums and cultural centers on their lands. It has also altered museums' practices of collecting, exhibiting, and interpreting. In effect, NAGPRA empowers source communities to control their own identity. Though some museums regret these changes, most see them as an opportunity for growth. Many go beyond the letter of the law to repatriate from an ethical standpoint. To shape mission and policy, museums with Native American collections now commonly employ Native American staff and actively partner with Native American academics and community leaders. The National Museum of the American Indian offers an internship program to train Native American students in museum theory and practice.[50]

Some museums with Native American collections have come up with innovative solutions that fulfill their own institutional missions and meet the needs of source communities at the same time. In the process, many of these museums have found that meeting the needs of source communities *is* their primary institutional mission. The University of Denver Museum of Anthropology isolates human remains and funerary objects into one NAGPRA vault and ceremonial objects into another. Access is restricted to certain museum staff and tribal representatives. Entry is limited to tribal visits and to cleaning and pest monitoring. Women who are menstruating are prohibited. No research is allowed on NAGPRA materials and their documentation is confidential. Human remains are wrapped in acid-free tissue or muslin, not stored in air-free containers, so they can breathe. Tribal members are welcome to make traditional offerings, called smudging, by burning sage, sweetgrass, and tobacco. The museum turns off its fire alarms when smudging takes place. The National Museum of the American Indian, which opened in late 2004 in its new building on the mall in Washington, DC, is attempting to set a model for treating photographs of Native peoples and their communities with dignity. Policy asserts that photographs are not to be used as mere illustrations or decorative objects. Photographs of religious or ceremonial significance are to be given the same respect as the ceremonies themselves and are only to be displayed or published with the permission of the source community.[51] Responsibility always rests with the researcher.

Other kinds of museums have prioritized humanitarian values as well. The Lower East Side Tenement Museum in New York, along with the Gulag Museum in Russia, the Slave House in Senegal, Terezin Concentration Camp in the Czech Republic, and six other institutions, has formed a consortium called the International Coalition of Historic Site Museums of Conscience. Member institutions share three goals: to show the contemporary applications of their historical sites; to prompt dialogue on social issues; and to promote democratic values. The Lower East Side Tenement Museum offers immigrants language classes where they learn English by reading the diaries and letters of past immigrants. It hosts topical web art, such as a project by Lauren Gill and Jenny Polak that allows users to enter and learn about the Immigration and Naturalization Detention Centers. The museum holds workshops for immigrants on issues such as housing conditions; participants role-play housing inspectors from the early 1900s and evaluate whether their own homes meet contemporary standards. It supports the Urban Museum Studies Program, which targets graduate students from minority, immigrant, and working-class families. Whether such initiatives evidence the rise of the post-museum is a controversial issue.

The Past, Present, and Future of the Museum: The Debate

Museum history

Some two decades of scholarship in museum theory have produced a new set of expectations for the museum, including greater accountability, sensitivity, and openness. To grasp the complexity of the moment – and to decide yourself whether museums have the potential for substantive change – it is crucial to look back at the history of museums to what Preziosi calls, as quoted at the beginning of this introduction, those "two centuries of museological meditations . . . [from] which our modernity has been generated, (en)gendered, and sustained." The writings of Michel Foucault provide a foundation for examining museum history.

Writing about the history of prisons, hospitals, and military barracks, Foucault identified three distinct epistemes or systems of knowledge created by ruptures in the economic, social, cultural, political, scientific, and theological status quo. These epistemes – Renaissance, classical, and modern – shaped

21

the formation and identity of institutions. Hooper-Greenhill has shown the relevance of Foucault's epistemes to the history of museums. She argues that only by acknowledging museum history as a series of ruptures, rather than an immutable continuity, can we imagine substantive change for museums today.[52]

Critics have noted the limitations of Foucault's notions of history. Museum theorist Andrea Witcomb has written that the Foucauldian approach is too monolithic to show the complexity of institutions and too static to allow for the possibility of change. As McClellan has detailed, museums have great flexibility and have been metamorphosing continually since their founding. Witcomb charges that the Foucauldian approach depicts the museum as conspiratorial, consciously engaging in duplicity to maintain systems of power. She argues that Foucauldian analysis portrays audiences as manipulated pawns, without agency. And she criticizes Foucault's followers for positioning the museum as a state-controlled environment of "exclusion and confinement" without examining its links to popular culture, where, as Bennett has shown, the museum, the amusement park, and the international exposition were all part of an "exhibitionary complex."[53] Recognizing these limitations, however, Hooper-Greenhill's analysis of museum history still provides a useful chronology for students of museum theory.

Foucault's Renaissance episteme is characterized by the humanist desire to understand the world through seeking universal knowledge. This is a time when beliefs are no longer controlled by theology but not yet dominated by science. Knowledge is acquired through discovering hidden relationships among objects. By identifying these relationships, humankind becomes a creator, a microcosm of the macrocosm that is God.

According to Hooper-Greenhill, the curiosity cabinet, commonly known as the *Wunderkammer* in northern Europe and the *studiolo* in Italy, mediates between the microcosm of humankind and the macrocosm of God and the universe. Aristocrats, scholars, wealthy merchants, artists, physicians, and apothecaries of the late sixteenth and seventeenth centuries created these precursors of the museum to represent the world in miniature. Referring both to a collection and to the particular piece of furniture in which the collection was housed, the curiosity cabinet was an arrangement of hundreds or thousands of objects of nature – *naturalia* – and of humankind – *artificialia*. Collectors filled their cabinets to capacity with a dizzying array of animal, plant, and mineral specimens, juxtaposed with antique statuary, ethnographic materials, elaborate metalwork, distorting mirrors, and the like. Most prized were objects of great rarity, such as the purported playing cards of a dwarf, and hybrids of nature/human in which artisans carved or refashioned unusual natural materials, such as ivory. Such objects were thought to proclaim both the diversity and the unity of the world and to assert humankind's central place within it. Arrangements of boxes within boxes, drawers within drawers, suggested that each microcosm was contained within another microcosm, eventually leading to the divine macrocosm of God's creation.

Collectors and their advisers typically based the organization of the cabinets on universalizing rubrics of the day, such as the four elements, the four continents, and the seven virtues. Iconographic programs were kept secret so that only the collector himself (almost all of such collectors were male) could animate, and thus control, his world in miniature by asserting correspondences among objects. And as the collector reified – or made real – the universe through the objects he amassed, the curiosity cabinet personified the Renaissance conception of a world created by both humankind and God.

The curiosity cabinet was a private space and not a museum. In fact, during the period in which the curiosity cabinet developed, the word "museum" was seldom used and refers to a reading room or other site where the "muses" can be studied. Nonetheless, certain activities of the curiosity cabinet prefigure those of the museum. Some curiosity cabinets provided access not just for dignitaries but for a cross-section of scholars, artists, bookbinders, jewelers, and other craftworkers as a professional resource. Many employed agents or "curators," well-connected merchants and scholars who procured objects for the collection. Curiosity cabinets commonly published inventories – precursors to the museum catalogue. And some had "conservators," artists hired to repair damage.[54]

In the mid-eighteenth century, a classical episteme emerged that pictured a world too complex, chaotic, and fragmented to be contained by the curiosity cabinet. Rationalism dominated; a need to impose order led to the development of and reliance on systems of classification. As Foucault makes clear, Linnaean taxonomy – the system Carl Linnaeus invented to classify the natural world by genus and species – was adapted to impose hierarchies on all aspects of experience. Such hierarchies provided an illusory sense of closure and containment. Complexities and contradictions were denied.

Hooper-Greenhill traces the impact of the classical episteme on collections – which became increasingly specialized. Repositories, study collections that were not public yet aimed to meet the needs of professional societies, were founded for scholarly research. Collections of natural history and art were separated and each genre developed its own protocols of display. The focus on rationalism and order created new priorities for collections.

23

The typical was valued as representative of the laws of nature; the rare – the anomaly – that did not "fit in" to classification systems was rejected as uncharacteristic or made to fit. Paintings were cut down or extended to conform to a standard of measurement; classical sculptures' missing limbs were completed. Objects were judged empirically, without taking context into consideration. Categories, though socially constructed, were seen as naturally determined and intrinsic to the physical world. Displays were linear and embraced an ideology of progress. Collections established a canon, a standard by which all was evaluated, and offered a single authoritative interpretation.

Foucault captured the essence of the modern episteme through the metaphor of discipline. Emerging in the late eighteenth and early nineteenth centuries with the French Revolution and the subsequent rise of Napoleon, the modern episteme embraces contradictory aims. On the one hand, it marks the end of the elitist institution and the beginning of a democratic culture. On the other hand, it denotes the rise of binary oppositions, most importantly between domination and subjugation, as the state attempted to shape the new class of the bourgeoisie. Military administration became the standard for professional practice throughout society. Clear boundaries were set between insiders, who maintained the power to make decisions, and outsiders, who became passive observers. Procedures and policies continued to be naturalized to justify paternalistic governance. Public spaces confined and controlled the populace through surveillance. In the modern episteme, the world was no longer seen as fixed but as ever-changing. The focus shifted from the surface of things to the larger questions of why phenomena occur. Researchers acknowledged the organic structure of matter and the complex relationships among objects and among issues. Fields of study such as biology and philosophy arose at this time.

The episteme produced a modern or "disciplinary" public museum whose vestiges are operational today. The paradigm, as Hooper-Greenhill, demonstrates, is what is now known as the Louvre Museum. The French Revolutionary government decreed in 1792 that a public museum should be opened in the former royal palace. The institution was in operation the following year and, after several name changes due to political turbulence, became in 1803 the Musée Napoleon. This was a museum accessible to all on several days of the week and thus ostensibly democratic. In practice, however, it was a carefully designed pedagogical tool to further nation building. It aimed to fashion modern citizens, without their being aware of it, who were patriotic, "civilized," aesthetically minded, homogenous, and easily controlled. Works of art were severed from their earlier royal, aristocratic, or ecclesiastical

contexts and reclaimed as national patrimony – object lessons to democrat-
ize and secularize the viewer. Displays articulated an evolutionary narrative
that used the past to validate the present. The collections were upheld as
canonical – representing a universal standard of excellence that should be
emulated. A history of art was fabricated as paintings were organized by
period, school (meaning country), and artist. The appearance of a work
became less important than chronology. Arts were separated from "crafts;"
western objects from non-western.

As Napoleon looted his way across Europe, a vast hierarchy was established to handle these new possessions. A community of curators was born,
specializing according to medium, to evaluate the worth of objects and to
make the Louvre the richest collection ever. Archivists, registrars, and conservators were organized as precisely as a military administration to document, classify, track, and repair objects destined for the Louvre and for a
network of provincial museums established across the empire. The great
number of objects amassed required that the museum exhibit only a representative sample and procure large storage areas for reserve collections.
Temporary exhibitions grew out of elaborate decorative schemes to celebrate
Napoleon's birthday and out of topical groupings to convey political messages
at times of war. To enhance the effectiveness of the museum's didacticism,
curators posted explanatory wall texts and published affordable catalogues
and guidebooks. Museum educators gave tours of the antiquities collections,
legitimizing current politics through ancient history and mythology.

In this model, which other cultural institutions in fledgling democracies
across Europe were quick to emulate, the museum wields great power. The
museum director and curators judge what's important and what's not and,
in so doing, define national identity. The visitor is authorized to acquire
knowledge but only through submission to the dominant power – the expert. Professional practices are hidden from view; nothing is transparent.
Museum architecture demarcates private, enclosed spaces for staff so that
their work is literally and figuratively hidden from view. It sets out wide
open spaces for the public to enable surveillance by museum guards and by
other museum visitors, who motivate the viewer to self-regulate.[55]

The skeptic's position: museums do not (cannot?) change

Some theorists, such as Mieke Bal and Carol Duncan, believe that museums
still conform to the Foucauldian modern or disciplinary model. Many cite a
1969 empirical study by sociologists Pierre Bourdieu and Alain Darbel as a

farsighted analysis; museums may be introducing new spaces, exhibitions, educational initiatives, and opportunities for consumption but, at heart, they remain elitist institutions. They obscure their decision-making processes and refrain from scrutinizing their own histories. As mission statements reveal, they aspire to unify their "publics," rather than to acknowledge multiple and shifting identities. They project an image of an ideal visitor to which the viewer is supposed to conform. They continue to attract an educated upper- and middle-class audience, remaining irrelevant and intimidating to margin- alized groups. A few museum directors have openly dismissed outreach efforts as unrealistic; James Cuno states baldly that art museums are "of inter- est to only a relative few (perhaps 20 percent of our population)."[56]

According to the skeptics, despite experiments in thematic and aesthetic hangs, most displays carry on the tradition of organizing works according to a canon that asserts evolutionary change. Objects are cut off from their context and fetishized. Artifacts from non-western cultures are still inter- preted through the lens of western cultural values. The subjectivity of con- servation is rarely acknowledged. Cameras and computers bolster traditional surveillance methods. New technologies, rather than creating a truly inter- active experience, merely distract the visitor from asking larger questions about the museum's authority and authenticity.

When new initiatives do take place, they occur most commonly in the realm of the temporary exhibition, which usually does not spark substantive change in the museum itself. And as the Enola Gay exhibit painfully demon- strates, museums still aim to generate consensus rather than conveying di- verse perspectives. Feminist art historian Griselda Pollock was so frustrated by the lack of commitment and rigor in a 1998–9 Mary Cassatt exhibition that she created what she calls a "virtual feminist space" in an essay where she imagined what the show could have been.[57] Contemporary artists grav- itate to installation, new media, performance art, and alternative sites because they see the traditional space of the museum as unwilling and/or unable to support ambiguity.

In the museum hierarchy, curators still make the important decisions, giving little voice to education departments – which are often sequestered in museum basements – and little attention to understanding audiences. Visitor studies are quantitative, rather than qualitative, and assume a passive audi- ence; results are used to offer statistics to funders, not to learn how visitors make meaning, and seldom shape museum policy. Citing a two-tiered sys- tem in which education departments create multicultural programming which goes unsupported by curatorial staff, installation artist Ernesto Pujol protested, "perhaps the most visionary – if not subversive – gesture that a museum director can make right now is to facilitate an empowering dialogue between educators and curators, and not after the fact but at the very outset of a new exhibition project."[58]

A vocal minority of theorists hold that museums, by definition, cannot change and that they are fast becoming obsolete. The mere act of display is always a political process that imposes a hierarchy. Ivan Gaskell remarks, about the art museum,

> Curators must make pragmatic judgments about the differential power of attraction of paintings placed in proximity to one another, for in any group of paintings to be hung together there is almost always a hierarchy of this kind . . . There is, in effect, a conventional hierarchy within any given gallery space, and of the relative power of visual attraction among paintings for viewers, both immediately and for sustained attention.[59]

The skeptics argue that the rhetoric of change does not create change.

The optimist's position: museums do (can) change

Other theorists argue that the museum is a contested site and that the jury is "still out." Some warn against idealizing the museum because the deconstruction of traditional value systems is only just beginning. Preziosi cautions,

> It is supremely disingenuous to proclaim that radical changes in scenography – whether under the rubric of a "new" museology or not – constitute effective social critique. A major problem with such evaluations is that as long as the aesthetic ideology of "originality" determines the "value" of social critique, the critique itself operates at a symbolic level, displaced from the actual social conditions that the critique aims to reform.[60]

Nonetheless, many theorists read as a healthy sign the gradual opening up of the "private" museum space to public scrutiny. Nick Prior estimates that "it has, at least, become possible for museums to inhabit a more democratic, open-ended 'third space,' beyond elitism and consumerism."[61] Those who see a post-museum taking shape point to the example of some curators who are eager to share power by initiating open dialogue and forging new partnerships with groups previously disenfranchised. These theorists are also encouraged by the variety of institutions, from neighborhood museums to community centers to university galleries, that have recently been established or have been given new life and that take diverse approaches to the representation of race, ethnicity, class, and gender. These are the institutions most likely to adopt the ideals of the post-museum, as they're more able to take risks than an established encyclopedic collection. They collaborate creatively with other institutions to meet their funding, scholarship, collection, and exhibition needs. And they sometimes bring in consultants, not just to save money on full-time salaries but also to gain insights and suggestions on the state of their institutions from outsiders without conflicts of interest.

The time of the museum as a "great" collector is past; most of the canonical works of western art are already in public collections and only a handful of museums, like the Getty in Los Angeles, have the funds to bid for the few that come on the market. Most museums also now do scrupulous research on provenance – the history of an object's ownership – before making an acquisition or accepting a donation. If there's any question of illicit activity, most curators, to avoid potential lawsuits and/or repatriation demands, will not complete a transaction. Partly as a result of this trend, the idea has become more important than the object in many museums. And as curators prioritize ideas over objects, they deconstruct the canon in the process. It is becoming more common for curators to reject "museum-speak" in favor of signed wall texts that convey the conflicts and contradictions of history. Installation design and text make connections and spark critical inquiry. Photography, graphics, and video provide context. Postmodern architecture or renovation, with its fragmented and self-referential style, offers visitors choice and supports the consideration of multiple viewpoints. Open storage areas and staff offices separated from the galleries only by glass create an environment of transparency.

Some museums are tackling formerly neglected issues such as domesticity, family, and sexuality. The Women's Museum of Aarhus, Denmark, includes exhibits on the history of obstetrics and gynecology, abortion and birth control, in the display of its permanent collections. It interjects into the mix installations on subjects including domestic violence. And it holds temporary exhibitions of work by subversive artists such as Yoko Ono. Run by a collective directorate of women with close community ties, the Women's Museum transforms what other institutions might see as disadvantage into great advantage. Most of the staff members have no museum studies training and many are temporary workers; the museum relies on them to think "out of the box." Most of its collections are of a personal, not public, nature; the museum uses them to initiate intimate conversations. Audiences range

from elderly visitors seeking nostalgia to hip young feminists wanting theoretical substance; the museum has adopted what Prior calls "double-coding"
to respond to diverse needs and desires simultaneously.[62] Such museums are
sometimes dismissed as quirky aberrations, yet they are becoming more and
more visible on the cultural landscape.

The emerging post-museum is finding culturally sensitive ways to treat
non-western objects. At the Seattle Art Museum, curator of African art Pamela
McCluskey embraces an expansive definition of African material culture in
the permanent collection galleries. She highlights not just West African artifacts, as is most typical of western art museums, but also objects from East
and South Africa and from Egypt. She displays a variety of media by women
and men including work that is contemporary and/or that subverts tradition. And she collaborates with community leaders from the cultures represented by the collection to create multi-faceted interpretive strategies. In a
2002 exhibition "Art from Africa: Long Steps Never Broke a Back," she
created a sense of immediacy through innovative acoustiguides. When visitors entered the galleries they found there were no labels or wall texts at all
– only the acoustiguides. And instead of spouting the usual "museum-speak"
that these devices often do, they relayed stories and proverbs, as told by
community elders and scholars. This was an effective way to show the
importance and complexity of oral history in traditional African cultures and
to provide museum education based on the priorities of source communities.

Other museum projects directly expose the subjectivity of museum activities. "Cultural Encounters," organized in 1996 by Elizabeth Hallam and Nicki
Levell at the Brighton Museum and Gallery, put on display the research
notes of anthropology graduate students from the University of Sussex, including work from the field, the archives, and the museum. By exposing this
usually private domain, the show revealed processes of constituting representations.[63] It also gave the anthropologists the chance to feel what it's like
to be put on display. Other projects have put the work of conservators on
display. "Altered States: Conservation, Analysis, and the Interpretation of
Works of Art," a 1994 exhibition at the Mount Holyoke College Museum of
Art, for instance, presented conservation as an art and a science.

Some museums in former colonized nations have set important precedents. District Six Museum in Cape Town was established in 1994 to honor
the memory of the District Six community, from which 60,000 people were
forcibly removed during the apartheid era. It stands as a memorial to all the
four million South African people forcibly removed to destroy mixed-race
neighborhoods. It also functions as a center to rebuild community by telling

29

stories. Due to the destruction of apartheid, very few artifacts, primarily road signs and photographs, have survived from District Six. Yet the founders of the institution saw that a museum is more than its material collections. District Six Museum collects memories and helps the healing process. It provides a community center for meetings and other group activities. The museum creates exhibits from oral histories. It has a sound archive. It facilitates the restitution of lands. It supports community development, including new housing that promotes interaction between neighbors. And, avoiding a triumphal narrative, the museum engages in self-critique.

Many museum theorists believe the most significant indicator of the rise in the post-museum is the changing nature of the relationship between institution and audience. Theorists cite the new status of educators, even at some more conservative museums like the Met, and the new attitude of respect for audience that puts the institution and the visitor on a more equal footing. Some museums are now making a concerted effort to get to know their audiences by assessing the quality of the visitor's experience. They engage in "front-end" evaluation to respond to visitors' suggestions before, not just after, an exhibition is complete. They support educational research that theorizes the museum experience. They acknowledge diverse learning styles and offer a variety of means by which to participate, such as lectures, performances, online exhibitions, video, art classes, workshops, and sometimes living history theater. There is now a recognition that visitors process the museum through the lens of their own experiences and value systems. As a result, some museums are prioritizing communication as one of their most important goals.[64]

In the emerging post-museum, educators work as a team with other museum staff, including curators and exhibition designers, to produce displays and coordinated programming that meet the needs of diverse audiences. The staff avoid crises by drawing constituencies into discussions at the earliest stages of a project. And the staff generate constructivist learning opportunities that empower the visitor to become an active and politicized participant in an open-ended educational experience.[65] Today, educators are using technology in innovative ways to show the complexities and contradictions of objects. When well designed, new media help visitors to ask questions, to challenge their preconceptions, and to stimulate dialogue. Museum websites, in particular, can provide new ways to interact with the museum. Most offer detailed context, archival data, and interactive activities. The best of them offer a glimpse into the museum's inner workings, including mission or director's statements, conservation efforts, and even curators' journals or logbooks for specific projects. A few host discussion pages where visitors can communicate directly with museum staff and even impact on exhibitions.[66]

According to Huyssen, such changes are "small but important steps toward a more genuinely heteronational culture. One that no longer feels the need to homogenize and is learning how to live pragmatically with real difference. We are far from that."[67] Part of the problem is that battles are fought locally, based on an individual institution's exhibition or policy. Understanding museum theory can help us to frame the debate from a larger perspective. What are the possibilities for museums in democratic culture? No one wants all museums to be the same. Artist Mark Dion argues that there's room for many kinds of institutions:

> When it comes to museums, I'm an ultra-conservative. To me the museum embodies the "official story" of a particular way of thinking at a particular time for a particular group of people. It is a time capsule. So I think once a museum is opened, it should remain unchanged as a window into the obsessions and prejudices of a period . . . If someone wants to update the museum, they should build a new one. An entire city of museums would be nice, each stuck in its own time.[68]

But because many museums do not provide transparency – do not articulate their agendas – visitors need to develop the critical skills to identify and challenge the choices being made. This book is dedicated to helping readers join the politically charged arena of discussion.

Notes

1 D. Preziosi. (1996). "Brain of the Earth's Body: Museums and the Framing of Modernity." In Paul Duro. (ed.). *The Rhetoric of the Frame: Essays on the Boundaries of the Artwork*. Cambridge: Cambridge University Press, 96–110, p. 97.

2 Much has been written on the Enola Gay controversy. See, for example, T. F. Gieryn. (1998). "Balancing Acts: Science, 'Enola Gay' and History Wars at the Smithsonian." In S. Macdonald. (ed.). *The Politics of Display: Museums, Science, Culture*. London and New York: Routledge, 197–228; S. C. Dubin. (1999). *Displays of Power: Memory and Amnesia in the American Museum*. New York and London: New York University Press, 186–226; J. W. Trent. (1997). "The Enola Gay on Display: Hiroshima and American Memory." *Positions: East Asian Cultures Critique*, 5: 3, 863–78; R. Kurin. (1997). "Exhibiting the Enola Gay." In *Reflections of a Culture Broker: A View from the Smithsonian*. Washington, DC, and London: Smithsonian Institution Press, 71–82;

S. A. Crane. (2004). "Memory, Distortion, and History in the Museum." In B. M. Carbonell. (ed.). *Museum Studies: An Anthology of Contexts*. Malden, MA, and Oxford: Blackwell, 328–32.

3   T. Webb. (2002). "Appropriating the Stones: The 'Elgin Marbles' and English National Taste." In E. Barkan and R. Bush. (eds.). *Claiming the Stones/Naming the Bones: Cultural Property and the Negotiation of National and Ethnic Identity*. Los Angeles: Getty Research Institute. Issues and Debates series, 51–96.

4   I. Gaskell. (2000). *Vermeer's Wager: Speculations on Art History, Theory and Art Museums*. London: Reaktion.

5   R. Handler and E. Gable. (1997). *The New History in an Old Museum: Creating the Past at Colonial Williamsburg*. Durham, NC, and London: Duke University Press. On authenticity, see D. Phillips. (1997). *Exhibiting Authenticity*. Manchester and New York: Manchester University Press; A. Huyssen. (1995). *Twilight Memories: Marking Time in a Culture of Amnesia*. London and New York: Routledge, pp. 32–5.

6   J. Cuno. (2004). "Introduction." In J. Cuno. (ed.). *Whose Muse? Art Museums and the Public Trust*. Princeton, NJ, and Oxford: Princeton University Press in association with Harvard University Art Museums, 11–25, p. 17.

7   Huyssen, *Twilight Memories*, 14–15, quote p. 15.

8   E. Hooper-Greenhill. (2004). "Changing Values in the Art Museum: Rethinking Communication and Learning." In Carbonell, *Museum Studies*, 556–75, p. 557; Cuno, "Introduction," p. 18.

9   See, for example, J. Clifford. (1988). *The Predicament of Culture: Twentieth-Century Ethnography, Literature, and Art*. Cambridge, MA: Harvard University Press, pp. 215–51; S. Vogel, A. Danto, R. M. Gramly, M. L. Hultgren, E. Schildkrout, and J. Zeidler (1988). *ART/Artifact: African Art in Anthropology Collections* (ex. cat. Center for African Art, New York).

10   For more on museums as a framing device, see Preziosi, "Brain of the Earth's Body," pp. 96–110; W. Ernst. (1996). "Framing the Fragment: Archaeology, Art, Museum." In Duro, *Rhetoric of the Frame*, 111–35. See also J. Derrida. (1987). "Parergon." In *The Truth in Painting*. G. Bennington and I. McLeod. (Trans.) Chicago: University of Chicago Press, 34–82.

11   P. Vergo. (1989). *The New Museology*. London: Reaktion.

12   For more on artists' impact on new museum theory, see D. Crimp. (1993). *On the Museum's Ruins*. Cambridge, MA, and London: MIT Press; J. C. Welchman. (1996). "In and Around the 'Second Frame.'" In Duro, *Rhetoric of the Frame*, 203–22. On Dada and Surrealist exhibitions, see M. A. Staniszewski. (1998). *The Power of Display: A History of Exhibition Installations at the Museum of Modern Art*. Cambridge, MA, and London: MIT Press. Though Benjamin's seminal essay "The Work of Art in the Age of Mechanical Reproduction" was first published in 1936, it was not widely available in English until 1968, at the time that many of these artists were formulating their positions; see W. Benjamin. (1968). *Illuminations*. H. Zohn. (trans.). H. Arendt. (ed.). New York: Schocken Books.

13   R. Smithson, "Cultural Confinement." Quoted in N. Holt. (ed.). (1972). *The Writings of Robert Smithson*. New York: New York University Press, p. 132.

14 On museums and digital art, see S. Delson. (2002). "Wiring into a Changing Climate: Museums and Digital Art." *Museum News*, 81: 2, 51–5, 63–4.

15 K. Clark. (1954). "The Ideal Museum." *Art News*, 52, 28–31, p. 29.

16 K. Clark. (1945). "Ideal Picture Galleries." *Museums Journal*, 45, 129–34, p. 133.

17 A. McClellan. (2003). "A Brief History of the Art Museum Public." In A. McClellan. (ed.). *Art and its Publics: Museum Studies at the Millennium*. Malden, MA, and Oxford: Blackwell, 1–49, p. 28.

18 P. de Montebello. (2004). "Art Museums: Inspiring Public Trust." In Cuno, *Whose Muse?*, 151–69, p. 155. For more on contemporary arguments for the museum as shrine, see the other essays in *Whose Muse?*

19 Clifford, *Predicament of Culture*, p. 2.

20 C. Duncan. (1995). *Civilizing Rituals: Inside Public Art Museums*. London and New York: Routledge, pp. 1–2.

21 D. Preziosi and C. Farago. (2004). "Introduction: Creating Historical Effects." In D. Preziosi and C. Farago. (eds.). *Grasping the World: The Idea of the Museum*. Aldershot and Burlington, VT: Ashgate, 13–21, p. 13. On museums and heritage sites as theater, see also B. Kirshenblatt-Gimblett. (1998). *Destination Culture: Tourism, Museums, and Heritage*. Berkeley, CA: University of California Press.

22 One of the first to put forth this argument is Duncan Cameron. See D. Cameron. (1972). "The Museum: A Temple or the Forum." *Journal of World History*, 14: 1, 189–202.

23 On museums and financial decision-making, see O. Robison, R. Freeman, and C. A. Riley II. (eds.). (1994). *The Arts in the World Economy: Public Policy and Private Philanthropy for a Global Cultural Community*. Hanover, NH, and London: University Press of New England. Salzburg Seminar; Gaskell, *Vermeer's Wager*, pp. 174–96; F. Ostrower. (2002). *Trustees of Culture: Power, Wealth and Status on Elite Art Boards*. Chicago and London: University of Chicago Press.

24 T. Hoving. (1994). *Making the Mummies Dance: Inside the Metropolitan Museum of Art*. New York: Touchstone.

25 Gaskell, *Vermeer's Wager*, pp. 165–73.

26 Kirschenblatt-Gimblett, *Destination Culture*, p. 151.

27 McClellan, "Brief History," p. 33.

28 N. Prior. (2003). "Having One's Tate and Eating It Too: Transformations of the Museum in a Hypermodern Era." In McClellan, *Art and its Publics*, 51–74, p. 54.

29 On the museum and marketing strategies, see C. Wu. (2002). *Privatising Culture: Corporate Art Intervention since the 1980s*. London and New York: Verso; McClellan, "Brief History," pp. 32–4. On the "Sensation" controversy, see G. Edelson. (2001). "Some Sensational Reflections." In L. Rothfield. (ed.). *Unsettling "Sensation": Arts-Policy Lessons from the Brooklyn Museum of Art Controversy*. New Brunswick, NJ, and London: Rutgers University Press, 171–80.

30 N. Harris. (1990). "Museums, Merchandising and Popular Taste: The Struggle for Influence." In *Cultural Excursions: Marketing Appetites and Cultural Tastes in Modern America*. Chicago and London: University of Chicago Press, 56–81; T. Bennett. (2004). "The Exhibitionary Complex." In Preziosi and Farago, *Grasping the World*, 413–41.

31 Kirschenblatt-Gimblett, *Destination Culture*; J. Baudrillard. (1982). "The Beauborg Effect: Implosion and Deterrence." *October*, 20, 3–13; R. Krauss. (2004). "The Cultural Logic of the Late Capitalist Museum." In Preziosi and Farago, *Grasping the World*, 600–14.

32 G. Debord. (1994). *The·Society of the Spectacle*. D. Nicholson-Smith. (trans.). New York: Zone Books, pp. 12–13.

33 I. Karp. (1991). "Culture and Representation." In I. Karp and S. D. Lavine. (eds.). *Exhibiting Cultures: The Poetics and Politics of Museum Displays*. Washington, DC: Smithsonian Institution Press, 11–24, p. 15. See also E. Hallam and B. V. Street. (2000). "Introduction: Cultural Encounters – Representing 'Otherness.'" In E. Hallam and B. V. Street. (eds.). *Cultural Encounters: Representing Othernesss*. London and New York: Routledge. Sussex Studies in Culture and Communication series, 1–10, pp. 5–6; A. Coombes. (1994). *Reinventing Africa: Museums, Material Culture and Popular Imagination in Late Victorian and Edwardian England*. New Haven, CT, and London: Yale University Press; M. Ames. (1992). *Cannibal Tours and Glass Boxes: The Anthropology of Museums*. Vancouver: University of British Columbia Press; G. Prakash. (2004). "Museum Matters." In Carbonell, *Museum Studies*, 208–15.

34 Hoving, *Making the Mummies Dance*.

35 On the history of exhibiting African art, see C. Clarke. (2003). "From Theory to Practice: Exhibiting African Art in the Twenty-First Century." In McClellan, *Art and its Publics*, 164–82.

36 J. N. Wood. (2004). "The Authorities of the American Art Museum" In Cuno, *Whose Muse?*, pp. 110, 113. On photography, see E. Edwards. (2003). "Talking Visual Histories: Introduction." In L. Peers and A. K. Brown. (eds.). *Museums and Source Communities: A Routledge Reader*. London and New York: Routledge, 83–99. On exhibiting human subjects, see Kirshenblatt-Gimblett, *Destination Culture*, pp. 7–78.

37 Quoted in R. Rugoff. (1995). "Beyond Belief: The Museum as Metaphor." In L. Cooke and P. Wollen. (eds.). *Visual Display: Culture Beyond Appearances*. New York: New Press. Dia Center for the Arts Discussions in Contemporary Culture series, 68–81, p. 81.

38 T. Adorno. (1976). "Valéry, Proust, Museum." In *Prisms*. S. and S. Weber. (trans.). Cambridge, MA: MIT Press, 173–86, p. 175. See also D. J. Sherman. (1994). "Quatremère/Benjamin/Marx: Art Museums, Aura, and Commodity Fetishism." In D. J. Sherman and Irit Rogoff. (eds.). *Museum Culture: Histories, Discourses, Spectacles*. Minneapolis: University of Minnesota Press. Media and Society series 6, 123–43; J. L. Déotte. "Rome, the Archetypal Museum, and the Louvre, the Negation of Division." In Preziosi and Farago, *Grasping the World*, 51–65.

39 Phillips, *Exhibiting Authenticity*, p. 165.

40 A. Konare. (1983). "Toward a New Type of Ethnographic Museum in Africa." *Museum*, 35: 3, 146–9, p. 146.

41 M. McLeod. (2004). "Museums without Collections: Museum Philosophy in West Africa." In Carbonell, *Museum Studies*, 455–60.

42 On repatriation, see E. Barkan. (2002). "Amending Historical Injustices: The Restitution of Cultural Property – An Overview." In Barkan and Bush, *Claiming the Stones/Naming the Bones*, 16–46.

43 C. Kreps. (2003). *Liberating Culture: Cross-Cultural Perspectives on Museums, Curation and Heritage Preservation*. London and New York: Routledge. Museum Meanings series.

44 L. Peers and A. K. Brown. (2003). "Introduction." In Peers and Brown, *Museums and Source Communities*, 1–10.

45 On feminism in the nineteenth-century museum, see J. Bailkin. (2004). "Picturing Feminism, Selling Liberalism: The Case of the Disappearing Holbein." In Carbonell, *Museum Studies*, 260–72. On feminist voices today, see G. Porter. (2004). "Seeing through Solidity: A Feminist Perspective on Museums." In Carbonell, *Museum Studies*, 107–9. On representation of gay and lesbian experience, see A. Vanegas. (2002). "Representing Lesbians and Gay Men in British Social History Museums." In R. Sandell. (ed.). *Museums, Society, Inequality*. London and New York: Routledge, Museum Meanings series, 98–109.

46 E. C. Hankins. (2003). "En/Gendering the Whitney's Collection of American Art." In L. Dillworth. (ed.). *Acts of Possession: Collecting in America*. New Brunswick, NJ, and London: Rutgers University Press, 163–89.

47 C. Duncan. (1989). "Hot Mamas in the MOMA." *Art Journal*, 48, 171–8; Duncan, *Civilizing Rituals*, 102–32.

48 B. Melosh. (1989). "Speaking of Women: Museums' Representations of Women's History." In W. Leon and R. Rosenzweig. (eds.). *History Museums in the United States: A Critical Assessment*. Champaign, IL: University of Illinois Press, 183–214.

49 Huyssen, *Twilight Memories*, 35. See also E. Hooper-Greenhill. (2001). *Museums and the Interpretation of Visual Culture*. London and New York: Routledge. Museum Meanings series; R. Sandell. (2002). "Museums and the Combating of Social Inequality: Roles, Responsibilities, Resistance." In Sandell, *Museums, Society, Inequality*, 3–23.

50 Kreps, *Liberating Culture*, pp. 79–91.

51 Kreps, *Liberating Culture*, pp. 94–5; Edwards, "Talking Visual Histories," pp. 95–7.

52 E. Hooper-Greenhill. (1992). *Museums and the Shaping of Knowledge*. London and New York: Routledge. See also M. Foucault. (1970). *The Order of Things: An Archaeology of the Human Sciences*. New York: Pantheon; M. Foucault. (1972). *The Archaeology of Knowledge and the Discourse on Language*. A. M. Sheridan-Smith. (trans.). New York: Pantheon; M. Foucault. (1973). *The Birth of the Clinic: An Archaeology of Medical Perception*. A. M. Sheridan-Smith. (trans.). New York: Pantheon; M. Foucault. (1977). *Discipline and Punish: The Birth of the Prison*. Alan Sheridan. (trans.). New York: Pantheon.

53 A. Witcomb. (2003). *Re-Imagining the Museum: Beyond the Mausoleum*. London and New York: Routledge. Museum Meanings series, pp. 13–18. See also McClellan, "Brief History," pp. 1–29; Bennett, "Exhibitionary Complex," pp. 413–41.

54 See also G. Olmi. (1985). "Science–Honor–Metaphor: Italian Cabinets of the Sixteenth and Seventeenth Centuries." In O. Impey and E. MacGregor. (eds.). *The Origin of Museums: The Cabinet of Curiosities in Sixteenth- and Seventeenth-Century Europe*. Oxford: Clarendon Press, 5–16, pp. 8–9; M. A. Meadow. (2002). "Merchants and Marvels: Hans Jacob Fugger and the Origins of the Wunderkammer." In P. H. Smith and P. Findlen. (eds.). *Merchants and Marvels: Commerce, Science, and Art in Early Modern Europe*. New York and London: Routledge, 182–200.

55 On the modern museum, see also Preziosi, "Brain of the Earth's Body," pp. 96–110; G. Perry and C. Cunningham. (1999). *Academies, Museums and Canons of Art*. New Haven, CT, and London: Yale University Press and Open University. Art and its Histories series, 207–37.

56 Quoted in McClellan, "Brief History," p. 36; see also pp. 29–40. And see M. Bal. (1996). *Double Exposures: The Subject of Cultural Analysis*. London and New York: Routledge; Duncan, *Civilizing Rituals*; P. Bourdieu and A. Darbel. (1991). *The Love of Art: European Art Museums and their Public*. C. Beattie and N. Merriman. (trans.). Cambridge: Polity.

57 G. Pollock. (2002). "A History of Absence Belatedly Addressed: Impressionism With and Without Mary Cassatt." In C. W. Haxthausen. (ed.). *The Two Art Histories: The Museum and the University*. Williamstown, MA: Sterling and Francine Clark Art Institute; New Haven, CT: Yale University Press, 123–41.

58 E. Pujol. (2001). "The Artist as Educator: Challenges in Museum-Based Residences." *Art Journal*, 60: 3, 4–6, p. 5. See also M. A. Lindauer. (2003). "Contesting Scientific Methods for Evaluating Museum Exhibitions: Arguing for an Arts-Based Approach." Paper presented at College Art Association Conference, New York; Hooper-Greenhill, *Museums and the Interpretation of Visual Culture*, 1–8.

59 Gaskell, *Vermeer's Wager*, p. 91. See also Crimp, *On the Museum's Ruins*; Krauss, "Cultural Logic of the Late Capitalist Museum."

60 D. Preziosi and C. Farago. (2004). "Introduction: Building Shared Imaginaries/Effacing Otherness." In Preziosi and Farago, *Grasping the World*, 229–36, p. 234.

61 Prior, "Having One's Tate," p. 68.

62 Prior, "Having One's Tate," p. 52. See also Porter, "Seeing through Solidity," pp. 113–16.

63 E. Hallam. (2000). "Texts, Objects and 'Otherness': Problems of Historical Process in Writing and Displaying Culture." In Hallam and Street, *Cultural Encounters*, 274–80.

64 Hooper-Greenhill,. "Changing Values," 570–2.

65 For more on new educational initiatives, see J. S. Hirsch and L. H. Silverman. (eds.). (2000). *Transforming Practice: Selections from the "Journal of Museum Education" 1992–1999*. Washington, DC: Museum Education Roundtable; L. C. Roberts. (1997). *From Knowledge to Narrative: Educators and the Changing Museum*. Washington, DC, and London: Smithsonian Institution Press; E. Hooper-Greenhill. (ed.). (1994). *The Educational Role of the Museum*. London and New York: Routledge. Leicester Readers in Museum Studies series.

66 On the potential of new technologies and of interactivity, see Witcomb, *Re-Imagining the Museum*, pp. 107–64.

67 Huyssen, *Twilight Memories*, p. 28.

68 Quoted in "Miwon Kwon in Conversation with Mark Dion." (1997). In L. G. Corrin, M. Kwon and N. Bryson. (eds.). *Mark Dion*. London: Phaidon Press, 6–33, p. 17.

Part I | Defining New Museum Theory

A Surveys and Groundwork

1 | THE ARCHITECTURE *IS* THE MUSEUM

Michaela Giebelhausen

Editor's Introduction

Michaela Giebelhausen is a lecturer in the Department of Art History and Theory and director of the MA in gallery studies at the University of Essex, UK. She has published several articles on prison architecture and has recently edited *The Architecture of the Museum: Symbolic Structures, Urban Contexts*. Her book *Painting the Bible: Representation and Belief in Mid-Victorian England* is forthcoming.

In the following chapter, Gielbelhausen traces the history of museum architecture, showing how "architecture *is* the museum," as her title attests. Looking at the disruptions rather than the continuities of this history, she isolates four paradigms, roughly associated with four time periods: arcadia and antiquity (late eighteenth to early nineteenth centuries); metropolis and modernity (mid- to late nineteenth century); a new century, a new aesthetic (early to mid-twentieth century); and recent reactions: fragmentation, contradiction, expression (late twentieth and early twenty-first centuries). In so doing, she relies on theorist Michel Foucault, who, in the 1970s and 1980s, isolated three historical epistemes, or systems of knowledge, based on the convergence of social, cultural, political, theological, scientific, and economic precepts, that led to major institutional shifts. Foucault was considering prisons, hospitals, and military barracks in his work but his ideas equally apply to museums. Giebelhausen argues that museum architecture is a highly symbolic building type that defines the institution. It is both sacred and modern, utopian and educational, and clearly represents the collections inside.

Most frequently compared to the temple or the cathedral, the museum is, in fact, closer in age to building types such as the prison, the railway station, or the department store. This crude juxtaposition, at first glance incidental and unflattering, highlights two issues that this chapter sets out to explore. The museum as a purpose-built structure is relatively recent: it dates back no further than the middle of the eighteenth century. Thus, it is not only contemporary with the prison but also less than a century older than the railway station and the department store. These seemingly accidental comparisons map a context for the museum that indicates both its spiritual heritage and its role in the formation of urban modernity. They also bring out the tensions inherent in that juxtaposition: a space both sacred and blatantly modern. This chapter charts the emergence of the museum as an independent building type and highlights some of the key stages of its architectural formation. I argue that the architecture *is* the museum: it is precisely the architectural configuration that gives the museum meaning. The architecture determines the viewing conditions both conceptually and physically. It not only frames the exhibits but also shapes our visitor experience.

From the beginning, the museum was conceptualized as a transformative space: at once educational and utopian, intended to celebrate the power of art and to display the authority of the state. Such intentions were intertwined in complex ways, as two seminal readings of the museum make clear. Carol Duncan and Alan Wallach first identified it as a space for the enactment of the "civilizing ritual," and, in Tony Bennett's Foucauldian interpretation, it figured as a disciplinary tool of the emerging nation state.[1] More recently, Charles Jencks has argued that the museum harbors spectacular contradictions and is, in fact, a schizophrenic monument to contemporary culture.[2] Despite such differences, the museum has mostly been understood as a building type that is poised to assess, define, and display the value of culture for the changing demands of contemporary society. This chapter explores just *how* such larger didactic and societal contexts are inscribed in the museum's architecture and display structures.

Arcadia and Antiquity

During the second half of the eighteenth century, a whole range of new building types was being developed in architectural competitions. These were mostly paper exercises: the submitted designs were not intended to be built. Instead, they sought to inspire debate and to visualize and organize complex new architectural forms. The public museum was a frequently set task in these problem-solving competitions. In 1763, George Dance the Younger won the gold medal of the Parma Academy for his design for a public gallery intended to display statues and pictures. Dance presented a richly decorated exterior with a colonnade and free-standing sculptures on the roof.[3] The sumptuous interiors were dominated by a sequence of large and small domed galleries. By the end of the decade, he had also designed the notorious Newgate Prison in London. Since neither building type had any precedents, Dance drew on the first-hand knowledge of antiquity that he had acquired during his time in Italy (1758–64). Both designs were inspired by specific Roman examples: the gallery's massing and detailing were based on the Baths of Caracalla; the prison's facade derived from the impressively rusticated wall that enclosed the forum of Nerva.[4] As influential reformers and thinkers such as John Howard and Jeremy Bentham turned their attention to the state of the prisons, humanitarian and economic concerns began to shape the long-term development of this building type. Consequently, prison design soon shed such antique elaborations and became increasingly utilitarian. By contrast, the museum continued to foster the resonances antiquity could bestow and developed into an overtly symbolic building type.

In 1800, the young Karl Friedrich Schinkel presented an important vision of the museum.[5] He situated the classical building – complete with temple-like portico and domed rotunda rupturing the roofline – in an antique landscape, which was peopled with classically draped figures and dotted with monuments and further classical buildings. There was nothing in Schinkel's oil sketch to indicate a possible contemporary context for the museum: his vision was truly Arcadian and ideal. While Schinkel's plan was closer to fiction than fact, such antique resonances did inspire contemporary museum architecture. The most impressive trace perhaps was to be found in Berlin's museum island: this cultural complex, which combined several important museums, was regarded as a "sacred and tranquil sanctuary for the sciences and the arts."[6] In an illustration of the early 1840s the scheme's outline recalled the Athenian Acropolis, antiquity's most famous cluster of cultural and ceremonial buildings.[7]

It is worth considering two further theoretical designs here which proved highly influential for the architectural articulation of the museum. Neither offered any contextual setting; instead, they concentrated on interior and exterior appearances. Etienne-Louis Boullée, a highly influential teacher in late eighteenth-century Paris, presented visionary and at times outright megalomaniac designs for different building types, of which the museum was one.[8] In line with his claim that architecture should be regarded as equal to painting, his designs often eschewed pragmatism and utility.[9] They were

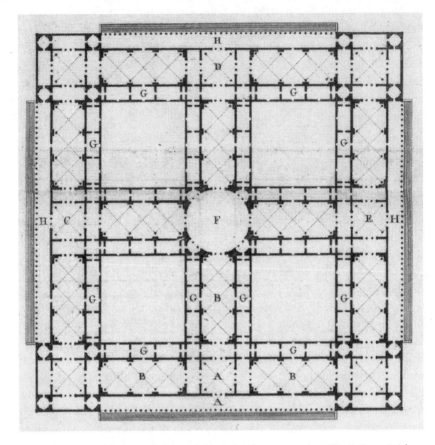

FIGURE 1.1 Jean-Nicolas-Louis Durand, ideal plan for a museum, 1802–5. From *Précis des Leçons de l'architecture données à l'École royale polytechnique*, 2 vols. (Paris, 1817–19, first published 1802–5)

daring and unfettered architectural visions: their sheer vastness was truly sublime; it inspired awe and dwarfed the human presence.

Boullée's designs required the modifications of his pupil, Jean-Nicolas-Louis Durand, to become practicable (figure 1.1). Durand's exemplary systematization of building types – published in the *Précis des Leçons* (1802–5) – provided early nineteenth-century architects with a blueprint for the museum. Durand retained the main characteristics of Boullée's design: a Greek cross inscribed into four wings of equal length; a central rotunda; four prominent entrances. But he scaled down all of these features considerably. A short accompanying text indicated the museum's chief functions:

they [museums] are built to conserve and to impart a precious treasure, and they must therefore be composed in the same spirit as libraries . . . The only difference that affects the disposition is that, since libraries hold only objects of a single kind and are designed throughout for a single use, they need no more than a single entrance . . . but museums, even those exclusively designed to hold the productions of the arts, contain objects of different kinds and are made up of parts intended for different kinds of study.[10]

Durand characterized the museum as both treasure house and repository of knowledge, containing different types of objects and serving different types of audiences. These inherently contradictory notions came into conflict in the debates that ensued over museums planned for Berlin and Munich. During the design stages, the architects crossed swords with a host of academic advisers in a protracted battle over the interior decoration and arrangement of the exhibits. While the architects demanded a treasure-house treatment to frame the precious objects, the academic advisers looked toward the conventions of the art academy – with its bare walls and even lighting – to ensure a focused viewing experience.

In 1815, Leo von Klenze won the competition to build a museum of sculpture, the Glyptothek, in a recently laid-out suburb of Bavaria's growing capital (figure 1.2).[11] The executed building was based on Durand's ideal design. It retained the four wings of equal length but omitted the Greek

FIGURE 1.2   Leo von Klenze, Glyptothek, Munich, 1815–30, main facade. Zentralinstitut für Kunstgeschichte, Phototek

cross and central rotunda. The main entrance was accentuated with a pedimented portico of eight Ionic columns. The Glyptothek's classicism was intended to reflect the collection's impressive holdings of genuine Greek antiquities. On entering the museum, the visitor turned left and passed through the galleries in which the history of sculpture unfolded in chronological sequence: ancient Egypt, Greece, the Roman Empire, and works by contemporary artists such as Schadow, Rauch, Thorvaldsen, and Canova. However, the chronology was punctuated by thematic and medium-based displays and by a set of banqueting rooms reserved for royal entertainment. Both were overhangs from previous modes of display: the thematic had long been favored by scholars and the reception rooms, of course, harked back to the representational functions of the palace. Thus, the Glyptothek was both modern and traditional in its modes of display.

Despite such idiosyncrasies, it proved a perfect space for the enactment of the "civilizing ritual": at once educational and processional. Accompanied by an explanatory catalogue and a contextual decorative scheme, the predominantly chronological displays culminated in a celebration of contemporary sculpture. Thus the museum not only made the art of antiquity available to a wider audience – more specifically, the citizens of the recent kingdom of Bavaria (founded as a result of the Napoleonic wars) – but also related past achievements to contemporary production. The potent claim to the continuity of artistic quality helped to represent the paternal power of the state. This represented a classic example of the "civilizing ritual," which – in the words of Duncan and Wallach – "equates state authority with the idea of civilization."[12] It was, after all, the benevolence of the Bavarian monarch which had made this educational experience possible, as a plaque in the entrance hall pointed out.

The year 1830 also saw the completion of Schinkel's Altes Museum in Berlin.[13] Here the displays comprised collections of antiquity and paintings arranged chronologically according to art-historical schools. They demonstrated a similar affirmation of contemporary culture's classical roots. Just as his colleague working in Munich had done, Schinkel adapted Durand's ideal museum design, even retaining the central rotunda. It was intended to change the visitor's register from the everyday to the contemplative: an echo of Arcadia in the city. In his visionary design of 1800, Schinkel had not only placed the museum in an antique setting but had also suggested the classical as the paradigmatic museum mode. As we have seen in the case of the Glyptothek, the architecture of ancient Greece offered the most immediate link with the art on display. Klenze made a similarly close symbolic connection in his subsequent museum building for Munich, the Pinakothek (1836), which was to house the royal collection of paintings.[14] Here he opted for the style of the High Renaissance, a period that epitomized the highest achievement in pictorial art. Special status was also accorded to the collection's works by the sixteenth-century painter Raphael, who was regarded as one of the most important artists of all times. His pictures were shown in a separate room and out of sequence with the otherwise broadly chronological arrangement in the other gallery spaces.

Even if not always Arcadian, typical museum buildings such as the Glyptothek and the Pinakothek, which was to become the blueprint for the nineteenth-century picture gallery, retained strong symbolic links with the collections. By looking backward to the golden ages of art – antiquity and the High Renaissance – they added historicizing and evocatively utopian dimensions to the modern city.

Metropolis and Modernity

"In great cities," Durand wrote in the *Précis*, "there may be several museums, some to hold the rarest productions of nature, others to contain the masterpieces of the arts. In lesser places, a single museum can serve these separate purposes simultaneously."[15] Accordingly, the number of museums indicated a city's true metropolitan status. This matter-of-fact observation contained the germ of the nineteenth-century museum mania that manifested itself in the aggressive accumulation and public display of cultural capital throughout the cities of the western world. As a highly symbolic building type, the museum also added meaningful resonances to the urban fabric.[16]

Once more, the Glyptothek and the Altes Museum provide typical examples. Although their respective urban locations were very different, these nevertheless indicated two major roles the museum was to play in shaping the nineteenth-century metropolis. The Glyptothek formed part of the newly laid-out suburban development to the north-west of Munich's center. It was situated on the north side of the Königsplatz, a square designed to commemorate the inauguration of the Bavarian kingdom in 1806. The Propylaeum – inspired by the gateway to the Athenian Acropolis – marked the approach to the city. With its array of classical buildings, the Königsplatz created an urban atmosphere that was at once almost Arcadian, deeply political, and dedicated to the modern state. Equally symbolically charged was the location of the Altes Museum in Berlin. Situated on the newly created north side of the Schlossplatz, the museum faced the royal residence and was flanked by the cathedral, the arsenal, and the university. Thus, the recent urban building type of the museum had taken up its place among the defining institutions of the state. To the formation of bourgeois society it contributed both an educational encounter with high culture and a symbolic legitimization for the powers of the modern state. From the 1830s onward, impressive museum buildings started springing up in all major European and American cities. Some dates – relating to the opening of the respective buildings and not necessarily concurrent with the institution's foundation – might be enlightening here: National Gallery, London (1838); British Museum, London (1847); the New Hermitage, St Petersburg (1851); Picture Gallery, Dresden (1855); National Museum, Stockholm (1866); Pennsylvania Academy of Fine Arts, Philadelphia (1876); Metropolitan Museum, New York (1880); Kunsthistorisches Museum, Vienna (1889).

The museum-building boom of the second half of the nineteenth century was part of the transformation most major cities witnessed. The museum – in the varied forms mentioned by Durand – joined a range of new building types such as the railway station and the department store, which are more commonly regarded as typical markers of urban modernity. Railway stations became the city's new portals, replacing traditional gates and toll barriers. The exposed glass-and-iron construction of the impressive sheds was a testimony to the age of mass transport and industrial production. Simultaneously, the extensive collections of what Duncan and Wallach have termed "the universal survey museum" rivaled the material abundance of the modern consumer society. This found its typical expression in the international exhibitions and world's fairs – held regularly in major European and American cities from 1851 – and in the department store, which sold "everything from pins to elephants."[17] The proliferation of material production which characterized nascent consumer culture also impacted on the museum. In addition to functioning as a traditional training ground for fine artists, the museum began to focus on the applied arts. This is most clearly demonstrated in the case of the South Kensington Museum (later renamed the Victoria and Albert Museum).[18] It was founded as a direct result of the Great Exhibition of 1851, held in the Crystal Palace, and it served as a sample collection for artisans and designers to inspire contemporary production. In some ways, the civilizing ritual inscribed in the museum visit, which turned citizenship into a performative exercise and thus embodied and visualized the power of the state, was also being harnessed to enhance the nation's output of material goods. Civic rivalry – so clearly indicated in Durand's equation between a city's status and the number of museums it possessed – was taken a step further in the international competition over economic hegemony.

The national displays at world's fairs and the abundance of goods in the department store both catered to a consumer society and its attendant inevitability: the crowd. The architecture of the museum also developed an affinity with these sites of modern mass culture. The much-maligned iron structures of the South Kensington Museum, the so-called Brompton Boilers erected in 1856, would have been inconceivable as museum spaces prior to the Great Exhibition of 1851. Their unadorned appearance was partly dictated by economy and partly by an unspoken sense of modernity expressed in buildings such as the Crystal Palace. Museum architecture also increasingly responded to the need for crowd control. The atrium design, with encircling galleries that defined the architecture of the department store, first appeared – albeit in modified form – in building types such as the exhibition building and the prison.[19]

These multi-leveled and galleried spaces offered multiple vantage points from which crowds could be surveilled. Such technologies of control either operated overtly, as in the prison, or were inherent in the behavior of the shopper and the museum visitor, who were both locked in a controlling exchange of gazes with others. Control and peer control alleviated the fears of unruly crowds which arose in the museum's effort to extend the civilizing rituals of citizenship to educate the working classes. Firmly established as a governmental tool, the museum no longer just confirmed the fledgling bourgeois assumption of citizenry – mostly modeled on some notion of the antique – but also became the space for self-improvement and societal self-regulation.

These diverse strands came together in the South Kensington Museum's South Court, which was built to house the Loan Exhibition of art that accompanied the 1862 International Exhibition (figure 1.3).[20] Both structures were designed by Francis Fowke. The South Court consisted of two lavishly decorated halls of double height, which were separated by a central gallery and flanked on either side by further galleries. The architecture combined the iron-and-glass structure of the train shed – recently made popular also for exhibition buildings – with a Renaissance-inspired decorative scheme for which Richard Sykes had drawn on the objects in the museum's collections. Arcaded on ground level, the walls were decorated with a set of mosaics which represented artists – painters, sculptors, potters, and other craftsmen and designers, and even a few architects – from antiquity to the present.

FIGURE 1.3 Interior of the South Kensington Museum (now the Victoria and Albert Museum), South Court, eastern portion, from the south, c.1876, showing the copy by F. W. Moody of Raphael's *School of Athens*, proposed for the gallery. Drawing by John Watkins. Victoria and Albert Museum, Print Room, no. 8089.L

This idiosyncratic selection reflected the diversity of the collections. Under the balconies at either end of the South Court, portrait roundels of politicians were installed. This rather sober line-up of officials complemented the roll-call of art workers and served as a potent reminder of governmental power inscribed in the project. The central Prince Consort Gallery, which dissected the South Court and housed some of the collection's main treasures, was dedicated to the memory of Prince Albert, who had been a staunch supporter of the museum. In the huge lunettes above the balconies Frederic Leighton was commissioned to paint two frescoes, *The Arts of Industry as Applied to War* (1880) and *The Arts of Industry as Applied to Peace* (1886). They illustrated the application of the arts to the states of the nation. From the balconies, visitors could not only get a closer look at the decoration but also survey both the displays and other visitors in the court below. The decorative scheme of the South Court represented the workings and aspirations of the museum. The celebration of artistic production and industry was an acknowledgment of consumer society and of the museum's role in raising the nation's productivity through inspiring sample collections.

The gradual diversification of museums reflected the wealth of the material and natural worlds and favored systems of classification that focused on the typical rather than the singular; objects deemed to exemplify categories were displayed and those judged to be anomalies were rejected. Narratives of development characterized the predominantly chronological display of art and – in the words of Bennett – "conferred a new codified visibility on the history of the nation and the history of art."[21] These narratives were applied to all man-made objects and to specimens of natural history as well. The modern age had shattered traditional certainties and questioned humankind's central position in the universe. According to Michel Foucault, the new order of things depended on "a history restored to the irruptive violence of time."[22] The taxonomies that dominated the rational museum stemmed from a desire to assert control in this disorienting age. Knowledge was based on an evolutionary narrative that unfolded over time, and expertise was acquired through the study of an object's development. As Bennett's Foucauldian analysis asserts: "The museum functions as a site in which the figure of 'Man' is reassembled from his fragments."[23] The architecture of the museum not only enabled developmental displays which unfolded along a processional route, but also provided symbolic architectural decoration which helped to frame the elaborate classification of the collections.

The Natural History Museum, London, which opened in 1881, might serve as an example here (figure 1.4). When taking over from the late Francis Fowke in 1865, Alfred Waterhouse made significant changes to the design. Most noticeably, he replaced the Renaissance style with the Romanesque, which not only allowed more scope for figurative decoration but also added sacred resonances.[24] With its arched portal and huge flanking towers, the main entrance evoked the great examples of Romanesque ecclesiastical architecture. This was taken further in a spectacular entrance hall that stretched into the distance like the main nave of a cathedral. Such deliberate substitution of the classical allowed the wonders of creation to be placed in a Christian framework. Everywhere in the museum, the figurative decoration constituted a mixture of heraldic, extinct, and extant creatures, represented in repeating terracotta molds. Additionally, the west half – dedicated to zoological displays – was decorated with examples of living species; the east side, which contained the geological displays, was decorated with extinct specimens. Standing on the central gable of the main portal, the statue of Adam presided over creation. Here the figure of Man was indeed reassembled from his fragments. His presence could be read as both the pinnacle of Christian creation – symbolically framed by the cathedral front – and the

FIGURE 1.4 Alfred Waterhouse, Natural History Museum, London, 1871–81. Photograph by Michaela Giebelhausen

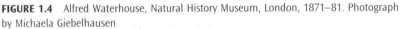

result of the evolutionary process inscribed in the overall decorative scheme. According to the biblical account, Adam named all the animals in the Garden of Eden. Consequently, he was the first collector and classifier of natural phenomena: the prototype of the curator. The architecture of the museum continued to be symbolically resonant: the secularized cathedral setting celebrated the wonders of the natural world while simultaneously allowing conventional Christian and modern scientific readings.

The nineteenth-century museum not only shared some traits with unequivocal markers of urban modernity such as the department store, the railway station, and even the prison, but also continued to present the viewing of objects – both man-made and natural – as an almost sacred experience. Architecturally its inspirations ranged from the temple of classical antiquity and its attendant civilizing rituals to the cathedral of the Middle Ages, whose diverse historical styles offered a wider scope for figurative and educational decoration to illustrate the order of things.

A New Century, a New Aesthetic

By the end of the nineteenth century the museum had been firmly established as an indispensable urban building type. Over the course of the century, it had proliferated just as Durand had suggested in the *Précis des Leçons*. The museum had become an emblem not only of culture but also of nation and increasingly of industrial prowess and modernity. The year 1929 saw two very different museum ventures: Clarence Stein's Museum of Tomorrow and the Museum of Modern Art in New York, which came to dominate the aesthetics of display for much of the twentieth century.

Clarence Stein drew up a detailed set of plans outlining his vision for the Museum of Tomorrow.[25] Although never built, the design captured two important issues. Stylistically, it had left behind the classical temple. The Museum of Tomorrow looked toward the latest architectural evocation of modernity: the skyscraper. At the core of the massive structure stood a central tower surrounded by display galleries on seven levels. This stepped massing made the elevation less soaring and gave the building the gravitas of a Gothic cathedral. The ground-floor plan combined several earlier configurations of the museum. Into the octagonal layout, eight wings were inscribed which radiated from the central information space. The scheme thus combined Durand's classic layout – central rotunda and Greek cross inscribed into a square of galleries – with the typical formation of early reform prisons, in which a flexible number of wings radiated from a central surveillance space.

Despite such derivative combinations, Stein's design contained an important innovation. The galleries were divided into those of interest to a general visitor and those housing reserve and study collections. Although the possibility of such a division had previously been discussed (for example, in the arrangement of galleries in London's Natural History Museum), Stein's design clearly distinguished between the needs of different visitor groups. The museum-going public was no longer perceived as homogenous: ideal citizens who shared a similar degree of knowledge and interest. At the museum's center Stein put the information area. The general visitor was most likely to remain close to the center and traverse the galleries that radiated from here. These contained contextual displays arranged in period rooms. Along the octagonal circumference of the vast building ran the reserve galleries and study collections which served a specialist audience.

The design offered strategies to cope with the immense accumulation of artifacts that increasingly characterized North America's prestigious museums. Gone were the days when the history of art unfolded in a processional route through a single sequence of galleries as had been the case in, for example, the Glyptothek. Stein's cathedral-like museum skyscraper responded to the overwhelming size of collections, and the arrangement of galleries acknowledged the different needs of audiences which had to be accommodated alongside each other. Its symbolic resonances incorporated the nineteenth-century legacy: as both skyscraper and cathedral, it combined tradition and modernity.

In contrast, the Museum of Modern Art (MoMA) in New York constituted a truly new departure.[26] It was founded with the aim of displaying contemporary art and staying abreast of developments. Alfred H. Barr, Jr, the first director, conceived of the museum as a torpedo moving through time. As it acquired and displayed contemporary art, it also handed over works which had been validated by the passage of time to its sister institution, the Metropolitan Museum, where they took up their respective places in the art-historical canon. This initial arrangement ensured that MoMA's collections remained up to the minute. Conceptually, MoMA was a museum in flux. Unlike its nineteenth-century predecessors, it had no desire to write permanent histories. During the first ten years of its existence, before moving to its brand-new building on West 53rd Street, it staged seminal exhibitions such as "Machine Art" (1934), "Cubism and Abstract Art" (1936), and "Fantastic Art, Dada, Surrealism" (1936). It introduced American audiences to a wide range of European avant-garde movements, including functionalist architectural design inspired by the Bauhaus. The 1932 show, "International Style," brought Europe's modernist architecture to the attention of American museum-goers. Through its exhibitions, collection policy, and outreach programs, MoMA promoted an understanding of modernism across a range of disciplines such as painting, sculpture, print media, film, photography, architecture, and design. Given this vigorous and holistic approach, it is not surprising to find that the permanent building into which MoMA finally moved in 1939 was in fact its prime exhibit.

Philip L. Goodwin and Edward Durell Stone designed an elegant modernist structure which sat flush amongst the nineteenth-century residential brown-

stones on West 53rd Street. The entrance – on street level and accentuated by an outward-curving canopy – gently receded and thus drew the
visitor into the main lobby. With its industrial materials, horizontal window
bands, and vertical lettering that identified the institution, the facade presented a departure from traditional museum architecture. Despite such stylistic contrasts, the building continued to function symbolically: its modernist
articulation spoke clearly of the collections it housed. The dedication to the
contemporary was reflected in the diverse exhibition program and ever-
changing collections. This required display spaces of unprecedented flexibility.
The open-plan space could be subdivided with partitions according to the
specific needs of each exhibition. For the inaugural show, "Art in Our Time,"
slender partitions created a sequence of mostly square rooms, which mapped
a prescribed route. The flexibility of MoMA's displays focused on the construction of the specific exhibition narrative, not on increasing visitor choice, or
indeed differentiating between the needs of different groups of museum-goers.

MoMA invented a new display aesthetic, which Brian O'Doherty has
called the white cube: spaces that aimed to focus attention on the individual
work of art.[27] Plain white walls, neutral floors, no architectural decoration:
in short, nothing to distract from the delicate act of contemplation. The
white cube, in which works are hung in a single line at a respectable distance
from each other, became the ubiquitous and normative form of display for
most of the twentieth century.

Previous types of display aimed to construct a contextual, educational, or
illustrative connection between the objects and the overall gallery space.
They presented the history of art as part of a larger celebratory history of
national achievement. In contrast, MoMA's galleries suggested the art work's
independence from the outside world. Emphasis was on the work and its relation to artistic movements, which were characterized by formal similarities.
The art was presented not as a product of a specific social order but as the
work of individual genius. MoMA sought to separate the story of modern
art from the competitive histories of nations.

Recent Reactions: Fragmentation, Contradiction, Expression

From the early days, the museum was torn between different possible modes
of display, different rhetorics of self-representation, and the need to serve
different user-groups. The early debates, in which the notions of treasure house and monument to culture were pitched against those of the art

academy and the studio, highlighted the tensions inherent in this diverse and complex building type. However, more often than not, the museum succeeded in demonstrating a coherent purpose which was expressed in its symbolically charged architecture. It is only relatively recently that the architecture of the museum has acknowledged the contradictions inherent in the building type. "The contemporary museum," observed Jencks in 1997, "is a spectacular contradiction of old requirements and new, mutant opportunities."[28] How then did the museum become a building type of *spectacular* contradiction during the 1990s?

The modernist white cube which dominated, in particular, the architecture of the art museum was the paradigm that superseded the classical. Its abstract and purified spaces provided the new secular sanctuary in which to celebrate an unadulterated encounter with art. During the 1970s, an anti-museum movement began to challenge this allegedly neutral environment.[29] So-called alternative spaces provided opportunities for artists to experiment and escape the overt commercialization of their work. One of the most influential was P.S.1, a contemporary art center located in a former school in New York City's borough of Queens. To this day, the flair of the abandoned informs the display spaces, which retain a degree of makeshift immediacy absent from the over-aestheticized museum environment.

The first major reconceptualization of the museum was the Centre Pompidou (1977) by Renzo Piano and Richard Rogers. Situated in a historical part of Paris, the building ruptured the immediate urban environment. Its scale, high-tech vernacular, and unusual color scheme were bold and discordant. The project represented a new departure: a cultural center that combined diverse functions such as a library, videotheque, temporary exhibition spaces, a bookshop, cafés, and restaurants, and the city's museum of modern art. The Pompidou functions as a multidisciplinary cultural factory which attracts a variety of audiences. Here the viewing of art becomes just one of a range of cultural activities. This emphasis on diversity creates a metropolitan buzz which also characterizes the atmosphere of the center's huge main lobby and the adjacent public square. The architecture displays functional elements such as ventilation ducts and escalators on the outside: an emblem of cultural production that emphasizes use, flux, and change rather than stasis and timelessness.

With the rise of postmodernism, the museum not only began to reclaim its historical roots but also to celebrate an architecture of what Robert Venturi termed the "Both-And," which increasingly acknowledged complexities and contradictions.[30] In many ways, James Stirling's extension to the Staatsgalerie in Stuttgart (1983) may best epitomize the museum's new-found historicity and conceptual playfulness.

Stirling reinterpreted the archetypal layout of Schinkel's Altes Museum: the traditional sequence of galleries and the central rotunda.[31] This ensemble he prefixed with an undulating facade whose main elements are boldly colorful. Pink and blue oversized railings flank the ramped approach; the main front – glazed and framed in grass-green – refracts and fragments any reflections; and the entrance is bright red and off-center. While these details are far from traditional, the approach still retains elements of the processional, almost ceremonial.

Inside, the main lobby exudes the functional atmosphere of an airport lounge, which is accentuated by the grass-green floor and the colorful high-tech lifts, reminiscent of the Centre Pompidou. In contrast, the display galleries are arranged in a processional route and draw on the "white cube" aesthetic, which, however, they modulate through adding historicized detailing. A further inflection occurs in the central rotunda (figure 1.5). Not only is it open to the sky and overhung with ivy but it also remains inaccessible from inside the museum. More ruin than traditional spiritual core, the rotunda invites contemplation on the role of culture in the postmodern age.

FIGURE 1.5 James Stirling, extension to the Neue Staatsgalerie, Stuttgart, 1977–83, view of central rotunda. Photograph by Michaela Giebelhausen

Simultaneously built on Schinkel's plan and reflecting "on the museum's ruins" – as Douglas Crimp[32] had so evocatively done in his essay of 1980 – Stirling's Staatsgalerie extension effectively visualizes what is true of most modern museums: "the history of the building type is always expected to be available in the mind."[33]

This overt return of history generated a wide range of responses to the architecture of the museum. Consequently, several interesting ways to break away from the mostly classical or modernist expressions of cultural universality developed. Fragmentation and playfulness erupted most forcefully in the Groninger Museum (1995) in the Netherlands. Alessandro Mendini, together with a team of designers and architects – among them Philippe Starck and the architectural practice Coop Himmelb(l)au – conceived of the museum as a series of distinct, yet connected, pavilions.[34] Each clearly displays the signature of its maker. For example, the high-tech deconstructivism of Coop Himmelb(l)au contrasts sharply with the cool chic we have come to expect from Philippe Starck. The Groninger Museum acknowledged that the contemporary museum could no longer be conceived as a unified and unifying representation of culture. The museum had to accommodate diverse collections (fine art, decorative arts, and local history), provide spaces for temporary exhibitions, and meet the needs of different audiences. It did so by inviting architects and designers to collaborate in producing a vibrant and controversial complex of independent yet related units, each of which provides a unique visitor experience. The Groninger Museum celebrates the contradictions inherent in the building type in a very immediate and flamboyant fashion.

More recently, a new expressionism has taken two forms: formal and conceptual. Frank Gehry's exuberant architecture has invigorated museum design.[35] In particular, the Bilbao Guggenheim, which opened in 1997, functions as urban landmark and global indicator. Not only did it anchor a whole new cultural precinct designed to rejuvenate the Basque capital and postindustrial port town, but it also sought to attract global interest. The city's facelift included a new subway system and an airport expansion, which was instrumental in making it a low-budget airline destination. Such combined policies helped put Bilbao firmly on the map of cultural tourism.

While Gehry's museums are spectacular landmarks, Daniel Libeskind's designs aim to give expressive form to the specific nature of the museum. This is evident in Berlin's Jewish Museum (2001) and the more recent Imperial War Museum of the North, which opened in Manchester in 2002. In both, Libeskind provided a symbolic and emotive expression of the museum's specific historical contents and display narratives. The architecture is evocative and resonant: it visualizes the museum's main themes. In the case of the Jewish Museum, which focuses on the history of Berlin's Jewish population, voids inscribed into the architecture function as memorial to the terrible absence the Holocaust created.[36] The museum's memorial aspect is also brought out in the Holocaust tower – a dark and chilling space of meditation – and the E. T. A. Hoffmann Garden, whose 49 concrete stele commemorate the recognition of Israel's independence in 1949. Recent examples such as these speak of a clear involvement: the architecture of the museum remains charged with symbolic meaning.

Over time, these meanings have, of course, changed. We no longer accept a universal approach to culture, embodied in the temple-like structures that referenced classical antiquity as both an artistic and a political ideal. Nor do we share the nineteenth-century museum's aspiration to totality, which was impressively captured in the classification and decorative schemes of London's Natural History Museum. More recently, the museum has come to depend on a multiplicity of meanings. Consequently, the architectural configurations have fragmented and proliferated.

While new buildings continue to reflect contemporary concerns, it is much harder for existing museums to adapt to changing conventions of display. Most of the examples discussed in this chapter have undergone some form of transformation, but three best exemplify the changes museum architecture has witnessed since the second half of the twentieth century. The Victoria and Albert Museum's lavishly decorated South Court is no longer visible to today's visitor. In 1949–50, it disappeared behind whitewashed partition walls and false ceilings to create a new restaurant.[37] It has since become the museum's largest temporary exhibition space. The balconies at either end of the South Court have been transformed into dimly lit corridors. Here Leighton's frescoes seem out of scale and out of place. A small peephole in the corridor wall allows a glimpse of the South Court's upper tier of decoration and glass-and-iron roof construction. This view also reveals the brutality of the architectural intervention. The original symbolic scheme has been obliterated and has given way to a multi-purpose space which has since served several different functions.

Given the close relationship between the architecture of the museum and its symbolical meanings and display paradigms, change is always fraught with difficulty. Ian Ritchie's provocative Ecology Gallery – installed in the Natural History Museum in 1991 – is a significant example of such an architectural intervention. The new structure is free-standing and inscribed into the existing galleries; it is dramatically lit and connects the displays via bridges. The Victorian shell is a ghostly presence. The museum's nineteenth-century narrative has been over-written, its didactic decorative scheme a faint echo. According to Ritchie, the gallery "creates another image within the magnificent romanesque building."[38] Unlike the South Court's obliteration, Ritchie's additional layer does not destroy, it invites discovery. Here the museum, whose original architecture was resonant, rich, and symbolic, acquires further layers.

Recently, MoMA has undergone the most extensive restructuring process in its long history. The new galleries were inaugurated in November 2004, in time for MoMA's seventy-fifth anniversary. Yoshio Taniguchi's design relates to both the museum's original display philosophy, the "white box," and the several architectural layers that have accumulated on the site since the Goodwin/Stone building opened to the public in 1939. Taniguchi believes that "architecture should not compete with the work of art." Instead, he claims: "The architecture should disappear."[39] This of course it never does. Further architectural layers may serve to obliterate, obscure, or enhance the original architecture. Nevertheless, such structures within structures, reminiscent of a Russian doll, guarantee that the architecture *is* the museum.

Questions for Discussion

1   Characterize the four paradigm shifts in the history of museum architecture, as Giebelhausen identifies them. Cite some museums that you're familiar with and discuss how each was shaped by one of the four.
2   What does Giebelhausen mean when she claims "the architecture *is* the museum"? Do you agree or not?
3   How does museum architecture represent the collections inside?
4   How has the "white cube" influenced the way we understand modern art? What is its legacy?
5   How does postmodern museum architecture meet the goals of museums trying to redefine themselves?
6   Is museum architecture today still a space for the enactment of the "civilizing ritual"? Is it a disciplinary tool? Does museum architecture continue to surveille? Is it still influenced by the department store and the world's fair?

Notes

1   C. Duncan and A. Wallach. (1980). "The Universal Survey Museum." *Art History*, 3: 4, 448–69. Duncan has subsequently developed the notion of the "civilizing ritual"

in, for example, (1995). *Civilizing Rituals: Inside Public Art Museums*. London and New York: Routledge. See also T. Bennett. (1995). *The Birth of the Museum: History, Theory, Politics*. London and New York: Routledge, pp. 15–105.

2   C. Jencks. (1997). "The Contemporary Museum." *AD Profile*, 130, 9–13.

3   J. Lever. (2003). *Catalogue of the Drawings of George Dance the Younger (1741–1825) and of George Dance the Elder (1695–1768), from the Collection of Sir John Soane's Museum*. London: Azimuth Editions, pp. 73–8.

4   Knowledge of antique architecture was also mediated through G. B. Piranesi's extremely popular print series. The forum of Nerva, for example, was evocatively captured in *Vedute di Roma* (1740s onward). For an illustration, see L. Ficacci. (2000). *Giovanni Battista Piranesi: The Complete Etchings*. Cologne: Benedikt Taschen Verlag, p. 712.

5   For an illustration, see B. Bergdoll. (1994). *Karl Friedrich Schinkel: An Architect for Prussia*. New York: Rizzoli, pp. 16–17.

6   V. Plagemann. (1967). *Das deutsche Kunstmuseum, 1790–1870: Lage, Baukörper, Raumorganisation, Bildprogramm* [The German Art Museum, 1790–1870]. Munich: Prestel Verlag, p. 118 (my translation).

7   See lithograph after Friedrich August Stüler, in Zentralinstitut für Kunstgeschichte München. (ed.). 1994. *Berlins Museen: Geschichte und Zukunft* [Berlin's Museums: History and Future]. Munich: Deutscher Kunstverlag, p. 59.

8   For elevation, ground-floor plan, and section, see N. Pevsner. (1976). *A History of Building Types*. London: Thames and Hudson, p. 119. For more on Boullée, see A. McClellan. (2002). "From Boullée to Bilbao: The Museum as Utopian Space." In E. Mansfield. (ed.). *Art History and its Institutions: Foundations of a Discipline*. London and New York: Routledge, 46–64.

9   H. Rosenau. (ed.). (1953). *Boullée's Treatise on Architecture*. London: Alec Tiranti. The epigram on the title page shows that Boullée regarded himself as a painter, p. 25.

10 J. N. L. Durand. (2000). *Précis of the Lectures on Architecture*. D. Britt (trans.). Los Angeles: Getty Research Institute, p. 160. (Original work published 1802–5.)

11 For a thorough account of the museum's history, consult the catalogue that accompanied the Glyptothek's 150th anniversary exhibition, K. Vierneisel and G. Leinz. (eds.). (1980). *Glyptothek München 1830–1980* [Glyptothek Munich, 1830–1980]. Munich: Glyptothek München.

12 Duncan and Wallach, "Universal Survey Museum", p. 450.

13 For an illustration of the main facade, see Pevsner, *History of Building Types*, p. 127.

14 For an illustration of the main facade, see Pevsner, *History of Building Types*, p. 129.

15 Durand, *Précis*, p. 160.

16 For an exploration of the museum's relationship with the city, see the essays in M. Giebelhausen. (ed.). (2003). *The Architecture of the Museum: Symbolic Structures, Urban Contexts*. Manchester: Manchester University Press.

17 Pevsner, *History of Building Types*, p. 267. For a useful survey of international exhibitions and world's fairs, see P. Greenhalgh. (1988). *Ephemeral Vistas: The Expositions Universelles, Great Exhibitions and World's Fairs, 1851–1939*. Manchester: Manchester University Press.

18   For an architectural history of the museum, see J. Physick. (1982). *The Victoria and Albert Museum: The History of its Building*. Oxford: Phaidon and Christie's.

19   For illustrations of such display spaces, see Bennett, *Birth of the Museum*, pp. 50–4. For an illustration of a comparable prison wing, see Pevsner, *History of Building Types*, p. 167.

20   For a succinct analysis of the South Court, see T. Barringer. (1998). "Re-presenting the Imperial Archive: South Kensington and its Museums." *Journal of Victorian Culture*, 3: 2, 357–73.

21   Bennett, *Birth of the Museum*, p. 36.

22   M. Foucault. (1970). *The Order of Things: An Archaeology of the Human Sciences*. New York: Pantheon, p. 132. (Original work published 1966.)

23   Bennett, *Birth of the Museum*, p. 39.

24   C. Cunningham and P. Waterhouse. (1992). *Alfred Waterhouse 1830–1905: Biography of a Practice*. Oxford: Clarendon Press, pp. 72–6. See also M. Girouard. (1981). *Alfred Waterhouse and the Natural History Museum*. London: British Museum (Natural History).

25   For illustrations of Stein's designs, see H. Searing. (1982). *New American Art Museums*. New York: Whitney Museum of American Art; Berkeley: University of California Press, pp. 47–8.

26   Useful further reading on MoMA: C. Grunenberg. (1994). "The Politics of Presentation: The Museum of Modern Art, New York." In M. Pointon. (ed.). *Art Apart: Art Institutions and Ideology Across England and North America*. Manchester: Manchester University Press, 192–211; M. A. Staniszewski. (1998). *The Power of Display: A History of Exhibition Installations at the Museum of Modern Art*. Cambridge, MA, and London: MIT Press.

27   In a series of influential articles that first appeared in *Artforum* magazine in 1976 and 1986, Brian O'Doherty analyzed and critiqued the aesthetic of the white cube gallery. These were subsequently reprinted in O'Doherty. (1999). *Inside the White Cube: The Ideology of the Gallery Space*. Expanded edition. Berkeley, CA, and Los Angeles: University of California Press.

28   Jencks, "Contemporary Museum," p. 9.

29   For a useful account of post-1970s developments, see D. Davis. (1990). *The Museum Transformed: Design and Culture in the Post-Pompidou Age*. New York: Abbeville Press.

30   R. Venturi. (1966). *Complexity and Contradiction in Architecture*. New York: Museum of Modern Art.

31   For ground-floor plans of both the Altes Museum and Stirling's extension to the Staatsgalerie, see V. Newhouse. (1998). *Towards a New Museum*. New York: Monacelli Press, pp. 180–1.

32   Reprinted in D. Crimp. (1993). *On the Museum's Ruins*. Cambridge, MA, and London: MIT Press.

33   C. S. Smith. (1995). "Architecture and the Museum: The Seventh Reyner Banham Memorial Lecture." *Journal of Design History*, 8: 4, 243–56, quote p. 243.

34   M. Martin, C. Wagenaar, and A. Welkamp. (eds.). (n.d.). *Alessandro and Francesco Mendini, Philippe Starck, Michele de Lucchi, Coop Himmelb(l)au in Groningen*. Groningen: Groninger Museum.

35 For a useful "official" summary history with ample illustrations, see C. Van Bruggen. (1997). *Frank O. Gehry: Guggenheim Museum Bilbao*. New York: Solomon R. Guggenheim Foundation.

36 For a succinct description with illustrations, see B. Schneider. (1999). *Daniel Libeskind: Jewish Museum Berlin*. Munich: Prestel Verlag. See also D. Libeskind. (1997). "Between the Lines." In *Radix–Matrix: Architecture and Writings*. P. Green (trans.). Munich: Prestel Verlag, 34–55.

37 Barringer, "Re-presenting the Imperial Archive," p. 366.

38 I. Ritchie. (1994). "An Architect's View." In R. Miles and L. Zavala (eds.). (1994). *Towards the Museum of the Future: New European Perspectives*. London and New York: Routledge. New Visions, New Approaches series, 7–30, p. 27.

39 S. Swanson (2004). "Museum of Modern Art Gains New Space, Style." Quoted from http://seattletimes.nwsource.com/html/artsentertainment/2002092019_moma16.html (accessed December 12, 2004).

2 | FEMINIST CURATORIAL STRATEGIES AND PRACTICES SINCE THE 1970s

Katy Deepwell

Editor's Introduction

Katy Deepwell, who lives in London, UK, is editor of *n.paradoxa: international feminist art journal* and author of *Dialogues: Women Artists from Ireland*. She has edited *New Feminist Art Criticism: Critical Strategies, Art Criticism and Africa*, and *Women Artists and Modernism*.

In this chapter, Deepwell traces the development of feminist curation, demonstrating the symbiotic relationship among feminism, feminist art history, and feminist curatorial practice. She provides a strong theoretical foundation for understanding the work of curation and emphasizes that feminist curation is not biologically determined.

Casting a wide net to convey the international scope of feminist curation, Deepwell discusses three distinct yet overlapping approaches. The first strategy relies on historical survey shows to gain visibility for women artists and to establish women's worth within the canon. The second looks to social and historical analysis to contextualize women's cultural production. This mode of feminist curation rejects the canon and critiques the institutional space that authorizes it. The third strategy concerns itself with the critique of femininity. In this case, feminist curation subverts visitors' preconceptions of art and the museum.

According to Deepwell, the overarching issue today in feminist curatorial practice is how to balance the desire to be polemical in making women artists more visible by emphasizing their differences from the dominant culture with a strong sense of the contribution women artists make to culture as a whole. She argues that it is unrealistic to think that feminism will become irrelevant in a world where gender doesn't matter; she holds that feminism will change over time but will continue to be a powerful force challenging the gendered state of power relations.

What does it mean to describe or label a curatorial practice as feminist? Feminist curation is most commonly identified with the organization of exhibitions of women artists. Such exhibitions have primarily been the work of women curators or groups of women artists, critics, or art historians coming together to present feminist research work. Feminism, as a body of ideas and political perspectives developed since the 1970s, also has an indirect presence in art exhibitions and museums where, as Canadian curator Renee Baert has pointed out, "feminist research, issues and methodologies may be folded into other projects, rather than existing in a designated space apart".[1] So how can we define what is feminist in curatorial terms about particular exhibitions, and what has been the challenge offered by feminist ideas in exhibitions where women artists' work has been shown in a space apart?

Curation itself is a modern practice, a late twentieth-century specialty linking arts management, knowledge of art history/criticism, and close collaborations with artists toward the production of an exhibition. Most "curators" of contemporary art exhibitions act on a freelance basis (in the sense of being without institutional affiliation). They work on *ad hoc* projects, often self-initiated, or as the organizers of events which have found institutional support after a proposal has been put forward. This freelance role differs from the most common use of the term "curator" – as a job description – for people who manage, "keep," and present collections of art in museums and galleries. Freelance curation is common in the galleries and museums which present exhibitions of contemporary art, especially where there is no permanent collection or where, if there is one, it is not used as the basis for organizing temporary exhibitions. It is also common when art-historical expertise is used to introduce "ground-breaking" scholarship. The in-house curators of most museums and galleries of contemporary art today increasingly rely on this kind of "freelance" creativity for new initiatives in their programs, while they generally concentrate on managing the housing and marketing side of a particular institutional space and collection.

Curation in museums and galleries of contemporary art is a female-dominated profession, a fact which often leads the woman curator to be regarded as a "keeper of culture" (rather than a producer) or, as Elizabeth Macgregor argues with some irony, a "hostess."[2] As in many other professions, there is an asymmetrical pyramid in operation in museum curation with regard to gender. Many of the positions at the top of the pyramid – in the hierarchy of national museums – are still held by men.[3] Nevertheless, the management of many independent galleries and museums of contemporary art around the world is today in the hands of women. This does not mean their programs necessarily have a commitment to the work of women artists or to presenting feminist art exhibitions. I make these remarks to unsettle the simplistic relation or automatic assumption that programming women artists or feminist projects will come only from women museum staff or curators, as very often this support has come from men who hold the positions of power within an institution. Since the early 1970s, many museum curators have shown themselves open to feminist initiatives within their programs. The question of who controls our institutions and who decides what is shown has feminist implications with regard to the gender (im)balance in museums as institutions. While there are optimistic signs of change evident in the occasional feminist exhibition in a museum program, this does not mean that an "equality" quota for showing women artists has been initiated. Discrimination against women artists still exists and curators must wrestle with historical collections in which women artists' work is in a minority.[4]

To speak of feminist curation might suggest simultaneously the programming of feminist or women's art exhibitions in an institutional space and the creative work of organizing such an exhibition. However, in this chapter, it is principally the latter which is discussed as feminist curation, while the former is regarded as the institutional context which makes these possibilities a reality. I want to direct attention to art history and criticism as the "structure of knowledge" through which museums operate and programs are organized. I will also consider here the impact of the relationship between feminism and art history/criticism in determining questions for feminist curation, especially its position as a practice designed to intervene or to challenge existing bodies of knowledge.

Art Historical Knowledge and Museum Display

Museum collections have been formed and informed by art history and its creation of a canon of great artists and significant schools or movements. As Griselda Pollock suggests, "canons may be understood . . . as the retrospectively legitimating backbone of a cultural and political identity, a consolidated narrative of origin, conferring authority on the texts selected to naturalise this function."[5] Collections of twentieth-century art around the world have developed their standards of display with a view to the canon, particularly in the way modernism defines major and minor artists in the progression of art through a succession of avant-garde practices, movements, and schools.

Where these displays differ is primarily in the attention paid to regional schools or movements in their collections. Fresh evaluations by academics of artists and movements often have a direct effect upon which works are shown as well as how works are shown. The museum's role as a study collection for scholars and as a repository of accumulated knowledge might suggest that museums have a comprehensive purchase on their areas of expertise, but it would be more correct to say that museums "authorize" works within academic discourse, as much as the same discourse informs collecting policy. Any investigation into acquisitions policies quickly reveals the partial and fragmented character of most collections and their dependence on art-historical knowledge. This situation, in the context of a museum's own self-image as an authority on what is great and good, determines the space and significance that museums give to women artists and the value attributed to these artists' work.

Until the late 1960s, the presence of women artists in most major museum collections would lead one to think that women existed only as a minority of practitioners. Their work formed less than 10–20 percent of most major art collections, a figure which does not equate with their increasing presence in galleries of contemporary art or temporary exhibitions. It is still quite common to see museum displays of early twentieth-century movements such as Surrealism, Futurism, or Constructivism in which women artists' presence is marginal or non-existent. At the Tate, for example, where a significant part of the collection is responsible for representing British artists, women artists represent 10 percent in the collection of British art. Very few women artists have more than one work in this collection (the exceptions are Barbara Hepworth and Dame Ethel Walker, whose estates were accepted as bequests) and, until the 1980s, solo exhibitions of women artists were a rare event.[6]

Since the early 1970s, feminist art history has been raising questions about how this pattern of marginalization has occurred and researching the lives and works of women artists, providing evidence which contradicts the dominant story of art. Feminist scholars have been analyzing art history and museums not as neutral institutions or guardians of the great and good but as both ideological and gendered in their construction and operation. Feminist art historians have re-evaluated the works of many women artists, and the research has often been directly critical of museum displays. This inquiry began with a critique of the male bias invested in the canon and an analysis of the gendering of "genius" as predominantly masculine, white (Euro-American), and middle-class.[7] Recovering a history of women artists

67

in different regions, movements, and schools was initially dependent on locating women artists' works in museum basements and private collections; this, in itself, revealed the partial and tendentious character of collecting in public museums.[8] What became more important was the means through which feminist art history questioned the basis for initial and often derogatory judgments of women's work. Feminist scholarship provided evidence of women's innovations in formal and technical terms, re-examining the relationships between gender and genres.[9] This led to a reassessment of women's contribution to changing the nature of art's discourse. It also prompted a re-evaluation of art history's methods and categories, because feminist art history provided new and comparative analyses of work produced by women in the same peer groups, movements, or schools as their male counterparts. In addition, feminist perspectives have introduced new forms of analysis by focusing on the gendered relations between the subject-in-representation and that of the artist and/or viewer.[10] As museum studies itself developed, the gendering of the space within the museum became a further object of feminist inquiry.[11]

The emergence of feminist art exhibitions in the early 1970s can be clearly located in the rise of feminist art history as a distinct area within and contesting the discipline of art history. Such exhibitions were equally shaped by developments within the political and politicized women's movement in Europe and America. Both feminist art history and the women's art movement (which was initially connected closely with the women's movement) were determined to gain visibility for the cultural production of women artists in a context where little scholarship and museum display space had been dedicated to their work.[12] Did women artists have a different history from their male counterparts? What was their contribution to the direction of culture and art as a whole? Was it the discourses of art history which led to their marginalization, or was it the type of work which women produced? What determined the type of work women artists produced?

It is necessary to draw careful distinctions here between a category known as "women's art;" the work of all women artists; and feminist perspectives in art history, curation, and art criticism. Where the content of an exhibition is art made by women, this does not of itself make the exhibition a feminist one. This is not only because many male curators have organized solo and group exhibitions of women artists, but also because women artists themselves have been coming together to organize group exhibitions of their own work since the middle of the nineteenth century in clubs, societies, and other organizations. Not all of these projects have been feminist in either conception or impact, nor have they always been "curated" events in the sense of advancing aesthetic, political, and social arguments through the works chosen and their arrangement. To define what is feminist in the curation of women artists' work, we have to look to the relationships between feminist theory and feminist art history in the planning of a curatorial project (as much as to its reception, and most particularly to the work of the women's movement of the 1970s; through its political debates, the women's movement raised new questions, issues, and subjects for art. The next section explores historical survey shows of women artists and what these shows owe to changing methods in feminist art history and theory. The last section explores some contemporary exhibitions by women artists and analyzes their relation to developing feminist theories and agendas.

Feminist Art History and the Making of Historical Feminist Exhibitions

Some of the earliest feminist art-historical exhibitions were sweeping chronological surveys of women artists' work, often drawn from the basements of museum collections and private collections. Ground-breaking projects include Linda Nochlin and Ann Sutherland Harris's "Women Artists, 1550–1950" (1976, Los Angeles County Museum of Art) and "Kunstlerinnen International, 1877–1977: Frauen in der Kunst" (1977, Schloss Charlottenberg, Berlin).[13] As both a curatorial strategy and art history, what these two exhibitions shared was a reforming approach which had one radical end: to insert women artists into the standard narrative of art history and correct the bias which had contributed to their neglect.

The exhibitions were not identical in terms of the artists selected. The differences between them reflect both different models of the "history" of art (beyond their separate time frames) and the availability to each exhibition of certain works for loan. The latter show, for example, emphasized women's involvement in modern movements from Impressionism to tendencies in contemporary art. For feminist art historians, one of the most striking effects of these and other survey shows was to reveal how much women artists shared with their immediate male peers in terms of style and approach. This highlighted feminist art history's need for greater comparative analysis to situate the work more precisely in its historical context, and to bring out the specific differences that gender (and race and class) made in the creation or the reading of the work.

69

In an attempt to offer a reassessment of women's art production, the catalogues accompanying these survey shows outlined the lives of these women artists, alongside reasons for their posthumous neglect, for the misattribution of their works, and for the themes and issues which the works themselves tackled. The authors of both catalogues maintained a strong biographical emphasis on the "obstacles" faced by women artists while emphasizing their achievements, often using biographical details to explain the work. The "obstacles" included among others: lack of access to formal academic education (in the eighteenth and nineteenth centuries); poverty; family commitments or attitudes; direct and indirect forms of discrimination; and personal tragedies. A picture of the heroic struggle for a woman to be an artist emerged, as did an assessment of what made her interesting or "great." Certain trends in liberal arts education which developed through the 1980s have promoted this version of a history of "great women artists" as a supplement to art history. This thinking encourages students to study Frida Kahlo and Georgia O'Keefe for their achievements as women while acknowledging Vincent Van Gogh and Pablo Picasso, despite (or rather because of) their equally turbulent lives, for their contributions to "Art." This ambivalent relation to art history through the production of a "great" woman artist – who is often seen in isolation from her sex (other women) as well as the history of art – characterizes much of the popular reception of "great women artists" today. The selective presentation of and over-investment in a handful of individual women as another "artistic" product in the culture industry is fueled by the popularization of their work through videos of the artist's life, calendars, mugs, bookmarks, and gift-cards.

Griselda Pollock has suggested that Nochlin and Sutherland Harris's approach in art history was open to criticism for its focus on biography, and that their account did not offer an adequate social or historical explanation for the marginalization of women artists or for the cultural production of art.[14] Pollock's critique and purpose were to argue for a social history of art – informed by both Marxist and feminist theory – which would reveal the social, political, and aesthetic circumstances in which women produced art and chose their subjects and methods. Her arguments positioned the operation of gender itself at the heart of feminist inquiry, exploring how "difference" functions in cultural, social, and political terms.[15] The following analysis explores the difference between the approaches of Pollock and of both Nochlin and Nochlin and Sutherland Harris.

In an early essay, Nochlin cited the formal exclusion of women from art education in the academies of Europe until the turn of the twentieth century as a clear case of institutional discrimination and the reason why so few women emerged as artists prior to the twentieth century.[16] However, the exclusion from academic training and specifically from studying the nude did not stop women from training as artists in private studios or from attending the newly founded academies for women in the late nineteenth century, even though it did encourage many more women to work in what were considered "minor" genres of portrait painting, still life, landscape, or miniatures. What it supposedly excluded them from producing, in many cases, was the "highest" genre, allegorical and historical painting, on which the reputation of "great artists" relied; yet some women artists did study the nude (privately) and were able to work as historical and allegorical painters. Nochlin's and Sutherland Harris's exhibition was intended to refocus readers and visitors away from explanations resting on women's biological or psychological capability. However, "Women Artists, 1550–1950" presented so many different women artists working in diverse periods and countries that the survey approach reinforced a personal or individual explanation for the work.

For Griselda Pollock and Roszika Parker, by contrast, nineteenth-century industrialization produced new categories of work and leisure and new distinctions among professional groups.[17] Access to academic training contributed to a renewed privileging of the work of men over the work of women at a time when the romantic myth of the artist itself developed as the antithesis of waged labor and bourgeois morality. Pollock and Parker argued in *Old Mistresses* that these distinctions had the ideological effect of separating Art (with a capital A) from women's work (unskilled, repetitive labor, often produced in the home or seen as amateurish). This nineteenth-century association of women painters with amateurism, and the related assessment of their exhibitions as an extension of a private hobby into the public sphere, continue precisely because of the alignment of women artists only with their sex and rarely with any quality in art, except the "feminine" or the "Other." This distinction has persisted in ideological terms even though, in both Europe and America, women artists have had access to professional training on the same terms as men since the 1890s, often dominating the student body of many art schools. Claudia Strom ironically titled her review of the "Kunstlerinnen International" project in Berlin, "Do Not Bake Cakes, Try Art!"[18]

Critical recognition through participation in major exhibitions of work in significant venues is an important part of how an artist emerges as a figure of interest to collectors, to museum collections, and to art history itself. The

71

numbers of women artists within the profession as a whole across Europe and America has risen steadily since the beginning of the twentieth century, averaging one-tenth to one-third of all artists in group exhibitions pre-1945 and rising thereafter to roughly one-third to one-half of the profession by the late 1960s.[19] But women's physical presence as artists has not always been matched by critical or art-historical recognition. This is why art history and art criticism bear further examination for their gender bias. For Griselda Pollock, the role that "femininity" plays as a marker of difference in the binaries which structure how we think about men/women, public/private, work/leisure, between Woman (a constructed ideological figure) and women (historical and social located beings), between the artist-as-producer and the chosen subject-in-representation, has now become central to the project of feminist art history.[20] This is a different project from an investment in a history of "great women artists," one designed to reveal the contribution of women artists' work to culture as a whole through an analysis of art's discourses.

The challenge presented by the initial wave of feminist art-historical scholarship has led to some significant revisions in the way women artists are now presented in museum collections, even to reattribution of works. It has spurred many museums to rehang "neglected" works by women and to organize significantly more one-person shows of women artists.[21] The groundbreaking exhibitions of Nochlin and Sutherland Harris and of the group behind the Berlin project did much to raise the visibility of women artists in art history. They provided a rich source for teaching feminist art history, and their catalogues quickly became core teaching material. Feminist art historians began to write more monographic studies of individual women artists included in these early shows and major comparative historical studies of the relationship between gender and genre (the nude/body, self-portraiture, art/craft, for example). As a consequence of the sweeping time frame the two shows employed, curators organized more specialist exhibitions based on a reassessment of "regional" or "nation-based" schools or histories (women Pre-Raphaelites, women expressionists, for example). Indirectly, the two early exhibitions also inspired the establishment of women's museums (for individual artists as well as for the private survey collections which became the National Museum of Women in the Arts, Washington, DC, and das Verborgene Museum in Berlin) and of archives documenting women artists' work. The two catalogues are now important precedents for the major survey exhibitions of women's art which have been organized since the early 1990s in countries as diverse as Australia, Ireland, India, Taiwan, Russia, and Hungary.[22]

Feminist art history has shifted since the early 1980s, and detailed analysis of women artists' works in specific historical and theoretical case studies has become the norm. Yet in permanent collection displays and survey exhibitions, chronological organization has more recently given way to thematic rehangs which introduce new criteria for why a work should be shown. These have consequences for women; for example, marginalizing their work in exhibits about war or social crisis, where war is defined solely as the soldier's experience on the front line (an experience few women have had but one which many male artists have received commissions to depict). If war in the twentieth and early twenty-first centuries were defined as a social-political crisis which affects the civilian population of a war zone, this perspective would open up more opportunities to present work by women artists. However, when the "body" – a major preoccupation of exhibitions in the 1980s–90s – is chosen, significant space is given to work by women artists, especially feminist art works from the 1970s, for what they reveal of women's experiences and viewpoints when compared to the dominant genre of male artist–female nude.

In 1996 Catherine de Zegher attempted a different strategy in order to present a history of twentieth-century women artists in "Inside the Visible: An Elliptical Traverse of Twentieth Century Art In, Of, and From the Feminine."[23] Baert, reviewing de Zegher's strategies as a model for feminist curation, argued that de Zegher's purpose was "not . . . to 'correct' an existing canon, nor to accumulate 'great women' but to identify and articulate a body of practice that doesn't 'fit' past histories and current debates, which has existed in its byways, and whose 'non-fit' speaks to aporias within modernism, and indeed within contemporary feminist theory."[24] De Zegher selected works from periods of aesthetic and social crisis she identified in the twentieth century – the 1940s, the 1960s/70s, and the 1990s – and created a thematic hang to demonstrate links and correspondences within the art practices. She divided the exhibition into four sections and made use of chronological contrasts between works within each; for example, juxtaposing works by Charlotte Salamon (from the 1940s) with those of Nancy Spero (from the 1970s) in the section entitled "The Blank in the Page." The exhibition catalogue had a critical or theoretical essay on every artist, each by a different writer; all focused on the significance of the works selected to the history of art. The exhibition was international, drawing on de Zegher's earlier work with Latin American contemporary artists, and designed to break the dominant Euro-American agenda in feminist art history. Using the feminine not as the mark of an essential femininity or a means to define women, but as a

73

mark of difference, her ambition was to show how women artists had generated distinct practices which explored, critiqued, and questioned concepts of the feminine and "otherness" in aesthetic terms. As Baert suggested, this had the effect of highlighting the work's different "materialities, spacialities, haptic properties, iconography, etc. (rather than, as too often the case, the other way around, art pressed into service as illustration to a pre-established theoretical argument). Thus the exhibition is not a mere 'fastening' of art and theory but is itself a necessary form." [25] De Zegher worked to accommodate a sense of the multiple perspectives and aesthetic strategies that women artists employ, developing a framework fluid enough to avoid creating artificial constructs which would be read as "fixed," while ensuring her choices conveyed meaning. Similarly, she attempted to negotiate the difficult tension involved in acknowledging each woman's individuality in her practice without firmly establishing a category known as "women's art," in which the concept of "outsider" or "other" would become the mark for women artists.[26] This was critical, given that the majority of the selected artists had mainstream professional careers and significant national or international reputations.

De Zegher's transnational approach in "Inside the Visible" stands in contrast to the collective presentation of women artists (largely by feminist art historians) in exhibitions such as "Mind and Spirit" (1998, Taipei) and "Glasgow Girls" (1990, Glasgow and Washington, DC), which tried to overcome the relegation of women artists to the margins of national art histories. Very little focus has been given to the framing of these national accounts; a region or national boundary has seemingly presented itself as a self-evident fact. Yet, from the second half of the twentieth century, this model has broken down for many artists who live, work, and travel internationally or between two or three major metropolitan centers. The art world invests its time and energy in creating international platforms for contemporary art even when its activities largely remain organized through nation-based structures for funding and exhibition support in the very same international forums. However, there is an important distinction between the nation as an indicator of place – a location where a work may be made and a context in which its concerns may be grounded – and a nationalist ideology which is used as a means of advancing national (often racist) pride, nationalist sentiment, or political ambitions. Women artists' relation to nationalism and to embodying or representing the nation remains particularly problematic. Until the 1980s, few women artists had the privilege of "representing" their country in national pavilions at international biennials, though this situation is rapidly changing. In addition, some women artists have provoked great controversy when they have exhibited work which critiques models of nationalism; for example, Joyce Wieland's exhibition "True Patriot Love/Veritable Amour Patriotique" (1971, National Gallery of Canada) and Marina Abramovic's presentation "Balkan Baroque" (1997, Venice Biennale). If the premise of an exhibition is to produce a separate history of women artists as a corrective to a nation's art history and to make visible again work which was erased from a particular historical account, isn't a critique of the model of nationalism and national schools now also fundamental for art history and museum practice? Many exhibitions of contemporary art have continued to propagate the views of a modernist internationalism, particularly the desire for a "universal" or singular model of art history. Women artists and feminist art historians must also negotiate their relationship to these models.

Contemporary Feminist Art Exhibitions, Modernism, and Feminist Theory

Women's exhibitions of contemporary art since the 1960s have used the modernist gambit of the art exhibition as an argument, a statement, and a polemical space. Yet a critique of the status quo – especially of modernism, which was the dominant theory and practice in the late 1960s for both the production of the art work and its means of display – has been central to the emergence of feminist art practices. The women's art movement emerged through group exhibitions and actions by women artists organized thematically and polemically around feminist issues, often self-organized and not "curated" by others. Women artists coming together collectively questioned the effect of the solo show in the culture industry and instead chose to develop through a politics of collaboration. The artists became their own curators. These events also challenged the idea that the only place for exhibitions of art is in the art gallery or the museum; many of these shows were organized outside such institutional spaces. The exhibition site became an opportunity for public debate about the possibilities of new forms of art practice, new spaces, and new audiences.

The feminist challenge to modernism was multi-faceted, as it re-examined art practices, methods of display, and exhibition organization. In modernist terms, the art work was perceived as a self-contained entity, literally a world held inside the frame and on the surface of the canvas. What surrounded the frame was often seen as a distraction; modernists developed the "white cube" to minimize distraction from the surroundings, allowing the viewer to focus on the internal space of the work. The white walls and minimal flooring themselves became an institutional model, an aesthetic, for how to present contemporary art in museums founded after the 1930s.[27] Modernist expectations about appropriate criteria were often combined with seemingly rigorous selection on the basis of "quality." Works were grouped to generate a coherent formal effect or series view and to enable audiences to understand stylistic similarities and differences across an artist's oeuvre through visual comparisons. In modernist terms formal or aesthetic innovation was seen as the key to "success," and critical judgment was geared to discerning and comprehending these shifts, especially in the one-person retrospective. Displays of "development" in the progression through rooms in an exhibition assisted these judgments. In the second half of the twentieth century, changing concepts of art (challenging the key modernist assumptions outlined above) produced new models for exhibition. These models prioritized context (the social, political, and aesthetic debates informing and determining the work as much as the space, catalogue, and presentation) in reading a work of art. The gallery or museum itself has become recognized as one of the frames for defining art and its discourses.

Feminist art practice positioned itself against modernism's so-called norms and assumptions *and* the stereotypes often used to describe women's work or Woman (in representation). Reversing expectations of "women's work" by redeploying methods or media in new ways and by challenging conventions in representation, content, form, and display became standard tropes. The focus on women's shared experiences as the content, and as a determining factor in the form of the work itself, became the distinguishing mark of feminist art practices. The sheer diversity of feminist art practices across media forms and modes of representation did not conform to the modernist expectation that a new movement be defined by a "style" or a singular type of practice. Instead, the question of what constituted the work as feminist became a social, political, and cultural issue. The "feminist problematic" is a term used by Annette Kuhn to question where the feminism of an art work is located: in the sex of the artist, in the content of the work, or in the reception by its audience.[28] In her essay "Reviewing Modernist Criticism," Mary Kelly outlined how modernist values were structurally embedded in museum and exhibition practice, and discussed the feminist problematic as constructed by reading together the sociality (social, historical, and cultural ideas employed), materiality (physical presence of the work, context of exhibition), and sexuality (sex/gender relations) embodied in the work of art.[29]

These factors were not, in Kelly's mind, separate from the institutional context or presentation of the work of art. Her argument usefully emphasized the role that a feminist strategy might play as an intervention within the established or conventional arguments of exhibitions and the social-political-aesthetic structure of the museum or gallery.

The 1972 "Womanhouse" project, for example, began as a collaboration among women students working on Judy Chicago's and Miriam Schapiro's Feminist Art Program at Cal Arts.[30] The exploration of women's associations with the home resulted from a critique of "normative" forms of femininity. This is what made the "Womanhouse" project such a powerful model for exploring women's consciousness from a feminist perspective. The students collectively took over a disused house in Los Angeles and each woman claimed a room within it to create an installation and a series of performances about women's use of the house. The installations included a bridal staircase, a menstruation bathroom, a nurturing kitchen, and a bedroom in which a woman constantly made up and cleaned off her face. The house became a venue for other performances and discussions, a temporary exhibition space as well as an installation.[31]

The feminist critique of domesticity and its alliance with women's "normative" femininity was also the subject of many of the works in the project and exhibition "Feministo."[32] This began as a mail art project between women in the mid-1970s and became an exhibition of the work generated by the project at the ICA in London in 1977–8. The exhibition was built like an installation, again a domestic space, to accommodate the work. This project, like "Womanhouse," exemplifies the trend of artists organizing and curating exhibitions themselves.

A different model of public art practice which emerged through feminist work is Suzanne Lacy's "Three Weeks in May" (1977, Los Angeles): a program of public events, conferences, dinners, and performances, presented primarily in public spaces outside the gallery. The project spiraled out from the presentation of two maps in a city mall, one which documented the locations of rape in the city in one three-week period, the other the locations of women's organizations which offered assistance to victims of rape. These events culminated in *In Mourning and In Rage* (Leslie Labowitz and Suzanne Lacy), a public performance on the steps of the city hall highlighting the incidents of rape in the city and women's resistance to this. The event was widely reported in the TV and broadcast media. While Lacy created specific works within the program – the maps and several performances – she also acted effectively as curator to other collaborating artists' projects, becoming involved in debates and discussions (as an activist) and presenting the project widely to a range of groups (as a publicist). Lacy's art practice today continues to utilize this expanded role of the artist in the public sphere, negotiating between different constituencies to generate art as a public discourse while remaining a model for art practice outside the conventional exhibition space of gallery or museum.[33]

Other early feminist exhibitions like "Frauen-Kunst-Neue Tendenzen" (1975, Galerie Krinzinger, Innsbruck) and Magma (1975–6, curated by Romana Loda and Valie Export in Brescia, Castello Oldofredi; toured to Vienna) presented a different strategy in women's art practice. They chose to align the work of women with the use of new media – photography, perform-ance, video, installation (rather than painting or sculpture) – as modes of expression and as a feminist avant-garde. Such exhibitions either explored the conditions of femininity or analyzed the myth of "Woman." Annemarie Sauzeau Boetti termed this critical investigation of the condition of femininity "Negative Capability as Practice in Women's Art" (1976).[34]

Large survey shows of contemporary women artists' work have been organized periodically since the 1970s, analyzing emerging tendencies in women's art production and their relationship to the legacies of feminism.[35] Many feminist exhibitions of women artists inside the gallery have tried to reverse the expectations which conventional audiences may have of "Art."[36] The danger is always that this challenge will not be understood and that feminine stereotypes about women's work will be reinforced. "The Subvers-ive Stitch" exhibitions in Manchester in 1986, one historical, the other con-temporary, exemplify this situation. They made use of Roszika Parker's feminist research into embroidery as a craft or trade in which women spe-cialized, and of her analysis of its association with "natural" femininity as an "appropriate pastime" for genteel women. Pennina Barnett, the curator of the contemporary exhibition, selected works by women artists which used textiles to subvert or question this medium's historical associations with femininity and communicate a resistant, often feminist, perspective. She found that, despite the clarity of her own (feminist) strategy, the media quickly neutralized her intervention and sought to reinstall precisely the stereotypes about textiles and obedient femininity that the works she had selected were challenging.[37]

A second problem that has arisen with major group exhibitions of women artists' works concerns the criteria of selection, and whether works which are often diverse and represent many different aesthetic tendencies can be meaningfully linked, as gender alone is inadequate as a criterion. As one

English critic, Guy Brett, cautioned in 1985, "the phenomenon of 'minimal critical standards' in exhibitions open to all women or exhibitions with the sociological aim of proving that 'women can do it' only act[s] as brake and confirm[s] the treatment of women as a special category, like a minority."[38] Brett was reviewing positively as a new "advanced" strategy a survey of contemporary art by 200 women artists from across the world, "Kunst Mit Eigen-Sinn" (1985, Museum der 20 Jahrhunderts, Vienna). He contrasted this exhibition with that year's "Documenta" and "Zeitgeist" exhibitions, in which women artists were a minority.[39] "As you began to look at the work in more detail you realised what the imposition of an average art-show atmosphere was really hiding: the range and depth of the challenge the work of women artists is making to cultural conditioning," he wrote. For Brett, this challenge had many facets which went beyond what any programmatic definition of (liberal or radical) feminism (as a bid for equality) could offer. Brett's comment highlights the problem faced by such exhibitions; to avoid marginalization, women artists' exhibitions need to be polemical and informed by feminism, yet they must also reassess not just women's presence as artists but their contribution to art itself.

What is the lasting impact of women's survey shows? An increase in the number of women artists at "Documenta"?[40] The choice between integrating more women into the system – a greater slice of the rotten pie, as Lucy Lippard described it[41] – and pursuing a strategy of temporary segregation to gain visibility remains important for many women curators. The "gap" between the numbers of women artists working and the selection of a limited minority in major exhibitions has been the focus of much agitation by women artists since the 1970s. This includes street protests against the limited numbers of women selected for the Whitney Biennial (in 1969, when only 8 women were selected amongst 143 artists);[42] the *Info-Dienst/Information Service* archive on women artists built by Ute Meta Bauer, Tine Geissler, and Sandra Hastenteufel as a public protest against the very limited selection of women in "Documenta 9" (1992);[43] and the poster and flyer protests of the Guerilla Girls against the selection policies of contemporary art galleries and collections.[44] Rosa Martinez selected 60 percent women for her Istanbul Biennial in 1997; this was the only time that a woman curator has succeeded in achieving such a high level of representation. A female successor to the post in 2001, Yuko Hasegawa, selected only 20 percent women, even though the cyborg sculptures of Lee Bul, a woman artist from South Korea, stood as the principal artistic concept for the show. In 1997, Hasegawa organized an exhibition called "Degenderism" (Setagaya Art Museum, Tokyo) displaying work by male and female artists that conveyed slippage between fixed gender distinctions, but where gender was only one of many sources of information about the body. However, despite her aspirations to move beyond rigid gendered distinctions, as suggested by the title, the exhibition did not demonstrate their collapse. The title echoes an often-expressed liberal attitude that, "after feminism," gender will no longer count or will just stop being an issue. This is a misplaced hope, given the current power relations of the art market and the world in general, where a clear asymmetry exists between men and women.

If the issue for women's exhibitions is not about numbers or visible representation for women artists, then it is really a battle for ideas. The tension continues for many (feminist) curators between the need for specialism (in women artists' exhibitions and publications) and the attempt to dissolve distinctions altogether with the aim of "normalizing" the situation. The question of what value is given to the term "feminism" as opposed to "femininity" remains a defining feature in exhibitions such as "Bad Girls" (1994–5, New Museum of Contemporary Art, New York)[45] and "Cross-Female" (1999, Kunstlerhaus Bethanien, Berlin). To organize a feminist art exhibition is often thought of as taking too high a risk of failing, and this is something that some museums curators are reluctant to do. This risk is worth reassessing, as it has no rational basis. Feminist art exhibitions have been hugely popular with museum audiences (which usually are dominated by women), often bringing new kinds of audiences to galleries; and they have frequently broken the box-office records of museums where they have been organized.[46] The critique of "femininity" in representation, as integral to the aesthetic sensibility manifest within the work and considered as a socially determined or a socio-psychoanalytic construction, has become a strong feature of many feminist exhibitions since the early 1980s. The need for feminist art exhibitions is not over, even though such projects will continue to be reinvented as feminist scholarship itself develops and as women continue to produce work about their own and other women's experiences in the world.

Questions for Discussion

1 What is curation? What is feminist curation? How is this different from women's curating of art? Why is most feminist curation done on a freelance basis? Why do feminist artists sometimes curate their own shows?

2 Discuss the relationship between feminist art history and feminist curatorial practice.

3 What is the canon? How do museums authorize works of art? What is the relationship between feminist curation and new museum theory?

4 Why does Deepwell provide such a broad international survey of feminist curation?

5 Compare and contrast the diverse approaches of feminist historical exhibitions. How would you characterize feminist curation today?

6 What is the "feminist problematic"?

7 If you were involved with feminist curation, what would your goals be? Where do you stand on the question of "segregating" feminist art to consider difference versus "integrating" it to show its contributions to culture as a whole? Why is "quality" such a political issue?

8 If you were engaged in feminist curation, how would you respond to museum architecture (see chapter 1)? How is museum architecture gendered? Does contemporary museum architecture show sensitivity to gender issues?

Notes

1 R. Baert. Contribution to "Historiography/Feminism/Strategy" College Art Association conference (New York, February 26, 2000). Published online in *n.paradoxa: international feminist art journal* at http://web.ukonline.co.uk/n.paradoxa/panel1.htm.

2 E. Macgregor. (1995). "The Situation of Women Curators." In K. Deepwell. (ed.). *New Feminist Art Criticism: Critical Strategies*. Manchester: Manchester University Press, 70–5, p. 72.

3 For figures and analysis, see Women in the Arts Project. (1992). *Women Working in the Arts*. London: Arts Council of England; D. Cliche, R. Mitchell, and A. Joh. Weisand. (eds.). (2000). *Pyramid or Pillars: Unveiling the Status of Women in the Arts and Media Professions in Europe*. Bonn: ARCult Media, pp. 19–20.

4 For figures on proportion of male to female artists in museum and gallery exhibitions, see: for America – R. Rosen and C. Brauer. (1989). *Making Their Mark: Women Enter the Mainstream*. New York: Abbeville Press, pp. 203–36; Guerrilla Girls. (1987). *The Banana Report: The Guerrilla Girls Review the Whitney*. New York: Clocktower; for Europe – Cliche et al., *Pyramid or Pillars*; for Australia – A. Van Den Bosch. (1998). "Women Artists' Careers: Public Policy and the Market." In A. Beale and Bosch. (eds.). *Ghosts in the Machine: Women and Cultural Policy in Canada and Australia*. Ontario: Garamond Press, 211–29.

5 G. Pollock. (1999). *Differencing the Canon: Feminist Desire and the Writing of Art's Histories*. New York: Routledge, p. 3.

6 Of the 206 solo exhibitions at the Tate between 1910 and 1986, only eight were of women artists, and five of these were held between 1980 and 1986. See P. Barrie. (1987–8). "The Art Machine." *Women Artists Slide Library Journal*, 20, 8–9; A. Framis. (2004). *Women Artists at the Tate*. London: Tate Gallery.

7   L. Nochlin. (1971). "Why Have There Been No Great Women Artists?" In (1989). *Women, Art and Power*. London: Thames and Hudson, 145–78.

8   For a bibliography of feminist research on women modernists, see K. Deepwell. (ed.). (1998). *Women Artists and Modernism*. Manchester: Manchester University Press.

9   See, for example, G. Pollock and R. Parker. (1981). *Old Mistresses: Women, Art and Ideology*. London: Routledge, Kegan and Paul.

10 See, for instance, T. Hess and L. Nochlin. (eds.) (1972). *Woman as Sex Object: Studies in Erotic Art, 1730–1970. Art News Annual*, 38. New York: Newsweek; L. Mulvey. (1975). "Visual Pleasure and Narrative Cinema." *Screen*, 16: 3, 6–18; L. Nead. (1992). *The Female Nude: Women, Art and Obscenity*. London: Routledge.

11 See C. Duncan. (1993). *Aesthetics and Power*. Cambridge: Cambridge University Press; S. Hyde. (1997). *Exhibiting Gender*. Manchester: Manchester University Press.

12 See also A. Higonnet. (1994). "A New Center: The National Museum of Women in the Arts." In D. J. Sherman and I. Rogoff. (eds.). *Museum Culture: Histories, Discourses, Spectacles*. Minneapolis: University of Minnesota Press. And for an account of feminist curatorial practices at the Women's Museum in Aarhus, Denmark, see G. Porter. (1996). "Seeing through Solidity: A Feminist Perspective on Museums." In S. MacDonald and G. Fyfe. (eds.). *Theorizing Museums: Representing Identity and Diversity in a Changing World*. Oxford and Cambridge, MA: Blackwell. On the impact of feminist historical research on museum practice, see G. Porter. (1990). "Gender Bias: Representations of Work in History Museums." *Continuum: The Australian Journal of Media & Culture*, 3: 1, 70–83. Space * Meaning * Politics issue. Institute for Cultural Policy Studies, Griffith University, Australia (ed.).

13 "Kunstlerinnen International" was organized by Ursula Bierther, Evelyn Kuwertz, Karin Petersen, Inge Schumacher, Sarah Schumann, Ulrike Stelzl, and Petra Zöfelt.

14 G. Pollock. (1982). "Vision, Voice and Power: Feminist Art History and Marxism." *Block*, 6, 2–21.

15 Pollock, *Differencing the Canon*; G. Pollock. (1988). *Vision and Difference: Feminism, Femininity and Histories of Art*. London: Routledge.

16 See Nochlin, "Why Have There Been No Great Women Artists?"

17 See G. Pollock, "Vision, Voice and Power." See also Pollock and Parker, *Old Mistresses*, pp. 8–9.

18 C. Strom. (1977). "Backe nicht mehr kuchen – Kunst musst du vershuchen!" *Tendenzen*, 114, 49–50.

19 See K. Deepwell. (1994). "A Fair Field and No Favour: Women Artists in Britain." In S. Oldfield (ed.). *This Working Day World: Women's Lives and Culture in Britain 1914–1945*. Brighton: Falmer Press, 141–55.

20 Pollock, *Differencing the Canon*.

21 See Tate figures quoted above in note 6.

22 See, for example, W. Ryan-Smolin, E. Mayes, and J. Rogers. (eds.). (1987). *Irish Women Artists: From the Eighteenth Century to the Present Day*. Dublin: National Gallery of Ireland and Douglas Hyde Gallery; G. Sinha. (ed.). (1997). *Expressions and Evocations*. New Delhi: National Gallery of India and Marg Press; S-. L. Chen. (ed.).

(1999). *Mind and Spirit*. Taiwan: Taipei Museum; K. Keseru. (ed.). (2000). *Women's Art in Hungary, 1960–2000*. Budapest: Ernst Museum; C. Muyser. (ed.). (1992). *Profession ohne Tradition*. Berlin: Martin–Gropius–Bau; N. Kamenetskaya and L. Iovleva. (2002). *Femme Art: Women Painting in Russia, XV–XX Centuries*. Moscow: Tretyakov Gallery. The "Profession ohne Tradition" exhibition built an archive of the Berlin Women Artists Association at the museum. "Femme Art" has led to new courses in Moscow University on women and art. See also J. Kerr and J. Holder. (eds.). (1999). *Past Present: The National Women's Art Anthology*. Sydney: Craftsman House, documenting a historical exhibition and a festival of 150 shows in 1995.

23 M. Catherine de Zegher. (1996). *Inside the Visible: An Elliptical Traverse of Twentieth Century Art In, Of, and From the Feminine*. Boston: ICA, MIT, and Kanaal Art Foundation. This exhibition toured to the Whitechapel Gallery in London and to Perth ICA in Australia.

24 Baert, Contribution to "Historiography / Feminism / Strategy."

25 Baert, Contribution to "Historiography / Feminism / Strategy."

26 See K. Deepwell. (1998). "Inside the Visible: Interview with Catherine de Zegher." *n.paradoxa*, 1, 15–23.

27 B. O'Doherty. (1986). *Inside the White Cube: The Ideology of the Gallery Space*. Santa Monica: Lapis Press. First published 1976 in *Artforum* in a somewhat different form.

28 A. Kuhn, cited in R. Parker and G. Pollock. (eds.). (1987). *Framing Feminism*. London: Routledge, p. 93.

29 See M. Kelly. (1996). "Reviewing Modernist Criticism." In *Imaging Desire*. Boston: MIT Press, 79–105.

30 See A. Raven. (1994). "Womanhouse." In M. Garrard and N. Broude. (eds.). *The Power of Feminist Art: Emergence, Impact and Triumph of the American Feminist Art Movement*. New York: Harry N. Abrams, 48–65.

31 In 1997, a virtual "WomEnhouse" online was created. See www.cmp.ucr.edu/womenhouse.

32 A. M. Kokoli. (2004). "Undoing 'Homeliness' in Feminist Art: Feministo: Portrait of the Artist as Housewife, 1975–1977." *n.paradoxa. Domestic Politics*, 13, 75–83.

33 K. Deepwell. (1999). "New Genre Public Art: Suzanne Lacy Interview." *n.paradoxa*, 4, 25–33; S. Lacy. (1995). *Mapping the Terrain: New Genre Public Art*. Seattle: Bay Press.

34 A. Sauzeau Boetti. (1976). "Negative Capability as Practice in Women's Art." *Studio International*, 191.

35 Significant examples of these include "Feministische kunst international" (1979, Geemente Museum, The Hague); "The Revolutionary Power of Women's Laughter" (1983, Protech Gallery, New York); "Art et feminisme" (1982, Musée d'Art Contemporain, Quebec); "Dialogue with the Other" (1996, Kunsthallen Brandts Klaedefabrik, Odense); *Sexual Politics: Judy Chicago's "The Dinner Party" in Feminist Art History* (Berkeley, CA: University of California Press, 1996); "Cherchez les Femmes" (1995, Kunsthaus, Hamburg); "Oh Boy! It's a Girl: Feminisme in der kunst" (1994–5, Kunstverein, Munich); "Some Kind of Heaven" (1997, Kunsthalle Nurnberg, Nurnberg); "Text and Sub-Text" (2001, Lasalle–SIA, Singapore). For more, see http://web.ukonline.co.uk/n.paradoxa/booksa.htm.

36 *Women's Images of Men.* (1980). ICA, London, for example, reversed the expectations of the conventional male artist's show where women are the subject of representation, selecting, from an open submission, women artists' images of men.

37 See P. Barnett. (1995). "Afterthoughts on Curating 'The Subversive Stitch.'" In Deepwell, *New Feminist Art Criticism,* 76–86. Parker's book is R. Parker. (1984). *The Subversive Stitch: Embroidery and the Making of the Feminine.* London: Women's Press.

38 G. Brett. (1985). "Kunst mit Eigen-Sinn." *Studio International,* 198: 1009, 31–4, p. 31.

39 Of the 350 artists selected for "Documenta" in 1977, 46 were women (c.13 percent). See P. Barrie, "Art Machine," pp. 16–17.

40 Among the 116 artists and 15 artists' groups presented at "Documenta 11" in 2002, 31 were women artists and 8 of the groups had women members (37 percent of all artists/34 percent overall; see *n.paradoxa* (July 2002), 10, 44). Although the highest percentage ever of women at "Documenta," these numbers do not reflect the curators' transnational, transgenerational, and transmedial ambitions, or the spread of work from 34 countries, as most women selected lived and worked in Europe and America (90 percent), regardless of their country of origin.

41 L. Lippard. (1976). "The Women's Art Movement – What Next?" In *From the Center: Feminist Essays on Women's Art.* New York: Dutton, 139–48, p. 141. This book also documents Lippard's work as a feminist curator.

42 Whitney protests were organized by the Ad Hoc Group from 1970; see L. Lippard. (1971). "Sexual Politics: Art Style." In Lippard, *From the Center,* 28–37; Garrard and Broude, *Power of Feminist Art,* pp. 90–1.

43 See S. Buchmann. (1995). "Information Service: Infowork." *October,* 71, 103–19; K. Deepwell. (2002). "Curating New Narratives: Ute Meta Bauer Interview." *n.paradoxa,* 10, 65–74

44 See Guerrilla Girls website, www.guerrillagirls.com, and their publications.

45 "Bad Girls" (October 7–December 5, 1995, ICA, London) showed six women artists. "Bad Girls" (part 1, January 14–February 27, 1994, and part 2, March 5–April 10, 1994, Museum of Contemporary Art, New York), curated by Marcia Tanner, included around 90 artists. See also "Bad Girls West" (January 25–March 20, 1994, UCLA, Wight Art Gallery, California). For discussion see, K. Deepwell. (1996). "Bad Girls? Feminist Identity Politics in the 1990s." In J. Steyn. *Other than Identity.* Manchester: Manchester University Press, 152–68.

46 Examples include: "Judy Chicago's The Dinner Party" in 1979, and the three shows "Women's Images of Men" and "About Time and Issues" (both 1980, ICA, London), and "The Glasgow Girls: Women in Art and Design 1880–1920" (1990, Canongate, Edinburgh).

3 | NEW ART, NEW CHALLENGES: THE CHANGING FACE OF CONSERVATION IN THE TWENTY-FIRST CENTURY

Rachel Barker and Patricia Smithen

Editor's Introduction

Rachel Barker and Patricia Smithen have been conservators of modern and contemporary paintings at the Tate in London, UK, since 1999. Barker worked in regional museums in the UK for 10 years and in 1998 was awarded a Winston Churchill Scholarship to study the conservation of contemporary art at the National Gallery of Canada. Smithen was a Fellow at the Canadian Conservation Institute and an intern at the Detroit Institute of Art.

In "New Art, New Challenges," Barker and Smithen use their experience at the Tate as a model on which to explore the changing face of conservation in the twenty-first century. They show that modern and contemporary art is prompting conservators to assume an increasingly pivotal role in the museum, collaborating with artists, curators, and educators and advising on major policy issues from acquisitions to display. Conceptual, ephemeral, and digital art and works using fragile and/or composite materials have challenged the notion that art, and the museum itself, are eternal. Today, conservators accept that the object changes over time, though they continue to act as defenders of a work's "integrity." The conservator has to negotiate continually the needs of use versus preservation at a time when many artists and curators are prioritizing the former. Barker and Smithen depict conservators as wearing many hats, including those of artist, scientist, mediator, educator, financial adviser, ethicist, and information manager. In the treatment of objects, conservators think of the piece over its lifetime, following the principles of minimal and reversible intervention and careful documentation. And in setting policies on collection care – considering the larger body of works in a museum – they determine museum-wide initiatives for storage, display, handling, and maintenance. Conservators also now have a public voice. In the past, to preserve the myth of timelessness, museums made conservators and conservation virtually invisible to viewers. But as Barker and Smithen suggest, many conservators of modern and contemporary art aim to convey to the visitor the complexities of objects and collections, including physical and theoretical aspects and questions in treatment and display. This chapter demonstrates the critical role that the conservator plays in transforming the museum from a temple to a forum.

Bequeathed to the Tate in 1910, *Dedham Lock and Mill* (1819) by British artist John Constable is a framed landscape painting perceived by the modern eye as traditional. This oil on canvas has been lined (to strengthen the original canvas) and cleaned and has undergone minor restoration, but is generally well preserved for its age. From a conservation perspective it has fallen within an established practical and theoretical framework for its conservation and care. Constable's intention was that this work would have longevity, as he was hopeful that it would enter a national collection and remain in perpetuity.[1] Paintings naturally change most rapidly in the first few decades of their lives, and *Dedham Lock and Mill* may have once undergone such transformation; nonetheless, the visual appearance of this painting is now changing slowly and will be seen as unaltered by visitors to the Tate.

In 2002 the Tate acquired the painting *Let a Thousand Flowers Bloom* (2000) by the German artist Anselm Kiefer. This work, at the start of its life – thus at a stage of rapid change – and created with unstable materials, challenges every aspect of a conservator's remit. Over a linen canvas supporting a thick film of artist-made oil paint, emulsion, clay, and shellac, Kiefer wired woody brambles that extend beyond the borders of the support, and inserted dried long-stemmed roses among their tangles. The heavy paint film cracked and split as it dried, forming craters across the surface under the brambles. The work appears stable on the gallery wall. Yet, each time it is moved, the canvas sways under the uneven weight of the structure; brambles wave, bounce, break off, and shed material and the odd rose head falls to the ground. Soon after the acquisition, dormant spider beetle eggs in the brambles hatched and larvae began eating through the woody structures.

What is the artist's intention regarding the preservation of existing unstable material? What do we do about the material that is already lost? How do we interpret the intent of the work when the artist suggests that the level of conservation intervention should be judged by the conservator's own conscience? How will the work change throughout its existence? Will the visitor who sees the work today return and be shocked by its altered appearance in 20 years time? How do such issues change the nature of conservation and the notion of the museum itself?

Controversies in the past century over long-term damage caused by some early restoration – the attempt to "restore" an object to its "original" condition – have led to the field of conservation – the act of conserving the original and providing thorough documentation of all intervention. Conservators today accept that objects change and that there is no one "pure" state. They work to a code of ethics[2] and in an environment of increased public accountability. With each treatment, there are choices to be made – how far to take an intervention and how to ascertain what is most important. Balancing primacy of original material, including stretchers and frames, over elements traditionally considered more critical, such as a perfectly flat picture plane or a more contemporary but aesthetically pleasing frame, is a frequent intellectual dilemma. Within a single gallery, such choices can pose display quandaries; a cleaned and heavily restored painting may look odd or even overcleaned next to a yellowed painting that is showing its years. But which is of greater value: the patina of age or something that might be closer to how the work originally appeared? Advocates are not lacking in either camp and each treatment is a compromise between these two poles. At the Tate, variety is accepted within the collection, and choices can be made based on the needs of an individual object rather than on a desire to create a cohesive look for a grouping.

As suggested by the Kiefer example, modern and contemporary art pose significant challenges to the field of conservation. The professional museum conservator has always had to respond to the conceptual and creative demands of artists. Traditionally made paintings may begin to fall apart during an artist's lifetime; and artists throughout the centuries have experimented with the unconventional media of their day. So what is unique about the role of the conservator dealing specifically with modern and contemporary works? First, she or he faces a larger array of materials employed in this "anything goes" era than ever before, including some which will have a relatively short life span. Second, living artists are frequently involved in the care of their museum objects, both intellectually and practically. This creates the possibility for conservators to interact with artists through discussion, interviews, and questionnaires in an attempt to document the concept of the work and attitudes of its maker regarding preservation, intervention, and display. Such contact informs conservators and ensures treatments are ethically as well as physically appropriate.[3] Finally, the ever-evolving science of conservation has led to new materials and procedures that are highly reversible, thus minimizing intervention. This allows for a wide range of options concerning the future care of these objects that are at their most vulnerable to change.

Using as a case study the Tate, which houses British art from the fifteenth to the twenty-first centuries and international modern and contemporary art, this chapter will show that modern conservation can successfully react to modifications imposed by changes in the art-making world and, in turn, transform the character of the museum. The conservation demands of art teach us that objects are ever-changing, that they require constant attention and occasional revision. As well as treating individual objects, the museum conservator is challenged by the conservation of a collection and all the issues dealing with its acquisition, display, and use. Through these activities, conservators are assuming an increasingly prominent role in making the museum an arena of discourse. They collaborate with artists, curators, and other museum staff to create the theater of the museum experience. Conservators' input helps shape the scenery of the museum and make the props communicate their complex stories.

The Changing Role of the Museum Conservator

The Tate is representative of trends in monumental museums of international scope. The history of conservation at the Tate charts the dramatic changes in conservation policy that similar encyclopedic institutions collecting contemporary art have undergone. Established in 1897 as a museum of paintings, sculpture, and unique works on paper, for its first 60 years the Tate used private restorers to treat its objects. The conservation department officially opened in 1958; one conservator and two assistants treated the entire collection of approximately 5,900 objects. In the early 1970s the print and archive departments were created and specialists in paper conservation were hired to care for those collections. In 1984 a sculpture conservator was added to deal with the growing specialty in that direction. As the permanent collection expanded to include more modern and contemporary art, the conservation department underwent a corresponding growth with diverse specialties. The Tate now encompasses a "family" of four galleries, including its original London Millbank site, now called Tate Britain, a second location in London, Tate Modern, a third in Liverpool, and one in Cornwall. As well, works can be viewed upon request at Tate Stores, a London storage site. The conservation department employs over 60 professionals, including specialists and technicians in frames conservation, electronic media, modern and contemporary paintings, and conservation science. The department is responsible for thousands of pieces with complex conservation issues, such as ephemeral works, conceptual art, new technologies, installations, and composite objects with problematic materials. The conservator's mission is both to care for the collection and to facilitate its desired usage.

Restoration/conservation has always been a key part of the museum machinery at the Tate and elsewhere, although originally the role focused on individual objects. The restorer's unique training, a marriage of art and science, was utilized to present the collection at its "best." As restoration evolved into the conservation profession,[4] the position broadened to encompass the diverse remit of collections care and all that the term entails. The principals of "do no harm" and "reversibility of materials and procedures" inspired a new era of conservation research to complement and support treatments. Preventive conservation developed and flourished, as cost-effective measures convinced administrations to support policies developed to minimize damage to objects and to utilize conservators as advisers. In 1991, the Tate's Conservation Department, in partnership with the National Gallery of Art (Washington, DC), the Canadian Conservation Institute, and the Smithsonian Institution, organized an international conference entitled "Art in Transit." There, the Tate showcased its policy for and research in improving and facilitating the safe transit of works of art in what is now a "global" exchange. The publication of the conference proceedings is now a reference standard for all aspects related to this key museum activity, facilitating the work of registrars, curators, and conservators of all disciplines.[5]

While an independent conservator, not associated with a museum, must, by necessity, address the condition of an object at a particular moment in time, in-house conservation departments like that at the Tate allow a greater versatility in the care and treatment of the objects. A museum conservator treats the object over its life span, continually assessing and revisiting the work. This perpetual care encourages minimal intervention, as more invasive work can be performed if further deterioration is indicated. Documentation is essential to the process in order to transmit information accurately. Looking over gallery records, one can chart the rise in the conservation profession with increased levels of treatment information. Eighty years ago, the cleaning of a painting might be briefly noted in a file or a restorer's invoice. Forty years ago, the method of cleaning would likely be recorded with all the materials used, possibly in conjunction with before-and-after treatment photography. Today, documentation also might include analytical reports identifying pigments and media, and records of imaging methods like infra-red reflectography and X-radiography. Comprehensive treatment reports include assessments of an intervention's success and notes for future considerations. Conservators and conservation scientists are responsible for collating and interpreting this complex technical data, which provides a comprehensive dossier on the object's continued care and maintenance. As well, conservators write summary reports and post them on the gallery's intranet to be used by curators and education staff engaged in interpreting the work.

Further to treating individual objects, collections care also means treating the collection as a whole. The conservator's role in this area tends to be advisory, and his or her influence infiltrates other departments and impacts on museum policy. Feasible standards of care are assessed, proposed, and implemented. This may include recommendations for storage facilities, display environments, handling techniques, and maintenance programs. As these actions require a budget and interdepartmental participation, preventive conservation measures become museum-wide procedures supporting the policies for protection of works of art. At the Tate, for instance, conservators recently introduced a transit frame, developed and tested in-house, to be used for all unframed or delicately framed paintings. It addresses one particular problem with large modern paintings: the accumulation of fingerprint grime along unframed edges and the dents caused by grasping works by their stretchers. It can be difficult or impossible to clean and invisibly repair color field surfaces or matte paint; prevention is essential. The introduction of the transit frame, an open wooden framework for storing and transporting works between sites and within galleries, has had a huge impact on the preservation of the appearance of these works by allowing them to be safely handled. Such innovations must be practical. Ideally, each work would have a climate-controlled case; practically, however, the cost of building, handling, and storing cases is prohibitive. The cost of the transit frame compares favorably with the cost of repairing and maintaining the objects. There is also added value in the increased reputation of an institution that cares for its works; such a profile makes it easier to convince other museums to loan valuable or fragile objects to the borrowing institution.

Cutting-edge collections care today is dependent on an ambitious program of research. Museum conservators are in a privileged position, often afforded resources unavailable to private conservators in the form of time, equipment, materials, and expertise. The sheer volume of works in a collection supplies statistics for research into procedures and often provides a solid body of works by an artist or group of artists for historical research. Research offers value to the collection, as the transit frame demonstrates, and links conservation with other museum departments. Research also leads to a more public role for the conservator. At the Tate conservators respond to general inquiries from the public, give talks to education department staff, and assume leading roles in the larger conservation community and in training programs.

The broader remit of collections care demands a corresponding increase in the administration that supports each task. Institutional conservators tend to spend more time in front of computers, in meetings, and at desks than their colleagues in private practice. These tasks are essential to maintain some semblance of order to the information generated about the objects, collection, and treatments. Information technology enhances communication among different departments. For example, conservation condition surveys are available on a database, allowing other departments to access information on display suitability and environmental requirements. This system enables curators to plan effectively for their exhibitions in terms of resources required. Even the rise in conservation administration influences the workings of the museum.

Acquiring Art in a Public Collection

A broad array of activities within a museum requires input from conservators. Chief among these is the acquisition of works for the collection. The process of acquiring an art work can take years, hundreds of labor-hours, and pages of correspondence. How does a museum acquisition occur and what might cause complications? The Tate's acquisitions process illustrates some of the difficult issues. Along with historical works, the Tate collects modern and contemporary objects that subvert traditional notions of fine arts media. The Tate relies on conservators to develop innovative approaches that make known the risks and responsibilities of acquiring such objects.

The process begins when the curator selects an object for the museum. The curator bases his or her decision on how well the piece fulfills the collections strategy of the institution and represents the work of the artist. At the Tate the curator submits a report on the object to the acquisitions board for its consideration. The document contains a one-page condition statement written by the conservator; it outlines current condition, concerns about the object's condition and maintenance, and cost estimates for treatment and housing. If the board chooses to acquire the work, further processing takes place, including registration and photographing of the object, writing a full conservation report, and executing any necessary remedial treatments.

These steps sound straightforward and for many objects they are. However, certain categories of work require additional consideration and negotiation before the implications of acquisition are established.

A major consideration of acquisition is accountability to the tax-payers who essentially own the collection. Are they getting good value for money? What are the costs involved in acquiring an art work? How well will the work fulfill its role in terms of usage and longevity? One of the Tate's stated aims is to "strengthen a world-class collection by adding works of outstanding aesthetic and historical significance," a deliberately broad remit.[6] Viewed in conjunction with the other major goals of the museum – presenting innovative exhibitions and programs and serving the public – a picture emerges of a collection to be used and displayed. However, although works are rotated regularly between storage and display, less than 10 percent of the collection is on view at any one time. The museum has an important role as a storehouse for valuables.

The cost of an object is more than the purchase price. There is cost associated with conservation treatment, storage, shipping, installation, and display. An enormous sculpture might require outsized vehicles and cranes to be hired for transport and installation; a video work may need specially trained technicians to install and maintain the media and supporting technology required to view it. Additional costs accrue when an installation demands that the artist set up the work over a series of days or weeks. One can reasonably add a few percentage points to the purchase price for basic extras in an uncomplicated acquisition. For a complex one, the overall cost may far outstrip the initial price within a few years.

Part of the job of the conservator is to estimate these costs, occasionally in conjunction with the curator; this entails a bit of fortune-telling as problems are anticipated. Consider our Kiefer acquisition again. While it was easy to foresee the need for a travelling frame to contain and support the work during its most vulnerable transit periods, the infestation of spider beetles went undetected and, thus, no funds were allocated for fumigation. In an object of that size, treatment can run to thousands of pounds.[7] Conservators are now considering a change in policy whereby all works with vegetable matter are automatically fumigated once acquired, thus minimizing the possibility of infecting the collection. However, a cost-benefit analysis must be undertaken first, outlining the risks to the art and the collection.

When the process works well, solutions can be negotiated to keep costs down. The artist who initially insists on installing his or her own work may be brought into the gallery to set up the piece for the first time and then agree on a particular configuration to guide preparators in future. Often it is the conservator's job to create an installation file which holds written descriptions, images, diagrams, and sometimes even videos that detail the criteria needed to reproduce a display.

A certain degree of robustness is required for objects at the Tate, as it is a multi-sited institution. An object may reside at the storage facility but should be capable of being transported and displayed at Tate Britain, Tate Modern, Tate Liverpool, and Tate St Ives. In addition, the gallery also has a strong commitment to lending; many art works are constantly travelling and on display. The collection includes some incredibly fragile objects, however, that may have restrictions on their usage.

Works that may be difficult to justify for acquisition are those that are intended to have a short life span: "ephemeral art." Examples include an ice sculpture with a life of only a few days, a liquid display that evaporates in a few months, and a wall painting that will be destroyed at the end of a fixed term. These objects are not conceived to be preserved; their inevitable decay is intrinsic to their meaning. It can be difficult to justify the use of public funds to invest in such a short-lived object. Thus, this type of work is not often well represented in collections, though it reflects a significant direction in contemporary art. It is much easier to collect ephemera when the works are given or bequeathed to the gallery than when they are purchased.[8] The need to build a national collection for future generations must be balanced against the desire to include a wide range of current trends and artists.

Even more problematic than ephemeral objects are those works that were intended to have longevity but that were constructed with materials or by methods that will change or degrade in a foreseeable manner and time frame. While they may be short-lived, these works do not embrace self-destruction as fundamental to their meaning. Conservators must attempt to preserve them in some displayable condition for as long as possible. It can be difficult for a conservator to determine acceptable levels of intervention that still allow the preservation of physical and theoretical integrity.

Sean Rainbird, senior curator at the Tate, has remarked that in the 1970s it was difficult to collect works by Joseph Beuys, one of the most influential leaders of avant-garde art in Europe. Through discussions and correspondence, decision-makers at the museum labeled one work under consideration too fragile and sought to acquire something more substantial. Then, when a substantial work did come up for sale, it was deemed not representative enough of the artist's body of work because it wasn't made of something sticky![9] The Tate's first purchase of a Beuys was *Bed*, a relatively robust bronze sculpture in 1972. In contrast, the Tate acquired *Fat Battery*, made of felt, fat, tin, wood, and board, only through a 1974 long-term loan that in 1984 became a bequest. The fat in the piece has infused throughout the materials, acting as a preservative but radically changing the initial appearance of the object.

Currently, museums of modern and contemporary art accept that change in a work is inevitable and need not always be disguised. The taste of today no longer requires a pristine surface; the preference for viewing the history and patina of age means that visible cracks, small damages, and losses in a modern work might not be restored to the same level as in a traditional work. In the past few years, the Tate has purchased objects comprising a wide range of unstable materials including balloons, organic matter, foam rubber, and digital prints. While these materials will alter in appearance, probably within 50 years, conservators and curators accept the transformation, as long as the artistic vision of the work is intact.

It is thus important to educate the public on matters related to conservation so that the appearance of objects on display can be fully appreciated and interpreted. To this end, some museums have staged exhibitions – both real and virtual – about conservation and/or have published their research in accessible language. The Tate Conservation Department's *Paint and Purpose*, *Material Matters*, and *The Impact of Modern Paints* have proved extremely popular and suggest that the visiting public is keen to know more about the nature of a conservator's work.[10] Nevertheless, the subjective nature of judgment complicates the decision-making process. What changes are deemed acceptable? At what point is the artistic vision compromised? Who makes that call and what should happen to the work at that point?[11] In some ways, conservators are the least accepting of visual change as they are trained to look carefully and identify flaws, cracks, damages, and deviations on a surface. An average visitor is able to appreciate a picture's appearance without being consciously aware that its surface is obscured by yellowed varnish or ingrained dirt. It is often only in contrast to other similar works, or when these flaws are brought to their attention, that many viewers start to notice the physical structure.

To manage the changing states of objects, conservators conceptualize each work in their collection as having two states of existence. One is the state of the work when it enters the collection. This moment in time serves as the reference for the rest of the object's existence. A "snapshot" is recorded: its condition, its display parameters, and its image. Often the conservator interviews the artist or his or her estate representative to add to this knowledge-base. This interview provides information on materials and construction of the work. It also allows the artist to state his or her views on display conditions, acceptable levels of intervention, and possible changes to the work. The second state is an object's continuous existence, incorporating all the changes since the acquisition. Conservators must constantly evaluate the balance between these two states to ensure that the integrity of the art work is maintained.

Conservators at the Tate have had to engage in such careful monitoring with works by Constructivist Naum Gabo (1890–1977). The museum owns a series of his small sculptures from the 1920s through 1940s that incorporate early plastics. Some of the sculptures have deteriorated and degraded in ways that were unpredictable at the time of their manufacture. Most have significantly yellowed, altering the transparency and color balance of the works. Curators and sculpture conservators work closely with the Gabo Trust to maintain the integrity of the artist's vision and to make decisions on when to retire objects from public view. In most cases, changes have been deemed acceptable and the majority of the fragile works continue to be exhibited. Conservation information is incorporated into wall texts when the works go on display to inform the public of their changing condition. In a few of the sculptures, the plastics have physically deformed to such an extent that they are no longer approved for display. As the objects continue to change, documentation becomes ever more important to retain information about their existence. Conservators have recorded some of the works with a three-dimensional laser scanner so that, when the sculptures are no longer viable, their form and appearance will still be available to scholars and publics of the future.

Building a relevant contemporary collection can be difficult as a time-lag exists between the introduction of new forms and the ability to accept and cope with them. However, as collections have grown to encompass art objects beyond physically traditional works, the philosophies and methods of conservators have also developed, making it easier to accommodate changes appropriately. Rather than constantly looking back, conservators are now emphasizing the future by managing technology and predicting, as far as possible, how objects might be used and when they might retire. Conservators make a significant contribution to the museum policies on access and display, balancing the needs of objects with the intentions of the artist and the demands of a working collection.

Meeting the Challenge of Displaying Modern and Contemporary Work

Displays are the interface between the visitor and the machinery of the museum. It is here that the expertise and capability of museum staff must fulfill the expectations of the visiting public, the curator, and the artist, while, in the case of the Tate, ensuring the reputation of a museum of international stature. At the Tate, we hold that the visitor should be afforded the opportunity to appreciate the physical and conceptual aspects of the art work, no matter how complex these might be; and yet modern and contemporary artists are challenging the museum like never before.

Tomoko Takahashi's *Drawing Room*, a Tate purchase of 2002, comprises 9,000 sheets of paper as part of an installation that fills a gallery room. The result is a cacophony of material; the work screams out chaos to the viewer, leaving little hint of the carefully orchestrated care that conservators have accorded it to provide effective display and preservation. In fact, every installation of this piece must reproduce exactly the initial arrangement by the artist. This requires the construction of a room specified to within a few millimeters. Each fragile element must be placed perfectly in its assigned position. If any measurements are off, some of the paper will simply not fit and the installation will fail.[12]

In practice, displays are an integral part of gallery life and their preparation, installation, maintenance, and removal exemplify the systematic teamwork of numerous departments. Once curators select a work from the collection for display, registrars verify its availability and conservators confirm its suitability. Suitability is largely determined by a work's stability: can the work be safely moved, installed, and exhibited without undergoing damage? Once an object is cleared for display, conservators make recommendations concerning installation, light levels, security levels, display length, and other factors to maintain the physical well-being of the object. At the Tate, aesthetic considerations may be secondary for some works. For example, while it might be desirable to clean a painting, the work may still be displayed until the treatment can be performed.

Installation

Conservation input at installation varies enormously with each object. At the Tate, once a painting is cleared for display, a conservator rarely needs to be present as it goes on the wall. Exceptions will include fragile works like Kiefer's *Let a Thousand Flowers Bloom*, where the conservator is needed to collect and re-adhere shedding material. Most sculptures and all installations will require conservators to advise on appropriate handling, placement, and, for technology-based items, operational parameters.

Works on loan at the Tate require conservators to be present at several junctures. Non-collection works must be fully documented to confirm an object's condition upon entry into the institution. This requires the conservator to write a condition report, often supplemented with photography or imaging. An important aspect of a conservator's job is to foster collaboration with the courier who might accompany the work. Together, they must establish that both parties are comfortable with the levels of protection offered to the object and agree on the state of a work before the borrowing institution accepts responsibility. The conservator and installation team must follow special instructions relayed by the lending institution through the courier to safely install and display objects on loan. This exchange of information, often quite complex in cases of modern and contemporary art, must be of the highest professional standard; professionalism preserves the trust between lender and borrower, as even the most minor of concerns will be reported back to the owners. The importance of lenders cannot be overestimated. It is a rare collection that can infinitely perpetuate itself in displays without being enhanced by external sources.

Display

International conservation standards spell out suitable conditions for display in public museums and galleries.[13] However, variations exist within each institution, depending on physical environment, resources available, and visitor profiles.

Consider the differences between Tate Britain and Tate Modern, both large, busy London institutions drawing on the same collection and core staff. Tate Britain exhibits British art from 1500 through today and draws the usual gallery-going visitors: art lovers, tourists, and school children. Tate Modern, opened in 2000 as part of the national millennium celebrations, has become a phenomenon extending far beyond its initial conception of serving

FIGURE 3.1   "Nature into Action" Gallery, Tate Modern, London, 2004. © Tate, London 2004

as a gallery of international stature. Tate Modern is a tourist attraction, a social and celebratory space in its own right; people who have never been to an art museum before are compelled to witness the transformation of a power station into a cultural icon (figure 3.1). The phenomenon has had a significant effect on how the space needs to be managed, especially given the number of unstable objects exhibited. Understandably, many viewers to Tate Modern were not used to being spatially aware of themselves around delicate artifacts; many reached out to touch the tactile surfaces and three-dimensional forms.

In response, conservators collaborated with curators in adjusting displays to assist behavioral cues around vulnerable works: signage was improved, more extensive barriers were installed, and works were removed to improve visitor flow. These steps were essential, but not made without lengthy discussion and negotiation. Curators understandably wanted spare, clean displays with as much visitor access as possible. "Do Not Touch" signs, which must be large and visible to be effective, can set an aggressive tone and visually interfere with the layout of objects in space.

One aspect of conservation which many curators find restrictive is the recommendation to use barriers and glass or acrylic in frames.[14] The exhibition of Leonardo da Vinci's *Mona Lisa* at the Louvre in Paris exemplifies the drawbacks of such restrictions. This rather small painting, given its history of theft and status as an international icon, hangs behind thick, bullet-proof glass with guards posted nearby. A queue of visitors parades past the work, unable to fully contemplate the beauty of the surface because of the extreme protective measures. The level of protection becomes part of the spectacle, adding to the experience, but not to the understanding of the object.

The need to protect works can interfere with artistic intention, particularly in modern and contemporary works which rely on visitor participation. An untitled Tate work by Robert Morris (1965/71) consists of four wooden cubes covered with mirrored plate glass, placed directly on the floor. When first installed at Tate Modern, the work had no barriers, allowing visitors to walk among the cubes. This interaction is important, as it functions to reflect the space and activity that the piece generates. Viewers were unable to keep their hands off the shiny, seductive surfaces, however. Fingerprints can be corrosive and may permanently imprint on some metals, glass, and paint when left in place. The edges of the cubes were subject to bumps and hits from visitors and their personal effects, causing small losses to the fragile surfaces. Damage to pristine surfaces can amount to a compromise of the artistic vision. Conservators responded by introducing a low barrier that allowed people to walk around the perimeter of the cubes and see the changing reflections yet limited their experience, contrary to previous installations of the work. This solution compromised the artistic vision of the work but allowed the piece to be safely displayed. This is a best-practice yet still somewhat unsatisfactory response to balancing use and preservation of the object.

To offer more options satisfactory to all parties, conservators are developing and testing new approaches. Conservators at the Tate have looked at different types of barriers, such as standard elasticized versions, floor markers with a slight profile, and infra-red alarm barriers. None is ideal and all must be used in combination with other methods, such as video surveillance, static and roaming gallery assistants, random security checks, and secure wall and plinth fastenings. New technology holds promise for future generations; invisible force-fields might one day be a practical and safe option.

Alternately, museums might undergo a change in philosophy. They might choose to shift the balance in favor of greater interaction with works, increasing the levels of acceptance of compromised appearances. Works will certainly suffer from fading, soiling, cracking, and vandalism but institutions may decide that they have so many objects that some attrition or damage is acceptable. Few works would be completely destroyed. What is our obligation to present future generations with pristine works, rather than well-used objects? Some artists are lobbying for museums to prioritize use over preservation; they have a clear vision of how they want their works to function and accept that pieces may change and deteriorate as a result. In the negotiation of display conditions, conservators impact policy by predicting consequences to a range of scenarios and providing recommendations to curators.

Lighting is an area in which conservation input is key. Organic objects are subject to deterioration upon exposure to high or prolonged periods of light. This deterioration can manifest itself as fading, discoloration, embrittlement, and decomposition. Studies have determined the optimum balance between visual access for the majority of visitors and appropriate levels for lighting vulnerable objects. Leeway does exist – some works may be lit at higher levels but for shorter periods than is typical. And innovative exhibitions may require compromise of conservation standards to fulfill curatorial intention. For example, *The Sun is God*, a 2000 exhibit of J. M. W. Turner oils and watercolors at Tate Liverpool, displayed unframed works in natural light to show how they might have looked in the artist's studio.[15] This installation imbued traditional paintings with a modern, almost abstract sensibility, playing with notions of how museum spaces function. In order to accommodate the concept, usual standards of constant light levels were altered. Levels were still monitored to measure the total amount of light hitting the works; the levels rose and fell throughout the days and season, sometimes too low to properly view works and sometimes much brighter than normally would be allowed. While not recommended for all objects or displays, occasional concessions are possible to accommodate new ways of situating works in galleries.

Sympathetic lighting can be used as conservation tool. A large color field painting must appear pristine to the average viewer, but many such works from the 1960s have been heavily displayed and have undergone serious damage due to handling and accidents. Some of Barnett Newman's works, for instance, are cracked, scuffed, and soiled with fingerprints. Many of his paintings are extremely difficult to restore, as surface variations, due to damage or restoration, become highly visible under harsh lighting conditions. These variations can be minimized if soft, diffuse light illuminates the work; the scatter of electrons fools the visitor into seeing a continuous field of color, rather than a broken, variegated surface. Good lighting can assist in minimizing levels of intervention.

Once a work is installed and display conditions set, a conservator sets up a routine of maintenance. Gallery assistants, art handlers, and security tend to be the eyes and ears of the gallery, reporting back on unauthorized visitor interactions with works, noting visible changes, and generally keeping tabs on things. Maintenance of objects on display consists of monitoring the environment, dusting and polishing works on display as required, and ensuring equipment is operational. Dust, like fingerprints, can be corrosive and needs to be dealt with daily. Tate Modern has a layered approach to object maintenance, essential in a large institution. Specially trained gallery assistants, art handlers, conservation technicians, and conservators work together to ensure each object is cared for.

Modern and contemporary works can pose tricky problems, even concerning something as simple as accumulation of surface dust while on display. *Shooting Picture* (1961) by Niki de Saint Phalle has accumulated a layer of dust and some ingrained dirt; bits of plaster are loose and dangling from its surface. The conservator is obviously tempted to perform a light surface cleaning and consolidation, but the artist's process of construction precludes this action. The artist made the work by filling polyethylene bags with liquid paint, securing them to wire mesh over block-board with string, and covering the entire surface with white textured plaster. At the show's opening, guests, including artists Jasper Johns and Robert Rauschenberg, were invited to shoot the picture. The bullets pierced through plaster, plastic, and wood, allowing the paint to spill out across the surface.[16] As a result, bits of plaster dangle precariously from loosened string; crumpled plastic fills the craters. Over its 30-plus years, the porous plaster surface has imbibed environmental dirt, but this is now indistinguishable from the original gunshot powder. While loose dust can be brushed from the surface, newly imbibed dirt must remain in order to preserve the residues from the original performance of its creation. New loose plaster bits can be consolidated into place, but the original bits loosened by the bullet impact must remain in their current state. In this case, photographic documentation is essential to allow original damage from creation to be distinguished from the later damage of existence and usage. A large proportion of museum dust is composed of dead human skin cells and fibers from visitor clothing. In future, technology may be available to separate this matter from other dirt composition, enabling conservators to clean problematic objects. Once again, the object dictates restricted intervention, yet its continued preservation in such a state as to be appropriately experienced will require increasingly high levels of preventive conservation and perhaps some invasive measures. Contemporary art requires versatility in approach to its care.

Conclusion

Modern and contemporary art introduces new ideas manifested in innovative materials and forms which can provide a multi-sensory experience for the museum visitor. No longer is "the art" necessarily what is hanging on the wall or what is positioned carefully in the gallery: its context, historical, aesthetic, and intellectual, can equally be what is "on show." No longer is it necessarily constructed in a way intended to last for future generations: the materials employed can be so ephemeral that they decay even before the fickle finger of fashion points to a new orthodoxy.

Furthermore, confusion can arise when traditional displays – hands-off, view-from-a-distance installations – are mixed in spaces adjacent to interactive and participatory works. Museums must be prepared to accommodate different experiences within their spaces, while still fulfilling their role as the guardians of the works. The conservator is an important and indispensable part of this scene, providing expertise and information on the physical nature of the work and often on its theoretical nature as well. The future of the museum depends on the ability of the conservator to collate the needs of the object – its physical nature, function, intent, and historical context, – to record these needs, and to ensure that, as far as possible, the object is not compromised on any of these levels.

This chapter has highlighted some of the changes already implemented by museums to provide appropriate care for modern and contemporary collections. And as to the future? While we cannot predict the future expectations of visitors to museum collections, as we have neither social nor political context, we can make assumptions based on the past. "Authenticity" has always been highly sought after but perhaps values may shift. Perhaps authenticity will be downgraded in importance and replicas will take the place of original objects.[17] Or maybe access and intention will be paramount and art works will simply be used as desired and discarded more frequently and easily. Alternatively, original objects might become so sacred that they will be housed in protective boxes and there will be a return to the exaggerated reverence of the Victorian picture salon. It is more likely, though, that some middle way will be pursued and that, as now, each display and each object must be considered anew whenever demands are made upon them. The conservator will likely remain guardian of the "ideal" state of an object, and indeed will continue to add his or her voice to the debate on what this "ideal" state is; in practice, though, she or he will be prepared to accommodate less than ideal conditions so that the work completes its function by being seen and experienced. Together with other museum professionals, united in the need to balance preservation and use, conservators continue to facilitate the complete experience of the museum object.

Questions for Discussion

1　If you were the director of a museum of contemporary art and were looking to hire a conservator, how would the job description read? If you had been looking to hire a conservator 30 years ago, how would the description have read?
2　Describe the collaborative relationship between conservator and artist and between conservator and curator. How does the conservator impact on museum policy? What is the difference between care of individual objects and collections care?
3　Why are conservators usually less accepting of physical change in a work than are the curator and the artist? How do conservators define the phrase "integrity of the object"? Do you think the balance between use and preservation will change in the future? If so, how?
4　Discuss the increasingly public voice of the conservator. In what way does the conservator have an educational mission? And what is meant by a conservator's "public accountability"?
5　Why do the authors use the metaphor of the museum experience as theater? What role does the conservator play in the performance? How does the new role of the conservator color the way we conceptualize the museum?
6　Do you think that many of the artists working with ephemeral and fragile materials are purposely trying to critique or change the museum? If so, how and why?
7　In what way do chapters 1, 2, and 3 of this volume together provide a general history of museums? How would you characterize this history?

Notes

1　S. Daniels. (1994). *Fields of Vision: Landscape Imagery and National Identity in England and the United States*. Cambridge: Polity, 201–2.
2　Development of preventive conservation and summaries of published conservation ethics can be found in S. Williams. (1997). "Preventive Conservation: The Evolution of a Museum Ethic" and R. E. Child. (1997). "Ethics and Museum Conservation." Both in G. Edson. (ed.). *Museum Ethics*. London: Routledge, 196–206, 207–15.
3　A good example of contemporary interactions between artists and conservators is found in L. Davies and J. Heumann. (2004). "Meaning Matters: Collaborating with Contemporary Artists." In R. Ashok and P. Smith. (eds.). *Modern Art, New Museums*. London: IIC, 30–3.

4 For an overview of historical developments of cleaning and retouching processes, see D. Bomford. (1994). "Changing Taste in the Restoration of Paintings." In A. Oddy. (ed.). *Restoration: Is It Acceptable?* London: British Museum, 33–40.

5 M. F. Mecklenburg. (ed.). (1991). *Art in Transit: Studies in the Transport of Paintings.* Washington, DC: National Gallery of Art.

6 (1994). *Tate Report 2000–2002.* London: Tate Gallery Publishing, p. 4.

7 The fumigation *of Let a Thousand Flowers Bloom* by Kiefer is completed but the treatment to stabilize the support is ongoing. Currently, when brambles shed or break, conservators save and, if possible, reattach the material using reversible methods. This is subject to revision, pending an interview with the artist.

8 N. Serota. Interview with Rachel Barker and Patricia Smithen. London, July 29, 2003.

9 S. Rainbird. Interview with Patricia Smithen. London, October 7, 2003.

10 For exhibitions on conservation, see, for example, "Conserving the Past for the Future" (2001, Cleveland Museum of Art); "Beyond the Visible: A Conservator's Perspective" (2002–3, Princeton University Art Museum); "Statue of an Emperor: A Conservation Partnership" (2004, Getty Center). For Tate conservation publications, see S. Hackney, R. Jones, and J. Townsend. (eds.). (1999). *Paint and Purpose: A Study of Technique in British Art.* London: Tate Gallery Publishing; J. Heumann. (ed.). (1999). *Material Matters: The Conservation of Modern Sculpture.* London: Tate Gallery Publishing; J. Crook and T. Learner. (2000). *The Impact of Modern Paints.* London: Tate Gallery Publishing.

11 A recent example is documented in C. Stringari, E. Pratt, and C. McGlinchey. (2004). "Reversal vs. Retirement: Study and Treatment of Black Painting, 1960–66, by Ad Reinhardt." In Ashok and Smith, *Modern Art, New Museums,* 165–9. Another example concerns the fate of Mark Rothko's "Harvard Murals" from the early 1960s. The visual change due to pigment fading was so dramatic that the works were thought by many to be a tragic loss, yet they were displayed, without reference their changed appearance, at the Fondation Beyeler in Basel in 2001. Clearly the works still are considered to be representative of the artist's vision.

12 Calvin Winner, paper conservator at the Tate, is now completing an essay for publication on the conservation issues and treatment of Takahashi's *Drawing Room.*

13 The classic text on this topic is G. Thomson. (1986). *The Museum Environment.* London: Butterworth.

14 S. Rainbird. Interview with Smithen.

15 L. Biggs. (2000). "Preface." In *J. M. W. Turner: The Sun is God.* (ex. cat. Tate Liverpool), p. 8.

16 Letter from the artist. Published in: (1998). *The Tate Gallery 1984–86: Illustrated Catalogue of Acquisitions including Supplement to Catalogue of Acquisitions 1982–84.* London: Tate Gallery, pp. 559–61.

17 A case study resulting in the refabrication of an art work is discussed in S. Willcocks. (2002). "Transparent Tubes by William Turnbull: The Degradation of a Polymethyl Methacrylate Sculpture." *ICOM Preprints: 13th Triennial Meeting Rio de Janeiro 22–27*

September 2002, vol. 11. London: James & James, 935–9. For a philosophical discussion, see D. H. van Wegen. (1999). "Between Fetish and Score: The Position of the Curator of Contemporary Art." In I. Hummelen and D. Sillé. (eds.). *Modern Art: Who Cares*. Amsterdam: Foundation for the Conservation of Modern Art and the Netherlands Institute for Cultural Heritage, 201–9.

B Case Studies in Contemporary Practice

4 | HOW WE STUDY HISTORY MUSEUMS: OR CULTURAL STUDIES AT MONTICELLO

Eric Gable

Editor's Introduction

Eric Gable teaches cultural anthropology at the University of Mary Washington, USA. He is the author (with Richard Handler) of *The New History in an Old Museum: Creating the Past at Colonial Williamsburg* and has written several articles drawing upon his ethnographic research in Sulawesi, Indonesia, and Guinea-Bissau.

In "How We Study History Museums," Gable takes an ethnographic approach in order to examine the uneasy relationship between the history museum and its publics. He sees the museum as a stage where staff and visitors perform an elaborate dance about democracy and power. By studying these performances and acknowledging those publics who refuse to perform, Gable shows the contested nature of official history. He rejects the idea that audiences are merely passive consumers of the culture that museums package. Audiences agitate on many levels. And though museums may want to control social memory, to justify their existence they need to respond to constituents' concerns. The chapter uses as a case study the plantation museum of Thomas Jefferson's Monticello, where Gable once worked and where race has long been a contested issue. He interprets comments from and his observations of tour guides, visitors, administrators, and the larger community as they thrash out the institution's treatment of slavery and Jefferson's sexual relationship with slave Sally Hemings. Gable demonstrates that constituents have the power to create shifts in official history at the museum, yet suggests that the institution's desire to "steward" collective memory remains strong.

Since the 1980ss scholars from a variety of disciplines – historians, anthropologists, philosophers, sociologists, in sum scholars in cultural studies broadly conceived – have begun studying history museums as loci for cultural production and consumption.[1] History museums are places where versions of the past are produced through words, pictures, and artifacts, and where the messages they contain are consumed by visitors with a variety of motives for coming to the site. To take the United States as an example, history museums include everything from heritage sites such as historical houses and other buildings that have been "preserved" for the public, to reconstructed communities such as Colonial Williamsburg, not to mention more obvious institutions such as the Smithsonian's Museum of American History. Scholars of such sites (whether in the United States, or Europe, or indeed, anywhere) are fascinated with the relationship between history museums and the nation state. This is because history museums and heritage sites came into being as the modern nation state emerged. These scholars generally assume that stories, images, and artifacts of the past which are displayed in such museums shape national identity by creating an "imagined community" or a "community of memory."[2]

Museums, so the standard assertion goes, make "official history" in the service of the state.[3] They create an imagined community from the top down, in part because their caretakers wish to use public history as a tool for developing a better, more committed citizenry.[4] Likewise, imagined communities are created from the bottom up, as the people who visit museums sometimes argue back at the messengers. Moreover, museums in democratic nation states actively pursue their publics and occasionally cater to their desires because museums, like modern democracies, are premised on the willing participation of a citizenry. The history they produce is a cacophonous outcome of contest and compromise. The shape public history takes in a museum is a product of negotiations among the (at times deeply divided) professional historians and the (often factionalized) public at large.[5] Because it is generally assumed among the professionals who manage museums and among the people who visit that museums display or convey what is true and factual, arguments about what counts as "true" or "false" history reveal and even exacerbate troubling differences among communities of "experts" and the public they ostensibly serve and educate.[6] Museums may be in the business of producing official history packaged as the truth as the experts see it. But as the museum also tries to make democracy by eliciting the willing participation of its audiences, the history it makes is inherently messy.

Because the people who manage history museums feel that they must make a democracy as much as represent its collective past, they are constantly monitoring their ongoing engagement with the public, testing whether the site has a representative or suitably diverse following or whether it seems to cater to one audience and not another.[7] As such, a history museum's caretakers have a peculiar relationship with their public in this managed "regime of knowledge."[8] They are, as Tony Bennett argues, at once gatekeepers, judging a public's comportment, and facilitators, encouraging a public's participation. Members of a public whose understanding of "the past" diverges too widely from the caretakers' own understanding can be dismissed on grounds of comportment; in the context of the creation of a managed community of memory these dissenters count as a kind of rabble. But caretakers might also feel compelled to conform to their public's rearranging of the past even when the public's understanding seems at odds with authoritative knowledge. A museum or heritage site that a "significant" segment of the public does not visit, and that this public loudly criticizes for using the cloak of authority to hide "the truth," can come to be perceived by its caretakers as a failure and an embarrassment.

In recent years, at American slave-era heritage sites, black Americans have acted as such a public, pressuring such sites' caretakers to change the way slaves and slavery are incorporated into America's pedagogic landscape.[9] Their criticisms have had a large impact on the communities of memory such sites produce. To illustrate how the public influences the museum, I will look at Monticello – a plantation and the home of Thomas Jefferson – as I came to know it from 1988 to 1992 through occasional encounters with those who worked at the site and visited it. This chapter is an ethnography; it is based on observations of the ways visitors and the site's caretakers interact with one another, and on listening to what they say about such encounters. I base my analysis on the assumption that such interactions produce meaning through what in cultural studies comes under the rubric of "performance."[10] Because it is an ethnography based on the observation of impromptu performances, my interpretation of Monticello differs from much of the work on museums in cultural studies which depends on words and images to read what museums represent.[11]

My ethnographic account is, however, truncated. I began observing Monticello when I went to work there as a "visitor services specialist" from March 1988 to November 1988. I took notes of conversations I had with employees and visitors with an eye toward an ethnography of this American shrine. In 1989 Richard Handler and I wrote an article describing the dilemmas museums like Monticello and Colonial Williamsburg face as they attempt to enact contradictory egalitarian values in the ways they treat the visiting public. We also applied for funding to study these two institutions in depth. After reading our proposal and our paper, the leadership at Monticello decided that, because the museum was already "over-assessed," our study would not serve its interests, and therefore denied our request to carry out research there. We went on to carry out fieldwork at Colonial Williamsburg exclusively. Nevertheless, Dr Jordan, the current director of the Foundation, agreed to be formally interviewed on two occasions in 1992. This chapter combines elements from those interviews with what I learned while I worked at Monticello and what I continued to learn in subsequent years from friends and acquaintances among Monticello's employees, with whom I have stayed in close contact. It also includes what I have gathered from public sources. I should note that all quotations from conversations are from written notes I took at the time or from transcriptions of the tape-recorded conversations I had with Dr Jordan.

When I was working at Monticello, I witnessed the beginnings of a major shift. The site's caretakers were compelled not only to tell the celebratory story of Jefferson's life and achievements, but also to represent slaves as historical actors in their own right; and they began to quietly change what they were willing to entertain about Sally Hemings, a mulatto slave who many Americans, and especially African Americans, believe had a long-standing liaison with Thomas Jefferson. In early 1988 staff on the site were still treating this story as a myth not worthy of sustained discussion. By 1998 discussion of the liaison is a major theme in the site's verbal, textual, and visual reconstruction of antebellum race relations. This ostensibly is because of a DNA study publicized in that year that shows the genetic connection between Jefferson and the descendants of Hemings.[12] But that study would never have been done were it not for what happened a few years before as African Americans used the site to indict publicly the history of Monticello as a sham. I will focus on how the site's caretakers either were swayed by or dismissed public skepticism about the way the Foundation chose to deal with the purported liaison between Jefferson and Hemings. By looking at shifts in institutional policy on the liaison, I will illustrate the contested nature of official history in modern democracies and the way such contests are enacted in museum practice.

The Site

Monticello is but one of dozens of slave-era plantation houses which were bought in the first decades of the twentieth century by philanthropic organizations for the edification and enjoyment of the public.[13] Many are little more than three-dimensional versions of an "Architectural Digest" excursion. Their current beauty, manifested in rich decor, ostentatious buildings, and beautiful gardens, is an unheard echo of a past extraction of huge surpluses from enslaved workers whose own presence has usually long disappeared from the site. The people who visit such houses tend to be middle-class and white. While many may know quite a bit about American history, they are usually aesthetic tourists who are encouraged to appropriate for their own lives pieces of the past on display. They identify with the plantation's masters, not the slaves. The wealth they gaze at does not make them resentful.

Monticello is similarly attractive to the aesthetic tourist. Situated on a wooded hilltop overlooking the rolling farm country around Charlottesville, Virginia, its house and grounds are considered to be masterpieces. Its gift shops make more money, so I was once told, per square foot than any other equivalent museum shop in the country.

But Monticello is a unique slave-era plantation because it was the residence of Thomas Jefferson; and the motto of the Foundation that runs the heritage site is to "preserve and maintain Monticello . . . as a national shrine and to perpetuate the memory of Thomas Jefferson and those principles for which he contended." "Those principles," guides at Monticello will tell you, are embodied in the three things for which Jefferson wanted to be remembered. He wrote Virginia's statute for religious freedom; he was the founder of the University of Virginia – one of the first publicly funded institutions of higher education whose core moral principles emerged out of Enlightenment humanism rather than an association with a Christian faith; and, above all, he was the author of the Declaration of Independence. It is from these three acts, and primarily for the last of them, that the Foundation – and to some extent the public – adduces "those principles for which he contended." What is stressed is Jefferson's role as a founder of American political values – individual freedom, equality of opportunity, the pursuit of happiness.

The Foundation also stresses Jefferson's preoccupation with intellectual and aesthetic pleasure – his love of gadgets, art, literature, music, gardens, architecture, archeology, science, food. Indeed, the over half a million visitors a year who take a 25-minute tour of the house and spend perhaps an hour exploring the grounds are more likely to learn details of Jefferson's aesthetic interests than of his political principles. While in the house, they are treated to brief vignettes about mechanical wonders such as the Great Clock whose weights, one for each day, disappear into a hole cut into the floor. They are allowed a glimpse of the narrow stairways that lead to the "invisible" upper floors and the mysterious dome or "sky" room that none of the general public will ever see. But mainly there are books, paintings, musical instruments, furniture, wallpaper; and outside, flowers from around the world. Visitors receive a quintessential "house and garden" tour – with Jefferson playing invisible host.

At Monticello, Jefferson's pursuit of knowledge and aesthetic pleasures have been portrayed as both a sign of and a reward for his success at living a life according to the civic virtues he authored. Yet, because Thomas Jefferson was a slave-owner, this celebratory narrative has always been potentially threatened. Jefferson's particular freedom to pursue happiness for himself and his family could be linked to the emiseration of others. Or Jefferson could be dismissed as a hypocrite whose lofty words did not match his deeds. Over the years I was familiar with Monticello, these criticisms occasionally surfaced in encounters the site's staff had with scholars in the wider knowledge-producing community. In these encounters historians and archeologists suggested informally and privately that Monticello consider reconstructing slave quarters on the site to make it easier for visitors to experience Monticello as a "working plantation." In the 1980s and 1990s the criticisms of Monticello and Jefferson crystallized in the popular imagination, around an illicit sexual liaison he allegedly had with a slave, Sally Hemings. That Jefferson denied having a long affair with an enslaved woman and denied any substantive connection to their several offspring could exemplify, at once, the typical hypocrisies of the politically powerful, the particular duplicities and fundamental inequities of race-based slavery, and – as "official history" continued to dismiss these stories – a sign of an ongoing cover-up.

Interpreting a Performance: Defending Jefferson's Reputation

In 1988, when I began research at Monticello, I was intrigued by the Foundation's response to visitors' often pointed interrogation of Jefferson's relationship with Sally Hemings. I was interested in how the ongoing act of representing a particular version of the past compelled a certain comportment among the site's caretakers and visitors alike. My assumption was that Monticello's ongoing conversation with its public would also entail teaching and learning a particular etiquette. This etiquette is part and parcel of current museum practice, yet it emerged out of the place museums have typically occupied in modern democracies since the late nineteenth century – the "exhibitionary complex," as Bennett so deftly characterizes it.

To tease out the significance of museums in late nineteenth-century modernity, Bennett compares the "exhibitionary complex" (which includes art galleries, expositions, and department stores as well as museums) to Michel Foucault's "carceral archipelago" – the system of prisons, insane asylums, and the like – which also has its origins in modernity. Prisons, Foucault famously argued, turned an opaque populace – thieves, murderers, and other threats to public peace, hidden in the poor sections of the city or in the forests beyond the state's highways – into a visible and monitorable group. Museums, Bennett argues, made another populace into a citizenry – people who learned to look at the world through the eyes of power and as a result internalized that way of looking. Not that the proprietors of increasingly open museums trusted their citizenry to behave themselves. Bennett reminds us that the rise of the modern museum arose from an ongoing conflict between reformers, emphasizing that the crowd can be educated not to be unruly, and elitists, ever fearful that the crowd will act like a mob, that they will touch and do damage to, rather than look.

Because of this ambivalence about their public, Bennett notes, the democratizing museum inevitably fails to live up to an institution's own internally generated goals. The wish to "reform" is driven by two internally generated principles, "the first . . . sustaining the demand that museums should be open and accessible to all . . . the second . . . that museums should adequately represent the cultures and values of different sections of the public."[14] These institutional imperatives lead to "insatiable" (that is, never satisfied, but always crying out for satisfaction) demands for reform and endless talk (often self-serving) that reforms are occurring, that progress is, despite inevitable set-backs and obstacles, happening. Museums are supposed to be universal. If they are about "man," they are about all groups of human-beings. Groups who feel excluded can make claims – based on the museum's own morally binding goals – for inclusion. Moreover, museums not only want to represent everyone, but want all citizens to participate. They claim, as Bennett puts it, to address a "public made up of formal equals," but end up making distinctions.[15] The door is open, but not everyone seems willing or proves capable of going through. If museums are places where a public learns to look but not touch, if they are sites where a public learns to become bourgeois, they are also places where caretakers come to assume as inevitable specific ways of governing or managing a public.

At Monticello I was particularly interested in what in museum parlance are called frontline employees – guides and other staff who convey the site's stories to the public. Guides, during the period of my research, tended to be

115

middle-aged women of a certain cultured quality and education that would mark them as upper-middle-class. There were also young men and women – recent graduates of university history and literature departments – barely scraping by on a meager guide's salary, and some of the older women were divorcees or in otherwise straitened circumstances, but they all maintained a cultured look and comportment. They were invariably "courteous," but they looked down their noses at such places as Colonial Williamsburg, where guides had to be artificially friendly to visitors and had to dress in period costume and speak in period accents. At Monticello, they dressed up rather than down. Their "uniform" was an idealized borrowing from the style of the country gentlewoman or gentleman. And when they retired from the public eye to have lunch together in the guides' kitchen, they ate meals that required a fork and knife or spoon, not sloppy sandwiches and the like. I found them congenial company. I wanted to ascertain how their encounters with the public led them to incorporate a certain lived attitude toward "the public."

To hear them talk, hardly a day went by when the site's guides were not asked by some visitor about "Sally Hemings," Jefferson's "slave mistress," or Jefferson's "other" (meaning unacknowledged) children." Often as not, the visitor would phrase the question in an accusatory or mocking tone – the kind of tone I associate with reporters at White House press conferences when the event turns stonewalling into a kind of theater. And indeed, the guides' general response – the response their superiors encouraged them to make – sounded a lot like stonewalling. The guides I observed or talked with discounted the story as a kind of "rumor" by invoking the authority of "professional historians."

What they said emerged out of their appraisal of what motivated the public to ask such questions. But it also reflected what they had been taught. This is what they learned, for example, in the in-house compilation of frequently asked questions written specifically for guides, under the section, "What is the truth about Jefferson and the slave Sally Hemings?"

> Sally Hemings, a mulatto slave born in 1773, was a valued household servant at Monticello and served as lady's maid to Jefferson's daughters in France in the 1780s. The allegation that Sally was Jefferson's mistress and bore his children was first published by a vengeful journalist . . . in 1802. Fawn Brodie's biography of Jefferson and a novel by Barbara Chase-Riboud have recently reiterated this claim. Although it is impossible to prove either side of the question, serious Jefferson scholars are unanimous in discounting the truth of such a

liaison. In the opinion of Jefferson's biographer, Dumas Malone, it would have been totally out of character and "virtually unthinkable in a man of Jefferson's moral standards and habitual conduct." Two of Jefferson's grandchildren explained that one of Jefferson's nephews was the father of Sally's children.[16]

The official position the guides were taught was ostensibly non-committal – "impossible to prove either side of the question." Yet this training document juxtaposes the authority of "serious Jefferson scholars" with a "vengeful journalist," and a bestseller "novel" with the authority of Jefferson's most famous biographer.

It is not surprising that many of the guides interpreted visitors' persistent preoccupation with this sexual liaison as graphic evidence of the low appetite for scandal. As guides often put it, the public "wants to knock alabaster statues off their pedestals." Or the guides construed pestering queries as reflecting a barely concealed desire among the public to besmirch the Monticello Foundation's reputation. Guides often complained to me that aggressive if transparently sly questions such as "But what about Jefferson's other children?" made it "impossible" to do anything but react defensively. As one guide remarked, "a little while ago a visitor asked a guide [who had just finished her tour], 'what did you tell them about Thomas Jefferson screwing colored girls?' Now, how are you going to answer a question like that?" – without, the guide didn't need to add, becoming complicit in racial slurs or sexual crudities.

If an interest in discussing Sally Hemings's sexual liaison with Jefferson was a sign of poor manners that could occasionally be dismissed as bigoted, some guides also believed that such questions reflected as well a general, if misplaced, obsession with secrecy. Visitors often talked as if the upper floors of the house (especially the dome room), which are off limits to the general public, were secret chambers that contained important artifacts purposely kept hidden. People would get off the bus and want immediately to be directed to the "hidden" passages that they assumed honeycombed the house and grounds. These secret passageways and rooms were often associated in the popular imagination with Sally Hemings. Guides complained that visitors would occasionally pester them to show the "secret room" just above Jefferson's bed where Sally Hemings had remained hidden and waiting to answer his call. Some wanted the guides to show them the ingenious system of pulleys which allowed Jefferson to hoist his bed up into this secret cubby hole. Others asked to see the air tunnels they thought led to secret and distant locations for the love tryst. Usually such requests were countered

117

with a courteous, if often icy, resort to a "just-the-facts" accounting. For example, those underground air tunnels, they would tell the visitor, were "in fact" ingenious because they let fresh air circulate to privies situated close to the house. One guide remarked:

> After one tour a woman came up to me and *demanded* to know why we didn't mention anything about the secret passageway to Michie's Tavern. I would like just once to wink or to give some sign . . . to pretend just once that the secret does exist, that the Foundation is part of some vast secret conspiracy to keep the truth from the people [but] because of some flash of communion with this particular visitor I'm going to lift the veil and reveal it all.

As this guide saw it, visitors in pursuit of the secret of Sally Hemings were asserting the existence of a body of knowledge kept purposely out of the public domain. The guide also recognized that when she and her colleagues routinely dismissed the Hemings story as "fiction," or countered queries about the site's invisible passages and hidden chambers with a dry "just-the-facts" response, they simply confirmed this suspicion.

In sum, guides learned the implicit lesson that in any democracy, no matter how open, there will always be a minority who believe in "conspiracy theories." Monticello was the perfect terrain upon which to enact such theories. Guides, who stood in an intermediary position between the public and museum leadership, developed an exaggerated faith in the truth of official knowledge as they found themselves compelled to act as guardians of the reputation of an exemplary figure and of the institution itself.

African Americans and Monticello

During the years that Monticello's guides were incessantly pestered by white visitors about Sally Hemings, the Foundation's leadership was trying to make the site more congenial to African Americans. The site's caretakers were embarrassed that there were so few black visitors to the mountaintop. The Foundation's director Daniel Jordan, the research historian Lucia Stanton, and the site's archeologist William Kelso all argued that if Monticello would focus more on the contributions of the hundreds of slaves who shared the mountaintop with Jefferson, then more African Americans would visit. They set a goal of ensuring that every visitor knew that the site was a plantation based on slave-labor. During the period of my research, this fact usually received at best perfunctory attention in the house tour, which continued, perhaps out of inertia, to focus on aesthetic themes. Nevertheless, visitors could learn much more about plantation life on Mulberry Row – where in Jefferson's day most of the slaves lived – and at the permanent museum exhibit of Mulberry Row at Monticello's visitors' center.

In a 1992 interview, Jordan explained to me that for a long time "slavery was the 's' word" among the guides, who preferred the less explicit euphemism "servants." In the Foundation's early days, members of the often implicitly segregationist "white identity" organizations – the Daughters of the American Revolution and the United Daughters of the Confederacy – served in rotation on Saturdays, Sundays, and legal holidays, while black doormen in livery continued to greet tourists at the East Portico door. And gentility in whiteface continued to be a hallmark of the site long after these organizations ceased to have an official presence at Monticello.

Jordan and his colleagues assumed that if Monticello provided uplifting or positive stories about African Americans from Jefferson's time, African Americans would feel more at home there. Such a view is typical in current museology. It is a view that museum workers share with those who produce culture more generally; it drives much of the effort toward expanding the canon in literature in American schools, for example. During the interview with Jordan, he asked if I had visited the gift shop lately. The Foundation was, he emphasized, "now selling a postcard" (the first in a series commemorating the slaves) – the photographic portrait of Isaac the slave blacksmith. Isaac's portrait was also prominently featured on a new brochure dedicated to the slaves who lived and worked on Mulberry Row. To sum up why these new efforts had been a success, he noted that more African Americans were visiting Monticello. Then he told me about a conversation he'd recently had with a school-teacher "from Oklahoma" who remarked that now that there were slaves on the mountaintop, her black students were interested in history, when before they hadn't been.

White museum administrators such as Jordan feel that they are doing the right thing when they find and display black history for black audiences. To give them Isaac to identify with is, by extension, to give them a place in history from which they were once excluded. In saying this about Isaac, Jordan assumed that white people's identities are already taken care of at Monticello. If black schoolchildren need a postcard of Isaac to take home with them as a memento of their visit, white children have Thomas Jefferson. And, no matter how dignified, how hardworking, how noble is Isaac, he will always be a second-class citizen in comparison to Jefferson.

As the Foundation tried to represent slaves and slavery in the texts and images it produced, Monticello also made efforts to reach out to the African American community. Monticello invited prominent African Americans to speak at public events such as the July 4th naturalization ceremony. More importantly, in 1992, the museum hosted a reunion of the Woodson family, whose members claimed to be descendants of Tom Woodson, the putative first and purposely unrecorded child of Jefferson and Hemings. By looking at this event, we can see how Monticello, with its status as a site for the production of public history, could become a location for public contestation of that history, a contestation which is performed or enacted. During the reunion the Woodsons would question the official version of history to call attention to the generally disenfranchised status of African Americans in the national imagined community.

The Woodsons for their part insured that the event would be televised by NBC national news. There, the reunion was portrayed as an antagonistic encounter, with the Hemings story resonating as a kind of exposé. The Woodson family, so the announcer said, came to Monticello "to claim what they say is their plantation." As such the Woodsons echoed what the political activist Jesse Jackson had said about Monticello on a visit that occurred shortly before they made their appearance. Jackson accused Monticello of "throwing sand on the fires of history" because it failed to give credence to the love affair between Hemings and Jefferson or mention the offspring they created together. To Jackson (and to many other African American intellectuals), Monticello's squeamishness was symbolic of the inability of white America to accept black America as a part of the same overarching national family. Like Jackson, the Woodsons asserted that Monticello had not been forthcoming in addressing their claims. Exposing miscegenation kept secret could be seen as central to telling a story of kinship denied.

The Woodsons, in short, portrayed Monticello as a typical white establishment villain. And every Monticello employee I talked to after the event agreed that the Foundation had taken a public relations beating on national television. Yet Monticello did not expect the Woodsons to produce (with NBC's collusion) the generally derogatory sound-bites that would be broadcast to the nation. In an interview I had with Jordan several months before the event, he talked about the Woodson reunion with considerable enthusiasm – "a milestone in Monticello's dealing with this part of history." As he listed all the things Monticello was doing to focus more on slave life he exclaimed:

I think a wonderful thing is going to happen next spring. That is, we believe we're going to have a reunion here of the descendants of some Monticello slaves . . . We participated in Black History Week this year and [our research historian] gave a wonderful talk . . . to a packed house . . . And she led them on a walk along Mulberry Row and explained to them what took place when, and how much we do know about these people – a lot. And this guy [who plans the Woodson reunion] was in the audience and has become a friend. And he mentioned the possibility of a reunion and I said, "Gosh that's a wonderful idea." So he's coming next week, and we're having lunch. And we're going to plan this homecoming and we're going to do everything that we can to see that it happens.

The homecoming Jordan envisaged was to have been a quiet one. The Woodsons would get a private tour of Monticello, the kind of tour the Foundation gives routinely to people they call "persons of stature" – corporate and governmental VIPs, and the hundreds of Jefferson's legitimate descendants who hold their annual reunion at the family cemetery on Jefferson's birthday. The Woodsons would also be feted to a picnic lunch at the satellite plantation of Shadwell. But the discreet attempt at inclusion became, when the Woodsons invited the press, a public re-enactment of exclusion.

Why then did the televised version of this event become an antagonistic encounter, rather than the "homecoming" of new friends that Jordan portrayed himself anticipating in his interview with me? Initially I thought that it was because the Foundation was not aware of the Woodsons' genealogical claims. (Note that in the excerpt above the Woodsons are characterized as "the descendants of some Monticello slaves.") But in an interview after the visit, Jordan insisted that he knew all along about their putative ancestry. In that encounter I was impressed more than anything by his befuddlement with the public's continued preoccupation with the Sally Hemings story.

Jordan remarked that "Jefferson" (like the Foundation) "would never duck any tough questions like race. But, on the other hand, he's a man for the ages . . . and we don't want to be too provincial in this stewardship." And in some sense his status as slaveholder might count as a provincial issue, an issue that associated Monticello with "the South," as compared to, for example, his authorship of the Declaration of Independence, an achievement of global significance.

But just as importantly, Jordan simply believed that "serious scholars" were similarly dismissive of the issue. He reminded me that the historian John Chester Miller, who had often been a critic of Jefferson the slaveholder, and who had also privately criticized Monticello's treatment of the topic of slavery (he had been a "friendly gadfly," as one staff member put it to me), "wrote a whole chapter demolishing the liaison."[17] But he also noted that "Monticello sells more copies of Fawn Brodie than any bookstore in America." Jordan was referring to the bestselling work of "psychological history" that went a long way in publicizing the liaison as "fact," and that the Foundation explicitly dismissed as unsubstantiated guesswork. Jordan made this remark to emphasize that Monticello was tolerant of a diversity of opinions. But he stressed that Monticello did not modify the way it responded to the public's interest in the Hemings story either in reaction to criticism or in response to consumer preference. He said that if there were ever hard evidence of the liaison, then the Foundation would tell the truth no matter how controversial, but "right now, we just don't know." Nevertheless, in discussing the Woodson family's claims, he wanted to be sure that I knew that, "I respect their oral tradition."

Where the Truth Lies

To respect an oral tradition while at the same time maintaining a judicious "agnosticism" (as it is often described by historians writing on the topic) on the issue of the liaison entailed a peculiar construction of an official community of memory at the site. It privileged, if inadvertently, a certain kind of "serious scholarship" as standing for the final word as far as "professional knowledge" is concerned; it allowed for contestation of that knowledge, but only as the alternative is subtly marked as different, "other:" "oral" traditions passed down through the generations as a kind of collective memory among "other" people. Thus, long before the science of DNA testing made the oral traditions of the African American community seem far more accurate than the judicious opinions of the community of professional historians, Monticello would open up exhibition space (at the visitor center) for the Woodson family to tell its story, as long, however, as it was marked as "oral tradition."[18]

New evidence of the officially recognized kind was, however, eventually produced, in large measure because the Woodsons continued to press their claim, provoking a collection of DNA from themselves, other Hemings descendants, and descendants of Thomas Jefferson's "white" family. When the journal *Nature* published an analysis of the DNA evidence (along with an editorial by the historian Joseph Ellis, who compared Thomas Jefferson's sexual transgressions to President Clinton's) in November 1998, Dr Jordan (who knew about the article in advance) immediately held a news conference to accept the report as the truth. What Jordan did not address in that news conference was the fate of the Woodson family's claim to a connection to Jefferson, a claim which, ironically, was also ostensibly disproved by the same DNA evidence that proved the Hemings–Jefferson liaison. In the months following, the Woodsons would complain loudly to whoever listened that they trusted the DNA evidence as little as they had once trusted those who had relegated their memory to the status of rumor. As a result of their complaining, as much as because of the DNA results, the Woodsons would also quietly lose their cachet at Monticello.

I witnessed the last public occasion that the Woodson descendants would be invited to Monticello. Scholars were presenting evaluations of Monticello's role in remaking the American imagined community, in effecting, as one of the panelists, the director of Monticello's guides, put it, "healing" between blacks and whites. Another panelist, the legal scholar Annette Gordon-Reed, averred that it was Monticello's "duty . . . to make everybody feel as if they have a place at the table." Most of the panelists spoke in celebratory tones. Now that Sally Hemings had taken her place alongside Thomas Jefferson, black and white Americans could recognize that they were a single "family." By accepting the truth of the DNA tests, Monticello had become a locus of racial reconciliation.

Then Byron Woodson spoke. His story was more personal and far more critical – a narrative of the Woodsons' "family pride," of a grandmother "who started looking into the past" to tell their story to an unheeding public. He argued that the DNA test had been "hijacked" by Clinton supporters to "save his presidency" by comparing Clinton's peccadilloes with Monica Lewinsky to Jefferson's liaison with Hemings. Byron Woodson emphasized that this kind of hijacking of black history for white purposes "has been going on for too long." Reminding the audience of the Truth and Reconciliation Commission in post-apartheid South Africa, he concluded: "I'd like to see an America where people look at history objectively." "If the truth were told there could be a healing process . . . that's what the Woodson family is trying to do." Later, Byron Woodson would publish a book, *A President in the Family: Thomas Jefferson, Sally Hemings, and Thomas Woodson*, similarly combining embattled pride with critique. In it he would make several accusations of cover-up. Woodson concluded his book by reiterating the power of family memories against the duplicities of official history:

Ultimately, however, the Hemings/Jefferson controversy will not be resolved on the front page of the *Washington Post* or with a bogus headline in *Nature*,

123

not in a press conference called by the Thomas Jefferson Memorial Founda-
tion . . . and certainly not by the History Department of the University of
Virginia . . . It will be resolved by people with names like Michele, Lucian,
Shay . . . Colonel Woodson. It will be resolved by a family – my family.[19]

Conclusion

When cultural critics study history museums, they usually treat the site as a
collage of texts, to be read as "representations" of the ideology of official
history. But we can also consider the museum as a kind of theater where
guides and visitors alike perform. Such performances can be interpreted for
what they tell us about making citizens, and making publics in democracies.
In the first approach, a history museum produces the ideas about the past
that an "imagined community" holds (more or less) in common. In the
second approach, the museum produces a certain kind of comportment
which can be resisted or contested. It is this second methodological approach
that I have employed in this chapter. What can we learn from the two sets
of performances I have sketched above – first, the day-to-day encounters
that occurred between guides and visitors, and second, a dramatic event
involving African American appropriations of the site – about what kinds of
attitudes are made at Monticello?

Above all, it is clear that official history is being questioned all the time.
When the members of the Woodson family stand on Mulberry Row and
complain to Monticello's chief research historian that their tour has been a
"glaring disappointment" because their ancestor, Tom Woodson, was not
mentioned along with Jefferson's other children, they are questioning the
official terrain at Monticello. When visitors ask the niggling question about
Sally Hemings, they, too, are subverting official history. Some of these,
doubtless, want their suspicions confirmed that in things American there is
always a conspiracy afoot. Others probably get a certain bigoted pleasure in
being able to assert in public that even the sanctimonious are "screwing
colored girls." Such questioning has a variety of effects. One effect is that
Monticello has been able to dismiss much public criticism as evidence of
public inferiority, a symptom of a more pervasive ignorance among the
masses at large. As such, the performative space of Monticello confirms
what is often as not a standard (and secretly cynical) attitude that "experts"
in democracies have about the public in general. Its members are ignorant,
so they need guidance.

But occasionally public criticism has to be taken more seriously. If white visitors could be dismissed for believing in the liaison between Hemings and Jefferson, black visitors could not so easily be shrugged off, precisely because their absence from the site was itself an indictment of its democratic pretensions. Yet such efforts can also be interpreted by a cynical public and cynical insiders, as well, as no more than a public relations ploy. After the news conference in which Dr Jordan accepted the DNA evidence, a member of Monticello's staff would remark privately to me that the news allowed for a public relations windfall because, out of the hundreds of articles that were in the national press, most would remark favorably about Monticello's admirable lack of defensiveness in accepting with alacrity the verdict of science on an old and festering controversy.

Caretakers at Monticello cannot help but want to celebrate their own impartiality and to downplay the contested nature of history itself, even in the face of clear evidence to the contrary. A vernacular skepticism about the motives and truth of public history results. In the vernacular view, official history will always be a whitewash. Like the Stalinist history Milan Kundera exposes in *The Book of Laughter and Forgetting*, an official narrative is a photograph out of which the purged politico has been airbrushed. That Monticello produces official history in this pejorative sense is what many of Monticello's visitors persist in believing, even as the Foundation attempts to be more inclusive and more attentive to the sensitivities and demands of hitherto ignored constituencies. This, in the end, is the lesson the Woodsons learned. One imagines that their experience continues to exemplify what many African Americans believe about sites such as Monticello.

What can museum professionals do about this? Will they ever be able to produce a past that makes for a more inclusive community of memory? I would argue that the solution lies in a much more radical form of honesty than is current practice at Monticello and places like it. Monticello needs ultimately to convey its past complicities in history's inevitable erasures. To Jordan and other caretakers of Monticello, the landscape they preside over is a more or less accurate if partial facsimile of the truth. They strive, they constantly assert, to make a hitherto hidden landscape more visible, truer, as they sift through the evidence and listen to the testimony of experts. But they also want "the public" to applaud their efforts – to trust them as "stewards," as Jordan put it to me, of a collective past. This requires an inevitable erasure which is far more subtle than the crude airbrushing of totalitarian regimes. At Monticello, this erasure entails purging from the public memory of the site, not only the profundity of disagreements among

125

the public about what counts as history (whether slavery or the Declaration of Independence is the more important story), but the contested nature of history-making itself (which is never as disinterested and objective as Jordan's acceptance of the fait accompli of the DNA evidence would make it appear), in favor of commemorating its calculated objectivity. As a result, Monticello, perhaps because of its desire for consensus, ends up producing two parallel landscapes that together add up to the terrain of modern democracy: a visible landscape of shared knowledge without controversy or conflict, and an invisible landscape of suspicion, mistrust, and paranoia.

Questions for Discussion

1 What is an "imagined community"? How is it created from the top down and from the bottom up?

2 Discuss the ambivalent attitudes museum staff have traditionally held toward their publics. Why are museums compelled to listen to their constituents? What can museums learn from those who choose not to visit their institutions? How do museums "make democracy"? And how are they sites of social control?

3 What does it mean to do an ethnography of a museum? How does the metaphor of performance provide insight?

4 Why is Monticello such an important touchstone in American cultural politics?

5 Why did Gable focus on tour guides? What is their role in the museum? What does Gable mean by the "comportment" or "etiquette" of staff? Why did guides often have an adversarial relationship with the public?

6 What shifts in institutional policy took place at Monticello from 1988 through the time of Gable's study? What is the legacy from the museum's foundation in the early twentieth century? How did Monticello change and how did it stay the same?

7 Did Monticello's publics have an effective voice able to change official history at Monticello? What role did the Woodson family play in this discourse? What was director Jordan's justification for not listening?

8 What lessons does Monticello hold? How can museums be more sensitive and responsive to the needs of their publics? What are some of the special issues that historic house museums face?

9 Discuss conflicting public views of the museum as revealing "truth" and as cloaked in secrecy.

Notes

1 See J. Blatti. (ed.). (1987). *Past Meets Present: Essays about Historic Interpretation and Public Audiences*. Washington, DC, and London: Smithsonian Institution Press; I.

Karp and S. D. Lavine. (eds.). (1991). *Exhibiting Cultures: The Poetics and Politics of Museum Displays*. Washington, DC: Smithsonian Institution Press; I. Karp, C. Kraemer, and S. D. Lavine. (eds.). (1992). *Museums and Communities: The Politics of Public Culture*. Washington, DC: Smithsonian Institution Press; D. Sherman and I. Rogoff. (eds.). (1994). *Museum Culture: Histories, Discourses, Spectacles*. Minneapolis: University of Minnesota Press; J. Evans and D. Boswell. (eds.). (1999). *Representing the Nation: A Reader: Histories, Heritage, and Museums*. London and New York: Routledge.

2   D. Lowenthal. (1985). *The Past is a Foreign Country*. Cambridge and New York: Cambridge University Press; B. Anderson. (1991). *Imagined Communities: Reflections on the Origin and Spread of Nationalism*. New York and London: Verso; R. N. Bellah, R. Madsen, W. M. Sullivan, A. Swidler, and S. M. Tipton. (1985). *Habits of the Heart: Individualism and Commitment in American Life*. Berkeley, CA: University of California Press.

3   The study of history museums emerged at roughly the same time as the study of public history. In this literature the word "history" is often put in quotes to remind the reader that we are dealing with discourses about the past, but not with the past per se; "history" is always a construct, usually with an ideological axe to grind. See K. Yelvington. (2002). "History, Memory and Identity: A Programmatic Prolegomenon." *Critique of Anthropology*, 22: 3, 227–56.

4   See M. Kammen. (1997). *In the Past Lane: Historical Perspectives on American Culture*. New York and Oxford: Oxford University Press, p. ix, for a prominent historian's appraisal of current efforts in America to "mobilize perceptions of the past for political or commercial purposes."

5   R. Handler and E. Gable. (1997). *The New History in an Old Museum: Representing the Past at Colonial Williamsburg*. Durham, NC, and London: Duke University Press.

6   Professional historians and educated members of the public increasingly operate with a model of "history" in which history is not the past but a reflection of present-day concerns and prejudices. It is also generally assumed that contradictory versions often co-exist and reflect the concerns of different factions within the public institution. See E. Gable. (1997). "Making a Public to Remake the Past at Colonial Williamsburg." *Museum Anthropology*, 21: 2, 1–13; E. Gable and R. Handler. (1996). "After Authenticity at an American Heritage Site." *American Anthropologist*, 98: 3, 568–78.

7   R. Kurin. (1997). *Reflections of a Culture Broker: A View from the Smithsonian*. Washington, DC, and London: Smithsonian Institution Press.

8   T. Bennett. (1995). *The Birth of the Museum: History, Theory, Politics*. London and New York: Routledge.

9   J. O. Horton, J. Oliver, and S. R. Crew. (1989). "Afro-Americans and Museums: Towards a Policy of Inclusion." In W. Leon and R. Rosenzweig. (eds.). *History Museums in the United States: A Critical Assessment*. Urbana, IL, and Chicago: University of Illinois Press, 215–36.

10   For a good general introduction to performance studies and its place in cultural studies broadly conceived, see P. Phelan. (1997). *Mourning Sex: Performing Public Memories*. London and New York: Routledge.

11 For the examples of primarily textual readings of museum representations, see Sherman and Rogoff, *Museum Culture.*

12 E. A. Foster and C. Tyler-Smith. (1998). "Jefferson Fathered Slave's Last Child." *Nature* (November 5), 27–8.

13 M. Peterson. (1960). *The Jefferson Image in the American Mind.* New York: Oxford University Press. P. West. (1999). *Domesticating History: The Political Origins of America's House Museums.* Washington, DC, and London: Smithsonian Institution Press.

14 Bennett, *Birth of the Museum,* p. 90

15 Bennett, *Birth of the Museum,* p. 103.

16 L. Stanton. (1987). *Monticello: Facts and Figures.* Charlottesville, VA: Thomas Jefferson Memorial Foundation, p. 20. See also F. Brodie. (1974). *Thomas Jefferson: An Intimate History.* New York: W. W. Norton; B. Chase-Riboud. (1979). *Sally Hemings.* New York: St Martins Press.

17 J. C. Miller. (1977). *The Wolf by the Ears: Thomas Jefferson and Slavery.* Charlottesville, VA: University of Virginia Press.

18 It is instructive to compare white and black historians before the DNA evidence made it harder not to conclude that Jefferson and Hemings had a long sexual liaison. J. J. Ellis, while claiming a certain agnosticism on the topic, concluded that "within the scholarly world and especially within the community of Jefferson specialists, there seems to be clear consensus that the story is almost certainly not true. Within the much murkier world of popular opinion, especially within the black community, the story seems to have achieved the status of self-evident truth." Ellis counts himself as a member of what he calls "the scholarly world" because for him too the "likelihood of a liaison is remote." See J. J. Ellis. (1997). *American Sphinx: The Character of Thomas Jefferson.* New York: Alfred A. Knopf, pp. 305, 303. The African American legal scholar Annette Gordon-Reed's brilliant and meticulously argued case for Jefferson's paternity should be read as Ellis's opposite. See A. Gordon-Reed. (1997). *Thomas Jefferson and Sally Hemings: An American Controversy.* Charlottesville, VA: University of Virginia Press. It is a generally accepted argument among African American intellectuals and historians that Jefferson's liaison was a fact and its cover-up a signal example of the more general tendency in the white community to deny such relationships. Indeed, it could be argued that such a history of denial is at the root of the invention and maintenance of distinct racial categories in America.

19 See B. W. Woodson. (2001). *A President in the Family: Thomas Jefferson, Sally Hemings, and Thomas Woodson.* Westport, CT: Praeger, p. 251.

5 | SPECTACLE AND DEMOCRACY: EXPERIENCE MUSIC PROJECT AS A POST-MUSEUM

Chris Bruce

Editor's Introduction

Art historian Chris Bruce is director of the Washington State University (WSU) Museum of Art, USA. He was director of Curatorial and Collections at Experience Music Project (EMP) in Seattle from 1999 to 2002. His recent curatorial projects include "Jim Dine Sculpture, 1983–2004" for WSU and "Artist to Icon: Early Photographs of Elvis, the Beatles and Bob Dylan" for EMP.

In this chapter, Bruce discusses EMP, founded by billionaire Paul Allen and opened in June 2000, as a prototype of the post-museum. Bruce defines the post-museum as a utopian display institution that rejects patriarchal authority in order to become a flexible, constantly changing social space prioritizing audience choice, interactivity, and pleasure. Writing in a conversational tone characteristic of EMP's wall texts and educational programming, Bruce shows how EMP strives to emulate the populist ideal of the post-museum through technology-driven spectacle. The designation "project," rather than "museum," in the institution's title conveys Allen's aspirations to dynamism, accessibility, and collaboration. EMP's conception of spectacle as liberation challenges that of Marxist theorists such as Guy Debord; in his 1967 analysis *The Society of the Spectacle*, Debord posits that "spectacle is the self-portrait of power" wielded to induce passivity and maintain the status quo. Bruce considers how an entrepreneurial, consumer-oriented institutional model such as EMP can indeed empower audiences and how it falls short. He argues that, while the technology of EMP has the potential to create radical change, the institution remains bound to conventional notions of popular appeal through promoting creative genius.

> The museum has been transformed from a temple of beauty into a kind of cultural fair.[1]

To say "museum" used to call out notions of timelessness and unimpeachable standards; an institution that represented the culture's signature achievements and presented the highest expressions of the human spirit; a guiding light in a world of change, a stable point of reference amid chaos and commerce.

In the last two decades or so, museums have tried to shake their quiet, clean, well-behaved reputation and have explored a wide variety of methods and subject matter to expand audience, to become more populist in appeal, and to engage an increasingly digital and interactive age. A new generation of museum professionals has attempted to reinvent the museum, to bring it into the twenty-first century as a place that can compete with other recreational venues for leisure time, a place more identified with providing opportunities for celebration than for contemplation.

The thrust of today's museums is to attain *attraction status*, to be a *destination*, and to appeal to a mass audience. To achieve this, the direction of exhibition and education programs inevitably shies away from universal ideals and moves toward the familiar or commonplace. In the battle between high and low culture, low seems to have the upper hand. Examples abound, from the motorcycle exhibition that toured three Guggenheim Museum venues between 2000 and 2002 to the Metropolitan Museum of Art's showing of Jackie O's clothing in 2001. That same year, the Auckland Museum in New Zealand passed up the chance to display the Dead Sea Scrolls in favor of a show featuring photos of naked body painting and genital piercings. Said director Rodney Wilson, "The museum has a mandate to reflect all sections of society and body art is part of street culture."[2]

For making such decisions, museums have been derided by critics as capitulating to "fun house" factors and "theme park" ambitions, and one wonders whether members of a museum board and staff consider such criticism as a good thing or a bad thing. As the Cleveland *Plain Dealer* recently asked, "It cannot be denied that museums are dumbing down. But is this a failure of the arts or a success for marketing?"[3] Or, more likely, is it simply an idea whose time has come?

Philosopher Arthur Danto identifies the mid-1960s as a point in time when street and museum culture came together: "What Pop Art told [common people] was that commonplace, reassuring, mass-produced things of ordinary life were not to be despised . . . It was hardly matter for wonder that a new kind of museum should evolve in the years that followed . . . The new museum, inevitably, was to associate the consumption of art with the consumption of food and the purchase of goods in the gift shops."[4]

Others would say these changes came from outside the walls of the museum, that it was less a matter of institutions leading this sea-change, and more a matter of reacting to a changing audience, for whom distinctions of "high" and "low" ceased to matter and for whom Las Vegas historian Hal Rothman has stated: "In this new world, experience has become currency and entertainment has become culture. Experience is what Americans trade, how they define themselves. Entertainment is the storehouse of national values. Authentic and inauthentic have blurred."[5]

No museum can be considered a responsible citizen by being simply a bastion of high culture any more. The effect of mass media culture, in which the Discovery Channel is only a click away from MTV, E!, or CNN, is so pervasive that we are all equal under the broad banner of "Nobrow" culture. Museums have had to adjust, and are now in the "experience" business. For example, a recent poll in *Travel Holiday* magazine awarded a Top 25 ranking to American museums based on criteria in which strength of the collection was simply one category among Architecture, Presentation, Food, Shopping, and Fun.

Travel Holiday characterized "Fun Factor" as "how enjoyable, enlightening, or just plain welcoming the place is."[6] What that comes down to is a service economy ideal of putting the audience member at the center of the institution's mission; architectural environment, content, and presentation are inherently at the service of the visitor's pleasure. Just as the first rule of teaching is to get the pupil's attention, it is this focus on the proactive engagement of the visitor that defines the post-museum.

The issue is not whether we play to the audience, but *how much*. Even as most large museums in America have tried to reinvent their essentially elitist roots and to become popular, populist attractions, almost none of them started with this purpose from the ground up. In effect, the *Travel Holiday* article demonstrates how superficial this attempt to "reinvent" has been – basically an expansion of the gift shop and food services, with little structural change to the basic institution.

What would it look like if a new institution were to be *conceived* with something like *Travel Holiday*'s score-card in mind? And even more, what would it look like if this institution put "Fun Factor" at the top of the criteria?

It would look something like the Experience Music Project (EMP) in Seattle. EMP pushes the envelope of the museum-as-attraction – a place that has the beneficent educational motives of a traditional museum providing chronology and historical context, but set within the entertainment strategies of a theme park. It is a model of what a museum might look like when it gets every populist, technological, and interactive wish it ever dreamt of – a spectacle of architecture and multimedia displays that attract, inform, and seduce its visitors. What is EMP? What are the advantages and the trade-offs in going down this path?

EMP

EMP is one of the first museums of the new millennium, and it is one of the very few to undertake a re-evaluation of the museum concept and visitor experience from inception. With the vast private resources of Microsoft co-founder Paul Allen, it has realized an expansive vision that combines the most popular art form on earth (pop music) and an unprecedented use of technology, with visitor experience at the forefront.

EMP didn't start out trying to change the museum world, but it quickly moved in that direction, partly because the founder was inclined to, but also because he could afford to (Allen is consistently ranked among the world's wealthiest individuals). Like other entrepreneurs of his generation such as Steven Spielberg or Bill Gates, Allen has a deeply held belief that things can be both super popular and "good." This is a new generational attitude, one that considers that "influence is measured in the intelligent pleasure given to a huge audience."[7] Like Spielberg, who is perfectly comfortable moving between overtly entertaining films like *Indiana Jones* or *Jurassic Park* and more serious (and risky) works like *Schindler's List* or *A.I.*, EMP would link the vast popular appeal of rock music with higher educational intentions.

From the evidence that EMP provides, we might implicitly begin to answer the question, "Why would anyone want to build a new kind of museum?"

- *Generational attitude*: A dissatisfaction with "old" ways as being passé or irrelevant.
- *Impact on community*: A belief that the culture changes through popular connections with the mainstream audience (as opposed to the elite).
- *Entrepreneurial attitude*: The more relevant and enjoyable your institution is, the more tickets you can sell.
- *Timeliness*: We live in a world that is increasingly breaking down the distinctions of "high" and "low" culture.
- *Technocentric*: A belief in technology as a powerful, effective educational tool and model of information management.

■ *Hubris*: We can do it "better," particularly given Allen's reputation as a visionary.

EMP started like most museums – it started with *stuff*, specifically a felt hat with a turquoise-studded hat band, formerly owned by the late great guitarist Jimi Hendrix, that Allen bought at a Christie's auction in 1991.

Allen had been a huge Hendrix fan since junior high school. The computer programmer admired the musician's technical virtuosity, wild creativity, and flamboyant personal style. Like Hendrix, Allen (about fifteen years later) grew up in Seattle. Like Hendrix in music, Allen was an innovator who reached a world-wide audience in his own field. There was a logic in the dynamic. Soon after Allen began collecting Hendrix memorabilia, he asked his sister and business partner, Jody Allen Patton, to look into how he might share his collection with other fans. In part, this was the simple desire of a fan paying tribute to his artistic inspiration, and yet ultimately, it would be about "going beyond" – beyond the models that other cultural institutions furnished.

Patton began a three-year process of intensive brainstorming, bringing teams of experts together to look at the possibilities of a "Jimi Hendrix Museum." Museum professionals, educators, exhibit designers, architects, project managers, rock critics, and techies took on the task of examining and imagining possible scenarios. How can you get an audience involved in a hat? How can you reach an audience beyond the die-hard Hendrix freaks? Using Hendrix as a reference point, what are the wider cultural implications? What methods of engagement can you create to expand people's consciousness and even change lives?

By asking such open-ended questions, Patton and crew staked out a willingness to reinvent the paradigm of museum. Nothing was considered sacred, everything was questioned. Even the hat was potentially expendable. And indeed, the team questioned the old sanctity of the artifact in favor of compelling narratives and delivery systems. Members looked with irreverence at assumptions about protecting institutional authority. Perhaps most radical was the willingness to look at presentation models outside the museum realm altogether (websites, motion pictures, theme parks).

Ultimately, EMP would expand the mission beyond Hendrix into the implications of his music, which embraced virtually all American forms (blues, R & B, jazz, folk, and rock). It would simultaneously abandon the term "museum" in favor of the more dynamic "project" while still upholding and even extending the aura of rare artifacts. It would retain some traditional

133

museum aspects like interpretive, largely chronological exhibits: histories of the guitar and North-west music along with a fundamental Afro-blues grounding for its basic musical trajectory. But it would enhance all of the above by presenting ideas through a host of elements never before seen in combination, including a theme park ride, a concert venue, and state-of-the-art interactives that could teach you to play an instrument.

Four primary notions would implicitly guide EMP as it developed its conceptual base:

1   Rock 'n' roll is the world's most popular art form, and therefore EMP would have a built-in audience.
2   Jimi Hendrix manifested an expansive sense of freedom, flamboyance, and commitment to music that crossed musical genres and racial boundaries. The attitude of EMP should reflect the rebellious, irreverent nature of rock and the self-expression of Hendrix.
3   The term "museum" has biases that are not consistent with the dynamic quality of rock 'n' roll. Amusement parks are more successful at engaging large numbers of people than museums are, therefore EMP should borrow freely from such models. (In fact, EMP would come to be located adjacent to the "Fun Forest" ride-zone of the Seattle Center campus.)
4   People have diverse learning styles. Concurrently, technology has created multi-layered ways of dispensing information. Therefore EMP's presentations should engage people in as many different ways as possible.

Along with these EMP-specific assumptions, we should be able to extrapolate some general values and qualities that separate the "new museum" from the "old:"

What the new thinks of itself:	What the new thinks of the old:
"Project"	"Museum"

Values:	
Populist	*Elitist*
Experiential	Static
Fun	Serious
Entertaining	Educational
Play	Work

Visitor experience:

Interactive	*Contemplative*
Sensory	Mental
Immersive	Passive
Participation	Observation
Celebration	Edification
Social	Solitary

Institutional presentation:

Innovative	*Traditional*
High-tech, media	Artifacts
Discovery/multiple viewpoints	Authoritative/institutional viewpoint
Boisterous	Quiet

In educational terms, all this points to a goal of creating a space for the *participatory* experience, which can lead to moments of self-actualization for the visitor. Just as a traditional museum assumes that *exposure* to culture *edifies* the visitor and creates a better, more well-rounded citizen, EMP assumes that active involvement *empowers* the visitor to have the confidence to perhaps uncover untapped wells of creativity and self-expression. At heart, EMP asks the question, "If a poor black kid from Seattle (Hendrix) can change the world as we knew it, why not you?"

With this in mind, EMP positioned its initial mission statement beyond rock 'n' roll, to "celebrate and explore creativity and innovation as expressed through American popular music and exemplified by rock 'n' roll."[8] It thus deliberately set out to distinguish itself from its two most immediate progenitors, the Hard Rock Cafés all over the world and the Rock and Roll Hall of Fame and Museum in Cleveland, which capitalize on fans' nostalgia through straight presentations of rock 'n' roll memorabilia.

Packaging Content: The Architecture

OK. Let's put ourselves in the process of creating a new museum. You want to make an impact and you need to send a message that you're on the scene, big-time. How do you package your content to reach your consumers?

If you were making decisions in the 1990s, the first thing you did was hire Frank Gehry as your architect, which is to say, you used the building to announce your intentions and ambitions as bold, radical, visionary. This is not just an exercise in founder vanity. Architecture, in "new museum" terms, is important. Remember, we're talking about a *destination*, an *attraction*, not just a museum. We're not talking about a "temple" but a brash, expressive beacon for a new way of thinking!

Frank Lloyd Wright's dynamic, spiraling Guggenheim Museum in New York (opened in 1959) must certainly be considered a precursor, and yet it was probably Richard Rogers's and Renzo Piano's industrial-style Centre Pompidou in Paris (1988) that broke the mold in first expressing the full range of values of the "new museum." Then in 1997, Gehry's sweeping, titanium-clad Guggenheim Bilbao opened and instantly produced an "attraction," not only for the museum, but for the all-but-invisible Spanish city of Bilbao. By comparison, other recently built museums – Mario Botta's San Francisco Museum of Modern Art (1995), Josef Paul Kleihues's Museum of Contemporary Art in Chicago (1996), Richard Meier's Getty Center in Los Angeles (1997) – play off traditional museum vocabularies, even in their extensive use of brick and stone. Antonio Calatrava's soaring 2001 addition to the Milwaukee Art Museum is an American answer to Bilbao, in part because its focus is on the new public gathering spaces more than on the galleries.

All these museums established their roots before the populist imperative was set in place, and they house art and artifacts that were doing perfectly well in the older buildings. Even the "contemporary" museums base their holdings on paintings and sculptures that date back prior to mid-century. EMP may be most radical of all, for it created – by design – a totally immersive environment for the visitor in which its (architectural) form and (institutional) content are seamlessly combined.

Frank Gehry was the perfect choice, and the subject matter would push even this out-of-the-box architect to new extremes of color and form. Gehry's process is to work primarily from models (as opposed to drawings) and he began to design EMP by assembling pieces of broken guitars. He pulled in associations from rock 'n' roll: the gold section was inspired by a Les Paul "Gold Top" guitar, the blue from a Fender Thunderbird guitar, the red from old vans that bands would tour in, the purple reflective surface from Jimi Hendrix's famous song "Purple Haze." Gehry took the overarching formal concept from Hendrix's music, which Allen described as "swoopy," suggesting an organic, up-and-down, roller-coaster ride of a structure (figure 5.1). The key to Gehry's aesthetic is movement, which at EMP combines with a certain weight and gravity, all of which are qualities consistent with rock 'n' roll.

Without the use of advanced technology Gehry couldn't have made the Experience Music Project building. EMP's radically waving forms rely on the technology of the CATIA computer system used by French aviation

FIGURE 5.1   Frank O. Gehry, Experience Music Project, 2000. © Experience Music Project, Seattle. Photograph by Stanley Smith

designers. Every one of the 280 steel I-beams is a different shape, and the structure and metal cladding simply could not have been engineered let alone built a few years earlier. As Gehry would say, "We did a building by computer for a computer guy."[9] And indeed, Allen said, "I thought it would be great to do something really innovative – to use technology to push the architecture and include an aspect of people's creativity. This is, I think, an attempt to show what a museum can be."[10]

The building sends the initial message of the institution as destination, and acts as a very specific tool in connecting with and even *determining* an audience type that possesses a high curiosity quotient and sense of adventure. The building announces that you're going someplace different, someplace a little weird but also exciting.

Content and spectacle

Put the architecture and a certain *density of content* together and you have an overall spectacle, not unlike Las Vegas or Disneyland in nature and effect.

Spectacle as I am using the term has to do with the big, dazzling environment, which simultaneously wipes the slate clean for visitors and jacks up the expectations and adrenaline for the engagement with what is to come. Museums have long been in the business of creating context for artifacts. Spectacle is *hyper-context*.

Like a Las Vegas casino, EMP does not hold back once you get inside. In fact, once inside, you tend to forget the outside. Density of content complements the intensity of architecture. The effect is to obliterate the everyday world. You have entered a spectacle and you are in its grasp. Eyes open wider, space is no longer a grid – it is a pulsing, electronically enhanced labyrinth. EMP's signature element and grand hall "Sky Church," which contains the world's largest indoor LED screen and a host of theatrical lighting effects used in stadium-sized concerts, epitomizes the spectacular; all is dense-packed in a space that maxes-out at 900 people, compressing the intensity of an arena rock experience into the size of a club (figure 5.2).

Traditional museums generally employ a seemingly objective classification system combined with authoritative but non-attributed interpretive text to establish the institution's role as knowledge-provider. Content is spaced and paced. Within the museum as spectacle, density of content in all forms

FIGURE 5.2 Sky Church, Experience Music Project, 2000. © Experience Music Project, Seattle. Photograph by Stanley Smith

and media is crucial to setting up a sort of experiential free market in which artifacts, various forms of multimedia, and a multitude of recorded voices cry out for attention, both competing with and complementing each other. Exhibit design is aggressive. Forget about contemplation. Instead, think beyond Robert Venturi's architectural dictum, "Less is a bore."[11] The code here is: "Too much is not enough."

The strategic value of the overall spectacle lies in its ability to provide access to content in a way that suspends the visitor's sense that she or he is being given only what the house wants. In Las Vegas, the raison d'être (gambling for the audience, making money for the house) is subsumed in the spectacle of theme architecture, shows, food, drinks, rides, pools, weather. Inside the casinos, day becomes night; under the lights of the Strip, night becomes day. It is no wonder Marxist theorists led by Guy Debord see spectacle as a model of power and control, for its capitalist, consumerist agenda is pleasurably concealed by the distractions of life lived "24/7."[12]

Does this mean that EMP's agenda is similarly consumer-driven and manipulative? Yes and no. As more and more museums position themselves to compete for mainstream audience leisure time and dollars, they inevitably adopt some of the same crowd-pleasing methods as commercial entities. Part of this has to do with a cycle in which mounting costs require greater revenue streams; part is a simple belief in the broad public appeal of the product.

EMP is an example of an institution that was born out of a willingness to borrow proven ideas from recreational, entertainment, and museum sectors. It was intended to be a commercially viable organization in the service of a bottom-line educational good (to "celebrate innovation and creativity" and better understand American music). It is almost a pure hybrid education/entertainment center, and one of the ideas it learned from both fields is that audiences respond best by having many ways to connect with content, with as much self-selection as possible.

The content is pushed through such overt entertainments as "Artist's Journey" (a virtual "ride" featuring a motion platform) or live concerts. It is experienced first-hand in the remarkable interactive zones of "On Stage" and "Sound Lab" (where visitors play instruments and record their own music). Although most exhibits are set up in chronological fashion, audience members ultimately manipulate their own visits through the interactive computer stations and the self-directed Museum Exhibit Guides (MEGs: personal, hand-held computers available to every ticket-holder). A visitor leaves knowing a great deal more about music, but feeling less like having had a

139

"learning experience" than having participated in the whole experience of entertainment excess. And if that still wasn't enough, you can always log on to the elaborate website to "extend" the visit.

Disneyland used to be grudgingly admired by museum professionals for one thing: visitor services. To consider it as a larger model would have been blasphemous, and to utter "Las Vegas" in the same sentence as "museum" would have caused convulsions. But times change. Disney and Las Vegas have drawn closer together, for they both represent paradigms of middle-class American recreational ideals. And so – if you are serious about creating a populist attraction – it only stands to reason they must be given their due. While most museum administrators might still retain a residual shudder at the thought, EMP embraced such visitor-friendly consumer models wholeheartedly. You could say that, in a way, EMP maximizes some of the latent educational offerings of a Disneyland, while simultaneously pulling the modest thematic presentations of a museum blockbuster closer to Disneyesque packaging. It then mixes everything together in a big *edutainment*. In the new museum, learning should, above all, be fun – and full of options for the visitor's attention. In museum terms, these layers of information and experience mitigate institutional authority and allow core content to come through in a way that feels like it is simply part of an overall adventure.

If we were to learn one thing about audience from spectacle, whether it is Las Vegas, Disneyland, or EMP, it would be that most people enjoy being stimulated – and they can actually focus on certain kinds of content quite successfully within a host of "distractions." By contrast, the harmonious, classically inspired environment of the typical art museum is based on the assumption that people need to be *rid* of distractions for the consideration of serious aesthetic or educational experiences. The environment at EMP – the spectacle itself – gives visitors a manic sense of freedom to jump into the fray and participate in a way they might not otherwise. Sing out loud, bang on a drum: the museum becomes a social place like a festival ground, where many different kinds of activities take place simultaneously, and where collaboration often occurs. Less obviously but perhaps more significantly, spectacle makes potentially transgressive subjects more palatable for visitors. Because the entertaining spectacle provides an equal-opportunity safe haven, EMP is able to introduce mainstream audiences to its edgier exhibit content: basically Afrocentric in heritage, from blues and funk to hip-hop; along with white, "do-it-yourself" alternative rock forms, like punk and grunge.

Content Delivery: The Persistence of Technology

The pervasive presence of media and technology at EMP has everything to do with how visitors engage in the content. Indeed, it is here that EMP really walks the talk of its initial mission (to "explore creativity and innovation"). The MEG is literally an EMP invention, as are the interactive instruments in Sound Lab. All 50 films and the hours and hours of audio content were produced in-house. The Digital Lab collection program was a collaboration between EMP and Plumb Design in New York. The Sky Church screen offers a dozen different music videos, specially commissioned by EMP.

All this technology and multimedia is a big part of Allen's vision of EMP, but it is also in keeping with its content base, as rock 'n' roll has always been dependent on technology. For most museums technology remains a rather exotic addition, most often limited to special exhibitions. In the music industry, however, people were utilizing complicated recording devices and radio signals to deliver music to its audiences for decades before rock. Today, the extravagant arena show is all but commonplace.

Because of the demands of interactive elements, visitors are consistently active participants, as opposed to being passive receivers of information. What electronic technology does in the museum is open the crack in time beyond what would otherwise be an array of static, silent artifacts with interpretive text. Time-based interactive media sets up an immediate demand on the visitor to respond – either to participate or to choose not to. Even when the visitor chooses to forego the direct interactive experience, she or he is aware that the environment is alive with options for engagement, aware that the institution is there to be played with.

In terms of information, the media creates a layering to content that simply could not exist without the technology. EMP has utilized many of its more than 400 filmed interviews with musicians to create edited narratives for portions of the exhibits, as well as hiring other musical personalities to provide additional recorded commentary. This radically counteracts the single, institutional point of view in favor of multiple – and even contradictory – voices, all at the visitors' choice. The driving objective is to have visitors feel like they had been "inside" the content, so the experience is more immersive and conversational than passive and professorial. For the museums of the future, such first-hand narratives will be increasingly important in conveying information to generations who have grown up with the free-wheeling access to information of the internet.

Content and the role of artifacts

With time-based media insinuated everywhere, the artifacts take on a different role; neither primary nor subservient nor supportive, but a shifting point of reference between physical presence and other types of information. This equal stature of technology and artifact posits a regular and essential dialogue between the *ephemeral now* (time-based media) and the *immortal future* (the preserved and revered object).

And within the overall spectacle at EMP there are many moments of surprising intimacy. This can take the form of an individual experience of playing a guitar for the first time. It can also occur listening to your MEG narrator discuss the California punk scene in the 1970s while simultaneously you look at the inventive graphic design in the tattered flyers from clubs like Mabuhay Gardens or the Mask; or seeing the original sketches of New York graffiti along with films that show those sketches exuberantly realized on trains that rumbled through the Bronx and Harlem. For fans, the encounter with Bo Diddley's guitar, Janis Joplin's feather boa, or original hand-written lyrics by Kurt Cobain is a deeply personal experience.

At EMP – again, like Las Vegas or Disney's EPCOT Center – the artifacts function to lend a touch of the "real world" within the contrived spectacle. In Las Vegas, the "artifacts" range from real lions behind glass at the MGM Grand to porpoises swimming at the Mirage, from Britney Spears's costume at the Hard Rock to the celebrated collection of art masterpieces at the Belaggio – not to mention the entire Guggenheim galleries at the Venetian. These "real things" ground the artificial environment and lend credibility to the spectacle.

At EMP, Jimi Hendrix's guitar from his legendary performance at Woodstock lends a concrete reference to the film playing on the monitor below. His lyric notebook gives a personal, physical presence to the interactive computer nearby. The rare guitars in the guitar gallery establish a series of historic focal points for the recorded sounds of those same guitars coming through the audio tracks of the MEG, and provide an overall context of "the real" for the entertaining animated film on the evolution of the electric guitar that is repeatedly projected on the screen in the center of the room. In some ways, this is simply an extension of good, old-fashioned interpretive exhibitry. But if you combine the self-guiding quality of the media with regular doses of live music and the ultimate plum of being able to play music and express yourself, you have a new paradigm of museum experience which revolves not so much around the object as around *numero uno* (the museum visitor).

Ultimately, at EMP, "content" equals *the combined dialogue between artifacts and media/technology* in an environment that is dynamic, multi-sensory, and interactive.

Technology and flexibility

The good news about technology and multimedia is that it is engaging. The flip-side is that when institutional identity is based on technology, you have to keep up to date – and state-of-the-art technology changes so rapidly that it is all but impossible to keep up. EMP is wired beyond any other museum on earth, but what about the coming "wireless" revolution? Technology/media is not only a treat for the visitor but a beast that needs to be fed.

There is a fundamental difference between "having the capacity" to utilize technology and having it be absolutely integral to everything you do (as in EMP's case). Media is expensive and time-consuming to produce. Original audio-visual material often comes with high licensing fees. Contrary to the common notion that you should be able "just to push a button," the seamless integration of technology into exhibits means that every time you change a poster or a T-shirt, MEG content needs to be changed, possibly the computer program or the film that goes with it, and Digital Lab content needs to be updated.

Even if nothing changed, mere upkeep is a full-time job for highly paid information technology staff. Visitor service on the MEG alone adds up: visitors need to be trained in how to use them, the MEGs need to be downloaded for reference on home computers, batteries need to be constantly recharged. The bottom line is that EMP has a staff population at least double a normal museum's. In 2002, the Rock and Roll Hall of Fame (with the same square footage as EMP) had approximately 100 staff members. EMP had over 400.

The dream of technology is based on a democratic principle of open access to information, but the new museum must answer questions of cost-effectiveness: how much technology is enough; how much too much?

Reality vs. Vision: The Still Uneasy Dynamic between Institution and Public

Just like any new museum or non-profit organization, EMP has had to confront issues regarding the difference between *realizing a vision* of what a new museum can be and *creating a viable institution* that is part of its community. How has this new museum addressed its greatest test: operating for the public?

Virtually all new museums achieve their peak attendance during the first year of opening (or reopening in new buildings) – for a good reason: there's curiosity and excitement about the new, usually along with a tidal wave of publicity and promotions. The festivities that surround the opening of a new museum have become increasingly elaborate civic events. When the Museum of Contemporary Art Chicago opened in 1997, it welcomed anyone who wanted in to a festive, free, weekend open house, 24 hours a day. By 9.00 a.m. of the second day, over 12,000 Chicagoans had made it up the grand staircase to see art most of them had never thought about before – and might never again.

EMP opened with three days and nights of concerts featuring the likes of Metallica, Dr Dre, Snoop Dogg and Eminem, Alanis Morisette, Beck, No Doubt, Patti Smith, and the Red Hot Chili Peppers – all covered on MTV and VH-1. The summer of 2000 witnessed daily lines of two to three hours just to get inside the building. In the first 12 months 820,000 people visited, extraordinary numbers for a northern city of half a million.

Maintaining such expectations is difficult at best. Not surprisingly, the numbers for EMP's second year dropped by half. Now, an attendance of a few hundred thousand is not at all bad for a regional museum, but it's not great for an international tourist destination. EMP's insistence in being a one-of-a-kind place that conspicuously avoided being considered a museum put it in a position of being simultaneously unique and hard to define. From a marketing and branding standpoint, this presents a challenge.

Audiences: local versus tourist

Tourist audience is based on one-time visitorship; local museum attendance looks for repeat visitation. Even after two years of operations, EMP was still trying to come to grips with the wildly different issues connected with the goals of international branding and functioning as a tourist destination versus becoming a much-beloved local institution. Add to that the fact that Seattle is not one of the nation's tourist meccas, that its weather will never allow it to have much more than a three-month high season, and you get an idea how poorly positioned EMP was to deal with post-9/11 audience behavior, when most tourists opted to stay home and the recession hit the North-west particularly hard. You could rightly ask "Who was?" but EMP was in a unique spot. It did not emerge out of an existing cultural community as most museums do. Instead, it superimposed itself on what is a rather grassroots-oriented region, with almost no significant engagement with the traditional patronage community, and its closest audience group a thriving but aggressively anti-institutional club scene.

The ticket price of $19.95 is at least twice that of most other museums. That's one thing as part of an annual vacation budget, but quite another thing if you're a local trying to decide on a return visit to EMP or going to a movie. For an institution that sets out to welcome "everyone" and to appeal to the public at large, this is a philosophical and financial hurdle no matter what the actual value of the product is. Membership, on the other hand, is a bargain at an entry level of $40.

To attract local audiences, EMP began to focus on concerts, but concert-going tends to be a one-shot commitment: if you like Sleater Kinney or Air or Public Enemy, you go – but then again, if you're a fan, you'd go *anywhere* to see them. The regular presence of performances does reinforce the participatory, celebratory nature of the new museum as a potentially consciousness-raising, event-based experience. Concerts also help solve the problem of keeping up with an ever-changing art form. More pointedly for EMP, however, a concert-going crowd or those who patronize the bar for free live music rarely translate into loyal museum-goers.

The traditional way for museums to re-stimulate attendance of both tourist and local audiences is to present periodically the blockbuster exhibit. But EMP's Special Exhibition Gallery is small by any standards (2,700 square feet, versus over 9,000 at the Seattle Art Museum). Its size was squeezed during planning to fit within the overall footprint while being whittled away at the sides by the competing needs of other programs, like Sound Lab and exquisitely developed (and highly inflexible) permanent exhibits. The result is that EMP has only limited potential for hosting a high-profile show that can drive "destination" traffic, and that the special exhibitions feel more like a member perk than a "can't miss," crowd-pleasing attraction.

Target audience

Generally speaking, EMP's core audiences are baby-boomers and junior high school kids. For boomers, the appeal is largely nostalgic – reconnecting with their youth and seeing their heroes enshrined. For the 10–14-year-olds, EMP is basically a cool place to hang out that has parental approval. EMP is well situated for a general audience – on the grounds of Seattle Center, along with the Children's Theater, the Science Center, and the Children's Museum, as well as the Opera House and Key Arena. Since opening, EMP has regularly played to the mainstream with such programs as a series of Sunday *afternoon* family rock concerts – hardly representative of rock's rebellious nature.

It is one thing to plan out-of-the-box, and another to attain such a goal in a living institution. In fact, while the focus of its original mission statement was to "celebrate and explore creativity and innovation," a year after opening EMP refocused its direction (and mission statement) to being a place that provides "dynamic, multi-faceted, ever-changing experiences through new and exciting explorations of American popular music."[13]

The shift may sound subtle, but what is lost is the potential to realize some of the more adventurous aspects of EMP as a place that could shake up the field as a new kind of trans-disciplinary arts center. In practice, it now presents itself as more of an entertainment venue than an educational institution, and it has moved closer to that which it formerly distinguished itself from – the Rock and Roll Hall of Fame in Cleveland.

So the issue of populism places limits on what the institution can do and, in fact, takes a great many possibilities off the table as being potentially offensive or too sophisticated for mainstream America. Rock's blatant sexism and drug abuse are pushed to the side as being lifestyle issues, while exploring crossovers between pop and more experimental forms is seen as obscurist. Although it has retained its Afrocentric musical point of view, EMP has done little to confront issues of race head on. In responding to a broad mainstream audience, the populist museum can quickly find itself with what you might call a *"Star Wars* responsibility:" make it appealing, simplify content, and avoid any real controversy.

Conclusion

In considering whether EMP is a useful model for museums of the future, we must acknowledge the obvious: it is the product of the personal vision and financial backing of one of the wealthiest human beings on the planet. EMP is, in fact, a $250-million "gift" from Paul Allen to the city of Seattle and the rock 'n' roll universe. As such, it faces unique challenges as it attempts to bring traditional non-profit funding sources into the mix. Such pragmatic issues aside, there can be no doubt that EMP is a fascinating and valuable case study for museums of the future in two ways:

- the attempt to create a new museum as popular attraction;
- the utilization of an internet-like "networking" model of presenting content.

EMP *is* a new kind of hybrid entertainment/educational venue, one that comes out of a boomer mindset – and more specifically, a new technology culture – that identifies itself with the popular culture. It is a point of view that is less concerned with preserving the status quo through highbrow paradigms or pedigreed masterpieces than it is with plugging into the enormous wash of mass media that is covering the planet. The old guard has its opera houses and art museums; why not add a few museums dedicated to pop art forms? In EMP's case, what could be more relevant than the stuff Quincy Jones once called "music that was made to get somebody through the day"?[14]

In so doing, it has aligned itself with a new generation of specialty museums as diverse as the Peterson Automotive Museum in southern California and the Neon Sign Museum in Las Vegas – institutions which tend to confirm their visitors' pre-existing interests and knowledge-base. Arthur Danto states the difference from traditional museums as shifting "from [the presentation of] objective data for knowledge into subjective opportunities for communion with . . . the viewer's own group."[15] Thus, the encounter with Woody Guthrie's guitar at EMP becomes the occasion of a spiritual experience for hard-core folk music fans, but just another old acoustic guitar for everyone else. On a modest scale, these places can become quirky sites of pilgrimage (for example, the Buddy Holly Center in Lubbock, Texas, or the Delta Blues Museum in Clarksdale, Mississippi), but EMP is anything but modest. Its ambition is to be a broad-based tourist attraction and an educational institution that can inspire inquiry and creativity beyond a core audience.

The positive aspect of addressing a target group is that it guarantees a certain passionate connection with audience, but the trade-off is self-limiting in both visitorship and program scope. Places like the Smithsonian's Museum of American History or the Museum of Modern Art rely on a wide variety of evocative artifacts to draw crowds. In EMP's case, the musical expressions might be varied, but the artifacts all fit within a relatively limited range (guitars, posters, records, costumes). An artifact may serve as the representative of a song or the personalities who created the song, but it is peripheral to the reason the institution exists, which is to celebrate music. It would be as though the Georgia O'Keeffe Museum in Santa Fe showed her jewelry and paintbrushes, but not her paintings.

147

EMP faced this obvious disconnection – that the primary subject matter is music, not artifacts – and called on innovative systems of technology to bridge the gap. Indeed, EMP's real breakthrough is in the way it has integrated new learning and recreational models into its content-deployment systems based on personal technology and the web. This is where EMP's vision is perhaps most profound. And it is here that it provides an array of options for other institutions to pick and choose as might fit their needs and goals, irrespective of content.

The interactive instruments in Sound Lab and the collection program in the Digital Lab are far beyond their equivalents in other museums. The website has consistently received high marks. The MEG, though rather cumbersome in its current iteration, will undoubtedly get more user-friendly as it is developed further. As it is, visitors' access to information is set up as a series of many-layered self-discoveries, in which each personal choice can lead to often-unpredictable tangents and hyperlinks. This is most fully realized in the Digital Lab computer programs, specifically in the "Think Map" section, in which a click on a specific artifact automatically reconfigures a surrounding realm of associations on the timeline. Click on another and you have a new constellation of associations. Every artifact has the potential of being at the center of its own universe. In a way, this is the ideal of flexibility (constantly shifting focal points) that even EMP has yet to fully explore, especially in terms of actually *creating structures* of multi-directional content in its exhibits (exhibits are still essentially laid out chronologically). But clearly, the model EMP strives for is based on the ideal of democracy as represented by the personal computer and the internet – non-hierarchical and multi-layered in nature, with "browser" capabilities for vast amounts of information available to all.

In pursuing such a democratic ideal, EMP has just scratched the surface of its own possibilities. And although EMP has created a physical plant (which is, in effect, a big piece of interactive hardware) and vision that at the present time would be cost-prohibitive for almost any other institution to consider, technology has a way of getting less expensive and less cumbersome as it is refined. So, EMP provides a kind of petri dish of possibilities for the entire field. By committing to an overtly populist subject and giving visitors the technology to explore and discover multiple points of view, it has leaped beyond those other museums that have tried to shoe-horn contemporary learning modes into old institutional models. It has demonstrated some of the potential – and some of the pitfalls – in attempting to reimagine the museum.

Postscript

In October, 2003, an expanded Jimi Hendrix gallery opened in the space formerly devoted to hip-hop and punk music. This suggests a newfound willingness to play to its core attraction, an acceptance that EMP is primarily perceived as a destination for Hendrix fans, and that while hip-hop and alternative rock continue to be immensely popular, their audience is rather uninterested in museum-going.

Also in 2003, the "ride-like" attraction "Artist's Journey" was shut down. This one-of-a-kind mechanism/film project had proved to be less than cost-effective: maintenance was costly as was the production of new content. This space is now dedicated to a new Science Fiction Museum and Hall of Fame. How such content integrates into Experience *Music* Project remains to be seen: although Hendrix had some interest in science fiction, it seems to be developed as more of an "added attraction" for the post-*Star Wars*/ current-*Matrix* generation, and one that is equally the product of founder Allen's interests.

Through all the changes, EMP continues to balance its program between the overtly populist and the educational. It has retained a strong commitment to family groups through its family concert series, its teen workshops, and the summertime Experience Arts Camp. It contributed educational and content support to PBS's 2003 seven-part series on the blues, as well as producing a massive tribute concert to the blues at Radio City Music Hall. Since 2001, it has hosted an annual pop conference, which connects a broad range of academics, journalists, musicians, and industry figures, with a focus on new writing about popular music. EMP thus remains a fascinating hybrid institution that continues to negotiate a balance between the seriousness of a museum and the entertainment function of an amusement park.

Questions for Discussion

1. How does spectacle empower and how does it control audiences at EMP? What are the implications of EMP's brash adaptation of conventions from Las Vegas and Disneyland?
2. How does EMP hold fast to tradition? And how is it a post-museum? What is the significance of the designation "project" in the title of the institution?
3. Discuss EMP's original mission statement. What are the values that it promotes? Why did EMP revise the mission statement? What is the impact of these changes?

4 Evaluate Giebelhausen's phrase "the architecture *is* the museum" (chapter 1) in the context of EMP. What is the relationship between Gehry's architecture and EMP's mission? Between architecture and collections? Between architecture and education?

5 Describe the educational model of EMP. What is the theory grounding "Artist's Journey," Sound Lab, the MEG, and other features? Are these devices effective? What can we learn from EMP about technology as a pedagogical tool?

6 Compare attitudes toward audience at EMP and at Monticello (chapter 4). Why do these institutions avoid content that explores conflict and contradiction?

7 What were Paul Allen's motivations in creating EMP? Why did he choose Jimi Hendrix and American popular music as his subject? How does Allen situate himself in relation to Jimi Hendrix and to EMP itself? In what ways is EMP a museum that celebrates the achievements of its founder?

8 Does the specialization of EMP – popular music – engender a more daring approach than those of art, history, and anthropology museums? How is the case study of EMP relevant to other museums today? What is the future of museum–audience relationships? Is "post-museum" a useful term?

Notes

1 A. C. Danto. (1992). *Beyond the Brillo Box: The Visual Arts in Post-Historical Perspective*. New York: Farrar, Straus, Giroux, p. 11.

2 B. Orsman. (2001). "Tattoos Rate Over Dead Sea Scrolls." *New Zealand Times* (July 12).

3 Associated Press. (2001). "Pop Goes the Easel." *Plain Dealer* (December 27).

4 Danto, *Beyond the Brillo Box*, pp. 3, 4.

5 H. Rothman. (2002). *Neon Metropolis: How Las Vegas Started the Twenty-First Century*. New York and London: Routledge, p. xviii.

6 Anon. (2000). "Museum Smackdown: Who's the Champ of American Art Museums?" *Travel Holiday*, 183: 9, 108, 109.

7 R. Corliss. (2002). "Chuck Reducks." *Time*, 159: 9, 54.

8 C. Bruce. (ed.). (2000). *Experience Music Project: The Experience*. Seattle: Experience Music Project, p. 4.

9 C. Bruce. (ed.). (2000). *Experience Music Project: The Building*. Seattle: Experience Music Project, p. 17.

10 Bruce, *Experience Music Project: The Building*, p. 6.

11 G. Debord. (1994). *The Society of the Spectacle*. D. Nicholson-Smith (trans.). New York: Zone Books. (Original work published 1967.)

12 R. Venturi, D. Scott-Brown, and S. Izenour. (1977). *Learning from Las Vegas*. Cambridge, MA, and London: MIT Press, p. 101. (Revised edition; original work published 1972.)

13 www.Emplive.com (accessed November 16, 2002).

14 C. Bruce. (ed.). (2000). *Crossroads: The Experience Music Project Collection*. Seattle: Experience Music Project, p. 9.
15 A. C. Danto. (1999). "Postmodern Art and Concrete Selves." *Philosophizing Art: Selected Essays*. Berkeley, CA, Los Angeles, and London: University of California Press, p. 136.

6 | REVEALING AND CONCEALING: MUSEUMS, OBJECTS, AND THE TRANSMISSION OF KNOWLEDGE IN ABORIGINAL AUSTRALIA

Moira G. Simpson

Editor's Introduction

Moira Simpson is the author of *Making Representations: Museums in the Post-Colonial Era* and *Museums and Repatriation*. During the 1990s she acted as repatriation adviser to the Museums Association of Great Britain. Her research and recommendations led to the publication of *Restitution and Repatriation: Guidelines for Good Practice*. Now at Flinders University in South Australia, she is examining strategies for culturally appropriate management of sensitive objects in museum collections and developing new models of museums in culturally diverse contexts.

In "Revealing and Concealing," Simpson identifies conflicts between the values of Australian Aboriginal communities and of the Euro-American museum model. She examines the clash in beliefs about the dissemination of knowledge which impacts on issues of display, education, and conservation. Australian Aboriginal communities privilege the control and restriction of knowledge, as opposed to western-style museums, which stress accessibility. The colonialist approach to representation of Aboriginal cultures in western-style museums has resulted in cultural repression and loss of heritage. Simpson explains that Australian Aboriginal communities have rejected the wholesale use of the western museum model as inappropriate. She identifies a strategy of appropriation in which Australian Aboriginal communities adapt and transform western museum practice to meet local needs. Appropriation and transformation create culturally relevant means to encourage Australian Aboriginal beliefs and practices to flourish. This strategy has generated a broad range of institutions, from cultural centers to interpretive centers, commercial art centers to Keeping Places, that challenge the conventional parameters of the museum. As a group, these institutions mediate between the community and the outside world to protect Indigenous culture while seeking public support from non-Aboriginals. The diversity of these institutions and their power to convey the "complex lives of objects" and beliefs holds lessons for western-style museums striving to become integral to the communities they serve. Simpson calls for a more flexible conceptualization of the museum to meet the needs of all communities.

In Aboriginal Australian communities, knowledge is restricted according to cultural protocols and is revealed gradually, in keeping with an individual's age, status, and clan associations. An intrinsic conflict exists between traditional Aboriginal methods of controlling and communicating knowledge and the ideology and functions of the western museum, which is based on concepts of open display and dissemination of knowledge. Yet Australian Aboriginal communities are establishing community museums and cultural centers, as Indigenous peoples are in many other non-western cultures. What relevance, then, has the museum for Australian Aboriginal communities? What forms of museums do Indigenous communities require? How do Indigenous peoples balance the need to control and restrict knowledge with the communicative role of the museum? How do they weigh the needs of the community and their desire to protect their culture against the demands of tourists to learn about Aboriginal life? What are the implications of the choices made for our understanding of the museum?

The Inadequacies of the Western Museum Model

To many Indigenous peoples, western-style museums are laden with associations of colonialism, cultural repression, loss of heritage, and death. The associations with death take several forms.

During the eighteenth and nineteenth centuries, the impact of colonialism had a devastating effect on Indigenous populations; by the late nineteenth century, the decline in Indigenous populations in North America and Australia was so great that western observers believed that Indigenous peoples were dying races. Anthropologists and museums carried out massive collecting programs to acquire knowledge and physical evidence of artistic styles, material culture, lifestyles, and religious beliefs and practices before Indigenous communities disappeared altogether.

Even after it became apparent that Indigenous cultures were surviving, many ethnographic exhibitions consisted primarily of material collected in the nineteenth and early twentieth centuries. This implied either that the peoples represented continued to follow the lifestyle illustrated by the objects or that the cultures displayed had not survived into the latter half of the twentieth century.

Museums also acquired massive collections of human remains. They collected skeletal material, hair, and soft tissue samples, not only to study human migration, health, and burial customs, but also to engage in research on race and evolution. Museums collected, studied, measured, and compared both human and cultural "specimens" to support social and racial theories that justified oppression. The western fascination with the "exotic Other" reduced humans to mere objects of study and display.

The association of museums with death also refers to the death of the object. The process of museum collecting can be seen to remove the object from life and remove life from the object. Theodor Adorno notes that "the German word *museal* (museum like) has unpleasant overtones. It describes objects to which the observer no longer has a vital relationship and which are in the process of dying. They owe their preservation more to historical respect than to the needs of the present."[1] In their original cultural contexts, museum objects were fundamentally integrated within the life and social structure of the originating community. The appropriation of non-western cultural objects and their redefinition in the western museum as "artifacts" or "works of art" divorces them from the reality of their original context and alters their meaning and significance. The traditional role of such objects may have involved performance as a means of giving life to them. The objects may have acted as mediators between the human and spiritual domains. Removed and transformed by the process of collection and display in museums, these objects are deprived of essential cultural usage and social interactions and so seem drained of life.

As a result of these historical associations, the museum may seem like a repository of material of dead and dying races, and some communities deem museums an inappropriate means of preserving and transmitting knowledge. Yet community support is an essential component of a successful and culturally dynamic community museum that will continue to contribute to Indigenous life. In many instances, museums established in communities outside the Euro-American cultural tradition have been modeled explicitly on the western concept by the missionaries, government departments, or historic societies which established them. By failing to address community values and needs, these museums may not have served Indigenous communities well. As a consequence, such projects may fail due to community neglect, becoming dormant relics of fading aspirations. If a museum is to thrive, it must reflect the cultural and spiritual values of the community.

Successful relocation of the museum into diverse cultural contexts requires flexibility in conceptualization of what the museum is, what it does, and how it does it. In its statutes and constitution, the International Council of Museums (ICOM)[2] has consistently emphasized the primary activities of a museum as acquisition, conservation, research, communication, and exhibition of collections of objects of artistic, cultural, or scientific significance. In some societies, however, this codification is inappropriate. Cultural values, concepts of cultural preservation, and management and methods of knowledge transmission may not conform to the principles upon which the conventional western museum has been based.

While Indigenous communities are adopting conventional museum conservation techniques to preserve collections in community museums, traditional cultural practices may have placed little importance on the preservation of objects. In some communities, for example, ceremonial items may be deconstructed or destroyed after use. Others are stored by traditional custodians and reused on ceremonial occasions until they are beyond repair or are destroyed by the elements, insects, or bush-fire. What may be more important is the preservation of knowledge and customs.

In Australian Aboriginal cultures, traditional knowledge is strictly controlled and access restricted. The more sacred and significant an object, image, or story, the more it is shrouded in secrecy. In contrast, academic inquiry, public display, and the dissemination of knowledge are integral elements of conventional western museum functions. In a western museum, the more important an object, the more prominently it is displayed; it may be designated and promoted as a star item or masterpiece, a "must-see" for museum visitors.

Since the early 1970s, the museum community has broadened its concept of the museum somewhat. The ICOM Statutes, revised most recently in 2001, now embrace a diversity of approaches to cultural preservation and knowledge transmission and encourage technological advancements in data storage and communication. The museum definition now includes "cultural centres and other entities that facilitate the preservation, continuation and management of tangible or intangible heritage resources (living heritage and digital creative activity)." Museums Australia, the national organization representing museums in Australia, adopted this category in an amendment of its constitution in 2002.[3]

Nevertheless, conventional notions of the museum prevail in the thinking of many. Most professional museum organizations still use a definition of the museum which is based upon earlier, more limited ICOM versions, and this results in persisting expectations that a museum must be actively involved in collection, preservation, research, public display, and interpretation.

In this chapter, I will argue that the concept of the museum must become even more flexible. It must be pliant enough to suit local community needs, to reconcile differences between conventional museum methodology and Indigenous cultural practices, and to include institutions whose practices may seem to run counter to conventional museological functions. The chapter will show that some Indigenous communities are embracing the concept of the museum and adapting it to suit their own cultural and social needs. In doing so, they may adopt some aspects of mainstream professional practice and yet push the parameters, molding the institution to suit the requirements of communities in differing cultural contexts. The forms these museums take may be determined by limitations reflective of customary beliefs and economic factors, but these alternative perspectives convey the transformative nature of the museum and the complex lives of objects. Furthermore, while restricting access to culture in order to preserve it, communities are able to use the projection and interpretation of their culture as a mechanism for cultural preservation. Restrictions can, in themselves, be valuable communicators of the significance of objects. While the focus here is upon museums, cultural centers, and Keeping Places in Aboriginal Australia, the diverse cultural needs of communities in other parts of the world require similarly flexible solutions determined by local circumstances and cultural values.

Traditional Methods of Preserving and Transmitting Culture in Aboriginal Australia

In many non-western societies, cultural knowledge was recorded, communicated, and preserved, not through written language, but through visual and oral languages. In Australian Aboriginal societies, sacred rituals, designs, dances, songs, and stories were the traditional methods of recording and conveying knowledge. The preservation of culture and transmission of knowledge occurred through the act of production and the performance of culture or, in other words, through living culture. These methods continue to play a key role today.

Iconography makes artifacts a significant instrument of cultural knowledge transmission. For example, many Aboriginal acrylic paintings from the Western Desert region and bark paintings from Arnhem Land depict sacred images of Dreamings – stories incorporating knowledge passed down from individual to individual throughout the millennia. These Dreaming stories tell of ancestral beings, the formation of the world, and the creation of laws by which Aboriginal people have lived for thousands of years. The stories recount the journeys of ancestral beings and the creation of landscape features. In so doing, the stories represent knowledge essential for survival and cultural maintenance – the location of waterholes and food sources, the pattern of men's and women's ceremonies, and so forth. The images, like the stories, are sacred and were allocated to each of the clans. The paintings identify clan affiliations and show clan estates and the creatures associated with them. Members of specific moieties or clan groups have a right to make paintings of particular Dreamings and sing associated songs. For example, *Tjunti* (figure 6.1), an acrylic painting by Warlpiri/Ngalia artist David Corby Tjapaltjarri, depicts a story of the Tingari cycle of creation events. The Tingari men traveled throughout the Western Desert region performing ceremonies, initiating young men, and teaching tribal law. This image shows the tracks of a group of Wakalyarri or Wallaby Ancestors travelling between waterholes (shown by concentric circles) as they flee a bush-fire lit by Tingari men at the sacred site of Tjunti. Tingari stories, songs, and ceremonies are of great spiritual significance and many details cannot be publicly revealed.

The images have multiple layers of meaning, including increasingly detailed knowledge restricted to traditional owners of specific Dreamings. Unlike western culture, which invites and rewards inquiry and the unrestricted dissemination of knowledge, Aboriginal cultures restrict knowledge according to age, gender, and status. Children learn gradually by observing and assisting their elders, receiving instruction at key stages in their lives, and listening to stories and songs. At appropriate times, an individual may be taught deeper, sacred meanings of stories, songs, and images and participate in ceremonies, gradually increasing his or her understanding.

The dominance of visual imagery as a form of communication in Aboriginal cultures requires that one has knowledge of traditional iconography, in the same way as European medieval religious paintings and sculptures

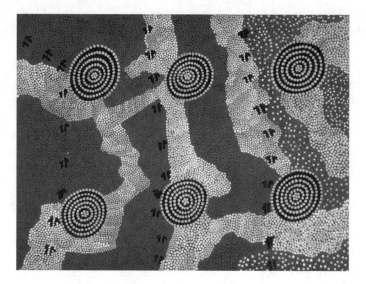

FIGURE 6.1 David Corby Tjapaltjarri, *Tjunti*, 1979. Acrylic painting. © David Corby Tjapaltjarri. Courtesy Aboriginal Artists Agency and Flinders University Art Museum

require knowledge of Christian iconography. Knowledge can thus be communicated and controlled by those with expertise. The viewer's familiarity with the symbolic nature of the iconography will determine the extent to which she or he can decipher meanings in the paintings and sculptures. In western museums, the uninitiated are flooded with information through captions, text panels, and catalogues, which provide the means to decipher the images. But in Aboriginal cultures, knowledge is earned or inherited. This has implications for the practice of museology in Indigenous communities.

In the past, the concept of preserving the fabric of material culture was largely confined to concealing sacred artifacts in places where only those with authority had access to them, and to caring for land and sacred places such as rock art sites. Sacred objects might be concealed in caves, under rocks, in trees, or hidden in the bush. While stone artifacts survived, wooden objects gradually eroded or might be destroyed by termites or bush-fire. These secret caches might also be jeopardized through inadvertent discovery by non-Aboriginals pastoralists, tourists, and others, or through deliberate looting by artifact collectors.

For thousands of years, Aboriginal people have decorated the walls of caves and rock faces with paintings in ochers and other pigments. These places functioned as sacred or ceremonial sites. In some communities, responsibility for care and maintenance of rock paintings includes ensuring that fading or damaged paintings are touched up and restored. It may also involve the reworking of compositions or painting over of old images.

These concepts of preservation and renewal are at odds with western conventions of conservation, in which the integrity of the original artist's work must be maintained – the work should not be distorted or modified. In Aboriginal cultures, it is the knowledge associated with images, rather than the images themselves, that is important. The preservation of culture and the transmission of traditional values involve the continuing practice of creating sacred images, telling sacred stories, singing sacred songs, and performing traditional dances and ceremonies. By tradition, the preservation of cultural heritage is the responsibility of the owners of individual Dreaming stories, whose curatorial training is provided through a lifetime of learning from elders.

The Growth of Museums and Related Institutions in Aboriginal Australia

Given the history and collecting patterns of museums – their record of cultural representation and the effect of cultural dislocation inherent in the collecting process – they may seem inappropriate models for Indigenous cultural institutions. Certainly, indigenous peoples may be ambivalent, uninterested, or even hostile toward museums. Nevertheless, by adopting what is essentially a European institution, adapting it to suit their needs and, when necessary, exploiting the administrative and curatorial skills of non-Indigenous staff, consultants, and state museum advisers, Aboriginal communities can use these cultural facilities to achieve their own agendas. Of those that have been established, mostly since the early 1970s, some actively promote cultural renewal and the transmission of knowledge within the community. Others serve as mediator between the local Indigenous community and the outside world, providing interpretive facilities for visitors and seeking to contribute to the process of reconciliation between Aboriginal and non-Aboriginal Australians. Some thrive, many struggle, and others have fallen into a state of neglect and disrepair.

Both economic and cultural factors influence the success of Aboriginal museums and related institutions. Activities and methods must be appropriate if institutions are to have relevance to the community and success as interpretive facilities. While providing access to public aspects of culture to teach visitors about Aboriginal values, such institutions must also adhere to community concepts of preserving and protecting culture, especially aspects that are secret and restricted.

Australian Aboriginal cultures have undergone tremendous change since European settlement. The survival of traditional practices in Aboriginal societies varies greatly, depending upon geographical location (figure 6.2) and the period and extent of white settlement. The influence of Christian missionaries, government resettlement programs, and the degree of involvement with non-Indigenous formal educational institutions have also impacted to varying degrees upon the (dis)continuity of connection with country and the loss of traditional languages and cultural practices. Even in the so-called "traditional" areas of North, Central, and Western Australia, communities have experienced dramatic transformations as they adapt to the modern world. Some influences have been destructive, introducing alcoholism, substance abuse, and poor health caused by high levels of carbohydrates and refined sugars in the western diet; Aboriginal populations now have a life expectancy 20–1 years lower than that of the total population of Australia.[4] Christianity, and western education and values, have also contributed to the erosion of the community framework and of the understanding of the roles, responsibilities, and relationships of each person. Other influences have been beneficial and empowering, enabling easier communication and offering opportunities to participate in global exchanges through access, albeit limited, to telephones, the internet, and transport.

In the face of these changes, Aboriginal communities endeavor to preserve the traditional values and knowledge of their communities while adapting to the pressures of modern life. Some see museums and cultural centers as helpful tools. By establishing their own museums, Indigenous communities have the opportunity to counteract aspects of conventional museology which have been the source of dissatisfaction and discrimination in the past.

The roles and forms of museum-like cultural institutions in Aboriginal communities are determined by local community needs and financial factors, as well as by the motivations and actions of non-Aboriginal curators, art coordinators, supporting institutions, and others involved in managing and maintaining such projects. Aboriginal heritage staff in state museums also provide technical support and training for staff of community museums and advise on basic conservation needs. Because of lack of training and low literacy levels, particularly in remote communities, some Aboriginal people may lack the necessary skills to handle the day-to-day administration and

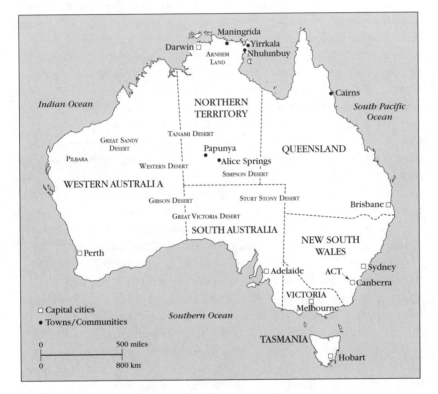

FIGURE 6.2 Map of Australia. © Moira G. Simpson

operation of Aboriginal museums and art centers. Consequently, community-based museums, art centers, and cultural centers in remote regions are often managed by non-Indigenous staff even though they are owned by Aboriginal communities.

Aboriginal people have been under-represented in the museum profession generally. When Dawn Casey was appointed as director of the National Museum of Australia in December 1999, she became the first Aboriginal museum director. While most state and national museums in Australia now employ a number of Aboriginal staff in curatorial positions, museum training has tended to neglect the needs of Aboriginal workers in community-based cultural institutions. In 2000, Museums Australia Queensland (MAQ) and the Regional Galleries Association of Queensland (RGAQ) commissioned a report which examined training and professional development needs of Indigenous people in museums and art galleries throughout Queensland. The report was prepared by Kombumerri Aboriginal Corporation for Culture and Yugambeh Museum, Language & Heritage Research Centre. The report identified a number of training needs, including "increased awareness of basic museum terminology and techniques . . . improved literacy levels . . . hands on, culturally appropriate and holistic training" and "training to provide individuals with real career prospects and opportunities."[5] It recommended that relevant adaptations be made to the existing National Museum Industry Training Package for implementation in Aboriginal communities.

Community-based museums incorporate aspects of the conventional museum but may omit or include activities or methods as pertinent to local agendas. In remote areas of central and northern Australia, communities have generally required secure storage or Keeping Places for the preservation of restricted, sacred materials and other important objects accessible only to those with appropriate standing within the community. Simultaneously, they have established commercially operated art centers which promote and sell Aboriginal art works to a growing international market. A small but growing number of cultural centers are being established, which fulfill a variety of additional roles such as archiving of collections or presenting exhibitions, and these cultural centers may include or be associated with Keeping Places and art centers. In the major cities and towns and the more densely populated or tourist-visited areas of regional Australia, museum-type facilities often take the form of interpretive centers which display and communicate unrestricted aspects of culture to visitors. Interpretive centers also preserve material culture and provide teaching opportunities within the community.

As oral history, dance, music, and visual expression were the primary forms of knowledge transmission, contemporary indigenous communities may prioritize the preservation and transmission of intangible cultural heritage over the preservation and interpretation of artifacts. Community members may seek to preserve and revitalize culture and religious beliefs through the continued production of visual imagery and the practice of intangible heritage, such as the performance of ceremony, music, dance, and storytelling, and the renewal of traditional languages. Indigenous museums and cultural centers may, therefore, highlight intangible aspects of cultural heritage. They may use storytelling, song, and recitation as the primary methods of interpretation, as these are more culturally appropriate than written texts.[6]

For example, Djomi Museum, a small community-based institution in Maningrida, Arnhem Land, in northern Australia, has introductory text panels but few object labels. The museum contains thematic displays using photographs and artifacts to convey aspects of material culture and public ceremonial life. It has a fine collection of bark paintings and fiber arts made by artists living in Maningrida and its outstations. The exhibits on bark paintings contain labels with artist and title but no explanation of their stories or the clan affiliations of the artists. The displays of fiber arts include photographs and text panels describing the processes involved in preparing and working plant fibers to make baskets, bags, and other objects, but individual artists are not named (figure 6.3). Unrestricted ceremonial items are also presented without explanation of their function or significance.

Staff of the Museum and Art Gallery of the Northern Territory in Darwin assisted with the design and construction of exhibits, and the absence of labeling is due, in part, to the community's lack of funding and full-time staff for museum activities. However, in a community where imagery is a traditional method of knowledge transmission, there is little necessity for or interest in labels. Indigenous community members with appropriate custodial rights can "read" the images. They are able to identify the works of individual artists through recognition of stylistic elements and technical workmanship, or their knowledge of clan associations and who own the rights to use specific stories and designs. Non-Indigenous visitors, however, will generally lack the knowledge to interpret images and may seek more detailed descriptions of the works and their meanings, as would be supplied in labels and catalogues in a western museum or art gallery. If staffing permits, the cultural heritage officer gives outsiders a guided tour. This enables visitors to learn about local Aboriginal culture from an Indigenous person directly.

FIGURE 6.3   Fiber arts display, Djomi Museum, Maningrida. Photograph by Moira G. Simpson. Courtesy of the artists and Maningrida Arts and Culture

Such direct contact between visitors and tourists is also occurring in the growing number of Aboriginal tourism enterprises being established, such as tours, dance performances, and demonstrations of traditional skills. While providing the interaction with Aboriginal Australians which many tourists seek, these events allow the community to set boundaries through control of information.

While exploitation of culture for tourism can create economic opportunities for Indigenous peoples, attracting tourists exposes community members and community life to the scrutiny of visitors. For communities in which ceremonial life has distinct elements of privacy and secrecy, the "tourist gaze" can be particularly intrusive and offensive.[7] When information of a religious or sacred nature must be restricted, there exists a potential conflict between the public dimension of a museum and the private aspects of culture. Insensitive actions by tourists, such as photographing people without permission, recording ceremonial activities, and walking on sacred sites, have led many Aboriginal communities to restrict tourism. These communities are attempting to preserve their heritage by balancing the public presentation and interpretation of their culture with the need for protecting restricted knowledge and cultural practices. In communities where aspects of ceremonial life are highly secret, preserving culture can mean maintaining it in isolation from the public domain.

In a radio interview in 1997, Ian Clark, then a lecturer in marketing and tourism at Monash University, maintained that public presentation of culture by Indigenous people can serve to protect communities from further intrusions:

> Indigenous people need to be very deliberate about the construction of tourist spaces that involve their communities. What communities are realising is that if they provide tourists with a 30 minute take of a particular aspect of a ceremony, the tourist leaves satisfied and the communities can then get on with their lives away from the gaze of tourists. So they can get on with their ceremonies and practices and norms that don't involve tourists intruding into their private and domestic and community spaces. So in fact it's probably in their interest . . . [to] construct a deliberate tourist stage and perform on this stage in a fabricated space, and that way their integrity and culture can be not compromised by interacting with tourists.[8]

Community museums and cultural centers can serve this function by restricting visitors' access to the community and offering the information that tourists are seeking.

Aboriginal Keeping Places

In many communities across Australia, preservation of restricted ceremonial and sacred objects was a primary motivating force in the establishment of community-based cultural preservation facilities or Keeping Places. The simplest of these are designed to protect objects from theft and restrict access only to those with custodial rights. Tourists and other non-Aboriginal visitors are normally prohibited from entry, as are uninitiated community members and others not holding appropriate rights or status. Throughout the period of Australian settlement, Europeans saw Aboriginal artifacts as collectibles. Demand from settlers, traders, anthropologists, and tourists led to the growth of commercial trade in Aboriginal artifacts, including sacred objects. When discovered in traditional desert caches, artifacts were often looted by collectors and dealers. Some were acquired by anthropologists and museums wishing to collect and study evidence of ceremonial practices or to safeguard objects from damage or theft. During the early twentieth century, some elders, concerned that younger community members would not take on responsibilities for care, entrusted large collections of sacred material to anthropologists for safekeeping.

In the past, communities had little knowledge of the nature and extent of the Aboriginal materials held in museum collections. Since the 1970s, however, cultural renewal and a growing awareness of the extent and nature of Aboriginal material culture held in state and national museums have led some communities to seek the return of sacred and ceremonial objects. However, communities lacked secure storage for sacred objects which had become highly sought after on the international art market. Many objects had to remain in museums for safekeeping, often at the request of the traditional owners. To facilitate repatriation and protect the objects from theft, a number of communities established secure storage spaces, or "Keeping Places," with the assistance of anthropologists, state museums, and government departments responsible for Aboriginal affairs.

Initially, Keeping Places mainly stored culturally sensitive material such as *tjurunga* – the sacred, ceremonial objects from central Australia which are restricted on the basis of gender and initiation status. The first Keeping Places were simple locked storage facilities – tin sheds or buildings of cement-block construction. They were established primarily in communities in desert regions of central and western Australia, where traditional cultural practices have survived to a greater extent than in Aboriginal communities in the southern and eastern coastal regions.

In contrast, a substantial storage facility of rammed-earth construction was recently completed at a sacred site in the Pilbara desert region of Western Australia. Aboriginal elders were concerned about the lack of protection they were able to provide for sacred objects that they had been keeping on wire-mesh covered with branches in secret locations in the desert. The wooden objects were being destroyed by white ants, so the elders sought assistance from BHP Billiton, an Australian multinational company with operations in the Pilbara region. BHP Billiton's involvement in mining and mineral exploration on Indigenous lands has attracted much criticism, and the storage facility for sacred objects, referred to as a *pirmal*, was constructed as part of their environment and community relations program at a cost of $A500,000. The *pirmal* is designed to withstand weather, insects, cyclones, and ram-raiders. It now provides secure storage for the sacred objects and for others repatriated from museums.[9]

Repatriation is now generally recognized as a critical factor in maintaining and revitalizing community identity by returning cultural material from museum collections to the communities from which it originated. Australian national heritage policy promotes repatriation, if communities wish it. In recent years, state museums and some other collectors have repatriated many sacred objects and other important community materials, such as genealogical information and historical documentation, and this is increasing the need for Keeping Places in communities across Australia.

As well as sacred objects, Keeping Places often contain other sensitive material not considered to be appropriate for general access, such as genealogical documents or photographs of secret ceremonies and deceased persons. Unlike western museums, these Keeping Places are not publicly accessible and do not organize exhibitions. Material may be viewed only by those with the rights or status to do so. Keeping Places share with museums, however, the function of preservation of objects for future generations. They also play an educational role through the transmission of ceremonial and other forms of cultural knowledge.

In other areas, Indigenous communities have established publicly accessible museums in which they present displays of cultural material. These may include a locked cupboard or room serving as a Keeping Place for restricted material. This is the situation in Djomi Museum. Its primary functions are the preservation and display of cultural materials, unrestricted ceremonial objects, and art works produced by members of the community. A locked room holds restricted material, although it contains few sacred objects. The destructive aspects of European settlement have been far less aggressive in Arnhem Land than in many other parts of Australia. Culture is strong, ceremonial life continues, and ceremonial materials are made, used, discarded, and dismantled or kept by participants as appropriate to their function and the protocols of cultural tradition. When objects were repatriated to Maningrida from state museums and private collections in the mid-1990s, sacred ceremonial items were returned to the care of traditional custodians or their descendants, rather than remaining in the museum. The only restricted materials now in Djomi Museum are selected books considered to convey details of ceremonies and other activities of a secret nature.

Most Australian state, national, and university museums have adopted the notion of the restricted Keeping Place, where sacred material is still held at the request of traditional owners or because the appropriate custodians have not yet been identified or cannot be identified due to lack of documentation. It may be that such items will never be displayed in public again. These museums, nonetheless, maintain their responsibility to provide culturally appropriate care for objects which, through their acquisition and use by the museum for many years, have been dislocated from their community and original purpose.

The continuing importance of ritual objects to contemporary religious practitioners may, however, demand their use in ceremonies. Unlike conventional museum practice, which restricts the handling and use of museum objects, Indigenous museums and Keeping Places may provide a secure store for sacred and ceremonial objects in their collections which are removed for use on special occasions. Recognition of the ongoing relevance of ceremonial material has led some mainstream museums to adopt similar lending practices while continuing to provide storage and conservation. This philosophy may be relatively new in museums with ethnographic holdings, but it is an accepted protocol applied to objects required for ceremonial purposes by the British monarchy and parliament. On ceremonial occasions these objects are removed from their normal places of storage and display in locations such as the Tower of London and Westminster Abbey.

While Keeping Places began as simple storage facilities, recent developments in digital data storage have revolutionized the notion of the Indigenous museum and Keeping Place, providing opportunities for remote accessing of information as well as for controlling this access. Today, the Keeping Place is being conceived of not only as a physical storeroom, but also as a complex multimedia storage and retrieval system that operates in the real and virtual worlds. The library services of the Northern Territory and Queensland are working with remote Aboriginal communities in the development of Indigenous knowledge centers, a form of actual and virtual archives. These will utilize multimedia technology "to deliver traditional library services in an interactive medium, accommodating cultural diversity" by blending western and Indigenous knowledge. The concept of the knowledge center "seeks to shift library services from the predominantly print-based western tradition to services based on the oral / visual traditions of Indigenous cultures," and will include materials in the traditional language of each community.[10] In addition to archival resources being copied and returned to communities, images and associated information from museum collections will be made available to the community from which the material originates, using electronic databases with different levels of access built in to protect restricted aspects of culture. Museums will continue to provide care of original films and audio tapes in a stable environment, while the Indigenous knowledge centers will provide a form of "virtual repatriation."[11]

Aboriginal Art Centers

A growing network of commercial art centers operates in Aboriginal communities across Australia. These centers promote wholesale and retail art, provide training opportunities for artists and schoolchildren, and supply artists with commercial art materials and transportation to visit country (traditional lands) or to collect bush materials such as bark and pandanus leaves. Socioeconomic disadvantage impacts heavily on many living in the remote Aboriginal communities scattered across the tropical north of Australia and vast desert regions of central and western Australia. With a severe lack of employment opportunities, the production of art works now provides one of the few means by which individuals can generate income. Activities are not limited to visual arts but include cultural, social, and welfare activities. Some art centers engage in cultural maintenance projects, such as recording oral histories, documenting and maintaining rock art sites, promoting language maintenance, and operating local museums and archives. Art center staff may also be involved in traditional ceremonial life and "sorry business" (funeral ceremonies) by making cash donations, assisting with transport arrangements, or donating art materials.

Acrylic paints, board, and canvas were introduced into remote communities of Australia's central regions in the 1970s, enabling artists to create permanent and portable – and therefore saleable – renderings of ceremonial designs which had previously been painted on bodies or the ground. As artists attain prominence, their paintings, sculptures, and other works – previously produced primarily for ceremonial purposes – take on new meaning as art works. Some art centers are seeking to develop archives to document traditional and evolving techniques and images as well as the styles and development of individual artists. As time transforms commercially produced art into items of cultural heritage, failure to archive works created within communities may perpetuate the imbalance in community control of cultural heritage, with non-Aboriginal museums and galleries continuing to hold the most important collections.

In communities that function at subsistence level, the retention of commercially produced art is very difficult.[12] In central Arnhem Land, for example, Maningrida Arts and Culture provides a wholesale outlet for artists, some of them nationally recognized. Djomi Museum, which like the art center is operated under the umbrella of Bawinanga Aboriginal Corporation, has a strong collection of bark paintings from the 1960s and 1970s. Unfortunately, the corporation lacks the financial resources to sustain an active acquisition program that would enable the museum to collect a representative sample of the evolving styles of the 1980s, 1990s, and 2000s.

The commercial role of Aboriginal art centers may seem to be at odds with the definition of the western museum as a "non-profit" organization that collects and conserves. Aboriginal communities have come to recognize, nevertheless, that art centers can effectively showcase the communicative power of their art, assert cultural autonomy, and articulate Indigenous political and social concerns to non-Aboriginal people. The Dreaming stories depicted on the bark paintings of Arnhem Land and the acrylic paintings of the Western Desert demonstrate the Aboriginal spiritual relationship to land.

Aboriginal communities have submitted bark paintings as evidence to support claims for land and fishing rights and to establish Native Title under Australian law. For instance, the Yolngu of Eastern Arnhem Land sent a "bark petition" to the Commonwealth Government in 1963, demanding that their rights be recognized and protected when a French aluminum company was granted leases and mining rights to a large area of traditional lands. In 1996, clan elders and artists of the Yolngu people of Yirrkala, following the illegal fishing and defiling of a sacred site, produced 80 bark paintings and recorded declarations in an effort to explain their traditional law and beliefs. An exhibition of the paintings, entitled "Saltwater: Yirrkala Bark Paintings of Sea Country," with an accompanying catalogue containing the declarations by five artists, toured Australia in 1999–2001.[13] In this way, the production and exhibition of art works is part of a process of protecting and preserving culture. The sale of art works is seen as a means of communicating traditional values and asserting Aboriginal identity to the outside world.

This educational objective has become an important part of the process of reconciliation in Australia. Many Aboriginal communities present tourism activities and exhibitions in community museums and cultural centers to provide visitors with a greater understanding of Aboriginal culture and laws. By making some aspects of their culture accessible, they hope that greater understanding by non-Aboriginal people will help communities to preserve their traditional lands, hunting and fishing rights, and value systems, in the face of increasing commercial and political pressures.

Displaying and Interpreting Aboriginal History and Culture

While, in the remote communities of Australia, Keeping Places and art centers have been the most relevant facilities for preserving and communicating culture, in communities closer to areas of urban development, museums and cultural centers that conform more closely to the conventional concept of the museum have been useful. Most of these western-style cultural centers and museums serve a dual purpose. They provide resources for the preservation and transmission of culture within the community, and simultaneously fulfill the educational function of displaying and interpreting Indigenous histories and cultures to non-Indigenous visitors.

Traditionally, Australian museums have neglected Indigenous histories in favor of the display of material culture. Dr Gaye Sculthorpe, an Indigenous Tasmanian who is director of the Indigenous Cultures Program at Museum Victoria in Melbourne, has noted that "it is perhaps too easy to be led by our existing ethnographic collections to present 'Indigenous cultures' rather than Indigenous histories."[14] Through a local museum or cultural center, Aboriginal communities have the opportunity to contest official histories and present alternative narratives to non-Indigenous visitors. They can also control the extent to which cultural knowledge is communicated.

Community-operated museums enable Indigenous people to tell their stories, give their views of the historical record, and actively counteract negative perceptions of Aboriginal culture. Some may incorporate material that is unsettling to non-Indigenous visitors. These museums may examine culturally repressive government policies in past decades and challenge visitors' existing knowledge of events that took place during the period of white settlement. Brambuk Aboriginal Cultural Centre in Victoria, for instance, presents excerpts from the papers of white settlers and military personnel detailing poisonings and shootings intended to clear the land of Aboriginal people.[15] Such atrocities have been largely omitted from the official historical record, including museum displays, in what has been termed the "Great Australian Silence."[16] Other Indigenous communities are developing exhibitions on difficult aspects of Aboriginal life under colonialism, such as the history of the Aboriginal police in the Kimberley region of Western Australia and the effects of the 1952–63 British atomic tests in the Maralinga area of the Great Victorian Desert.

Increasingly, Australian state and national museums are responding by rejecting celebratory colonialist narratives that gloss over the horrors of conquest. Many are incorporating Aboriginal views of history into their exhibitions. Bunjilaka, the Aboriginal center in Museum Victoria, Melbourne, includes an audio-visual presentation with excerpts from historical documents that provide shocking accounts of settlers' callous behavior toward Indigenous peoples.

This sensitivity toward Aboriginal points of view is not occurring without some debate. Critics oppose what they call the "Black Armband View of

History," a phrase first used by historian Geoffrey Blainey in 1993 to describe what he regarded as too much emphasis upon the negative or "gloomy" aspects of Australian history since European settlement. This contrasts with what Blainey calls the dominant "Three Cheers View of History," which ignores uncomfortable aspects of history such as the treatment of Aboriginal Australians.[17] The National Museum of Australia (NMA), which opened in March, 2001, has been the subject of particular criticism. It was established as a result of the 1975 Report of the Committee of Inquiry on Museums and National Collections (the Pigott Report), which called for the establishment of a national museum that would include the history of Aboriginal Australia as one of three central themes.[18] Conservative critics have attacked the new museum, accusing staff of political bias in the presentation of Indigenous "cultural propaganda" and challenging the accuracy of content on frontier history and Aboriginal deaths.[19] In December, 2002, the Council of the National Museum of Australia announced that the museum's exhibitions and public programs were to be reviewed and that the contract of the Aboriginal director, Dawn Casey, would be extended for just one year rather than the expected three.

Liberals, on the other hand, believe that curators have been restricted by political pressure from fully addressing the historical truths and the effects of government policies in Indigenous affairs. In assessing the National Museum's First Australians gallery, Kester Tong of the Australian National University asserted that "The political binds placed on curators have created a gallery that does not address important political issues such as a government apology to aboriginal people, conflicts between mining and land rights, mandatory sentencing and many others. It is not lack of space that excludes these political issues but a fear of retribution."[20]

The 2003 review concluded that "political or cultural bias is not a systemic problem at the NMA. Rather, it exists in pockets, which may be fairly easily remedied."[21] However, the announcement of Casey's one-year extension and the undertaking of a review so early in the museum's history are seen by some to justify fears of a backlash and to confirm direct political interference by conservatives.

Conclusion

Because Aboriginal community circumstances vary greatly across the nation, the needs and agendas of communities also vary. The cultural and spiritual values of the community must shape the museum if it is to survive and provide a significant role in future cultural preservation practices. The parallel processes of globalization and indigenization of the museum offer communities and the museum profession new models of preserving, presenting, and transmitting culture, challenging conventional models of what constitutes a museum and how knowledge is preserved and transmitted. The activities of community-based cultural institutions and the gradual infusion of Aboriginal staff into the museum profession are beginning to change museum practice. Through the incorporation of Indigenous concepts of cultural heritage, curation, and preservation, the idea of the museum is evolving to accommodate the needs of diverse cultural groups, both as audiences for museums and as presenters of culture and custodians of tangible and intangible heritage. While these developments can be seen in a growing number of mainstream or public museums, they are essential elements of community-based museums.

The establishment of Aboriginal community museums and cultural centers has enabled Indigenous peoples to appropriate the museum and the exhibition as a means of both preserving and transmitting culture. While adopting the conventions of the museum, some communities have simultaneously rejected the nomenclature of "museum," with its ancestry of colonial domination and cultural appropriation, and its inherent associations with antiquity and death. Instead, communities may favor a term which better reflects the museum's localized role, the significance of the cultural material it contains, and a desire to proclaim their cultural continuity. Increasingly, Indigenous people are recognizing the value that these institutions can have in communicating their histories, cultural values, and political concerns to the outside world. Indigenous communities wishing to provide interpretation to non-Aboriginal visitors are trying to find a balance between exposure of culture to public scrutiny and the need to protect cultural practices that are not meant to be open. By enabling the community to control the transmission of knowledge, the community museum, Keeping Place, or art center becomes a mediator between the Aboriginal community and the outside world. By limiting access to restricted aspects of culture, communities can preserve that which should not be public and, by presenting public aspects of culture, they can seek support for the preservation of their cultural practices.

So the forms which museums and cultural centers take in indigenous communities reflect the limitations of customary beliefs and economic factors, and these alternative perspectives illustrate the transformative nature of the museum and the complex lives of objects. Such developments extend the notion of the museum from an institution that collects and preserves *objects* to one which also assists in the preservation of *traditions and cultural practices*. In other words, its concerns are not just with the *artifacts or tangible heritage* of cultures but also with *intangible* heritage and the *peoples* of those cultures. As Hooper-Greenhill has noted, "in the modern age, the function of the museum is to research and demonstrate the social and cultural context of artefacts and to foster relationships between objects and peoples."[22]

As the notion of the museum spreads, then, the conceptualization of the museum is changing and adopting new roles and forms. As asserted by Appadurai, "at least as rapidly as forces from various metropolises are brought into new societies they tend to become indigenized in one or other way."[23] In concept and practice, the museum, like other forces from the metropolis, can be "indigenized," its functions and methods adapted to suit the needs of the local context. In 1989, the revised ICOM Statutes provided for inclusion of "such other institutions as the Executive Council . . . considers as having some or all of the characteristics of a museum." This opened the door for the inclusion of a variety of cultural models. On paper at least, this allows for the inclusion of diverse forms of cultural institutions, some of which may appear to challenge or even reject conventional museum practice.

When adapted to suit the needs of individual communities, the indigenized museum offers the potential to play a key role in the enhancement of Aboriginal cultural life in terms of both preserving valued aspects of traditional life and evolving new forms. Flexibility in the conceptualization of the museum will facilitate this process by ensuring that the roles of these various cultural models are recognized, accepted, and supported by government agencies, financial institutions, and the broader museum sector.

Questions for Discussion

1 Discuss the quotation above from Adorno concerning the German word *museal*. Why have some linked the museum with death? Have you ever experienced this association? Why have indigenous communities, in particular, rejected the Euro-American museum as a mausoleum? What has been the impact of colonialism on the representation of Australian Aboriginal communities?

2 How do Aboriginal Australian cultural protocols clash with those of the Euro-American museum model?

3 What is the significance of the verb "appropriate"? What aspects of the western museum have Aboriginal Australian communities appropriated? How have

communities transformed these aspects to meet their own needs? Have they had to make compromises?

4   Discuss the diversity of cultural institutions in Aboriginal Australian communities that have resulted from appropriating aspects of the western model. How have Australian state and national museums or libraries helped and/or hindered the process? Have Australian state and national museums themselves changed as a result? What is the difference between exhibiting indigenous cultures and exhibiting indigenous histories? How do Aboriginal Australian cultural institutions promote reconciliation?

5   How is the indigenous museum a mediator between the indigenous community and the outside world?

6   What changes does Simpson call for in reconceptualizing the museum? What can western museums learn from the example of Aboriginal Australian cultural institutions?

7   When is the museum so totally transformed that it becomes something else altogether? When has the Aboriginal model moved beyond the point where it is useful to assert parallels with the "museum"?

Notes

1   T. W. Adorno. (1967). *Prisms.* S. and S. Weber (trans.). London: Neville Spearman.

2   Article 2, ICOM Statutes of 2001. http://icom.museum/statutes.html.

3   Museums Australia. (2002). *Museums Australia Constitution 2002.* Canberra: Museums Australia. www.museumsaustralia.org.au/structure/ma_constit.pdf.

4   Australian Bureau of Statistics. (2003). "Health – Mortality and Morbidity: Mortality of Aboriginal and Torres Strait Islander Peoples." *Australian Social Trends 2002.* www.abs.gov.au/Ausstats/abs@.nsf/0/cd784ff808c14658ca256bcd008272f6.

5   Museums Australia Queensland. (2000). *Training and Professional Development Needs of Indigenous People in Museums and Art Galleries throughout Queensland.* Final report prepared by the Kombumerri Aboriginal Corporation for Culture on behalf of Museums Australia Queensland and Regional Galleries Association Queensland. www.maq.org.au/profdev.

6   In North America, the Hatathli Museum, run by the Navajo Community College in Arizona, displays murals, sand-paintings, and other objects with no labels; the associated stories and their meanings are told and discussed by tutors and their students. Traditional oral methods of communication have also been used on occasion in western museums as a means of providing evocative and culturally appropriate forms of interpretation in exhibitions of non-western art or ethnography. For example, the exhibition "Art from Africa: Long Steps Never Broke a Back" at Seattle Art Museum, 2002, used oral narrative rather than labels. Incorporating traditional methods of knowledge transmission enables Indigenous views to be articulated and voices to be heard, and provides visitors with the opportunity to see and hear the

Indigenous presence in the exhibition, providing a fuller, multi-dimensional representation of a culture.

7   J. Urry. (2002). *The Tourist Gaze.* Thousand Oaks, CA, London, and New Delhi: Sage. (2nd edition.)

8   I. Clark. (1997). Comments made in an interview in "Sacred Sites," Program 7 of the Australian Broadcasting Commission's "Australian Tourism" series.

9   C. Wilson-Clark. (2003). "Sacred Aboriginal Artefacts Kept in Secret Pilbara Safehouse." *West Australian* (May 30), p. 10.

10 *Inquiry into the Role of Libraries in the Online Environment. Submission to the Senate Environment, Communications, Information Technology and the Arts References Committee from the Department of Community Development, Sport and Cultural Affairs through the Northern Territory Library and Information Service.* (2002). Darwin: Northern Territory Department of Community Development, Sport and Cultural Affairs, p. 6

11 Tom Redstone, project consultant, quoted in Anon. (2002). "Galiwin'ku Knowledge Centre." *Land Rights News*, 8.

12 While 33 of the art centers surveyed in 1996–7 were said to hold an archive, only 1 was described by the respondent as "excellent" (Djomi Museum), 7 as "good," and 11 as "reasonable" or "OK." Ten others reported that the conditions of the archives were "poor" and some described them as "scattered," "very bad," or "appalling." F. Wright. (1999). "Appendix II, 11: The Status of Art Centre Archives." In *The Art and Craft Centre Story. Vol. 1: A Survey of Thirty-Nine Aboriginal Community Art and Craft Centres in Remote Australia, Undertaken by Desart Inc.* Canberra: ATSIC.

13 "Saltwater: Yirrkala Bark Paintings of Sea Country" (1999, Neutral Bay, NSW) Catalogue Yirrkala: Jennifer Isaacs Publishing in association with Buku-Larrnggay Mulka Centre, Yirrkala.

14 G. Sculthorpe. (2001). "Exhibiting Indigenous Histories in Australian Museums." In D. McIntyre and K. Wehner (eds.). *National Museums: Negotiating Histories.* Canberra: National Museum of Australia, 73–84.

15 Brambuk and this exhibition are described in some detail in M. Simpson. (2001). *Making Representations: Museums in the Post-Colonial Era.* London and New York: Routledge, pp. 31–4, 126–32. (First edition 1996.)

16 H. Reynolds. (1998). *This Whispering in Our Hearts.* St. Leonards: Allen & Unwin; H. Reynolds. (1999). *Why Weren't We Told?* Melbourne: Viking; Sculthorpe, "Exhibiting Indigenous Histories," pp. 73–84; W. E. H. Stanner. (1979). *White Man Got No Dreaming: Essays 1938–1973.* Canberra: Australian University Press, p. 207.

17 G. Blainey. (1993). "Drawing Up a Balance Sheet of Our History." *Quadrant*, 37: 7–8, 10–15; G. Blainey. (1993). "Goodbye to All That?" *Weekend Australian* (May 1–2), 16.

18 P. H. Pigott. (1975). *Museums in Australia 1975: Report of the Committee of Inquiry on Museums and National Collections including the Report of the Planning Committee on the Gallery of Aboriginal Australia.* Canberra: Australian Government Publishing Service.

19 J. Morgan. (2001). "Howard's Man: 'These People Are Not My Heroes.'" *Sydney Morning Herald* (5 June), accessed online, http://old.smh.com.au/news/0106/05/features/features1.html; K. Windshuttle. (2001). "How Not to Run a Museum: People's History at the Postmodern Museum." *Quadrant*, 45: 9, 11–19.

20   K. Tong. (2001). "The First Australians Gallery at the National Museum of Australia." *Australian Review of Political Economy*, 1. Electronic journal available online, www.anu.edu.au/polsci/arpe.

21   J. Carroll R. Longes, P. Jones, and P. Vickers-Rich. (2003). *Review of the National Museum of Australia, its Exhibitions and Public Programs. A Report to the Council of the National Museum of Australia*. Canberra: Commonwealth of Australia.

22   E. Hooper-Greenhill. (1992). *Museums and the Shaping of Knowledge*. London and New York: Routledge, p. 18.

23   A. Appadurai. (1990). "Disjuncture and Difference in the Global Economy." In M. Featherstone. (ed.). *Global Culture: Nationalism, Globalisation and Modernity*. London: Sage, p. 295.

7 | RESTRUCTURING SOUTH AFRICAN MUSEUMS: REALITY AND RHETORIC WITHIN CAPE TOWN
Julie L. McGee

Editor's Introduction

A visiting assistant professor of Africana studies and art history at Bowdoin College, USA, Julie McGee teaches and publishes on African American and African diasporic studies. The interviews discussed in this chapter form part of a recently completed documentary film on post-apartheid conditions for practicing black artists in South Africa, *The Luggage is Still Labeled: Blackness in South African Art*.

In her chapter, McGee explores the importance of social memory, as constructed by national museums, to identity and nation building. And she demonstrates the intransigence of institutions that keep intact their power structure when social memory is contested. McGee's definition of change in the museum is much more subversive than that of Chris Bruce (chapter 5). Through the case study of the South African National Gallery (SANG), she identifies what she calls "transformation ideology," a self-congratulatory rhetoric, however well intended, that never seriously engages in the kind of radical rethinking that engenders real change. She argues that the SANG is still entrenched in western value systems, the systems that brought colonial and apartheid injustices to South Africa. Like Moira Simpson (chapter 6), McGee holds that those represented must have the right to control their representations. But while Simpson believes that museums in Australia can reconcile differences between western museological practices and local needs, McGee sees no such reconciliation in Cape Town. She shows that black artists in South Africa have compelling ideas, such as increased accountability, changes in educational standards for staff, and deaccessioning, to create change; but, because some of these ideas challenge western notions of "professional" practice, these artists have been shut out of decision-making processes.

McGee asserts that museums such as the SANG must empower black South Africans to create new value systems for their institutions that meet the needs of the disenfranchised. She holds that black South Africans can and should reshape social memory through the museum to create lasting democracy.

One of the more memorable international stories of 1994 was the first democratic election in South Africa. Aerial photographs of long, snake-like queues formed by South Africans patiently waiting to vote, many for the first time in their lives, demonstrated globally the optimism within this new democracy and the patience of a population that had suffered for years under state-sanctioned apartheid. A system of racial segregation established under the National Party (NP) in power from 1948 to 1994, apartheid both legislated and strengthened a system of white minority rule and black disenfranchisement previously established by European colonizers and settlers. Arts and culture and the institutions that protect and promote them are vitally important to the internal formulations and external projections of a newly democratic South Africa. These are exciting yet difficult times for museums, economically, functionally, and ideologically. Museum staffs have been asked to re-examine purpose, mission, audience, collection, education, and exhibition planning, *and* to enact changes that move their institutions from their colonial and apartheid past to a newly democratic South African present. All *nationally* recognized heritage institutions are expected to develop new policies and undertake initiatives that transform these organizations into democratic entities reflecting and representing a plurality of South Africa's cultures.

The restructuring of South Africa's museums offers rich opportunities to consider the sociopolitical ramifications of cultural institutions and the complex relationship of theory and practice. An analysis of the choices being made provides insight into the process of constructing and contesting social memory. South African cultural narratives have reflected and privileged colonial values, and their revision requires advancing new narratives and shifting emphases away from western epistemologies and interpretations. This chapter considers the struggles of one national institution, the South African National Gallery (SANG), which is the earliest public collection of art in South Africa, and the responses of some of its stakeholders to its transformation process. In its continued attempt to control social memory, the SANG remains entrenched in the western value system that first disenfranchised the majority of South Africans. Radical reconfigurations may well be needed to significantly move the National Gallery away from the west and toward something that can justly be called South African.

In political and constitutional terms modern South Africa has been called the lineal descendant of Jan van Riebeeck, a Dutchman who established in 1652 a settlement in Cape Town, largely to service the supply needs of the Dutch East India Company. The Dutch were followed by the British (who conquered the Cape in 1795) and an influx of European immigrants (primarily British followed by German and French) who colonized the interior of South Africa. Modern South Africa's cultural heritage institutions, the oldest founded in the nineteenth century, are also lineal descendants of European colonization. They have followed Eurocentric models in the most fundamental aspects of their work: collecting, preservation, research, education, and ideology. Cultural bias and limited access have been defining characteristics of these cultural heritage sites, and under apartheid white privilege and black exclusion became a matter of law.

South Africa's first democratic general election brought a new government, black majority leadership, and a new constitution, among other things. Transformation and reconstruction are key words in post-1994 South African initiatives, especially government-sponsored ones. Yet museums and heritage sites vary tremendously in their abilities to embrace fully these initiatives and then undertake transformation and reconstruction. Staffing expertise, human and economic resources, and the collections themselves all play a role in the process. Some institutions began to redefine themselves in the early 1990s before legislative mandates while others, even after legislative directives, find it difficult to begin. The SANG falls somewhere in between, its efforts now seemingly both furthered and hindered by its present status as one of the 15 museums bundled together as South Africa's Southern Flagship Institution, or Iziko Museums of Cape Town.

What does it mean for an institution of European and colonial heritage embedded in South Africa to transform *and* incorporate more fully non-Eurocentric cultures? What are the measures of success vis-à-vis transformation, and who acts as jury? What kind of evaluative process should be implemented? Is success driven by national or international measures? Is there a point when transformation is concluded, the job is done, as it were? Or is it the nature of a public cultural institution to be constantly transforming? What is the impact of the Iziko umbrella on the SANG's day-to-day practices and ongoing effort to transform?

To understand the SANG one must first recognize that fine arts in South Africa have been and still are to a large degree defined by western European

epistemologies or theories of knowledge. Western Eurocentric models provided the foundation for the professionalization of the fine arts through
exhibitions, artists' and collectors' societies, galleries and museums, education and degree-granting programs, and the history of art history. Once
considered a canonical if not encyclopedic document of South African art
and its history, Berman's *Art and Artists of South Africa: An Illustrated Biographical Dictionary and Historical Survey of Painters, Sculptors and Graphic Artists
since 1875* was published in its first edition in 1970 and enlarged and revised
in 1983. Here one finds the "antecedents" of South African art laid out in
European terms – what the art interests and abilities were of early Dutch
colonists, European visitors, and later settlers. Distant from European art
centers, Berman noted, "the development of South African art pursued a
slow and stumbling course."[1] The assumption is that western standards of
art and its progress have legitimate universal application. Under this ration-
ale, visual material outside normative western categorizations is excluded
from history, or at best, awkwardly included. While Berman's text does
acknowledge that the "story of painting in South Africa had its beginnings
amid a hunter-culture in the distant past" with "artists of the rocks," it
asserts that the study of rock art largely interests archeologists and anthropologists, not artists or art historians:

> In recent years, scholars who are aware that South Africa's history has usually
> been presented from a European viewpoint, have become disposed to adopt a
> more Afro-centric attitude in examining the legacy of the past. Within that
> legacy, the indigenous contribution of the rock artists is undoubtedly a price-
> less heritage. It is also a source which might be drawn upon for inspiration in
> forging a common South African culture. Thus far . . . that fountainhead has
> not attracted much attention from artists, black or white. It is the scientists
> who demonstrate the greatest interest and concern regarding this cultural
> heritage.[2]

Presently, information and samples of work by "artists of the rocks" are in
the collection of the SANG's neighboring institution, the SA Museum (South
African Museum of Natural History).

The SANG is a product of the South African Fine Arts Association, considered the first "art society" to be established in South Africa and founded
in Cape Town's public library in 1850. While this designation ignores recognition of communities of artists among indigenous South Africans as comprising art societies, the SANG's kinship with the SA Fine Arts Association
clarifies the institution's early purpose and early collection, both of which

FIGURE 7.1   South African National Gallery, Cape Town. Photograph by Julie L. McGee

resonate today. The "first formally arranged art exhibition" took place in 1851 and consisted "largely of works of European art on loan from the wealthier Cape Town residents." An 1871 bequest from the estate of Thomas Butterworth Bayley, one of the society's members, formed the "national collection," which continued to receive gifts thereafter.[3] In 1895 the collection, then comprised of some 100 works of art, officially came under government control through the South African Art Gallery Act. The current home of the SANG opened in 1930 in Company Gardens, Government Avenue, and in 1932 became officially the South African National Gallery (figure 7.1).[4]

The museum building itself, designed by members of Cape Town's public works department, is aligned both in placement and in style with other government buildings situated on Government Avenue. The influence of Dutch colonial style and French Beaux-Arts planning is evident and the museum fits seamlessly in the park-like corridor, located in downtown Cape Town. At the time of its opening the national collection maintained its colonial resonance. Of the hundreds of works in the collection, only 30 were by South African artists – and these were artists of European ancestry. As curator Joe Dolby notes, "This state of affairs was both a reflection of the tastes current at the time and a heritage from bygone years."[5] Later bequests to the National Gallery would include more European art; long-term loans brought old master paintings and modern French and English paintings and drawings. Visitors to the gallery would find there a modest but clearly European museum model; in the 1960s traveling exhibitions brought works by Auguste Rodin, Henry Moore, Rembrandt van Rijn, and French Impressionists. Acquisition funds enabled the museum to collect work from what it perceived to be South Africa's "founder countries" – the Netherlands, Germany, England, and France. Acquisition funds have always been limited, but the collection of work from "founder countries" took priority over objects from African countries. Most of the South African artists represented were of European descent. The collection may well have been called national and indeed perceived as such by those who worked and visited the gallery – but in reality it was not.

Post-1994, both officially and ideologically, the National Gallery of South Africa is compelled to be nationally focused and relevant. Late nineteenth-century assumptions about what determines a "national collection" no longer hold. But twenty-first-century definitions of "national," shaped by and with the newly democratic South Africa in mind, remain elusive. For many, "national" is best defined by equal representation and participation – visible evidence of transformation. South African artists, in particular those who do not trace their family lineage to Europe, wish for and repeatedly ask for clearer signs that the SANG *is* the national gallery of South Africa. For black South Africans the promise of post-1994 reconciliation, the gift of a non-violent democratic transformation, came with the expectation that privileged white institutions such as the SANG take dramatic steps to address and rectify imbalances. This means seeing on a regular basis exhibitions presenting the work of contemporary South African art and the history and legacy of all indigenous South African artists. But the SANG does not have a comprehensive or deep historical collection of work in this area. Its initial steps to acquire African art and works by black South African artists began in the 1960s and 1970s. Acquisition policies prior to 1996 placed a priority on art from European founder countries and by the time this was reversed – perhaps under the influence of inadequate funding – there were, effectively, no funds set aside for acquisition.[6]

Developing strategies to overcome racist, classist, and entrenched colonial systems now appears on the visible agenda of previously white South African institutions. Recasting cultural heritage, rewriting, re-examining, and recontextualizing social memory, are not merely theoretical or academic dispositions in South Africa; rather, the gathering of history and the interpreting of culture are significant matters of democratization and nation building. Post-1994, reconstruction and transformation are seen as the all-important tools for building the "new South Africa." Yet some institutions seem to have embraced (and suffer from) what is best defined as "transformation ideology." Understanding ideology to be the ways in which certain belief systems sustain meaning, values, and thereby dominance, we begin to see how power relationships within art institutions have failed to change, although much has been done under the rubric of reconstruction and change. Legitimacy is maintained by those who have always been in power and who are now able to legitimize the transformation process through the same channels and resources used prior to 1994: that is, creating, documenting, proclaiming, writing, publishing, and speaking – in this case, the language of change.

Colonization of Southern Africa by the Dutch, British, and Germans has had a lasting impact on South African art, both its production and its documented (a.k.a. known) history. As such it affects all practicing artists, present and future, most particularly those who interface with the more formal art institutions such as Cape Town's Michaelis School of Fine Arts or the SANG. What this means in very real terms is that the art-historical record of South African art, both in written and in visual terms, has been and continues to be dominated by colonial art, its history and structure, and its aesthetic and validating influences. Provincial and national arts collections, where they exist, are dominated by European art or South African art inspired by European and American standards of style, content, and aesthetic values. Many, like the SANG, have been historically "white own affairs" institutions far longer than not, meaning European history and culture were privileged over those of indigenous Africans.

Since 1991, the SANG has undertaken several measures intended to shift the direction of the institution, and these inform the collection and exhibition policies. The year 1990 brought a new director, Marilyn Martin, and a new acquisitions policy that emphasized the collection of South African art and material culture, including the repatriation of objects taken out of South Africa. Presently the SANG both promotes and exhibits itself as an institution willing to explore, explain, and critique its past. A newly installed permanent exhibition that greets today's visitors to the SANG provides an apt introduction to this very situation. Titled "ReCollection: 130 Years of Acquiring Art for the Nation (1871–2001)," the exhibit seeks to contextualize the SANG collection and as such restates, visually and in English-only wall text, the dominant place of South African "white artists responding to European tradition and innovation."[7]

In presenting a visual and historical outline of the collection, the exhibition illuminates but neither subverts nor transforms the space of the SANG. "The permanent collection of any art museum is the centre of its existence," wall text informs us. And so, a small number of recently collected works by contemporary black South African artists accompany hanging Ndebele *Liphotho* (beaded marriage aprons of the Ndebele peoples), West African artifacts, and European and white South African art, works that date back to the nineteenth century. From "ReCollection" we learn that "black artists enter[ed] from the margins," and that the SANG acquired its first work by a black South African artist in 1964. "The first steps to represent the *art of Africa* in the collection were made in the 1960s and 1970s by Assistant Director Bruce Arnott."[8]

Exhibits such as "ReCollection" attempt to happily marry a colonial legacy to a black African present under the rubric of honesty in representation of the so-called "rainbow nation." Again, good intentions aside, the presentation represents the South African paradox. Without destabilizing institutional power, the exhibition provides an honest account of the SANG collection history, noting the preference for European tradition and the difficulty of acquiring black South African art. Wall text informs us that it was only after the work of black artists was "given exposure and legitimacy by its inclusion in new publications" that the SANG took notice: "Political isolation made this no easy task. Since the 1980s, reclaiming the neglected history of black art has been undertaken by research and exhibitions. The high market prices demanded for the works of the 'first generation' of black artists has now placed them beyond the reach of the SANG's meagre acquisitions budget."

In the first instance, this is a remarkably honest, up-front, and important presentation – a look behind the scenes, as it were. But what else does it tell us? First, the language and installation tell us that just what is *African* art and what is *South African* art are unresolved issues. This has tremendous significance for a national gallery. "African" can and has been used expediently to protect and legitimize white South African artistic production. Simultaneously, "African" means black, non-Eurocentric, or indigenously African. In terms of art, only black artists in this exhibition are referred to as "emergent" or "first generation." This suggests a point of origin for black art, while such is not the case for non-black artists. The inclusion of Ndebele *Liphotho* and other "artifacts" alongside paintings, prints, and sculptures acknowledges new policy and acquisition changes and the museum's desire to break down traditional barriers between fine art and craft. Hung together as a group are Ndebele marriage aprons (purchased 1991), an Akan linguist's staff from Ghana (purchased 1994), a Shona headrest from Zimbabwe (purchased 1995),

185

and two sculpted portraits of Chief Albert Luthuli, created by black South African modernist Dumile Feni in 1968 (purchased 2002). The grouping is confusing at best. On the one hand, Feni is presented as another black African artist working in 3D. On the other hand, his works have little practical relationship to marriage aprons, headrests, and the linguist's staff. His work embodies the formal qualities of Cubist reductionism and abstraction, a European modernist style influenced itself by African and other non-western art forms. Unfortunately the African artifacts and sculptures are hung and presented like nearby paintings, doing little to destabilize canonical hierarchies. Moreover, exhibition wall text defines black artists who produced paintings, sculpture, and graphic arts as "first generation black artists." Last and perhaps most problematic is the continued sense that it is the SANG itself that legitimizes the mainstream. We are told that since the 1960s, the SANG has "markedly increased its holdings of work by black [meaning South African] artists. The marginal was at last becoming mainstream."[9] The power of mainstreaming and legitimizing which the SANG as an institution repeatedly bestows upon itself is its Achilles heel.

Despite this supposed academic integrity or gesture of good faith, today's black artists continue to feel excluded, as I learned in a 2002 collaboration with Vuyile C. Voyiya, artist and education officer at the SANG.[10] Together we collected over 50 hours of interviews with artists, curators, educators, and gallery directors whom we asked to consider the meaning of "black" in so far as it related to or framed their professional life. Because we considered our interviewees to be among the most important of the SANG's stakeholders, we asked for frank comments about the institution and its efforts to change.

Our interviews with black South African artists suggest little has changed for them in terms of their relationship with and attitudes toward the SANG and other art institutions. A privileged system that first denied black artists equal opportunities, resources, and education still controls the history of South African art. Black South Africans are not equal partners in the endeavor to collect, curate, write, preserve, and thus construct this history. When they share the platform they are not equally heard, for they rarely project the same point of view as non-blacks.

Visits to the National Gallery, when they are undertaken at all, have repeatedly failed to capture the imagination or address the history and concerns of many black artists. In combination with a required entry fee that most find unfair – "it is after all the *nation's collection, our collection*," we heard often – this has successfully deterred most black artists from visiting the SANG. Students with valid student cards from recognized educational institutions are allowed free entry, but students who study art at the Community Arts Project or other informal workshops targeting black artists in particular do not have student identification cards and must pay.[11] Other deterrences include transport, language, ineffective systems of communication, and lingering suspicions about any previously "white own affairs" institution. Most black South Africans, thanks to apartheid engineering, live some distance from Cape Town's city center and must bear the costs of transportation to visit the gallery. Although the SANG purports to be a trilingual institution (English, Afrikaans, Xhosa, the three dominant languages of the Cape), this is rarely the case. Only major exhibitions have information in three languages and, even then, typically only the introductory wall text appears in three languages.[12] In terms of communication, the SANG's most effective outreach is to those on its mailing lists, that is, the Friends of the National Gallery (FONG) who have made a donation, those affiliated with other art institutions, and, to some extent, those who live in the city center and read mainstream newspapers. Educational outreach to outlying schools does exist, but the SANG has no consistent and distinct budget for educational programming. Thus, educational programming, as with many aspects of the SANG, largely depends upon outside funding and volunteer guides (typically white women). Much of the infrastructure of apartheid-era South Africa remains intact; the legacy of the apartheid engineered environment, physical and socioeconomic, places significant demands on institutions wishing to appreciably reflect and attract a plurality. Rearranging or changing the furniture inside the museum walls, as it were, is simply not enough. It is the SANG's responsibility to inform and bring into the institution those who have been excluded or marginalized.

The task of transformation is not easy and the SANG is hampered in its work by a number of issues, not the least of which is a lack of the resources necessary to evolve more dynamically. State funding is sparse and the institution today relies on lottery money and on private and corporate support. In late 2001, Martin noted that the SANG had had no acquisition budget since 1997 and that state funding had been static since 1994. Additionally she said, "I do not know where we would be today without the contribution of business and foreign governments."[13] On the other hand, individuals make choices about how money is used and money alone will not bring the change envisioned by our interviewees.

Some artists and critics propose deaccessioning as a means toward visible change and helping to finance new acquisitions. In a recent public exchange of letters between Gavin Anderson, of the *Natal Witness*, and Brenden Bell, director of the Tatham Art Gallery (TAG) in Pietermaritzburg, Anderson chastised the TAG for the display dominance of its European collection at the expense of more national and local examples. Anderson suggested that the gallery sell "a sizeable batch of works from the collection back to Europe, in order to finance the purchase of more relevant, immediate, powerful and interesting works to supplant them." TAG director Bell responded:

> Anderson's concern about the central prominence of the British and French collections . . . is justified and is being dealt with. That the issue has not already been finalised is purely a matter of logistics and capacity. His contention of selling off part of the collection to fund more relevant purchases suggests a misunderstanding of the purpose of museums. Art museum collections reflect histories and modes of cultural production. They are a collective memory for future generations of both positive and negative histories and as such have to be left intact. Censoring a collection is not, in my view, a healthy transformation tool.[14]

Clearly deaccessioning is too radical an action to consider at this time for those in control at most art museums in South Africa, including the SANG.

But if art museums function as the collective memory for future generations, what if that memory is flawed, or composed of too few voices, or remembered in ways that are accessible to only a few – and who decides? Leaving a collection intact seems to imply that it represents a whole, in and of itself, or that censoring was not inherent to the institution's initial collection policies. If museums such as the TAG and the SANG legitimize their exhibition priorities on the basis of their past collections, then they must admit to being and remaining flawed "white institutions" with good intentions but inadequate means to be otherwise. In play here is the shape of social memory as constructed by cultural objects and legitimized by cultural institutions. For some, cultural memory is best shaped by adding previously ignored objects to established systems of classification and meaning. But, for others, a more dramatic reshaping based on new and differing values is necessary, and deaccessioning, considered taboo by western standards, is a viable means of questioning and perhaps financing what would be a more equitable and representational collection. In his critique of the Tatham, Anderson states,

> It seems to me that the TAG has done too little over the last decade that is visible externally to make the majority of the work on display from its collection, the collection itself, and the various exhibitions that it hosts more

relevant and hospitable to the immediate life-world of the majority of our community, and to other important minorities within it.[15]

Reactions are remarkably similar with respect to the display of European art at the SANG. Bound by gift restrictions, the SANG permanently displays a significant portion of the Sir Abe Bailey Bequest of over 400 items, acquired by the SANG in 1947. The paintings of the Bequest are largely British portraits and hunting and horseracing scenes. A wealthy mining magnate and businessman, South African born and British educated, Bailey envisioned his Anglophile collection as a worthy addition to the National Gallery. And at the time of its bequest it was indeed a welcome gift, providing the museum with works by Sir Thomas Lawrence, Sir Joshua Reynolds, and George Stubbs, among others.[16] Because the SANG is legally bound to exhibit the collection, its presence provides ample fodder for criticism. Some detractors favor deaccessioning and the use of such funds to redress the imbalances and inadequacies of the SANG collection. In a 1995 essay, American art historian Linda Nochlin juxtaposed the Bailey Bequest with a concurrent temporary SANG exhibition, "IGugu lamaNdebele (Pride of the Ndebele)," to critique the historical pride of place of the western tradition.[17]

When asked about the relevance of the European collection to the SANG, current director Martin said she believed the standard for a "national gallery" was that which one finds internationally; first-rate national galleries traditionally provide an internationally representative collection for educational purposes alongside its nation's art. While this is widely accepted among Euro-American museum professionals and visitors, this definition of a "national gallery" is recognized and has been experienced by only very privileged South Africans who have had the opportunity to travel outside the continent. Artists we speak to express a genuine desire to see themselves reflected in these national institutions first and foremost; indeed most recognize and subscribe to the historical importance and legitimacy of museums and galleries.

This disappointment with the collection and exhibition policies should not be perceived as a threat to the institution as a whole, but rather as a revalidation of its place and significance. At issue is just how "national" is made manifest and by whom. As expressed by Cape Town artist and art history graduate student Thembinkosi Goniwe, "who and on whose taste or aesthetic habits was and is the black culture or art selected and represented? In fact, who is legitimate to negotiate and take charge in selecting and representing or recasting the culture and identity of the 'other' in such a national institution?"[18] Goniwe, studying at Cornell University, aspires to be among the first black South Africans with a doctorate in art history. His position reiterates the South African paradox, namely that South Africa's system of art-historical legitimization is Eurocentric; blacks without recognized credentials continue to be excluded from decision-making processes.

At the moment, too few black voices participate in constructing South Africa's art-historical history and national art collections, but those in power rationalize the situation in the name of western notions of professionalization. According to Martin, "South Africa lacks the black researchers, art historians and curators who can fulfil the task of reclaiming and representing history and art history."[19] There is an awkward excusing of the dominant white voice in the transformation process.

When one compares actions and statements, written and spoken, by those running art institutions with those by black artists, it seems evident that transformation and reconstruction mean quite different things. Some black artists contrast the failure to transform art museums with processes fostering the transforming of national sports teams. The racial makeup of national sports teams and their leadership is highly visible and the rate of change in this area is nearly a daily news feature, often front-page news. Artists see no high-profile governmental advocate (like the minister of sport, Ngconde Balfour), however, lobbying for genuine reform within and by art institutions. There appears to be no external pressure from the media or from politicians on arts organizations and institutions to change; these artists wish for but see no real accountability.

One of our interviewees, artist and educator Garth Erasmus, describes accountability in ways that are more profound and more troubling than the sports analogy:

> Our art institutions still have not come to terms with the problems black artists have faced over the years and now there does not seem to be the need. Nothing has actually happened since 1994; the people who are responsible did not take their responsibility seriously; now the urgency is not there. There is a greater interest in being part of the world. Galleries, be they commercial or public, have the freedom *not* to be responsible for the past; they have now a freedom from the past. Post-1994 South Africa and its art institutions have become part of the global world.[20]

Many black artists believe that responsibility for the past has been abandoned in the push to join a global and commercialized art market. As Erasmus noted, the Truth and Reconciliation Commission has had little impact on artists and art institutions.[21] In other words, political and moral responsibilities vis-à-vis the art arena have not been aired publicly, let alone met.

Since her hiring in 1990, SANG director Martin has worked to craft a transformation narrative for the National Gallery that first acknowledges its past as a colonial and apartheid cultural institution, and then posits the institution as a genuine partner for change, fully engaged in facing, confronting, and rewriting South Africa's history. Repeatedly and prolifically, she defends the choices of the museum, as in a 1995 catalogue: "The Board of Trustees and staff of the SANG worked tirelessly on transforming the institution, on redressing imbalances of the past and involving the broader community in out activities." Her concrete evidence is a series of "groundbreaking exhibitions" curated at the SANG, each one appealing to specific but new audiences for the museum. Martin provided a similar narrative in our recent interview with her. There is sincerity in the voice and certainty on the part of the narrator in the following: "The people of South Africa are laying claim to their national art museum, and we are proud to be part of the generation and definition of a national identity and a shared destiny."[22]

Martin writes and reports frequently on the activities of the SANG geared toward transformation. In essays such as "Transforming the National Gallery," or "Art in the *Now* South Africa: Facing Truth and Transformation," Martin writes and rewrites the history of the SANG. A number of devices appear consistently: optimism and idealism tempered by caution; acknowledgment of the "spectre of internal neo-colonialist practices and appropriation which admits artistic pluralism in order to gain control;" claims of internal self-policing within the SANG; and a chronicle of the museum's "transformational" activities over the past decade or so, recounted primarily as a series of exhibitions.[23] Among the exhibitions commonly listed are: "Ezakwantu: Beadwork from the Eastern Cape," "IGugu lamaNdebele (Pride of the Ndebele)," "Muslim Art in the Western Cape," "District Six: Image and Representation," and two exhibitions designed by art professors from Michealis School of Fine Arts that sought to recontextualize objects of material culture from the SA Museum.[24] The language Martin uses to describe the actions of the museum is powerful: "We believe we are doing more than passively holding up a mirror to society. We inform, construct, change, and direct the narrative of our lives and our experiences – aesthetically, culturally, historically, politically. The national art museum is integral to the refiguring and reinventing of South African art and identity."[25]

Thus, the story of the SANG's transformation focuses on temporary or one-off exhibitions and, when possible, the collection and repatriation of

South African material culture. In the preface to the exhibition catalogue for "Ezakwantu: Beadwork from the Eastern Cape," Martin made note of the revised acquisition policies adopted in 1990 by the Board of Trustees regarding the collection of the "material culture" of Africa, and especially southern Africa: "This meant that the national art museum was to become actively involved in the preservation and presentation of a multiplicity of cultural manifestations, and that it would be instrumental in altering the status of objects which initially had been regarded by the West as curiosities, and later as ethnographic specimens."[26] The power to "alter the status of an object" recalls the ideology of the museum as temple, not the museum as forum. The institution itself is not altered, only the status of the object. In other words, the institution is transformative but not transforming, and claims to the alteration reinscribe a Eurocentric ideology.

Why do Garth Erasmus and others profess not to see any change in South Africa's art institutions? Has there really been no change and, if not, why has there been so much done and written in the context of purported changes? Realistically, the centers of power and the individuals who are in power have changed very little if at all. The flow of information, as well as decisions about and definitions of what reconstruction and change are, remain defined by the same stakeholders and decision-makers.

The SANG provides a salient example of institutional recentering or the "transformation ideology" that is the *changing same* confronting black artists. The institution proclaims its commitment to reconstruction, taking both a visible and a vocal position as challenger to the status quo, but reconstructive power is not shared let alone given over to a majority black population. Some things change: the museum collection and temporary exhibitions expand to include objects from material culture and new works of art. Some things don't change: directors, curators, the power to define what change is and means. From a practical point of view, questions about deaccessioning and recentering, redefining a national collection from a democratic South African perspective, are never seriously considered. Museums continue to apply western art ideologies and practices universally. In the same vein, the museum profession, as a western invention and institution, has become a universal standard. Curators arrange objects on the basis of chronology, nationality, and aesthetic values rather than function. The past is interrogated, critiqued, and occasionally altered but only in so far as it fits comfortably within professionally determined boundaries and ideologies. To return to wall text provided by SANG exhibition "ReCollection," "Our first art museums were colonial inventions that were slow to acknowledge the creativity of black artists. Until the 1950s there were in fact few black artists working in western techniques." Herein the use of western techniques is an implicit criterion for inclusion in a South African art museum. For black South Africans this universal means little more than white domination and/or determination.

Rather than being transformed through new influences, the institution purports to change that which it brings into the institution. A transformation ideology that is event-centered can easily mask or justify fundamental or underlying issues or policies sorely in need of change. Exhibition-centered transformation develops new and discrete audiences around each event but does little to sustain these new relationships once the event has concluded. The museum walls are temporarily penetrated by new voices and viewers but the institutional structures are free to remain intact. To suggest that there are no black voices adequately equipped for the "task of reclaiming and representing history and art history" is specious if not naïve. This view privileges past epistemologies and methods, the very systems that rendered black history invisible or "other" – or worse, presumes that these systems are the only means of claiming and presenting South African history. It is, therefore, not surprising that many of our interviewees do not see the arts climate today as better and some believe it has deteriorated.[27]

The process of reconstruction for the SANG is indeed complex and two key factors in it must be acknowledged before closing – the first a political legacy and the last a new structural dynamic. Historically, a white minority whose tastes were formed by European and American models has supported formal arts and cultural institutions in South Africa. To this we must add the recent politicized history of the arts in South Africa. Under apartheid the Department of Arts and Culture (DAC) of the African National Congress (ANC), operating from exile, supported a cultural boycott of South Africa (formally instituted by the United Nations in 1980) and, equally important, promoted art as a *cultural weapon*. Within South Africa, the United Democratic Front (UDF), an internal operative for the ANC, sought to censor arts production that was not in support of the struggle against apartheid and the National Party. Both of these histories – white minority control of culture and art in the service of resistance – devalued black South African creativity and freedom, and rendered a substantial part of black artistic productivity invisible, if not moot. Building visibility for the arts and promoting arts education that can transcend these rooted and differing barriers is a task that extends beyond the SANG itself.

Last, on April 1, 1999, the government of South Africa created a management structure for its heritage and cultural instructions that effectively defined and combined what were considered South Africa's *national institutions*. Established at that time were the Southern Flagship Institution (Western Cape) and the Northern Flagship Institution (Gauteng Province). Intrinsic to and underlying the bureaucratic and institutional restructuring is the implicit understanding that this was both an economic and a democratic necessity. In the Western Cape the Southern Flagship Institution was effectively renamed Iziko Museums of Cape Town. Iziko, a Xhosa word for "hearth," is meant to imply "the center of cultural activity." The SANG maintains its national status, but from an operating standpoint it is bundled with 14 other institutions of like and unlike natures including the South African (SA) Museum, established in 1825 and considered the oldest museum in sub-Saharan Africa, and the South African Cultural History Museum (also known as the Slave Lodge).[28]

The value of the Southern Flagship Institution, or Iziko Museums of Cape Town, to each institution's individual transformation remains to be seen. The present CEO of Iziko is a South African historian, Professor H. C. Bredekamp, but what his legacy will be is as yet unclear. The first CEO, Jack Lohman, who was British, had a short and controversial tenure. He came aboard in 2000 and worked hard to foster international partnerships for Iziko institutions. He also sought to introduce new museological practices and innovations from European institutions to Iziko, and to establish internships for South African citizens in European museums. Under Lohman, Iziko Museums sponsored an international conference, "Blurring the Boundaries: Training for Transformation," and innovative museum professionals such as Mikko Myllykoski of the Finnish Heureka Museum were brought to Cape Town as consultants.[29] But both the need for a foreign CEO of the nation's museum and Lohman's leadership style have been severely criticized.[30] In South Africa, skepticism is never distant when national institutions rely on European leadership and funding. Indeed one should question continued reliance on European models in the reshaping of South African national institutions. Partnerships are important, but not at the expense of South African conceptualizations of proficient and superior *national* museums.

At its best, the Iziko concept offers opportunities for varying museums to work collectively and in so doing break down the academic and ideological walls that define the distinct collections. Partnerships between Iziko institutions just might bring examples of rock art into the SANG. Two recent exhibitions at the SANG demonstrate this kind of collaboration: "Birds of a Feather . . ." (2001–2) and "The Loom of Life: African Attire from the Iziko Collections" (2002). In the former, ethnographic, zoological, historical, and visual material relating to birds was all brought together for a comprehensive exhibition at the SANG that even included a live owl on display in the museum's atrium. The juxtaposition of numerous preserved bird specimens in archival cases and works of art that include birds certainly did demonstrate collaboration. But Lallitha Jawahirilal, a South African artist whose thematic concerns include personal agency and exile, was unhappy that the SANG exhibited her works in this particular exhibition, thereby reducing their meaning to a relationship with birds.

At its worst, the Iziko umbrella may detract from focus, energies, and funds necessary for individual institutional democratization. The shuffling, redistribution, and redisplay of collections is useful, especially if it dislodges or destabilizes stale, static, and outmoded museologies. But the cultural institutions that make up Iziko have divergent histories when it comes to collection, exhibition, research, and staffing, and some of these need to be addressed independently. The initiatives undertaken by the SANG to date are important and instructive in this light. Seen from an internal perspective, things have changed with regard to some museological practices. But these changes have not yet configured the institution in such a way that it seems to belong to previously disenfranchised South Africans, especially black artists.

Prior to 1994 the SANG had already begun its transformation process; this beginning brought optimism, hope for the future, and some tangible changes. Today, however, much of this optimism has been tempered if not lost; critical oral history exposes the fallacy of the written narrative. The constructed and at times congratulatory written history of transformation by cultural institutions participates in an ideology that does little more than solidify the center and the periphery. Many of the most difficult questions remain unaddressed institutionally, yet they are of critical importance to black South Africans. In the absence of alternative histories and voices and shifting loci of power, the concerns of black constituents remain marginalized at the same time they are assumed to be a major impetus for transformation. A redefining must occur before South Africa's national cultural institutions do more than reflect colonial and apartheid histories. It remains to be seen whether a fundamentally European system of professionalization and status vis-à-vis fine arts can become *national* and *South African* in both word and deed. A museological model is not to be found for this, but rather to be made. The openness of the debate and the strength of contesting voices inspire optimism – for here one finds a true plurality of people who care deeply about South Africa's cultural heritage. In South Africa today the recasting of social memory within heritage institutions is far more than a theoretical gesture; it is a social, political, and national imperative. To this end, the processes undertaken and responses to them have much to teach all of us concerned with the intersections of theory and practice within museums today and in the future.

Questions for Discussion

1   What is social memory? What is the relationship between social memory and the museum? Describe social memory as constructed by the SANG in the past and in the present. How might cultural narratives be reconstrued by the black artists that McGee interviewed?
2   What is the significance of the SANG's designation as a "national" gallery? What responsibilities does it entail? Compare Marilyn Martin's definition of a national museum with that of the black artists surveyed. How do you define a "national" gallery?
3   How is the SANG now changing? Why does McGee refer to this as the "changing same"? Why are museums in South Africa behind other institutions, such as professional sports, in making transformation? What is the significance of the term "white own affairs" institution?
4   What practical problems do Martin and her colleagues cite? Do you think these practical issues are valid reasons for not pressing forward? Who should evaluate change at the SANG?
5   What kinds of new museum practices do black artists call for to create substantive change at the SANG? How can partnerships with other Iziko museums have an impact? Do you agree with McGee that taboo conventional museum practice should be examined and perhaps utilized to meet the needs of black South Africans? Why is deaccessioning considered taboo in most western museums? Discuss the impact, both positive and negative, of deaccessioning at the SANG.
6   Compare the approaches of McGee and Moira Simpson (chapter 6) to cultural self-determination. Does McGee advocate a more radical response to neocolonialism than does Simpson? Or are the focuses of McGee (challenge/rethink all aspects of the museum) and Simpson (appropriate what's useful and transform it to meet the community's needs) more similar than different?
7   How is McGee's definition of transformation in the museum different from that of Chris Bruce (chapter 5)? What would the administration at Experience Music Project have to do to create the kind of revolutionary change McGee calls for in South Africa? Or are the contexts of the two museums so different that comparing them is inappropriate?
8   What lessons does McGee's discussion of the SANG hold for other museums trying to affect change? What about Monticello (chapter 4)? Should museums always be in a state of change?

Notes

1   E. Berman. (1983). *Art and Artists of South Africa: An Illustrated Biographical Dictionary and Historical Survey of Painters, Sculptors and Graphic Artists since 1875*. Halfway House: Southern Book Publishers, pp. 1–2.

2   Berman, *Art and Artists of South Africa*, p. 366.

3   Twenty-one of the original 45 works in the Butterworth Bayley Bequest remain in the SANG collection. Works deemed of low quality were sold during the directorship of Edward Roworth in 1947.

4   In 1895 the collection was under the control of the Cape Colonial government and in 1932, as the SANG, it became a state-aided institution. The history of the SANG is described in various places. See Berman, *Art and Artists of South Africa*, pp. 376–8; M. Bull. (1975). *One Hundred Years Ago: An Exhibition to Commemorate the Opening of the "Cape Town Art Gallery" in New Street*. Cape Town: SANG; M. Martin. (1997). *Contemporary South African Art 1985–1995 from the South African National Gallery Permanent Collection*. Cape Town: SANG, p. 17; J. Dolby. (1981). "A Short History of the South African National Gallery," *Lantern* (December), 37–50.

5   Dolby, "Short History," p. 42.

6   For the history of acquisitions and the policies established in 1980 and 1996, see Martin, *Contemporary South African Art*, pp. 38–9.

7   "ReCollection: 130 Years of Acquiring Art for the Nation (1871–2001)," curated by Hayden Proud.

8   Emphasis added. Wall text, "ReCollection," SANG, 2002.

9   Wall text, "ReCollection," SANG, 2002.

10 In addition to our own interviews, an October 2002 survey of practicing black artists in Cape Town produced similar results. The survey was commissioned by BLAC, Cape Town, and executed and written by Mgcineni Sobopha.

11 The Community Art Project (CAP), an NGO once identified as a "struggle institution," is the oldest fine and performing arts education center in Cape Town with an open admissions policy. Its student population consists primarily of black South Africans, with a growing number of non-black students. Almost all practicing black fine and performing artists in Cape Town today spent part of their early career at CAP. The SANG admissions policy was a constant issue for the artists we interviewed and was reiterated in a recent survey of black visual artists in Cape Town (October, 2002) undertaken by BLAC and Mgcineni Sobopha. Presently, admission to the gallery is free on Sundays.

12 The SANG does not employ full-time translators, or outsource translation, which would be needed if all educational material were to be in three languages. Additionally, the language of art itself requires knowledge of art and its history.

13 M. Martin. (2001). "What's Wrong With Us?" *Mail and Guardian* (October 19–25), 4–5.

14 G. Anderson. (2002). "Transforming the 'White Giant Building,'" and B. Bell. (2002). "Transforming the 'White Giant Building:' The Tatham's Director Responds."

Artthrob, 2. www.artthrob.co.za/02mar/news/tatham_bell.html. Both essays previously published in the *Natal Witness*.

15 Anderson, "Transforming the 'White Giant Building.'"

16 Details of Sir Abe Bailey's life, the Bequest, and its significance to the SANG collection are discussed in A. Tietze (2001). "The Culture of the Countryside: Sir Abe Bailey and his Collection." In *The Sir Abe Bailey Bequest: A Reappraisal*. Cape Town: SANG, 2–21. The publication was prepared in conjunction with a new installation of a portion of the Bequest, curated by Hayden Proud.

17 Nochlin referred to the works in the Bailey Bequest as "tenth-rate foxhunting scenes." L. Nochlin. (1995). "Learning from the 'Black Male,'" *Art in America*, 83: 3, 91. Both Hayden Proud and Anna Tietze note criticisms prompted by the Bequest and Proud quotes at length from Nochlin's *Art in America* review. See *The Sir Abe Bailey Bequest*, p. 1.

18 T. Goniwe. (2001). "South African Art: Institutional Control," *BLAC On-Line* (August 4), www.mweb.co.za.blaconline.

19 M. Martin. (1991). "Transforming the National Gallery." In B. Atkinson and C. Breitz (eds.). *Grey Areas: Representation, Identity and Politics in Contemporary South African Art*. Johannesburg: Chalkham Hill Press, 145–52, p. 146.

20 Garth Erasmus, personal interview, Cape Town, 2002.

21 Now concluded, the Truth and Reconciliation Commission (TRC) was created in 1995 "to enable South Africans to come to terms with the past on a morally accepted basis." Mission as defined by former minister of justice Dullah Omar, quoted on the Commission's website www.doj.gov.za/trc.

22 M. Martin. (1995). "Introduction." In *District Six: Image and Representation*. Cape Town: South African National Gallery, 7.

23 M. Martin. (1997). "Art in the *Now* South Africa: Facing Truth and Transformation." In K. Geers. (ed.). *Contemporary South African Art: The Gencor Collection*. Johannesburg: Jonathan Ball, 131–49, p. 136; and Martin, "Transforming the National Gallery," pp. 145–52.

24 The latter two exhibitions, "FACE VALUE: Old Heads in Modern Masks," curated by Malcolm Payne (November, 1993), and "Miscast: Negotiating Khoisan History and Material Culture," created by Pippa Skotnes (April, 1996) are creative and intellectually crafty. Yet, though they have attracted significant attention from academics interested in the contested terrain of exhibition theory, they, along with the other exhibitions, appear to have done little to engender real change institutionally.

25 Martin, "Transforming the National Gallery," p. 145.

26 M. Martin. (1993). "Foreword." In *Ezakwantu: Beadwork from the Eastern Cape*. Cape Town: SANG, 6–7. Martin discusses the post-1990 acquisition of beadwork and the "African Art Heritage Collection" in "Introduction," *Contemporary South African Art 1985–1995*, 17–25, pp. 19, 25 note 4.

27 To summarize their responses: so little, really too little, has changed. Whites who were in control remain in control. The power to shape, control, and shift art practices still belongs to whites in South Africa. Blacks are not central to the intellectual input of

arts institutions and their supporting, legitimizing educational bodies. These institutions remain "too white" in terms of power and "too foreign" and unwelcoming.

28 While Iziko differentiates 15 museums or sites, these divisions are less apparent to museum visitors. For example, to visit the Planetarium one enters the SA Museum. The South African Cultural History Museum is the Slave Lodge, but also is the name for some satellite museums, such as the Bo-Kaap Museum and the Maritime Museum. Iziko groups the 15 into 3 collection types: South African social history collections, art collections, and natural history collections. See www.museums.org.za/iziko.

29 One of the most publicly noticeable and controversial decisions under Lohman's directorship was the closing of the notorious "Bushman" diorama. On display for some 42 years, the exhibit included casts of hunter-gatherers indigenous to the Cape, made in 1912 to represent racial types, and placed before a diorama representing a natural landscape. On view in the SA Museum, which specializes in animal and plant species, the diorama offended many, most notably the Cape Khosian community. Both the arts and culture minister, Ben Ngubane, and the National Khoisan Consultative Conference called for its closure, and both Lohman and the minister used the closure as an opportunity to demonstrate moves toward more democratic institutions.

30 R. Greig. (2001). "Foreign Hotshot Pulls Cape Town's Museums into the 21st Century." *Sunday Independent* (August 19), 11; W. Snyman. (2001). "Sharing Ideas with Iziko. Finnish Finesse for Our Museums." *Cape Times* (November 29), 13; L. Pollak. (2002). "Jack Lohman: Star or Damp Squib?" *Artthrob* (August 2), www.artthrob.co.za. For the "Bushman" diorama, see: (2001). "Museum Defends Closure of 'Bushman' Exhibition." *Dispatch Online* (April 6), www.dispatch.co.za/2001/04/06/southafrica/MUSEUM.html; Sapa. "Parliament, November 2, 2000." http://www.anc.org.za/newsbrief/2000/news1103.txt; P. Skotnes. "'Civilised off the Face of the Earth': Museum Display and the Silencing of the /Xam." In L. de Kock, L. Bethlehem, and S. Laden (eds.). (2004). *South Africa in the Global Imaginary*. Pretoria: UNISA Press, 32–56.

Part II | Looking to the Future: Theory into Practice

8 | THE CRITICAL MUSEUM VISITOR
Margaret Lindauer

Editor's Introduction

Margaret Lindauer is an associate professor at Virginia Commonwealth University, USA, teaching museum studies in the Department of Art History. She was awarded a 2004 postdoctoral Smithsonian Fellowship in Museum Practice to explore relationships among educational philosophies, museum practice, and new museum theory.

Lindauer takes us on a trip through the Heard Museum in Phoenix, focusing on the temporary exhibition "A Revolution in the Making: The Pottery of Maria and Julian Martinez." Using a first-person narrative, peppered with relevant facts from her own intellectual autobiography, she demonstrates how to be a critical consumer of the museum. Influenced by semiotic theory, Lindauer sees the museum as a text or script to be decoded. She looks at her prior assumptions. She engages in careful observation of details, from wall texts to spatial pathways, from websites to commemorative plaques, identifying patterns and posing questions along the way. She shows how assessing these patterns leads to insights about an institution's stated and unstated goals. In the process, she distinguishes between the ideal visitor, as imagined by the creators of the exhibition, and the critical museum visitor, informed by museum theory. Lindauer argues that visitors who embrace critical museum theory have the power to effect change in the institution. She envisions a new museum model that declares institutional purpose, acknowledges a point of view, provides cultural context, reveals contradiction, and inspires debate.

When you visit a museum, do you ever ask yourself, "What am I doing here?" I don't mean, do you consider whether or not you would prefer to be someplace else? But rather, have you ever consciously thought about what kind of experience the museum staff has designed for you? How do you participate in that experience? Do you play the role of ideal visitor?

Exhibit developers recognize that no two individuals go through an exhibition in exactly the same way. But developers also conduct market analyses and assess audience demographics as a means to envision a typical and/or ideal visitor to whom the museum tailors its programs. A typical visitor represents the average of all visitors in terms of education, socioeconomic status, racial or ethnic identity, and previous museum experience, whereas an ideal visitor is one who would be ideologically and culturally at home in the exhibition or politically comfortable with the information that is presented.

I'm interested in fostering a third category: the critical museum visitor, who studies how the visual, written, and spatial features of an exhibition collectively implicate an ideal visitor. This is entirely different from assessing actual audience reactions and characterizing the typical visitor. The critical museum visitor notes what objects are presented, in what ways, and for what purposes. She or he also explores what is left unspoken or kept off display. And she or he asks, who has the most to gain or the most to lose from having this information, collection, or interpretation publicly presented?

This chapter takes students through the preliminary process of creating an exhibition critique. I've structured the chapter to go back and forth between posing investigative questions and responding to those questions with observations from my own visit to "A Revolution in the Making: The Pottery of Maria and Julian Martinez," a temporary exhibition displayed at the Heard Museum in Phoenix, Arizona, May 5–September 14, 2003. I conclude with brief comments regarding the transition from gathering observations to structuring a critique. I also characterize the relationship of critical museum visitors to new museum theory and exhibition practice.

Before the Visit

After you've selected an exhibit to visit but before you go, consciously describe your expectations, hopes, and assumptions. (In fact, during every stage of observation, notice what you are doing, thinking, and deciding as you proceed.) Think both broadly, about museums in general, and specifically, about the exhibit you've selected. For example, what does the very word "museum" mean to you? In 1985, archeologist and museum curator Nick Merriman asked museum visitors and non-visitors across Britain to identify what type of institution most closely resembles museums – school, church, library, monument to the dead, department store, community center, or something else.[1] Do any of these comparisons resonate with you? In the realm of popular culture, movies and novels cast the museum as a place of mystery, intrigue, monsters, and murder. Do these descriptions more accurately describe your attitude toward (or hope for) museums?

Think about the title of the exhibit you're going to see. What do the individual words, phrases, and names mean to you? Why have you selected this particular display? Does it appeal to a special interest or hobby of yours? Does it sound like a fun place to take your family or out-of-town guests? Would you likely invite your friends to go along? If you're going for the sole purpose of completing a class assignment, what specifically draws you to one exhibition over all possible others, and why would you otherwise not attend?

My pre-visit observations

I carry lots of professional baggage to my museum visits. I began my museum career in the mid-1980s as a graduate assistant in a university art museum while I was working on a Master of Fine Arts degree in studio art. I helped install short-term traveling art exhibitions and displays of faculty and graduate student work. In retrospect, I would characterize my job as creating aesthetic experiences for visitors. Shortly after completing my MFA, I began working in an anthropology museum, where the primary purpose of exhibits was to explain anthropological concepts or phenomena. Aesthetics still mattered, but in the service of explanatory effectiveness. I initially embraced the new challenge but gradually grew bored with the aesthetics of didacticism. So I started visiting other museums in search of new ideas for presenting objects, histories, and people.

My quest for professional inspiration coincided with the emergence of new museum theory, which explained how exhibits that illustrate aesthetic concepts, cultural phenomena, and historical events also enact social relations of power. Essays on new museum theory affected my visits; I became a critical museum visitor. I began noticing when exhibits presented a European, masculine, and/or economically privileged perspective as if it were a singularly authoritative account of diverse arts, histories, and cultures around the world. And I occasionally discovered displays that addressed a call from new museum theory for curators to clarify the perspectives from which they present knowledge and/or invite alternative, multiple, or contradictory points of view.

205

Overall, I like going to museums because, regardless of whether or not I like the exhibitions, they're always a catalyst for interesting conversations. I'm drawn to visiting "A Revolution in the Making: The Pottery of Maria and Julian Martinez" partly because I know a little bit about Maria and Julian Martinez, whose valuable ceramic creations played a significant role in the historical development of the Native American art market. But I'm not familiar with the details of their lives or the specific ways in which their pottery contributed to broader aesthetic trends during a complex historical period of US–Native American social and political relations. So I expect that I'll learn something new.

The exhibition title, however, has me a bit bewildered. "Revolution" is a strong word – connoting either something radically new (a ground-breaking change, development, or transformation) or a dramatic, usually violent overthrow of governmental administration (synonymous with rebellion, insurrection, or mutiny). Of course, when I consider the exhibit title in relationship to what I already know about Maria and Julian Martinez, I assume that the intended meaning relates to a development in the Native American art market. But I wonder why museum staff would select a word with such strong connotations. Did they intend to circumscribe an audience that already has some knowledge about the history of the south-western Native American pottery market? Did they also intend to titillate the imaginations of out-of-town and international visitors (a primary audience for the Heard Museum) who may harbor outdated stereotypes of south-western US history as a sequence of battles, mutinies, and revolts among cowboys and Indians?

I put these questions in the back of my mind as I embark on my visit, reminding myself that my main goal is to understand how the individual features of an exhibition work together to create a whole. The slightly ambiguous title is one feature. And while I may find other characteristics to be confusing, unsettling, or even perhaps prejudiced in some way, I also will look for aspects of the exhibition that are impressive, interesting, or creatively executed.

Museum Architecture

When you hear the word "museum," does a particular architectural image come to mind? Does the museum you're visiting correspond to that image? As you embark on your visit, consider the building itself and its location within a community or region as part of your experience.

Does the building architecturally mimic another kind of institution? If so, what unspoken messages are sent? Art historians Carol Duncan and Alan Wallach have suggested that art museums with exterior facades inspired by Greco-Roman temples metaphorically allude to the beginning of western civilization. Duncan and Wallach argued that this temporal reference is politically significant when the sequence of primary exhibitions celebrates Euro-American art and marginalizes Oceanic, Native American, African, Asian, and Latino art works by exhibiting them in secondary galleries.[2] The spatial relationship between primary and secondary galleries connotes a cultural hierarchy (western civilization above all others) encased in a quintessentially Euro-American architectural structure. What cultural/temporal connotations are inscribed in the architectural facade of the museum you're visiting?

Perhaps you're visiting a museum in a renovated storefront, electrical plant, royal palace, office building, or private home. What are the implications of these transformations? Do they relate thematically to the exhibits presented inside? Maybe the museum you're visiting is architecturally distinct, a work of art in and of itself. Art critic Douglas Davis suggests that large urban museums built since the late twentieth century serve two purposes. They architecturally announce that they are unique places filled with irreplaceable objects, and they are designed to attract a demographically diverse audience with a suite of entertainment options including restaurants, outdoor gardens, shops, movie theaters, and auditoriums. However, as Davis notes, they don't always successfully communicate a union of exclusivity and populism.[3] They may intimidate non-visitors who are culturally ill at ease or unschooled in postmodern architectural appreciation.

Does the architectural design of the museum you're visiting inscribe any contradiction between style and intent? How do *you* feel as you approach and enter? Are you calm, agitated, contemplative, or confused? Do you feel cultured, sophisticated, herded, under surveillance, or enlightened? What specific architectural features instill your reactions?

Heard Museum architecture

The first time I visited the Heard Museum, in 1989, I recently had moved to the Phoenix area and was just learning my way around. Because of the museum's international reputation for having a pre-eminent collection of Native American art, I expected it to be prominently located and fairly easy to find. But I had some difficulty, partly because Phoenix did not have a distinct urban center but also because the museum was located on a minor

207

FIGURE 8.1   Heard Museum, Phoenix. Photograph by Margaret Lindauer

side street and adjacent to an affluent neighborhood of expansive homes and immaculately landscaped lawns.

Dwight and Maie Heard built the museum – a white stucco building with red tile roof, central courtyard, and arched promenade – on their estate grounds. It was designed to complement architecturally their 6,000-square-foot, Spanish-Colonial-revival-style house and blend into the neighborhood. The result, completed in 1928, accordingly embodied the human scale of a private (albeit upscale) home and epitomized the Spanish Colonial revival style. The museum has expanded several times since it first opened, most significantly in 1999 when it doubled in size (to its current 130,000 square feet) and reoriented its entrance to face Central Avenue, the main north–south street through downtown Phoenix. What it lost in intimacy it gained in street recognition and stature. The new building is set back from the street, with an enormous, grassy, open-air amphitheater separating it spatially and aurally from traffic noise (figure 8.1). The scale is now institutional rather than human and seems appropriate to the museum's international renown. But insofar as its exterior features (white walls, red tile roof, central courtyard, and arched promenade) mimic the museum's original Spanish Colonial revival style, it architecturally recalls the colonial invasion of North America which resulted, by the end of the nineteenth century, in the assumption that American Indians would soon be an extinct race. The cultural/temporal connotation metaphorically contradicts the museum's mission to celebrate and sustain Native American artists and communities, prompting the question: do the museum's displays reconcile and/or reiterate this contradiction?

The question lurks in my mind as I proceed beyond the U-shaped exterior facade that faces Central Avenue and into the distinctly south-western central courtyard, with shaded promenade surrounding desert landscaping, outdoor dining tables, and two linear water fountains (extending perhaps 75 feet) directed toward a life-size white marble sculpture of an Indian drummer situated in front of the museum's main entrance. The gentle sound of flowing water and the speckled light shining through the tiny leaves of desert trees ideally create a soothing transition from everyday urban life to contemplative art appreciation. But two small but conspicuous, silver-colored commemorative plaques that read "The Honorable & Mrs. John Pritzlaff Jr. Courtyard" and "Reflecting Pool made possible by Fred and Ann Lynn," as well as the large sign above the museum's main entrance, "Nina Mason Pulliam Pavilion," disrupt my aesthetic experience. I understand that museums typically honor individual and corporate donors, but when that honor *introduces* an appreciation of Native American art, who are the museum's primary constituents? Do these financial sponsors allude to the museum's ideal visitor? I file these questions alongside my uncertainty about the museum's architectural style and my reservations about the exhibition title as I continue making observations.

Display Style

When I enter an exhibit as a critical museum visitor, I begin by characterizing the display style. I often use the 1988 exhibit entitled "Art/artifact," produced at the Center for African Art in New York, as an initial frame of reference. Susan Vogel, the exhibit curator, explained that "Art/artifact" juxtaposed four approaches to displaying similar kinds of utilitarian and/or spiritually imbued African artifacts from diverse cultures.[4] In one section, objects were grouped together in display cases modeled after anthropology exhibits that explain technical, social, or religious functions. Another section represented an art exhibition – a room with white walls and pedestals upon which individual objects were placed, spatially isolated from one another to accentuate aesthetic qualities. A third section included a diorama displaying three life-size mannequins fabricated to look like African men adorned with and surrounded by artifacts. The diorama did not single out any particular object, or even the objects as a whole, but rather alluded generally to the interrelationships of material culture, social interaction, and environment. And finally, a collector's den re-created the c.1905 "curiosity room" at the Hampton Institute in Hampton, Virginia, presenting an abundance of artifacts in dark wooden cases and frames that matched the room's wainscoting and furniture. In this section, the collection as a whole connoted the Euro-American collector's wealth and presumed worldliness, overwhelming the diverse cultural significations associated with relationships between objects and their makers/users. Because similar kinds of artifacts were displayed in each of the four sections, "Art/artifact" demonstrated that display methods impose social, cultural, or historical meaning upon objects.

Does the exhibition you're critiquing invoke any of these display styles? Be aware that some installations may blur the lines between academic disciplines, and design trends have changed significantly since 1988, when "Art/artifact" was produced. For example, natural history museums have developed immersion environments in which visitors walk through larger-than-life dioramas. And hands-on manipulative devices and interactive computer programs, ubiquitous in science centers, often are incorporated into art, anthropology, or history exhibitions.

Focus on design elements – wall color, lighting, font style, physical barriers between audience and artifacts, and spatial relationships of objects to one another – and note how these elements influence the way you move through the display. At first, consider explanatory text panels and audiovisual components as spatial visual features, reserving close scrutiny of written messages until a second walk through the display. How does the display style influence the way you think about objects? And in what ways does it inscribe an ideal visitor who would be ideologically and culturally at home in the exhibition?

Display style of "A Revolution in the Making"

I see, immediately upon entering, that "A Revolution in the Making" models an art display style. An array of Native American pottery is presented individually or in small groups upon 10 freestanding pedestals covered with plexiglass vitrines. And a selection of shallow bowls is displayed on a two-sided vertical display case (figure 8.2). My gaze rests briefly on the largest pot, which stands slightly more than 2 feet high and is situated just inside the entrance. My eye then dances among the other vessels, which range from approximately 10 to 20 inches high and are dispersed throughout the relatively small gallery (measuring perhaps 40 feet by 40 feet). Highly polished black vessels decorated with matte black designs are interspersed among buff (yellowish) colored pots with black- and/or red-painted designs. Most of the shapes mimic historically utilitarian vessels – jars and bowls of various depths.

FIGURE 8.2 "A Revolution in the Making: The Pottery of Maria and Julian Martinez," exhibition, Heard Museum, Phoenix, 2003. Photograph by Margaret Lindauer

The visual impact of the pottery is so overwhelming that at first I don't even notice the didactic components – explanatory text panels, identification labels, black-and-white photographs, and a descriptive video placed in the corner behind the vertical display case. The introductory text panel is placed across the room from the entrance to the gallery. Thus I am not compelled to read and then look but rather encouraged to aesthetically appreciate and then, perhaps, investigate the written information. A single identification label is placed on each pedestal, angled slightly to make it easy to read through the plexiglass but not so much that the written words are visually obvious from a distance. When several pots are placed together on a single pedestal, small black circles with white numbers are placed slightly below and next to each vessel. These numbers – which also are not noticeable from a distance – correspond to a list on the single label inside each vitrine. Words again are set apart from objects, encouraging viewers to experience the size, shape, style, texture, and painted decoration of pots before reading descriptions.

While the presentation of pottery clearly follows an art-display style, the overall gallery ambience also subtly suggests (but does not mimic) a collector's den. Visitors enter through opened French doors, with glass panels framed

211

by dark wood. A second set of French doors, which leads to the exterior of the museum (but remains closed and is clearly labeled as an emergency exit), allows natural light into the gallery, diffusing the spotlights directed to each pedestal. The vertical surfaces of richly stained wooden pedestals have slightly raised central panels with beveled edges. Their horizontal surfaces (upon which the pots are displayed) extend slightly beyond the vertical panels, like a household table or buffet chest. Indeed they look more like fine pieces of Mission-style furniture than institutionally neutral display cases. Three of the walls are painted pale yellow – the room is not the stereotypic white cube sometimes found in art museums. The fourth wall is painted a dark slate blue that visually enlarges the small gallery space. The concrete floor is stained a brick-red color that visually softens the texture and mimics the hue of the *saltillo* clay tiles found inside countless south-western homes.

Even the descriptive video feels like a domestic accoutrement. A small television monitor stands on one of the richly stained wooden pedestals tucked into the last corner that visitors approach as they typically move through the gallery in a circular path. The black-and-white video, which plays only when visitors press the "start" button, obviously is dated, produced well before Maria's death in 1980. The monotone male narrator's voice reminds me of old public television presentations. Even when the video is playing, it does not overwhelm the ambience of the gallery, especially because there is very little room for visitors to gather in front of the monitor.

Insofar as the documentary film culturally contextualizes pottery making, it blurs the line between display styles, from an art display (with hints of domestic interior) to an anthropological approach. In the opening scene Maria Martinez speaks in her native language while gathering clay. The voice-over narration explains that she spiritually expresses gratitude to the earth. Scenes from San Ildefonso Pueblo, where the Martinez family has lived, visually reiterate cultural context. The narration, however, focuses on the pottery-making process, illustrated three-dimensionally on a wall shelf next to the video monitor (which I didn't notice until reaching the end of the exhibit). This shelf displays pottery-making tools in front of small black-and-white photos that illustrate stages of pottery production.

In terms of display style, the exhibition's ideal visitor would feel at home admiring Native American pottery and might be a little bit curious about how the pots were made. The occasional conversations among numerous actual visitors attending the exhibit while I am there bear this out. For example, one woman says to her companion, "Oh, I want that one. Isn't it beautiful." Another visitor asks her friend, "This reminds me of your collection; don't you have some like this?" And one man, while watching the video, says to his mate, "I wonder if she signed the pots before they were fired." The predominantly white middle-class visitors appear to be intellectually, aesthetically, and culturally satisfied with the visually conservative, domestically soothing display style. I file this observation in my mind, alongside my questions about the exhibition title, museum architecture, and primary constituents, as I turn my attention to the written text.

Written Texts and Unspoken Messages

In terms of writing style, museum exhibitions historically have tended to be didactic – asserting factual information and exuding an aura of truth or respected knowledge. Even when written text poses questions, queries may be merely rhetorical and followed by informative response. Literary critic Mieke Bal calls this museum didacticism "truth-speak" and argues that it invokes social/cultural relations of power, insofar as it shows off curatorial expertise while devaluing perspectives among people whose work is on display.[5]

New museum theory calls for exhibit developers to debate such questions as: whose knowledge should be disseminated? Who decides? How are the decisions made? These kinds of questions are absent from technically oriented publications outlining how to develop exhibits that effectively transmit information. For example, museum consultant Beverly Serrell states that introductory wall texts for exhibitions should focus on one "big idea [that] provides an unambiguous focus . . . stating in a noncompound sentence the scope and purpose of the exhibition."[6] She advises that object labels start with concrete visual information and extend to no more than 50 words. While this is sound technical advice, it does not encourage museum professionals to ask who benefits from having the selected "big idea" featured in a museum. Does the celebration of some "big ideas" implicitly sustain political inequities among people of diverse social, economic, cultural, or racial histories?

The critical museum visitor, drawing from new museum theory, focuses on the political implications of written text. As you study text panels and object labels, notice the writing style, word choice, and theme. Read between the lines. Whose knowledge is presented? What is explicitly asserted and what is implied or unspoken? Does the text invoke an anonymous expert's voice? To whom does it speak and for what purpose? Look at narrative structure and descriptive or explanatory content. Does it lead you to a state of intrigue, boredom, receptivity, devotion, anger, or reflexivity? If the exhibition includes multiple voices, do they represent a range of perspectives, a point/counterpoint, or a harmonious reiteration of a single point of view? Does the text *encourage* you to develop your own informed opinion? In what ways does the writing style invite and/or dissuade from a dialogue of ideas?

Written text in "A Revolution in the Making"

The first line of the introductory text panel in "A Revolution in the Making" proclaims, "Maria and Julian Martinez revolutionized the look of pottery when they created the black-on-black pottery style around 1918." As I suspected in advance of my visit, "revolution" refers to a ground-breaking development in the Native American art market, but I look to the written text in vain for an account of how that change came about. I'd like to know what social, cultural, or financial factors influenced and were influenced by the Martinezes' ceramic innovations. Instead the introductory text follows its pronouncement with disconnected reiterative details: polished blackware pottery had been made at San Ildefonso and nearby pueblos before 1918, but it was not decorated with matte black designs; Julian painted vessels that Maria made and polished; the black-on-black colored finish results from a particular outdoor firing process; and Maria and Julian Martinez "had a tremendous impact on Pueblo pottery making that continues today."

I am not surprised that the didactic text systematically answers unspoken questions of who, what, where, when, and how (but not why) with simple facts. But as a critical museum visitor I'd like to read an engaging narrative that encourages an exchange of ideas or fosters the development of individual opinions and various points of view. Instead, I am left wondering: why should I care? To whom is this litany of authoritative facts relevant?

The anonymous author seems to address me as if I were a potential collector who might learn to covet the celebrated artists' work. So I decide to adopt an imaginary persona of novice collector as I walk to one of two secondary text panels (located on a wall adjacent to the introductory text). The panel lists significant events in the artists' careers. "These are fun facts," I tell my make-believe self, "to share with friends who might admire the collection I plan to amass."

During my visit, a museum guide led a tour group into the gallery and whetted my imaginary-collector's appetite with slightly more embellished narratives than the reserved assertions offered by written text: Maria was known for making vessels of a particular shape that no one else could master; other artists commanded certain techniques but could not duplicate some of the colors that Julian created; and, fortunately, the couple's children and grand-children inherited great talent and have carried on the family pottery-making fame. As the guide escorted people out of the room, she pointed to the large pot near the entrance and delightfully shared some insider know-ledge: The museum purchased this Maria Martinez pot in 1926 for two hundred and fifty dollars; today it's worth at least a half-million! I fantasize, "Wouldn't it be great if I could invest so wisely? I wonder what bargains might be found in today's market."

I began to scrutinize the object labels for information that might inform my anticipated purchases and discovered that the exhibit subtitle, "The Pot-tery of Maria and Julian Martinez," had misled me to believe that all of the pots on display were made by the celebrated couple. In fact some of their descendants, many of whom are still alive but not yet famous, created perhaps as many as half of the exhibited works. The critical observer in me silently derided this bait-and-switch technique wherein unfamiliar names like Barbara and Cavan Gonzales gain the cachet of Martinez fame. But my imaginary persona relished the thought that their works might be affordable and appreciate monetarily, as did the work of their great-grandparents.

The object labels offer standard art-historical information (or provenance) including maker's name, cultural affiliation, years of birth and death (or just year of birth if the maker is still alive), object type (e.g., jar, bowl, plate), the year in which it was made, and name of the collector who donated or loaned the object to the Heard Museum.

I realized that approximately two-thirds of the pots are on loan to the museum and embellished my fantasy, "Wouldn't it be great if I had a collec-tion that the Heard Museum wanted to borrow and display?" But the critical observer in me (recalling the commemorative plaques displayed in the exte-rior courtyard) disparagingly mused: exactly who is being celebrated here, as the list of 19 donors and lenders outnumbers the list of 8 artists?

I continued to study the object labels, noting that they also indicate how each vessel is signed. This information relates to the other secondary text panel (across the room from the list of significant career events), which presents a chronology of signatures found on the pottery. This information appeals to collectors' interests, although the exhibition does not explain that signature and provenance partly determine monetary value. Some object labels also include a short paragraph, offering information about a particular design, where a pot was purchased, or further biographical information about the artists. All of these factual tidbits, quickly digested and easily regurgitated, are unquestionably of great interest to my make-believe persona. But the

215

critical observer in me, who repeatedly disrupts my fantasy, notes that neither the secondary text panels nor the object labels explicitly relate back to the purported exhibition theme of a revolution in the making. But they do complement the exhibition's display style, which emphasizes aesthetic qualities of the pots and alludes to a collector's den.

In brief, the text instills respect for connoisseurship, compels ideal visitors to admire the pots, and implicitly lauds the collectors who have lent or donated their purchases to the museum. For visitors who already have an aesthetic interest in south-western Native American pottery, the gallery is a visual delight augmented with delectably factual tidbits. Insofar as the exhibit does not support an academic assertion, tell an engaging story, encourage an exchange of informed opinions, or contextualize the pottery within a social, cultural, or political history, it situates the visitor as a passive consumer of simple, undisputed information rather than as intellectually engaged participant. I include this interpretation among my ongoing list of observations and questions as I proceed to investigate the social, cultural, and financial issues that the exhibition does not address.

Beyond the Display

Exhibit critiques that offer well-reasoned recommendations potentially can influence museum practice. This involves looking beyond the particular display you're critiquing in order to propose suggestions that seem compatible with the museum's mission, yet are not included in the exhibit.

Explore other resources – journal essays, monographs, newspapers, visual or literary art works, and other documents – to identify issues, ideas, and perspectives that are absent from the exhibit you are critiquing. Think about how to frame these ideas in ways that address the call from new museum theory for curators to clarify the perspectives from which they present knowledge and/or invite alternative, multiple, or contradictory points of view.

Look at the museum's brochures, gallery guides, and website to discern its mission. Does the literature identify an institutional purpose – perhaps to educate, memorialize, celebrate, explore, and/or protect? What is the museum's primary subject matter, collection, or range of academic disciplines? What audiences, cultural groups, or artists are identified as principal constituents?

Walk through other exhibits within the museum. Do you find a range of display styles under one roof, or does it appear as if the exhibit developers are constrained to follow a standard institutional approach? In what ways do extant styles accommodate the ideas you're recommending? In your opinion, what are the most daunting obstacles – in terms of mission and current practice – that museum staff receptive to your ideas likely would face? Given these obstacles, how would you characterize the museum's ability to enact new museum theory in its practice?

Beyond "A Revolution in the Making"

The pottery of Maria and Julian Martinez was part of an *economic* revolution that sustained aesthetic and cultural traditions, which cannot be fully appreciated without also acknowledging the ways in which nineteenth-century US policies economically devastated Native American communities.

By 1848, when the US seized Mexico's northern territories (including current-day New Mexico, in which San Ildefonso Pueblo is located), American Indians in the region had been fighting (first Spain, then Mexico) for three hundred years. They battled against their lands being expropriated, their religions targeted for extinction, and their community members sold into slavery. US conquest brought a new adversary, and American Indians resisted US squatters' claims just as fervently as they had fought Spanish and Mexican aggression.[7]

After the Civil War, US military tactics shifted from eradicating Native people to containing them on federally assigned reservations. Twenty years later, during the 1880s, official US policy shifted again, away from containment to assimilation. The federal government established Indian boarding schools located beyond reservations, in which Native Americans were required (sometimes through the imposition of physical force) to enroll their children.[8] When children arrived at the schools (some of which were hundreds or thousands of miles from their homes), they were constrained to dress in school uniforms; cut or style their hair according to Euro-American cultural standards; march military style from their beds to the parade grounds, cafeteria, and classrooms; relinquish all vestiges of their religious beliefs; and refrain from speaking their native languages.

Assimilation policies also included the 1887 General Allotment Act, through which reservations were broken into multiple tracts of land, each of which was assigned to an individual tribal member. The Act was designed to "teach" American Indians to think like property owners.[9] Once all tribal members had been allotted a tract, the "surplus" was available to non-Indian buyers. Prior to allotment, American Indian communities operated within subsistence economies in which they produced what they needed, cultivating food and making household tools, ceremonial materials, and trade goods from communal resources. Allotment left American Indian communities with an insufficient land base for subsistence production. By 1920 only six farmers in San Ildefenso Pueblo cultivated enough food to feed their families.[10] Thus many community members had little choice but to work away from home as wage laborers for industrial corporations or government agencies. Native American pottery, basket, and textile production declined at the same time as the US government issued annuity goods – industrially produced household products – to "compensate" for economic devastation. The vast, intercultural trade network that pre-dated the Spanish invasion of the region eventually dissolved.

Maria and Julian Martinez played a primary role in re-establishing the Native American pottery-making industry, through which some families rose above poverty without having to leave their communities to work for private corporations or government agencies. But this economic revolution also carried an intercultural political cost, because it developed alongside a burgeoning tourist industry spurred by the construction of cross-continental railroads and the rise of a Euro-American middle class. Travel brochures and advertisements featured romantic images of peaceful Indians producing handmade crafts in visually stunning landscapes.[11] These images supplanted stereotypes of savage, uncivilized people, which had circulated as the US enacted its policies of eradication, containment, and assimilation. But the images also inscribed stereotypes of static primitive cultures frozen in pre-industrial time. Tourist companies hired Native people to dress in traditional clothing, perform mock-ceremonial dances, and demonstrate traditional craft-making techniques.

The tourist industry bolsters Euro-American cultural domination, as sociologist Dean MacCannell argues, when it presents a "spectacle of a beautiful and frozen innocence lost."[12] In the realm of popular opinion, iconic stereotypes of American Indians put Native communities at a political disadvantage when historic and contemporary economic issues – water and mineral rights, land use, education, health care, and tribal sovereignty – are negotiated among US and Native American governments. Essayist and poet Gloria Bird, a member of the Spokane tribe, accordingly urges Native American writers to tell stories that serve a useful purpose rather than merely parading ethnicity.[13]

The presentation and ongoing production of traditional Native American arts inscribe a paradox, which poet and ceramicist Nora Noranjo-Morse, a member of Santa Clara Pueblo, mocks in her poems "Mudwoman's First Encounter with the World of Money and Business" and "The Living Exhibit Under the Museum's Portal."[14] On the one hand, American Indian artisans have generated prosperity from their business acumen, taking stock of what kinds of designs appeal to a tourist and collectors' market. On the other hand, their acumen often is overshadowed by a stereotypic notion that American Indian cultures are stuck in pre-industrial time and therefore less advanced than Euro-American social systems through which political issues are negotiated.

Could the Heard Museum present an exhibition that simultaneously instills admiration for the aesthetic beauty of Martinez family pottery, explores the historical context of a culturally, community-based economic revolution, and acknowledges the intercultural paradox in which contemporary Native American artists work? The museum's website explicitly states, "The mission and philosophy of the Heard Museum today is to educate the public about the heritage and the living cultures and arts of Native peoples, with an emphasis on the peoples of the Southwest."[15] This broad declaration certainly does not preclude such a presentation. And one of its long-term exhibitions, entitled "Remembering Our Indian School Days: The Boarding School Experience" (November 15, 2000–January 1, 2005), instills some optimism.

The display begins with a curved hallway, both sides of which are covered from floor to ceiling with collages of historic black-and-white photographs of Indian children depicted before and after they were removed from their families, enrolled in boarding schools, and forcibly dressed and coiffed in Euro-American cultural styles. A cacophony of voices recalling the children's experiences saturates the hallway. Text panels also present first-person accounts, juxtaposing various font sizes or styles in order to emphasize unsettling school policies. For example, the text panel situated behind an old barber's chair (below which the floor is covered with straight black hair) reads, in part:

The next day **the torture
began**. The first thing they did was cut our hair . . .
We'd **lost our hair
and we'd lost our clothes**.
With the bath we'd **lost our
identity as Indians**.

From the hallway, visitors proceed into a re-created dormitory room and classroom and then on to displays of athletic trophies, band uniforms, and

219

first-person accounts by former students who attended boarding schools in the mid-twentieth century. The horrific effect of the introduction to the exhibit gradually is assuaged as these former students reminisce fondly about school rivalries, a budding romance, academic accomplishments, old friends, and clandestine excursions off school grounds – events that might have happened at any school.

The exhibition presents a paradoxical history. On the one hand, the philosophy of assimilation enacted in Indian boarding schools is reprehensible in a nation that claims tolerance for cultural diversity. On the other hand, recent graduates appreciate the ways in which their education prepared them to live in two worlds. Thus the exhibit neither reduces American Indians to mere victims nor disavows Euro-American culpability for sociocultural injustices. But my hope – that the Heard Museum can practice new museum theory, creating a place where horrific historic events, social injustices, and cultural prejudices are analyzed, at the same time as art works are appreciated and visitors are encouraged to debate processes through which social inequalities might be disrupted – is guarded.

As I walk through other current exhibits, I find that the Heard Museum primarily addresses a non-Indian public and instills aesthetic appreciation of Native American art works. It appeals especially to children and families, with numerous hands-on craft projects scattered throughout two of its largest exhibits. These projects unfortunately risk reducing symbolic cultural production to facile activities in which anyone can participate. The museum purports to teach the public about living cultures, yet grossly simplifies concepts of identity and difference, especially in its long-term exhibition entitled "We Are! Arizona's First People" (January 1, 2000–January 1, 2005). This display includes 21 cubicle-like stations, each of which briefly characterizes one federally recognized tribe in Arizona with five to seven short paragraphs explaining the significance of place, language, or history; two or three small objects; a hands-on activity (e.g., bead weaving, puzzle assembly, or paper-basket making); and, in some stations, a child's voice offering instructions for completing the activity.

Thus the boarding school exhibit is unlike all other Heard Museum displays. And I wonder if coincidence accounts for the fact that it's installed in the East Gallery, one of only two display areas (among eleven) not yet designated by a patron, sponsor, or trustee, whose names appear prominently on the museum's walls and in its Gallery Guide and Map.[16] Visiting the Heard Museum is like going to a movie so saturated with blatant product endorsements that you wonder whether the story line is a vehicle for commercial advertising, or vice versa. For example, the Lovena Ohl Gallery, within which "A Revolution in the Making" is displayed, honors the former Heard Museum shop manager, who now owns a gallery featuring Native American art in Scottsdale, Arizona, also named the Lovena Ohl Gallery. Thus she gains not only personal recognition but also a perpetual advertisement within the museum. In addition to nine display areas and two commemorative plaques in the exterior courtyard (which I noticed as I entered the museum), six other non-display facilities bear the names of Heard Museum sponsors.[17]

The names of Native Americans whose art works, histories, and cultures are displayed visually are upstaged, especially in the museum's printed Gallery Guide and Map, by the acknowledgment of financial donors. And this, I suspect, alludes to one obstacle that museum staff interested in enacting new museum theory might face insofar as the person who signs the check often has decision-making clout.[18] I add this conjecture and information gathered from research beyond the display to my ongoing list of questions and observations and am now ready to begin constructing a critique.

From Observation to Critique

Transforming notes from an investigative process into an exhibit critique involves recasting explorative questions into assertions that address an overarching thesis statement and are supported by observations. Look at the salient issues that you have listed during the course of pre-visit, exhibit experience, and post-visit research. In what ways do your concerns or queries relate to one another? Is there a recurrent theme or a set of themes that resonate with one another? In what ways do those themes relate to new museum theory – are they represented in the exhibition as indisputable fact, as one point of view among many, or within a point/counterpoint discussion? If the curatorial perspective is not explicit, what social relations of power are enacted through the presentation and interpretation of art works or artifacts – who has the most to gain and who has the most to lose from the particular ways in which aesthetic concepts, cultural phenomena, and historical events are represented (or left unspoken)?

Relationships between theory and practice vary widely from one exhibition to another. So it's impossible to provide a universally applicable checklist or detailed step-by-step process for transforming observations into well-argued analysis. But I can briefly describe how I would frame a critique of "A Revolution in the Making."

As I review my notes, I generate a thesis statement that the Heard Museum is immersed in and manifests multiple paradoxical relations, which collectively inhibit its potential to put new museum theory into practice. I can make a case for this thesis by organizing my observations to support four assertions. First, the Heard Museum generally celebrates the fact that Native Americans have sustained cultural traditions that historically were targeted for extinction *within* a building whose architectural style recalls the history of European colonization followed by US federal policies of eradication and assimilation. Second, the museum casts its mission as a service to Native American artists and communities *but* appeals primarily to middle-class visitors, wealthy benefactors, and corporate sponsors. Third, "A Revolution in the Making" features art works created by Martinez family members *while also* implicitly celebrating the collecting acumen of museum donors and friends, thereby encouraging culturally decontextualized aesthetic appreciation and connoisseurship. And finally, the exhibit alludes to an economic revolution *but* disavows the complex cross-cultural historical context in which that revolution occurred.

The museum's primary constituents – people who have the most to gain from the ways in which the visual, written, and unspoken features of "A Revolution in the Making" work together – can be gleaned from these paradoxical relations. Artists whose work is on display and collectors whose property is exhibited gain recognition. Museum sponsors benefit from perpetual advertisements. Novice (or vicarious) collectors gain an education in connoisseurship. And middle-class consumers enjoy a leisure-time activity that is neither intellectually taxing nor politically engaging. The museum benefits from the various constituents whom it petitions. It receives subjects and objects for display, cross-cultural endorsement of its exhibitions, financial backing for exhibit production, and an audience with disposable income who may regularly patronize the museum. Striking such a complex balance among diverse constituents is a remarkable achievement, but it does not put new museum theory into practice.

An exhibition that enacts new museum theory simultaneously would instill admiration for the aesthetic beauty of art works created by members of the Martinez family; explore the historical context of a culturally and community-based economic revolution; acknowledge the intercultural paradox in which contemporary Native American artists work; and encourage visitors to develop their own opinions about the social, cultural, aesthetic, or economic ramifications of the early twentieth-century revolutionary development in the Native American pottery production. The people with the most to gain from such an approach are the same as those with the most to lose from "A Revolution in the Making": visitors who come to the museum with an interest in how art works resonate with complex cultural historical contexts; artists whose works are more historically, culturally, and politically complex than connoisseurship suggests; and people from various societies whose contemporary lives are misunderstood when entrenched cross-cultural stereotypes are sustained and relationships among past, present, and future are oversimplified.

The Critical Museum Visitor and New Museum Theory

The Heard Museum may not be able to enact new museum theory without risking its own economic survival. It clearly enjoys an established customer base (sponsors and visitors) that endorses and consumes its current approach. Museums are unique cultural institutions but they also operate like businesses, employing professionals to develop products that satisfy their clientele. Given extant customer satisfaction, enacting new museum theory would be a business risk as well as an ideological shift. So there must be a compelling justification for change before the risk seems worthwhile. Some museum professionals disdain new museum theory. Others may be more sympathetic to critiques of traditional museum practice, but find a dearth of professional development programs focusing on *how* to conceptualize and develop exhibitions informed by new museum theory. It is a daunting task – for which there are not a lot of models – to produce exhibits that encourage informed debate, grounded in explorations of social relations, inscribed in representations of multi-faceted social, cultural, and aesthetic histories. That's why I'm interested in fostering critical museum visitors. Insofar as museum professionals may shy away from forging new ground and *because* the museum is market driven, change relies partly on audience demand. Exhibition critique – thoughtful analysis accompanied by informed recommendations – is a process through which a critical mass of critical museum visitors might develop to become agents of change.

Questions for Discussion

1   What is the significance of Lindauer's designation "the ideal museum visitor"? How does the museum construct an image of the ideal visitor?

2 What does it mean to be a critical museum visitor? What responsibilities does the critical museum visitor have? Why is it essential to consider what's absent as well as what's present?

3 What is Lindauer's assessment of "A Revolution in the Making"? What elements does she note in her assessment? How does she pull together her many detailed observations to gain larger insights into the exhibition and the museum as a whole? And what conclusions does she come to as a critical museum visitor?

4 How does Lindauer characterize the Heard's projection of its ideal visitor? What is Monticello's perception of the ideal visitor (chapter 4)? EMP's (chapter 5)? The SANG's (chapter 7)?

5 What is Lindauer's assessment of the exhibition "Remembering our Indian School Days: The Boarding School Experience"? How is the exhibition informed by new museum theory?

6 What kinds of exhibitions does new museum theory call for? What are the most important characteristics of such exhibitions? What should be the goals of museum staff planning these exhibitions ?

7 Write a mission statement for a museum committed to new museum theory.

8 What are the primary obstacles to change in the museum? What can we do to promote change?

Notes

1 N. Merriman. (1991). "The Social Basis of Museum and Heritage Visiting." In S. Pearce. (ed.). *Museum Studies in Material Culture*. Leicester: Leicester University Press; Washington, DC: Smithsonian Institution Press.

2 C. Duncan and A. Wallach. (1980). "The Universal Survey Museum." *Art History*, 3: 4, 448–69.

3 D. Davis. (1990). *The Museum Transformed: Design and Culture in the Post-Pompidou Age*. New York: Abbeville Press.

4 S. Vogel. (1991). "Always True to the Object, in Our Fashion". In I. Karp and S. Lavine (eds.). *Exhibiting Cultures: The Poetics and Politics of Museum Display*. Washington, DC: Smithsonian Institution Press, 191–204.

5 M. Bal. (1996). *Double Exposures: The Subject of Cultural Analysis*. London and New York: Routledge.

6 B. Serrell. (1996). *Exhibit Labels: An Interpretive Approach*. Walnut Creek, CA: Altamira Press, p. 2.

7 See E. H. Spicer. (1962). *Cycles of Conquest: The Impact of Spain, Mexico, and the United States on the Indians of the Southwest, 1533–1960*. Tucson: University of Arizona Press.

8 See D. W. Adams. (1995). *Education for Extinction: American Indians and the Boarding School Experience, 1875–1928*. Lawrence, KS: University of Kansas Press.

9 See R. Thornton. (1998). *Studying Native America: Problems and Prospects*. Madison: University of Wisconsin Press.

10   H. K. Burton. (1936). *The Re-Establishment of the Indian in their Pueblo Life through the Revival of their Traditional Crafts.* New York: Teachers College, Columbia University.

11   See L. Dilworth. (1996). *Imagining Indians in the Southwest: Persistent Visions of a Primitive Past.* Washington, DC: Smithsonian Institution Press.

12   D. MacCannell. (1994). *The Tourist: A New Theory of the Leisure Class.* Berkeley, CA: University of California Press, 163.

13   G. Bird. (1998). "Breaking the Silence: Writing as 'Witness.'" In S. J. Ortiz, Jr. (ed.). *Speaking for the Generations: Native Writers on Writing.* Tucson: University of Arizona Press.

14   N. Naranjo-Morse. (1992). *Mud Woman: Poems from the Clay.* Tucson: University of Arizona Press.

15   See www.heard.org/about.php.

16   The nine display areas named after individual or corporate sponsors include the Lovena Ohl Gallery; Ullman Learning Center; Sandra Day O'Connor Gallery; Freeman Gallery; Edward Jacobsen Gallery of Indian Art; Dr. Dean Nichols Sculpture Courtyard; Kitchell Gallery; Russ Lyons Realty Crossroads Gallery; and the COMPAS gallery, named after a conglomeration of corporate and individual sponsors.

17   These are the Scott L. Libby Jr. Amphitheater; Steele Auditorium; Dorrance Education Center; Phelps Dodge Plaza; The Thunderbirds Children's Courtyard; and Billie Jane Baguley Library and Archives.

18   See, for example, V. Alexander. (1996). *Museums and Money: The Impact of Funding on Exhibitions, Scholarship, and Management.* Bloomington: Indiana University Press.

9 | VISITING THE VIRTUAL MUSEUM: ART AND EXPERIENCE ONLINE

Lianne McTavish

Editor's Introduction

Lianne McTavish is associate professor of visual culture at the University of New Brunswick, Canada, where she writes about and teaches critical museum studies. She is also an associate curator at the Beaverbrook Art Gallery, Fredericton, and the author of *Childbirth and the Display of Authority in Early Modern France*. She is now writing on museums and professionalization in Canada.

The following chapter explores how virtual museums both reinforce and challenge notions of authenticity and institutional authority. McTavish examines the virtual gallery – an online exhibition that a museum reproduces from its real-world installations – and the virtual exhibition or collection, which may or may not be part of a real-world museum or consortium and which contains exhibits or images that are only available online. Critical to her analysis is Jacques Derrida's concept of the *parergon* or framing device which makes meaning by establishing boundaries; the picture frame, museum architecture, and the museum itself are *parerga* that establish what is art and what is not. McTavish considers how the virtual museum operates as a *parergon*. The chapter also examines the conflicting aspirations of virtual museums to be commercial and to be subversive. Drawing from media studies theorist Lev Manovich, who critiques the assumption that the web is, by definition, interactive, McTavish asks whether the participation called for by museum websites is merely passive clicking or does indeed encourage new ways of thinking. She weighs the potential of the virtual museum to transform display institutions into entities of dialogue and debate, not unlike the post-museum that many theorists envision.

"Have you taken a virtual tour of the Rijksmuseum?" One of my colleagues displayed the website of the national museum in Amsterdam on his computer screen, inviting me to examine its digital format. I was expecting to see a home page with an image of the museum's facade overlaid with text links labeled "visitor information" and "current exhibitions." Instead, framed paintings adorned the walls of a three-dimensional gallery. My colleague used his mouse to move through this space, clicking on Rembrandt's *Night Watch* and zooming in for greater detail. The work's rich colors and contrasting light and dark tones were revealed. Accompanying text described the famous painting, providing information about its subject matter, artist, and date – 1642. Impressed with the quality of the reproduction, we agreed that the virtual museum could be used to teach university students about the content and style of seventeenth-century art. "There is at least one drawback," I conceded. "Now there is no reason to go to the real Rijksmuseum."

My statement was meant to be ridiculous, on the basis that the personal experience of art works in real space could not be replicated, no matter how sophisticated imaging devices became. But like all jokes, my comment also revealed a certain anxiety: perhaps the museum visit would be replaced or altered by increasingly complex virtual museums. Many art historians consider visits to museums and galleries an inspirational part of the learning process. Despite postmodern critiques of cultural categories such as authenticity and originality, art experts continue to reinforce distinctions between artistic creations and reproductions of them. The discipline of art history is founded on the use of copies, especially slides, yet an exclusive encounter with reproductions is still deemed less legitimate than immediate experiences of the "real thing."

My virtual tour of the Rijksmuseum raised many questions about the effects of the relatively new formation of museums online. Do virtual museums undermine or reinforce traditional conceptions of the authenticity of art works and museum visits? How are these websites experienced? Is the visitor offered greater freedom to engage with museum spaces and their contents online, or are the power dynamics of conventional institutions reaffirmed? How do digital collections affect both encounters with and understandings of museums? What happens when everyday people begin to produce the content of virtual museums, appropriating the roles of curator and even museum director? Does a more inclusive, global, and democratic conception of museums ultimately emerge? Furthermore, what is the relationship between virtual museums and teaching? Do online museums encourage active learning, or do they perpetuate passivity by inviting computer users simply to "point and click" on selected images? Are educational goals undermined when online visitors become consumers who purchase items from virtual museum shops?

In this chapter, I address these questions in relation to a range of virtual museums. After examining many websites, I realized my initial understanding of their contents and organization was outdated. Some small institutions still boast what might be called "glorified pamphlets" – providing information about hours and entry fees – but almost all museums and galleries now have extensive websites which portray an array of material, including digitized images of their collections. Though not all virtual museums are designed like the Rijksmuseum, major institutions such as the Louvre in Paris, the Museum of Anthropology in Vancouver, the National Gallery of Art in Washington, DC, and the Hermitage Museum in St Petersburg feature virtual tours of their galleries as part of more extensive sites. Other websites associated with established museums – notably the Museum of Modern Art (MOMA) in New York – present digital exhibitions and art works created exclusively for the internet. They portray the web itself as an artistic medium, instead of using it to enhance the experience of gallery spaces. Not all virtual museums, however, are linked with specific buildings; some exist exclusively on the world wide web – including the Alternative Museum, the Museum of the Person, and the Virtual Museum of Canada. Without providing an exhaustive survey of virtual museums, I consider their different incarnations, focusing on particular websites to address the significance of displaying cultural material online.

Constructing a website is almost always a group effort, drawing on the expertise of various museum staff – though wealthier institutions also hire professional designers and technology experts. It follows that most scholarly discussions of virtual museums stress issues important to museum workers, namely design, navigation, and utility.[1] The ways in which museums and their effects are refigured online can best be explored, however, in relation to a developing body of critical museum theory. Since at least the 1960s, sociologists, anthropologists, and art historians have been exploring the sociocultural role of museums, investigating how they sustain hierarchies of power, reframe art works, and mold the experiences of visitors. This scholarship has revealed that museums are far more than revered containers. As institutions of civil society, they participate in the way society is ordered, shaping politics, national identities, and distinctions between high and popular culture.

In some ways, virtual museums respond to museum theory. While certain critics insist that museums are elitist institutions that both exclude popular classes and attempt to fashion them into "civilized" members of society, museum administrators claim that online resources make collections more

accessible, offering diverse patrons an "interactive" experience.[2] These officials suggest that visitors of virtual museums are empowered by the sites,
and actively engaged with them – able to follow their own interests rather
than passively submit to institutional authority. In examining particular
websites, however, I find they are not exactly utopian spaces offering intellectual stimulation and freedom to visitors. I question the rhetoric of interactivity typically associated with virtual museums.

The websites are not, however, bereft of intriguing challenges. On the
contrary, virtual museums are riddled with contradictions, a feature they
share with traditional museums, which are often informed by multiple and
conflicting goals.[3] Virtual museums simultaneously undermine and reinforce
the traditional boundaries of museums. They also enable and constrain the
endeavors of virtual visitors. Virtual museums are thus paradoxical entities
ripe for analysis. They cannot be dismissed as mass marketing tools; nor can
they be championed as inventive mechanisms which engage and educate
patrons. Individual websites require critical evaluations which consider,
among other things, how virtual museums deploy technology, reshape collections, and envision the "proper" role of the museum.

Virtual Reality Galleries

The Rijksmuseum website offers users many options – they can pursue
information about the museum's collections and exhibitions – but its virtual
tour is arguably the most spectacular. After deciding which of the three
floors they would like to tour, online visitors are provided with a map of the
museum, color-coded to indicate the contents of particular galleries. Clicking
on a specific gallery initiates downloading of a 360-degree, panoramic view of
the room, with delays varying according to computer capability and internet
connection (figure 9.1). Using a mouse, visitors can then "turn around" to
survey the walls of the gallery, moving up to view the ceiling and down

FIGURE 9.1 View of QuickTime virtual reality gallery, www.rijksmuseum.nl. Courtesy of
the Rijksmuseum, Amsterdam

toward the floor. When adjoining galleries are also visible, they can be entered with another click of the mouse. At the same time, if particular paintings, sculptures, or objects are of interest, viewers are able to zoom in for a closer look. Clicking on an art work designated a "hot spot" produces a larger, overall view of it, as well as written text providing additional information.

Like most other virtual museum tours I encountered, the virtual Rijksmuseum was created with QuickTime virtual reality software, requiring QuickTime Player to view it. First a photographer stood in the center of every "real" gallery, rotating slightly before taking each shot in order to picture the entire room. These photographs were then digitized and reassembled, providing a cylindrical gallery available for viewing.[4] Apple Computer Inc. promotes the software as providing an immersive environment with which computer users can interact. Yet the QuickTime suite does not attempt to mimic bodily sensations as do other virtual reality technologies, which typically oblige users to don special equipment such as goggles, data gloves, or head-mounted displays.

The virtual Rijksmuseum is nevertheless meant to offer online visitors a simulated version of a visit to the "real" galleries. A statement appearing on the website suggests as much, apologizing because the virtual reality tour no longer corresponds with the current installation of art works in the museum. The virtual Rijksmuseum includes not just those spaces containing paintings and sculpture, but also passageways – virtual visitors confront turnstiles if they download images of the east entrance. Almost all the museum's public spaces are portrayed online.

The depiction of the art works in these spaces is, however, not entirely convincing. The texture of the images is barely represented even when projected by the most sophisticated computer system. Sometimes the details of particular paintings are blurry, with the zoom function revealing pixels instead of more precise views. Despite these problems, the virtual reality technology portrays two-dimensional art objects more effectively than those in three dimensions. It is impossible, for example, to survey all sides of sculptures in the round; viewers are offered static, frontal views of them.

Though the virtual reality technology favors two-dimensional objects, it is actually designed to create the illusion of space. In some ways, this emphasis on space directs attention away from the art objects. The polychrome floor, barrel-vaulted ceilings, and magnificent windows pictured in the Michelangelo gallery of the virtual Louvre Museum, for example, attract the viewer's eye – they are even more engaging than the sculptures. In the virtual Louvre as well as other virtual reality museums, visual emphasis is placed on seemingly insignificant items such as placards, exit signs, and climate-control devices. These details, however, are hardly irrelevant. They work to produce the reality effect of virtual galleries, convincing viewers they are encountering substantial spaces. According to media expert Ken Hillis, most virtual reality environments function this way. Surfaces saturated with visual detail engage the eye, disavowing the essential flatness of the technology.[5]

Though resulting from the virtual reality technology used, this effect potentially promotes critical appreciation of the role of museums. In virtual reality galleries, art works are not portrayed as independent entities, floating above earthly concerns. The galleries foreground how institutions frame works – producing their value. As details take precedence, the main subject of virtual galleries becomes less clear; distinctions between foreground and background are blurred. The boundaries of art works are implicitly questioned in a way that recalls French philosopher Jacques Derrida's critique of Immanuel Kant's concept of the *parergon*.[6] When, in the *Critique of Judgment*, Kant uses the term *parergon*, or "by-work," he refers to those adjuncts (like the frames around paintings or drapery on statues) that separate what properly belongs to a work from what remains outside of it. According to Derrida, however, these margins function as more than ornamental additions; they crucially differentiate between the intrinsic and extrinsic aspects of a work. The borders not only produce a bounded object of study (namely the work of art), but are fundamental to the becoming visible of the very concept of art and thus every discussion of art. The display of art and artifacts in virtual galleries reveals that museums are significantly bound up with the perception of art works – these institutions are also *parerga*, which simultaneously produce and challenge binary distinctions between essence and ornament, the art work and its exterior.

Virtual reality galleries represent museums that are not neutral spaces, fading into the background while viewers have immediate experiences of art works. This allusion to the way museum spaces mediate experience challenges traditional conceptions of the authentic museum visit – conceptions which affirm viewers should have personal, intellectual, and spiritual encounters with art works, without distraction. Some critics have argued, however, that such experiences have never been possible in museums: by de- and re-contextualizing art works, museums can only offer inauthentic experiences. During the eighteenth century, art historian Quatremère de Quincy, for example, charged the newly founded Louvre Museum with estranging culture from its true context in living history.[7] More recently, English professor Susan Stewart claimed that museums destroy the object's

231

context of origin, replacing it with the context of the collection.[8] Stewart studied how new meanings were inscribed in displaced objects, but Quatremère de Quincy held that works removed from their original locations were devoid of meaning, encouraging viewers to adapt a detached and passive attitude toward them.

Despite drawing attention to how museums recontextualize art objects, virtual reality galleries are actually meant to encourage more authentic experiences of art works – experiences at odds with Quatremère de Quincy's characterization of the museum visit. Web designers typically describe the goals of virtual museums in terms of public service, claiming that visitors can engage directly with museum collections online. Administrators of Cybermuse – a website that features virtual reality galleries representing the National Gallery of Canada in Ottawa – promise viewers: "No more visiting hours. Anytime of the day or night, visit Cybermuse from your own home . . . Just click to visit."[9] The text accompanying virtual reality tours of the National Gallery of Art in Washington, DC, is a little different, focusing on individual choice and movement. It proclaims: "As you 'walk' through these QuickTime VR tours of NGA exhibitions, you can select specific works of art for larger image views, close-up details."[10] Virtual reality galleries are thus contradictory, simultaneously pointing to the museum's mediation of art works and attempting to overcome the effects of that mediation.

In some ways, then, descriptions of virtual reality galleries reinforce traditional notions of the ideal museum visit, with visitors having personal experiences with art online. At the same time, there is little emphasis on intellectual or spiritual engagement. Instead, accounts of the benefits of virtual reality galleries stress public access and activity, especially physical movement – visitors are urged to "walk" through the galleries and manipulate digital images. According to media expert Lev Manovich, such descriptions are not unusual. He argues that the rhetoric of computer interactivity emphasizes the physical interaction between user and media object, rather than psychological engagement.[11] In this discourse, pressing a button or choosing a link is often equated with mental processes. As a result, Manovich continues, individualized intellectual operations, such as remembering, identifying, and problem solving, are not encouraged by "interactive" computer software. Do virtual reality galleries promote the same kind of interactivity, supporting physical rather than intellectual endeavors?

Virtual reality galleries do stress movement, encouraging visitors to transgress the physical barriers of traditional museums. Internet users can jump from one corner of the building to the other, or between floors at will; they are not obliged to take a standard path through the museum. Nor are virtual visitors constrained by geographical boundaries. Anyone with access to and comprehension of the internet can view installations in Paris or Ottawa without incurring the cost of travel. Furthermore, online visitors can devise their own itineraries, avoiding limited museum hours, crowded spaces, and worry about whether or not specific galleries will be open.

Dynamic movement, however, is not part of the experience offered to visitors to virtual reality museums. Internet users do not so much "walk" through virtual spaces as occupy fixed positions in the center of galleries. The walls of these galleries rotate, creating the illusion that the stable viewer moves his or her "head" to survey three-dimensional spaces. While visitors can relocate to another fixed location, they are constrained by technological rather than strictly physical barriers. Only those viewing positions predetermined by software designers are available. The visitor's experience of movement is further restricted because reality is defined in exclusively visual terms in virtual reality galleries. Virtual viewers are offered a limited bodily experience, which stresses visual (and occasionally also aural) perception.[12] Awareness of the bodies of other visitors is equally limited in virtual reality museums. Instead of picturing different viewers enjoying the exhibitions, the virtual galleries are empty. Virtual visitors are supplied with an independent viewing situation – though various surveys indicate that people tend to visit museums in social groups.[13] This isolation reinforces the notion that viewers should engage in singular encounters with art works, focusing on them without distraction.

Overall, then, virtual reality galleries presuppose and may even produce an ideal visitor – one who is well behaved, predictable, and obliged to enjoy a primarily visual experience of gallery spaces. In this sense, the virtual museums do not offer visitors increased freedom of movement or thought; they reinforce rather than transform conventional relationships between museums and their public. According to Tony Bennett, during the nineteenth century museums were seen, along with public libraries and parks, as potential sites for reforming the habits, morals, and leisure activities of the subordinate classes – ostensibly replacing visits to ale houses with cultured experiences. Extending Michel Foucault's arguments about the development of the prison, Bennett argues that the museum was thus another disciplinary technology designed to produce a well-behaved public, encouraging self-surveillance and the incorporation of the values of the state.[14]

Though freedom and choice may be illusory in virtual reality galleries, visitors can nevertheless be empowered by them. Standing in the center of it all, the independent visitor is a masterful subject, surveying his or her domain. Exhibition spaces move at the visitor's command. He or she appears to occupy a position of seeing without being seen, like a guard in the Panopticon, a prison designed but never built during the nineteenth century.[15] The central tower of the Panopticon, Foucault explains, allowed guards to observe prisoners without themselves being observed. Subject to an unseen gaze, prisoners would begin to regulate their behavior at all times, whether guards were present or not. Bennett argues that something similar happens to visitors in modern museums – they adjust and adapt their manners even though alarm sensors, cameras, and guards are not present in every room. Yet virtual reality galleries apparently reverse this dynamic, equipping the visitor with a powerful gaze, so that he or she occupies the position of guard rather than prisoner. Of course, virtual visitors may only imagine they are unobserved, as their entrance to museum websites is often registered and added to the databanks of other computers.

Even as visitors to virtual reality museums experience constraints and surveillance, they can also enjoy an active gaze that provides pleasure. The voyeurism of the virtual visitor's viewing experience is enhanced by the way in which images are downloaded in QuickTime galleries. The viewer first sees a grid which is replaced by digitized images that eventually come into focus. The gradual revelation of particular spaces and art works produces a sense of anticipation. While enjoyable – if the internet connection is not especially slow – this unveiling also offers an intellectual opportunity to reflect critically on definitions of both museums and their contents. The way in which images are downloaded makes it appear as if technology, rather than architects, curators, and artists, has produced them.

This aspect of virtual reality software raises a longstanding art-historical dilemma, namely the relationship between copies and originals. In the case of virtual reality galleries, the debate is invoked not only in terms of art works, but also in relation to the museum itself. Distinctions between virtual and real museums are blurred on many websites which employ spatial metaphors, encouraging visitors to enter and tour virtual galleries. The overall implication is that institutions and their collections can be replaced by online representations of them, with the real and the virtual portrayed as congruent terms, not binary opposites.

Yet even as virtual and real museums are merged in rhetoric (including the term "virtual reality tour"), attention is drawn to differences between them – and not just by official apologies which note the imperfection of virtual reality galleries. Images of art works portrayed in virtual museums are often deficient, erasing distinctions of texture and scale. Despite striking images on the website of the Rijksmuseum, the disappointing quality of many reproductions in virtual reality galleries reaffirms differences between the objects exhibited in "real" museums and digital reproductions of them. This separation of original and copy is related to copyright issues. Various institutions do not want internet users downloading accurate images of works in their collections, illegally disseminating them at will without paying the appropriate fees.[16] While the relatively poor quality of the digital images in many virtual reality museums affirms that particular institutions retain control of their collections, it also implies that art works and artifacts cannot be experienced outside their "real" walls. This aspect of the galleries sends another mixed message, indicating that, in the end, authentic experiences of art works cannot be had online.

Virtual reality galleries are contradictory entities. Confusing distinctions between real and virtual, original and copy, these galleries simultaneously reaffirm traditional definitions of museums and suggest critical challenges to them. They imply that "real" museums are imbricated in definitions of art, and yet remain the appropriate locations in which to view it. At the same time, virtual reality tours both demonstrate and attempt to overcome the museum's mediation of art works. Even as they emphasize personal experience and choice, virtual reality galleries offer pre-programmed menus, potentially promoting the activities of pointing and clicking at the expense of thinking. Nevertheless, there are aspects of these galleries which encourage critical reflection on the role of the museum. Visitors can ponder how museums frame objects, as well as the relationship between "originals" and "copies." These viewers are, after all, not passive subjects manipulated by software designers. Visitors to virtual reality galleries can enjoy pleasures at once empowering and constraining. However, not all virtual museums boast virtual reality tours. Some websites reject the illusionism of this technology, representing different but no less contradictory virtual museums.

Virtual Exhibitions and Collections

Museums devoted to modern and contemporary art rarely feature virtual reality galleries on their websites. This situation is in some ways surprising. One might expect an institution such as MOMA in New York, for example, to embrace the "cutting-edge" technology, given the museum's longstanding support of avant-garde art works and new media. QuickTime virtual reality

235

technology is, however, actually at odds with the official image of MOMA. In an article discussing the museum's website, Greg Van Alstyne argues that it was designed to embody the museum's values of dignity and intellectual contemplation, while avoiding the look of commercial sites. The website, he affirms, "eschews *trompe l'oeil* effects and the kitsch of simulated 3-D dropshadows."[17] The illusionary space and realism promoted by virtual reality galleries is at odds with both the modernist aesthetic and the abstract art identified with the museum.

The website of MOMA nevertheless both describes exhibitions currently on view in New York and offers online versions of them. In contrast to the virtual reality galleries described above, however, it does not reproduce particular installations. Although presenting similar material and themes, online exhibitions are created specifically for the website, with images and text suited to its digital format. The MOMA site also boasts what are called "online projects," exhibitions produced exclusively for the internet and never installed in the "real" institution. The first show produced for online visitors was "Artists of Brücke: Themes in German Expressionist Prints," which digitized materials sensitive to light exposure. Explaining that such exhibitions "explore some of the properties and possibilities of the Web, such as interactivity, motion and sound," website designers used Macromedia Flash software to support animated images and music – effects not available in QuickTime.[18] Visitors to "Artists of Brücke" are greeted by the sound of a piano, and are then able to select specific artists or themes, clicking on them for information. The exhibition is flexible, with more links than the QuickTime virtual reality galleries. Yet interactivity is still primarily identified with the physical manipulation of digital objects, rather than an intellectual engagement with them. The web designers claim, however, to be more interested in form than content. Reinforcing this modernist preoccupation, they portray the web itself as a medium with unique characteristics. The MOMA website is thus presented as both part of and other than the "real" museum; it extends modernist ideals, but does not reproduce the institution.

The conception of the virtual museum as an exhibition venue for distinctively web-based productions is presented most clearly on the website of the Alternative Museum. This organization promotes artists who create, among other things, manipulated photographs, web-based sound art and pixel paintings. Asserting that digital art is "real art" worthy of appreciation, administrators of the site present the web itself as an artistic medium: "For web-based artists, the computer and the monitor are just one more set of tools and system for the delivery of their work."[19] The Alternative Museum was initially founded as a physical space in New York City in 1975 to support art and artists not yet embraced by other institutions. It is now, however, exclusively an internet institution. In this case, the virtual museum has indeed displaced its "bricks and mortar" predecessor. Administrators contend that this transformation reinforces the original mandate of the Alternative Museum. Striving for diversity and inclusion, the online Alternative Museum continues to promote artists from various countries, many of them non-western. Trustees and staff of the Alternative Museum describe the virtual museum as an experiment both in global democracy and in the "global sharing of art and culture in a way that has never been possible with traditional institutions."[20]

The current form of the Alternative Museum seems to offer the greatest challenge to the traditional museum thus far, dislodging rather than extending it. Yet the virtual institution is not entirely at odds with conventional institutions, given its utopian assertion that "geographical boundaries and cultural differences are a thing of the past."[21] According to Bennett, during the nineteenth century museum designers had similar aims, desiring to provide universal representations of the world. These exhibitions nevertheless offered necessarily partial views, a paradox that politicized the issues of inclusion and exclusion still relevant today.[22] While museums continue to struggle with the politics of inclusive representation, online institutions such as the Alternative Museum may in fact have the potential to respond most effectively to such issues.

Virtual museums appear to be more accessible not only to visitors and new kinds of artists, but also to those typically marginalized by museums. Brazil's Museu da Pessoa (Museum of the Person), for example, is another institution that exists exclusively on the web and strives to be inclusive. According to director Karen Worcman, the virtual museum was founded in 1992 because "in Brazil public and cultural institutions are complicated by money and politics."[23] The mandate of the Museum of the Person is to collect, preserve, and publish the life histories of average people, recognizing their importance. Using text, images, audio, and video, this virtual museum encourages anonymous people – many of them over 60 years of age, and from Brazil, Europe, and the United States – to become part of both history and the museum. The Museum of the Person is arguably not only the most inclusive but also the most interactive website discussed so far. Everyday people produce museum content. The website invites virtual visitors to email to the institution autobiographies and photographs; and staff members frequently stage events in which random individuals are asked to

FIGURE 9.2   Home page of the Virtual Museum of Canada, www.virtualmuseum.ca.
Courtesy of the Department of Heritage, Government of Canada

tell their stories on videotape. In contrast, the Alternative Museum is still primarily a site of display, distinguishing artists from audience.

The Virtual Museum of Canada is another online museum striving for diversity and inclusion (figure 9.2). Unlike the virtual museums discussed previously, this institution is a collective endeavor produced by hundreds of museums as well as other private- and public-sector cultural organizations. Like the Alternative Museum, the Virtual Museum of Canada exists exclusively online, but it reinforces some conventional understandings of museums. Instead of representing a particular kind of art work, the Virtual Museum of Canada portrays a nation. Inaugurated in 2001, the online museum is sponsored by the Canadian government and exists to stimulate Canadian cultural content on the internet, using this "powerful broadcasting tool" to "preserve, make known, and pass along our Canadian heritage."[24] Designating $75 million to the first three years of the project, the Department of Canadian Heritage invited museums across the country to produce digitized content in keeping with this mandate. Rhetoric associated with the Virtual Museum of Canada promotes the standard metaphor of Canada as a tapestry combining different strands to create a strong and colorful fabric which nevertheless

238

preserves distinctions – a deliberate contrast to the image of the melting pot traditionally identified with the United States of America. The original digital presentations certainly promoted this particular representation of the country, covering the voyages of explorer Samuel de Champlain in Québec and Ontario, Yukon photographers, black communities in Nova Scotia, Inuit art, and, of course, hockey as a national pastime.

A major goal of these digital exhibitions is educational, championing museums as part of the educational infrastructure – a longstanding perception of museums – and providing online resources for instructors as well as students. While aimed at the Canadian population in general, special emphasis is placed on teaching Canadian youth about the country in which they live. Audiences are offered lessons in citizenship which define Canada and what it means to be Canadian. According to art historians Carol Duncan and Alan Wallach, museums have traditionally promoted society's most revered beliefs and values, embodying the idea of the state. As visitors follow a ritual script through the ceremonial architecture of museums, these scholars contend, state authority comes to be equated with the idea of civilization.[25] The nationalistic agenda of the Virtual Museum of Canada is blatant, overtly embracing the government's policies of sustaining Canadian content and multiculturalism.

Nevertheless, like virtual reality museums, the Virtual Museum of Canada does not consist of architecture that would predetermine a ritual script for internet users. In keeping with descriptions of other online museums, the Canadian website is publicized as an interactive and accessible museum that promotes intellectual engagement as well as creativity. Its educational mandate is informed by the tenets of critical pedagogy, a teaching style that is student-centered and designed to liberate citizens, not indoctrinate them. According to Henry Giroux, an advocate of critical pedagogy, educators should facilitate the examination of conflicts over relations of power, identity, and culture, empowering students as critical and active citizens.[26] Many of the exhibitions comprising the Virtual Museum of Canada stress identity and politics – as well as activities meant to encourage thinking. Students of different ages are invited to participate in role-playing, games, and quizzes inspired by the material on the website.

Though promoting an engagement with online material that goes beyond pointing and clicking, few exhibitions in the Virtual Museum of Canada emphasize conflict. "The Making of Treaty 8 in Canada's Northwest," however, examines the impact of one of the treaties made between the Canadian government and First Nations Peoples in 1899. In addition to reproducing the terms of the treaty and discussing it as both an historical and a living agreement, sacred to Native peoples, the exhibition addresses misconceptions people may have about Aboriginals and their supposedly special treatment by the government of Canada. This discussion of treaty rights opens up questions about land claims and the use of natural resources – questions that can challenge notions of a unified Canada. Yet at the same time the digital exhibition continues to promote the federal government, portraying it as an enlightened entity that protects the rights of all Canadians.[27]

Itself a government program, the Virtual Museum of Canada exists to encourage increased knowledge and use of the internet. At the same time, it rewards with funding and recognition those museums which digitize their collections. The pressure to make collections available online is of course not exclusive to Canadian museums, but rather standard in much of the museum community, with funds sometimes reluctantly directed away from other activities in order to accomplish digitization. Virtual collections differ from virtual reality museums depicting gallery spaces, as well as online exhibitions devoted to particular themes. These collections consist of a wide range of objects from both the permanent installations and storage areas of museums, digitized and made available online. Many museum websites now include search engines able to access digitized images of their collections – collections not shown imbricated in museum spaces or arranged to tell stories of nationality.

The move to put most if not all of museum collections online is not uncontested. Detractors contend an uncritical embrace of digital technologies undermines the museum's established purpose – the preservation of original objects. Not all scholars, however, associate the digitization of museum collections with a loss of tradition. According to museum expert Wolfgang Ernst, digitization actually recalls those Renaissance cabinets of wonder which exhibited an astonishing mixture of natural specimens and human-made objects. Like those cabinets, Ernst argues, digital collections display objects that are co-present and discontinuous – not made to conform to an historical narrative. They thus return audiences to a time when "thinking with one's eyes . . . was not yet despised in favor of cognitive operations."[28] When digitized, the museum is revealed as a non-discursive and random collection of objects, not a final destination point that ensures the preservation of objects. In fact, digital collections encourage museums to function as temporary rather than permanent storage containers. Internet users download records of objects both on permanent display and in storage, breaking down distinctions between these areas. A new understanding of the museum emerges, one in keeping with the electronic inventory systems of commercial companies, which facilitate immediate access to commodities in the supply–demand relationship. Digitizing museum collections is thus related to consumer demands in late capitalism, with collections converted to a digital format in order to expedite the increasing consumption of culture.

Though virtual exhibitions such as those comprising the Virtual Museum of Canada assume a narrative form, digitized collections are indeed non-narrative. The website of the National Gallery of Art in Washington, DC, allows users to search the collection by artist, title, subject, theme, or accession number. This online collection encourages internet users to make connections between objects, outside of the chronological or geographical concerns that often preoccupy curators. The virtual visitor can even appropriate the role of curator, making his or her own museum. This possibility is advocated by the Virtual Museum of Canada, which includes an option entitled "My Personal Museum," a space for individuals to collect and exhibit those objects made available in the digitized image bank. Creating a personal museum may provide online participants with a sense of mastery, not unlike that afforded by virtual reality galleries. Despite concerns about copyright, digitized collections promote the public ownership of the museum in ways that can challenge the authority of both institutions and their staff.

Yet, as Ernst points out, the digitization of museum collections is intricately bound up with contemporary forms of consumption. After all, the Virtual Museum of Canada was designed in part to "sell" museums, giving institutions increased opportunities to generate revenues by attracting more visitors and marketing products online.[29] The home page of the virtual museum invites viewers to explore various museum boutiques as well as exhibitions, indicating that shopping is an important part of being a Canadian citizen. The association of museums with consumption on the Virtual Museum of Canada website is hardly unique; almost every virtual museum currently on the web promotes online shopping. The website of MOMA features an especially prominent virtual shop. Despite efforts to eschew commercial design, this shop resembles a standard shopping site, such as amazon.com, with its clean lines, detailed views of selected objects, advertisements, and virtual shopping basket. In this light, the "My Personal Museum" feature of the Virtual Museum of Canada seems less like an educational way to empower internet users and more like an online shopping cart, in which virtual shoppers deposit and exchange desired items.

Digitized collections may simply make museum objects available for personal consumption. This shift is implied in the rhetoric of interactivity, which emphasizes how visitors to virtual museums experience increased convenience, speed of access, and fulfillment of personal desires. If the online museum visitor is an individual consumer who picks and chooses items of personal interest, interactivity consists of more than pointing and clicking; it also promotes the quest for possession. Stewart argued that in museums the object's context of origin was replaced with the context of the collection. Digital collections go one step further, minimizing the context of the museum, and allowing visitors to inscribe objects with their own meanings. Affirmative accounts of the interactive and innovative nature of virtual museums thus reinforce utopian understandings of the capitalist consumer. The representation of autonomous visitors who select and manipulate objects, making them their own, is inseparable from the liberal individual imagined by capitalism. Insisting that digital exhibitions and collections empower visitors – serving their diverse desires and identities – reinforces a particularly western conception of the ideal visitor or "client."

The affiliation of visiting museums and shopping was noted by American artist Andy Warhol, who claimed: "When you think about it, department stores are kind of like museums." This quotation greets online visitors to the One Stop Warhol Shop, a virtual museum developed by the Andy Warhol Museum in Pittsburgh, and hosted by the collective virtual museum ArtMuseum.net. Advertised as the "single most comprehensive internet resource on Andy Warhol," the website is designed to mimic a grocery list, inviting visitors to "shop" the site and construct their own Warhol.[30] While teaching viewers about Warhol's method of collecting and reshaping popular culture in his work – breaking down distinctions between high and popular art – the One Stop Warhol Shop also presents shopping itself as a creative activity. This representation is in keeping with arguments made by French philosopher Michel de Certeau, who contends that shopping is a dynamic practice, with individuals selecting and resignifying given objects.[31] In this view, perusing digital collections and purchasing items from virtual shops go hand in hand; both are endeavors by which virtual museum patrons refashion the museum into their own image. De Certeau's theories offer a more positive vision of the activities promoted by digital collections. While visitors to virtual museums may indeed participate in a kind of shopping, this enterprise is neither sinful, nor without intellectual and creative content.

Virtual museums which promote digital exhibitions and collections exclusively available online are different from virtual reality galleries, but no less paradoxical. With emphasis placed on the web as a unique medium, these virtual museums are distinguished from "real" museums. Yet even those museums existing only on the internet often reinvigorate rather than challenge traditional conceptions of museums. Virtual museums may nevertheless be more inclusive than traditional "bricks-and-mortar" institutions. They potentially welcome a variety of viewpoints as well as visitors. Furthermore, they enable users to access collections both on display and in the storage areas of "real" museums. Even so, it is not certain that visitors have liberating experiences of virtual museums. While administrators of online institutions stress the opportunity for engaged education, the interactivity they promote often consists of the physical manipulation of digital objects and the opportunity to possess them. Though this kind of capitalist consumption is of questionable value, it does not entirely erase the creative opportunities available to online visitors.

Conclusions

This chapter has established that virtual museums send mixed messages, simultaneously reaffirming traditional aspects of museums and potentially encouraging critical evaluation of these institutions. I have focused on the ambiguity of museum websites in order to undermine both the wholesale rejection and the uncritical embrace of them. I have also discussed particular sites to avoid generalizing about virtual museums. Nevertheless, some overall comments are possible. There are many positive aspects of virtual museums; they provide educational materials for teachers, allow increased access to collections, and can include a broad array of voices – voices which challenge elitist museum practices. On the other hand, virtual museums tend to promote a restricted understanding of interactivity, one that mainly consists of the user pointing to and clicking on, or else attempting to possess, digital objects. In addition, virtual museums often continue to impose narrative structures on objects, while positioning visitors as either well-behaved individuals or clients desiring service. In their current form, virtual museums are at once intriguing and disappointing. The future of online museums is, however, difficult to predict. It remains to be seen how a new generation of virtual museums will reshape, reinforce, or undermine notions of authenticity, interactivity, and even the museum itself.

Questions for Discussion

1 Discuss the concept of authenticity in the context of the museum. Do virtual museums challenge this concept? How do museum websites blur the boundaries between the real and the virtual?
2 What is a *parergon*, as Derrida defined it? How do virtual museums function as *parerga*? Does conceptualizing the virtual museum as *parergon* lead to insights about the "real" museum as *parergon*?
3 Are museum websites useful? How does one become a critical visitor (chapter 8) to the virtual museum? How might one use virtual museums to enhance classroom learning? To help in research? To prepare oneself for museum-going?
4 What is the potential of the online site to create transformation in the museum? How are these sites conventional? And how are they subversive? Is a museum that exists only on the web really a museum at all? How might such an institution challenge commonly held assumptions about the "real" museum?
5 What is interactivity? Why is it important to education? Why does Lev Manovich critique what he sees as the rhetoric of interactivity? Do you think most museum websites are interactive, in the sense that Manovich would applaud? How could they become more interactive? How could educational programming within the museum itself become more interactive?
6 Why do museums of modern and contemporary art take a different approach to their websites than those with other kinds of collections? What is the result?
7 How does the digitization of museum collections impact on the way we view art and museums? What is the significance of the ability to design one's own museum from digitized collections on the web? How could designing your own museum in this way strengthen your skills as a critical thinker?
8 Assess the websites of some of the museums discussed in other chapters of this book. How do they compare with other aspects of the institution, as characterized by the contributors?

Acknowledgments

I would like to thank my colleague Gary Waite, the editor Janet Marstine, and all the museum professionals who responded to my inquiries about virtual museums. Funding for research was provided by the Social Sciences and Humanities Research Council of Canada.

Notes

1 D. Bearman and J. Trant. (eds.). (2001). *Museums and the Web 2001: Selected Papers from an International Conference.* Pittsburgh, PA: Archives and Museum Informatics;

D. Bearman. (ed.). (1995). *Multimedia Computing and Museums*. Pittsburgh, PA: Archives and Museum Informatics; J. Bowen. (2000). "The Virtual Museum." *Museum International*, 52: 1, 4–7.

2   P. Bourdieu and A. Darbel. (1991). *The Love of Art: European Art Museums and their Public*. C. Beattie and N. Merriman. (trans.). Cambridge: Polity. (Original work published 1969); C. Duncan. (1995). *Civilizing Rituals: Inside Public Art Museums*. London and New York: Routledge; T. Bennett. (1995). *The Birth of the Museum: History, Theory, Politics*. London and New York: Routledge.

3   Bennett, *Birth of the Museum*, p. 28.

4   For the history of virtual reality see K. Hillis. (1999). *Digital Sensations: Space, Identity, and Embodiment in Virtual Reality*. Minneapolis: University of Minnesota Press.

5   Hillis, *Digital Sensations*, p. 49.

6   J. Derrida. (1987). *The Truth in Painting*. G. Bennington and I. McLeod. (trans.). Chicago: University of Chicago Press, pp. 37–82.

7   For Quatremère de Quincy, see D. Maleuvre. (1999). *Museum Memories: History, Technology, Art*. Stanford, CA.: Stanford University Press, pp. 13–21.

8   S. Stewart. (1993). *On Longing: Narratives of the Miniature, the Gigantic, the Souvenir, the Collection*. Durham, NC: Duke University Press, pp. 151–4. (Originally published by Johns Hopkins University Press, 1984.)

9   See www.cybermuse.gallery.ca (accessed October 6, 2002).

10   See www.nga.gov/onlinetours/onlinetr.htm (accessed October 27, 2002).

11   L. Manovich. (2001). *The Language of New Media*. Cambridge, MA: MIT Press, pp. 55–61.

12   Hillis, *Digital Sensations*, pp. 90–132.

13   For surveys of virtual visitors see S. Sarraf. (1999). "A Survey of Museums on the Web: Who Uses Museum Websites?" *Curator*, 42: 3, 231–43; J. Chadwick. (1999). "A Survey of Characteristics and Patterns of Behavior in Visitors to a Museum Web Site." In D. Bearman and J. Trant. (eds.). *Museums and the Web 1999*. Pittsburgh, PA: Archives and Museum Informatics, 154–62.

14   Bennett, *Birth of the Museum*, p. 19.

15   M. Foucault. (1977). *Discipline and Punish: The Birth of the Prison*. A. Sheridan. (trans.). New York: Vintage Books, pp. 200–9.

16   Bowen, "Virtual Museum," p. 4, advises museum website designers to "avoid making high-quality graphic images available unless you are happy for them to be reused by others." For a classic discussion of the reproduction of art works see W. Benjamin. (1969). "The Work of Art in the Age of Mechanical Reproduction." In *Illuminations*. H. Zorn. (trans.). H. Arendt. (ed.). New York: Schocken Books, 217–52.

17   G. Van Alstyne. (2000). "Cybernetics, Modernism and Pleasure in www.moma.org." *Museum International*, 52: 1, 36–41, p. 38.

18   See www.moma.org/docs/onlineprojects/index.htm (accessed October 27, 2002).

19   See www.alternativemuseum.org/home.html (accessed October 6, 2002).

20   See www.alternativemuseum.org/home.html (accessed October 27, 2002).

21   See www.alternativemuseum.org/home_nodon.html (accessed October 27, 2002).

22   Bennett, *Birth of the Museum*, pp. 102–3.

23   See T. Gillespie. (1997). "Brazil's Museum of the Person." www.indiana.edu/
      ~slizzard/museum/article.html (accessed August 27, 2002); K. Worcman, J. S.
      Matos, and R. Henriques. (1999). "Museum of the Person: A Brazilian Experience of
      a Virtual Museum." In Bearman and Trant. *Museums and the Web 1999*, 46–52.
24   See www.virtualmuseum.ca/English/Pressroom/p-02-05-01.html (accessed October
      27, 2002) for the statements made by minister of Canadian heritage Sheila Copps.
25   C. Duncan and A. Wallach. (1980). "The Universal Survey Museum." *Art History*, 3:
      4, 448–69.
26   H. A. Giroux. (1997). *Pedagogy and the Politics of Hope: Theory, Culture and Schooling.*
      Boulder, CO: Westview Press, pp. 71, 102.
27   I thank Hannah Lane for suggesting that the federal government of Canada appears
      to support the rights of First Nations Peoples in order to enhance its image.
28   W. Ernst. (2000). "Archi(ve)textures of Museology." In S. A. Crane, (ed.). *Museums
      and Memory*. Stanford, CA: Stanford University Press, 17–34.
29   www.chin.gc.ca/English/Members/Vmc_Investment_Program/
      guidelines_overview.html#outcomes for the desired outcomes of the Virtual Mu-
      seum of Canada, under "VMC Program Guidelines" (accessed October 27, 2002). See
      also C. Tellis. (2000). "Building the Next Generation Collaborative Museum Shop-
      ping Site: Merging E-Commerce, E-Museums and Entrepreneurs." In D. Bearman and
      J. Trant. (eds.). *Museums and the Web 2000*. Pittsburgh, PA: Archives and Museum
      Informatics, 113–18.
30   See www.ArtMuseum.net (accessed August 1, 2002).
31   M. De Certeau. (1985). *The Practice of Everyday Life*. S. Rendall. (trans.). Berkeley, CA:
      University of California Press.

Websites

Alternative Museum, New York: www.alternativemuseum.org
Amazon: www.amazon.com
Andy Warhol Museum, Pittsburgh, PA: www.warhol.org
Cybermuse (National Gallery of Canada, Ottawa): www.cybermuse.gallery.ca
Hermitage Museum, St Petersburg: www.hermitagemuseum.com
Louvre Museum, Paris: www.louvre.fr
Museum of Anthropology, Vancouver: www.moa.ubc.ca
Museum of Modern Art, New York: www.moma.org
Museum of the Person, Brazil: www.museudapessoa.com.br
National Gallery of Art, Washington, DC: www.nga.gov
One Stop Warhol Shop: www.ArtMuseum.net
Rijksmuseum, Amsterdam: www.rijksmuseum.nl
Virtual Museum of Canada: www.virtualmuseum.ca

10 | REFRAMING STUDIO ART PRODUCTION AND CRITIQUE
Helen Klebesadel

Editor's Introduction

Helen Klebesadel headed the studio art program at Lawrence University, USA, for a decade before accepting her current position as director of the Women's Studies Consortium for the University of Wisconsin System. She is also a visiting professor in the Women's Studies Program at the University of Wisconsin, Madison. Her work has been featured in feminist journals such as *CALYX* and *Feminist Studies* and can be seen at www.varoregistry.com.

In "Reframing Studio Art Production and Critique," Klebesadel uses feminist strategies to assert that introducing museum theory into the studio art critique process can be empowering. She argues that the traditional "crit" is an outdated pedagogical model that perpetuates patriarchal systems of power. According to Klebesadel, new museum theory can highlight for emerging artists the mediating process that all objects, including their own, undergo when they enter a collection. It can also show that artists have choices and do not have to be controlled by the values that museums and galleries uphold. By understanding the inner workings of the museum, political and practical, students can position their art on the basis of their own beliefs, within or without the institution. And by learning to be critical consumers of the museum, students can work to create change in the institution both through their art and through their constituency. Klebesadel explains that some contemporary artists have long held a vested interest in museum theory, both shaping its precepts and using it to subvert museum systems. And she discusses the increasingly pivotal role that artists are playing in a particular type of museum that is seeking fresh perspectives. Citing her frustrations with her own traditional studio arts schooling, Klebesadel urges readers to take responsibility for their own education. Being informed by new museum theory, she says, leads to new possibilities for artists and for museums.

"What exactly do you mean when you say, 'teach me to be an artist'?" My students often look slightly scandalized when I ask them this question. They seem to believe that I should intuitively understand what it is that they imagine for themselves as "artists." This assumption begs a slew of other questions. Is art a calling or a career? Is it a profession or a discipline? Is an artist a small business operator, a visionary, a social critic, an entertainer, a scholar, or something else? I would argue that all of these possibilities are valid. Before students embark on their chosen career trajectories, however, they must wrestle with a number of challenges and preconceptions. This chapter will explore one aspect of what it means to be an artist: the often uneasy relationship between those who create and those who display works of art. The chapter addresses an imagined audience of studio art students, men and women who not only want to be trained in a profession but hope to engage in a critique of the discursive practices of art, particularly those associated with institutions of display, be they galleries, museums, or other less traditional venues.

This chapter is part of a volume devoted to contemporary museum theory because many art professionals are beginning to recognize the important connection between institutions of display and the education of artists. All institutions have established practices that are determined to be important by the people who control them. Institutional theories reflect the values and perspectives of the culture, class, race, sexuality, gender, and other politically significant life determinants of the individuals who populate them. Artists' sensibilities, as well, are developed in the context of their cultural, social, political, and economic positions. Artists' work can be considered to be historical, cultural, social, and political texts and practices that are interpreted by institutions of display, including the museums. To determine whether or not something is considered to be valuable art, or art at all, it is less product-ive to look at the object in question than to look at the way the object is being treated. Where is the object kept, and what is said about it and its maker? If our art institutions value the object highly enough to protect it, study it, exhibit it in art galleries and museums, and write about it in art magazines and art history books, then it's clear that the object is art and its maker an artist. Artists today must understand and be able to critique institu-tional practices to have the fullest range of possibility for their work.

This chapter will focus on changes in disciplinary discourses that have previously defined art education and presentation, using a feminist visual cultural theory. Primarily concerned with subjectivity and power dynamics, this perspective considers how visual culture contributes to the way gendered subjects are formed, valued, and experience their lives in cultural and social space. Feminist visual cultural theory blends feminist methods and analysis with a particular focus on the intersection of gender, race, class, and sexuality. This theory represents, in broad terms, the commingling of visual textual and social theory, within a commitment to progressive social change. Rather than limiting its focus to canonical works of art, feminist visual theory also devotes time to marginalized cultures, popular media, crafts and traditional arts, music, clothing, and visual spectacles like sport. This is a perspective that considers how institutions of display contribute to defining social values. Additionally, by looking at how visual culture is used and transformed by varied social groups, it takes the position that people from all cultural groups are not simply consumers, but also potential producers of new social values and cultural languages.[1] Using interdisciplinary feminist pedagogical perspectives to review the relationship between contemporary artistic practice and art education, the chapter will consider the potential of museum theory to transform the skill-oriented studio art critique that has traditionally been the central vehicle for teaching evaluative processes to undergraduate and MFA students. Further, the chapter will take a constructivist theoretical approach, arguing that artists construct rather than simply reproduce knowledge. This approach to art-making recognizes that art helps to create our culture rather than simply reflecting it. Students will be challenged to reject pedagogical perspectives that promote the myth of artists as passive conduits of inspired creativity, helplessly reliant upon other art professionals to define, evaluate, and position their art. Readers will be encouraged to adopt the position that art education should critically examine those professional practices that control how art is disciplined – how it is selected, organized, and distributed – and by whom.

It is no longer appropriate that the realities of "how the art world functions" are addressed exclusively in art history, arts administration, or museum studies programs. Studio artists must recognize the relevance of these realities to the distribution and reception of their own work. They must further understand that they and their art are part of larger systems that produce knowledge and define our world. Students can no longer accept an education that does not address these issues. Learning to interpret the contexts in which art is produced is the first step to developing agency as an artist.

Agency, the ability to act or exert power, requires an awareness of the dynamics of power operating within the spheres that affect your life. You can bring three levels of reflection to an analysis of your situation. You can interpret the meaning of your own personal experiences as brought to your work. You can also acknowledge the institutional contexts you find yourself working within and decipher the social, political, economic, and cultural agendas that guide those institutions. This awareness aids your ability to exert control over a given context when you are conscious of your intentions. Finally, you can reflect upon the larger global context for your art and your actions. You can view your experiences as shaped by patterns of political, social, and economic struggles; "the personal is political," as Carol Hanisch so succinctly put it.[2] If you understand the systems of power that surround you, you can consciously examine how the choices you make and the institutions you work within contribute to the value systems that define your society. These insights encourage you to realize that your actions in the world matter. With awareness, you gain agency as both an artist and a citizen.

The Author as Learner, Teacher, and Artist

Situating within larger social and political movements my own experiences as a learner, a teacher, and an artist has helped me gain agency. It has influenced the art I make, whom I make it for, where I choose to exhibit it, and how I teach. When I was 18, in the early 1970s, I attended a prominent mid-western art school with a solid visual arts program. My teachers were professional artists who strove to instill in their students the critical tools to appreciate, as well as the technical skills to make, "fine" art. Unfortunately, one by-product of this approach was the steadily growing realization that I did not fit their definition of a professional artist. None of my professors was a woman. No examples of artwork by women or people of color were discussed in any of my courses. It became increasingly apparent that people who looked like me and who were concerned with subjects and art forms that were valued by my community were not going to be found in the curriculum, in my textbooks, or in the museums and other institutions of display that I visited as a part of my training. The challenge I faced as a young white girl from a rural working-class background was to hold fast to the belief that I, too, had something to offer. Within the context of these institutions, my efforts and the work of other women artists were less valued than the creative work of male artists, particularly white male artists. Essentially, I was taught that my art was "worthless." Despite relative success in my courses, decent grades, and scholarship support, I dropped out of art school my freshman year. I had internalized the belief that people like me were not artists.

As I reflect upon my personal experiences, it is not difficult to see why I eventually chose to focus on subjects and themes that resonate for the women who are part of the audience for my work. It was one way to counter and resist the sexism I faced in the art institutions of my youth. It would take me a decade and a number of other challenges before I decided to return to college and, once again, take up the study of art, this time in conjunction with women's studies.

I wasn't aware at the time I dropped out of college that my experience was, in fact, quite common.[3] Neither was I aware of the opposition to "business as usual" that was mounting in art schools, museums, and other art institutions across the country; feminist, multicultural, and postmodern institutional critiques were launched against the art world, and against a broad spectrum of western society.[4] From the beginning of this movement, artists played an important role in molding the new museum theory which now informs studio art education. Conceptual artists of the late 1960s and early 1970s, including Joseph Kosuth, Marcel Broodthaers, and Hans Haacke, were among the first to question the idea of the museum as a neutral space.[5] Feminist artists like Miriam Shapiro and Judy Chicago and art historians such as Linda Nochlin and John Berger rejected the idea of the canon and of individual male genius.[6] In the 1980s and 1990s the activist art group the Guerrilla Girls demanded representation for women in the most prominent New York institutions of display, while artists such as Adrian Piper and Howardena Pindell made art-world racism the subject of their work.[7] Meanwhile, art historians like Lucy Lippard wrote texts that explored the breadth and depth of multicultural art in the United States, and artists such as Cindy Sherman and Sherrie Levin created works that questioned ideas of originality, authenticity, and the commodity value of art.[8] All of these artists and scholars were interested in reconceptualizing the function of art and examining the role of institutional context in producing meaning.

As a young student, I was not taught to think critically about the inherent bias of what was being presented in the classroom or the museum. It was a harsh lesson to realize that the prejudices and misconceptions that influence the rest of the world are not only reflected in cultural institutions but are, in part, created by them. I had grown up believing that museums were objective purveyors of truth and the caretakers of all that was exceptional in art. In school, I anticipated being let in on the secret that defined "good" art. I expected art museums and my instructors to disclose some objectively defined criteria for excellence that I could adopt to succeed. I learned, instead, that objectivity is as much a myth in institutions as it is within individuals and that everyone and everything exists within ever-fluctuating cultural contexts. I don't want to give the impression that individuals and institutions are incapable of acknowledging the dynamics of power within which they function or of recognizing that the perspectives they share are influenced by their cultural context. Rather, I want to emphasize that, to be a well-educated artist today, one must strive to understand the myriad contexts in which work is produced.

Who teaches you matters. What is taught to you matters. The diversity of art you see in your museums and public art collections matters. It matters which artists are held up as examples for you to emulate. It matters whose visual representations are displayed – and validated – for society at large. It matters who is represented as having agency and who is not. Agency is the ability to assert yourself on your own behalf. This means that students should be actively engaged in pursuing the education they need. It means that artists should be fully involved in shaping the direction of their art and careers. It means that consumers of visual culture should demand access to work that reflects cultural difference and exemplifies social and economic justice.

The Curricula

College, university, and museum faculty or staff have historically privileged narrow definitions of art and artistic success. At schools of art, the challenges of institutional philosophy are usually manifested in debates surrounding the curriculum. Depending on the size of the program, it is not unusual for curricula to be organized around media that traditionally have been sanctioned as "fine" art – painting, sculpture, drawing, printmaking, and, in recent decades, ceramics and photography. Larger programs may offer art metals, book arts, graphic arts, installation, performance, video, new media, and, increasingly, computer-generated art. Programs with a historical commitment to "craft" may also include woodworking and carving, pottery and various fiber arts.

Not surprisingly, the act of designating art media in a curriculum has political and social consequences. It is not unusual to find faculty teaching against the limits of the named curriculum by expanding the definition of traditional media; for example, defining "sculpture" as dealing with space, environment, and all things three-dimensional, or designating "painting" as the manipulation of color on a two-dimensional surface, be it with paint, fabric, thread, or something else altogether. In response, some art institutions have adopted a thematic approach to course offerings, prioritizing theory over the acquisition of media-specific skills.

Increasingly, progressive art programs have begun to adopt the term "visual culture" to describe content knowledge for teachers and facilitators of visual art. Visual culture encompasses multiple forms of cultural production which, taken together, constitute one's visual environment. By considering multiple forms, art programs reflect the range of cultural practices of a diverse citizenry and, some would argue, promote representations and interactions that are democratic and egalitarian. This approach encourages students to explore the functions of art within larger cultural and historical frameworks. Clearly, art and curricula are both products of history and potential sites for cultural change. While the parameters of a curriculum establish the thrust of an institution – theory or practice – it is the studio classroom that carries out this agenda.

Studio Art Critique

In all institutions of higher learning, some form of studio art critique has been, and continues to be, an essential component in the teaching of art at all levels. There are many ways to conduct a "crit," but critiques always involve an artist, a concept or object, and an audience. Whether the critique takes place in a classroom, a gallery, or a museum, in front of a large group of students and faculty or just between a student and an instructor, the main purpose of the critique is to evaluate an artist's work within an educational context.

Historically, studio art critiques were played out as skirmishes. They were modeled on an attack–defense interaction between faculty and students. In a traditional critique, the work of a few privileged students received the praise and attention of the instructor. More often than not, these pieces embodied approaches in technique or subject matter that characterized the teacher's own work. The instructor made observations and asked judgment-laden questions about the work while the students attempted to deflect the questions with acceptable responses. All too often these responses masked the work's actual intent for fear that with exposure would come humiliation. Interestingly enough, those who were chosen to "battle" the professor were actually the lucky ones. Negative attention, it seems, is better than no attention at all. The rest of the students' art works were largely ignored, banished as unworthy of the teacher's attention. For over a century, scenarios such as this have played out in schools, ateliers, universities, and art competitions.

In this manner, the social, political, aesthetic, and theoretical beliefs of the "master" artist determined what was worthy artistic practice.

Studio art education on the university level is changing as art programs build on new scholarship and consider perspectives shaped by critical theory from many disciplines – sociology, psychology, anthropology, history, art history, linguistics – and from interdisciplinary studies – including visual studies, women's studies, and ethnic studies.[9] Studio art critique is most useful when theories concerning "how we learn to value" are central to a pedagogical process that engenders student engagement. Just as much museum education has evolved away from viewing audiences as passive learners, so the studio art critique has increasingly tried to foster students' participation in their own learning. It is important that today's emerging artists take responsibility for shaping and defining their own intellectual, creative, and aesthetic work. It is the job of art faculty to cultivate not only art-making skills but also learning environments where student artists may address critical questions through the lens of their own concerns. Developing artists should be asking, "Where is good art found? How does context matter? Who can be a good artist? Who gets to judge?" Using a collaborative process to jointly determine the criteria of academic success helps engage student artists in meaningful evaluation.

The studio critique can also provide a forum in which to discuss issues of presentation and display. When you decide you want to become an artist, do you automatically mean you want to make objects of art that will be displayed in museums and galleries? If yes, then how can you best retain control over your work in that setting? Traditionally, the artist has had very little voice in the institutional setting. Once a work is acquired or accepted for exhibition, the curator, conservator, and educator often make all policy decisions about it. More recently, some museums have begun to recognize the usefulness of input from living artists and to seek out their advice. In either case, as an artist, you cannot demand complete control over the presentation of your work; you can, however, become an effective advocate for your art by understanding the protocols of museum work. Studio critiques can be geared to explore the principles that influence museum planning. By considering the philosophy and concerns of curators, conservators, museum educators, and other arts professionals (who serve as gatekeepers or, at the very least, influence the reception of your work), you are prepared to appreciate how the gallery or museum "frames" your work.[10]

Art does not exist in a vacuum; artists today have to take responsibility for negotiating the political minefields of display. Institutions of display impose meaning through context. Just as you frame a two-dimensional piece to control its presentation, reception, and interpretation, the institution as a whole frames objects, collections, and exhibitions.[11] Museums, galleries, and alternative spaces construct, deconstruct, and reconstitute the signification of art. Understanding display practices and theories of framing is critical to positioning your work in the art world and beyond.[12]

Artist and philosopher Adrian Piper argues that people learn their values, including aesthetic values, from others with the same social, economic, and ethnic background. She concludes that the art valorized in museums has historically represented the taste and values of the white upper class to the exclusion of art made by and for other groups or communities. Piper further contends that, to succeed in the system, an artist must adopt the aesthetic and cultural norms of the dominant group, discarding other values they may hold dear.[13] As a result, access to a broad range of art practices that represent diverse social values has been extremely limited.

The critique should help students to see that they have choices; rather than simply accepting the museum venue as their one and only goal, emerging artists should consider the range of options most appropriate for their work, be it gallery, alternative space, street corner, community center, or coffeehouse. Recognizing opportunities in alternative venues lets students know that they can produce work that is meaningful to them, instead of allowing institutions of display to dictate what is fitting. Having choices creates agency. The studio critique should introduce the work of diverse artists who have challenged or rejected the museum system.

Artist Faith Ringgold has devoted much of her career to resisting the hegemony of the gallery and museum systems. In the 1960s, she served as an advocate for African American artists, working tirelessly for the inclusion of their work in New York museums. When she subsequently found herself excluded from exhibitions of black artists because of her gender, she launched further feminist and multicultural critiques of museums. She organized public protests to demand increased representation and, at the same time, sought alternative venues for her work outside of New York. Ringgold subverted the mediating power of museums in effective ways. She chose as her primary art form painted quilts which featured visual and textual narratives; in merging the "craft" of quilting with the "fine" art of painting as she engaged in the folk art of storytelling, she challenged the longstanding divisions between "high" and "low." And, in adopting a medium that was inexpensive to ship (as against paintings or sculpture, which usually require expensive museum-quality crating), she was able to send her work all over the US, thus circumventing barriers to success in New York. Ringgold's willingness to explore new subjects and media, informed as they were by her personal and cultural background, and to creatively and irrepressibly seek out alternative venues for exhibition, particularly university and college galleries, helped launch a long and fruitful career.[14]

Other artists involved in questioning museum practices have actually made their work simulations of the museum or the processes of museum professionals.[15] Some artists, like Fred Wilson, who includes in his resumé employment in the education departments of the Metropolitan Museum of Art, the American Crafts Museum, and the Museum of Natural History, draw upon their experiences as museum educators to consider the museum's role in society.[16] Artists such as Andrea Fraser and Mark Dion use strategies of simulation to create institutional critiques from within (see chapter 11).

Some artists choose to circumvent the mainstream contemporary art world altogether, refusing to make saleable objects which typify a corporate aesthetic. Stepping outside the museum and gallery system can give artists freedom from the hierarchies and constraints imposed by these institutions. By making work that does not have a physical reality but exists only in the interconnected network that is cyberspace, digital artists consciously reject the system of the art market. By focusing on audiences who rarely visit art museums and galleries, public art brings art to the people. Artists are usually driven to public art as a form of social commentary. Muralist Judith Baca's work with young artists to depict an alternative history of LA, *The Great Wall of Los Angeles* (1976–84), functions as an instrument of change, as do performance artist Suzanne Lacy's *Crystal Quilt* (Minneapolis, 1987) a public celebration of older women, and environmental artist Betsy Damon's *Living Water Garden* (Chengdu, China, 1998), a large-scale project that brought together artists, business people, and governmental agencies to build a beautiful water-cleansing ecosystem. Other artists have rejected the commodification of the object by establishing organizations that promote social change through art. Photographer Jim Hubbard's "Shooting Back" (founded 1989), which gives disadvantaged children across the US cameras to document their own lives, is another example of art that does not define its value through acceptance by museum professionals or their audiences.[17]

Art aimed at social change often relies upon context to be effective. Curator Mary Jane Jacobs, who studies new public art, identifies three specific strategies of artists working outside traditional institutions of display. These artists typically employ emblematic displays or actions to inspire social change. Their works affect social systems by benefiting a particular group or generating monetary income to support social goals. Collaborative and participatory processes impact on the individuals involved and contribute to a remedying of social problems. Jacobs concludes that this approach usually does not give rise to a larger audience for art, but replaces the imagined "art world viewer" with a different one drawn by a connection with the subject matter, the community upon which the piece is focused, or the collaborative ideal.[18]

Some cultural commentators believe that, in seeking to effect social change outside of existing art systems, avant-garde artists are merely reinforcing the art world's endemic elitism.[19] According to these commentators, artists who refuse to engage with those institutions that determine cultural values end up delaying critiques that could one day bring a greater democracy of representation. I would argue, however, that it is possible for artists to critique museums and advocate change from both inside and outside the system, especially if curators, museum educators, and administrators become allies in the struggle.

New museum theory asks you to consider the interpretive practices that bring meaning or "life" to objects in the museum.[20] Introduced into the studio critique, museum theory can help you to generate ideas about lobbying for your own interests and influencing museum systems.

Transforming Studio Critique

The studio art critique, when it embraces student engagement in critical questioning, will continue to be an extremely useful pedagogical tool for the next generation of artists. Student artists can use the critique to think about the choices curators, exhibition designers, and conservators make and the ways that these professionals work with contemporary artists. Only when emerging artists know how the museum operates can they have an effective voice in the process. Furthermore, developing an understanding of museum practice and theory opens up employment options within the museum system. Working from within the system often provides opportunities to elicit substantive change.

It is no longer appropriate in studio critique to simply pass judgment on the iconography and execution of objects, by comparison with past visual art practice. More complex approaches to meaning and making are necessary. Student artists should expect to learn how to perform a visual analysis of their own and other artists' work in a way that recognizes the relationship of art to the cultural institutions that mediate its meaning. In so doing, they

257

should consider art works as cultural texts, examining how subject, material, form, and context come together to create the work. A four-pronged approach is useful in guiding inquiry. By following this approach, students discover that their work can be interpreted in multiple contexts – often in ways quite different from the artist's original intention. The broad range of questions often generates disparate and even contradictory responses.

Useful concerns in critiquing works of art include:

- *Subject*: Specifically, what is the piece about? Does it use images or objects associated with political perspectives, popular culture, or the history of art? Does the work address subjects you are accustomed to seeing in art? Does the subject challenge existing conventions in art or the larger culture?
- *Material*: From what is it made? What social, cultural, political, historical, and economic associations, as well as artistic conventions, does the material evoke?
- *Form*: How is the object made? How does the artist employ formal visual language? What historical and contemporary visual references does the handling of the medium imply? How does the method of its making indicate the artist's intentions and suggest appropriate criteria for analysis?
- *Context*: Who seems to be the intended audience for the work? Consider how the display of the work might influence its reading. Does the piece look like it's in discourse with other works you might find in an art museum (evidencing a concern with the art world), or does it resemble artifacts more often found in a museum of natural history, a craft museum, or other cultural and political institutions? What implications does this have? Would a shopping mall or a home be a more typical environment for the display of the object? How does the work change if it is removed from one context to another?

While all of the categories above are important, it is the fourth category, that of "context," that draws upon the potential of museum theory to transform the traditional studio art critique into a process where artists can be empowered as both producers and consumers of art. It is here that artists can begin to investigate the mediating and interpretive practices of institutions of display. Artists learn to see that art does not have a fixed meaning, that environment makes meaning. And they become educated consumers of the museum, capable of formulating a critique and asking for accountability.

The critique should be a venue in which to examine the assumptions on which the modern museum and commercial gallery are based. It is within your purview to be concerned with the complex and sophisticated relationships that exist among economics, social context, and aesthetics, as represented in the contested space of the gallery. Despite thirty years or more of ongoing critique, galleries, museums, and mainstream art organizations remain the arbiters of style. They still largely define and distinguish what art is perceived as valid. Museum professionals have the power to identify which makers of art will be supported; categorize art according to genre; evaluate art according to a hierarchy of media; assess quality upon the basis of standards they accept as most appropriate; and place art within a continuum of art history. They determine the display, interpretation, and publication of the art to which you have access. Objects have a complex afterlife when they leave the studio and enter the realm of display.

Critique exercises can pose questions that will help emerging artists gain agency within the gallery and museum systems. What venues are most appropriate to your work? By looking through museum or exhibition catalogues and websites (being a critical reader of these often commercialized resources) and by visiting alternative venues in your community, you can identify sites where you would like to show your art. Once you have made your choices it is important for you to examine why you've chosen as you have. What do these spaces you've selected represent to you and to others? And why did you reject other kinds of sites? How might the meaning of your work shift from one site to the other?

Planning and curating exhibitions of your own and others' work can be an invaluable part of your art education. This work helps you see that display includes discursive manipulations that impose classification systems and hierarchies which, themselves, assert meaning. You can get curatorial experience on a formal basis through university gallery internships, independent studies, and museum studies courses. You can get this experience informally by designing an exhibition plan of your work and/or that of your classmates. If you were to organize a show of these pieces, what choices would you make and why? How does the environment make meaning? What impact might a different scheme have? Compare your exhibition plan with those of your fellow students. In executing your plan, use university galleries and student display spaces to their fullest potential as laboratories. You can also create models, real and virtual, of your plans or simply arrange works around the classroom in alternative ways. In addition, you can make virtual exhibitions from available images of art works online, as long as

259

copyright-protected images are not published. (See chapter 9 for a site that allows you to produce your own virtual museum from its collection of digital images.)

Working on a conceptual basis, without "real-world" constraints or fear of failure, encourages risk-taking and can be a powerful learning experience. Such processes, with critical analysis embedded in the planning and execution, lead to insights about the museum as a framing device and guide you to make conscious decisions about your goals as an artist. These exercises may even generate ideas about how to subvert the museum as frame.

Other useful exercises focus on related questions. What kind of wall texts might be appropriate or inappropriate for the display of your art? How can the type and style of text strengthen the meaning you seek to evoke? How does the manipulation of lighting or the arrangement of space advance or impede your intentions? What would you want a tour guide or cassette guide to say about your art? Working and thinking in this way helps student artists realize why it is so important that they be able to talk and write about art in a clear and compelling fashion. Artists can no longer rely on someone else to define and position their work. Sometimes the artist's statement is the only opportunity they have to communicate to a curator or educator presenting their work. You must be prepared to make the most of it. Exercises aimed at articulating your vision will lay the groundwork for future success, as they reveal where your thinking about intentions might be a bit muddy and require further examination.

Studio curricula should also consider the new relationships developing between artist and curator. Indeed, curators of contemporary art now sometimes collaborate with artists to seek fresh perspectives and new audiences. Postcolonial theory has underlined the importance of giving voice to those represented. Feminist theory has put forth new models of curation as a collaborative process. Artists' rights, since the early 1980s, have been clarified through law. Alternative spaces, in which the artist plays a pivotal role, are influencing mainstream institutions. And, increasingly, more artists are graduating from MFA programs well versed in critical theory and prepared to make a contribution to museum discourse.

Many museums that want to inspire discourse will make sure the artist has a place at the planning table, knowing that she or he can help institutions become more vital to the communities they serve. It is not unusual today for artists to jury and curate exhibitions. Moreover, artists are calling for a stronger voice in the museum by creating installations, new media works, ephemeral pieces, and conceptual art that are dependent on collaboration with curators for display, storage, and/or care. Some artists are even designing whole environments for museums, essentially becoming curators as they plan and install their projects. Artists are becoming curators and curators are becoming artists as well, with display as their medium. Many curators today eschew the modernist purism of the "white cube" in favor of compelling design environments that acknowledge the gallery as a framing device.

Studio exercises can also investigate relationships between artists and conservators. Before making an acquisition, many museums will have their conservators write up a treatment and maintenance plan in conjunction with the artist or the artist's estate (see chapter 3). What kind of conservation and maintenance policy would you write for your own works? If you have used unstable materials or new technologies, consider how your work will fare over time. Will the materials require special care to keep from disintegrating? How would you define "artistic integrity" for your work? What interventions are acceptable to you? And which do you prioritize, use or protection? Can your sculpture be painted a different color? Can your painting be reframed in another material? What is or isn't allowed? What do you care about and why?

Beyond the Studio Critique

As student artists, you can make opportunities for yourselves outside of the critique classroom as well. Internships within museums, art centers, and galleries spur valuable insights while also providing training that might lead to future employment. Museum studies courses, both theoretical and practical, can further your understanding of context issues introduced in the progressive critique. Sometimes, museum studies is taught through a department of anthropology, American studies, or history, instead of art; don't let that stop you from taking these courses. Engaging in museum studies is a key means to create agency.

If you are willing to collaborate with fellow students, additional possibilities open up. Join forces to produce and display communal work. Seek out alternative spaces or establish new ones. Developing strategies to work collectively is one way to subvert the traditional museum system. Art work produced collaboratively challenges ideas of individual genius and conventions of isolation. Student art clubs and organizations can be useful resources and networks. Events can be organized under the auspices of an educational group that would be unavailable to you as an individual. Such groups can curate and mount exhibitions, on campus and off, to address the issues that matter most to their members. Student organizations can also arrange meetings with and talks by curators, conservators, museum educators, and gallery directors. These events introduce the theories and practice of museum professionals into students' own communities.

Your studio art education can be designed to help you build the analytical skills to both critique museums' systems of power and participate effectively within them. Whether you want to work with and within institutions of display or to subvert the museum system and larger social structures, your education should guide you to identify strategies that will improve your chances of success. Create a plan, grounded in self reflection and research, for making yourself known to the institutions you seek to work with, and act upon it. Determine your goals and identify what type of institutional or programmatic support you will need to accomplish them. If you aim to work with galleries, art centers, and/or museums, be proactive. (If the focus of your art is community based, or outside the realm of the art world altogether, you can apply a plan of action to the institutions you seek to influence.)

Research institutions by visiting them and gaining an understanding of their mission. Acquaint yourself with the systems of power at work there. Remember, administrators, curators, and other museum professionals have been drawn to the arts, too. Do them the honor of respecting their creative and critical work. Focus on the institutions and individuals with goals similar to yours and be ready to clearly articulate why your work complements their vision. Do not seek approval for your work from people who represent institutionalized value systems you do not share. Contact appropriate sites and ask about their process of review. Most institutions have organized review processes. Many arts professional will take the time to meet with you if you approach them in a way that is considerate of their time. When you have arranged a meeting, ask for feedback and recommendations on where to take your work. All organizations are based on relationships and, most often, relationships are developed over time. Once you have initiated contact with a curator or an arts program administrator, keep him or her updated on the progress of your work with exhibition announcements and personalized invitations.

If you seek to work outside the system, explore what legal steps are necessary to exhibit public art outside of traditional institutions of display. Discover the procedures of permission required to bring your work to the audiences you seek to engage in discourse. Become an active and knowledgeable participant in the art community and events that surround it. Do your art. Find opportunities to share it. Build relationships with like-minded members of the larger art communities that you wish to become a part of. Seek collaborative opportunities. Do not wait to be "discovered" and do not assume you will not find support for your work. Understand your art as part of a larger discourse that is enriched by your participation and the participation of other, broadly diverse voices.

Through your art work you translate your understanding of the world into patterns of meaning that could broaden our cultural dialogues. No matter what audience you choose for your art or what becomes your chosen media, as an engaged practitioner you may construct new knowledge through your and your works' interaction with cultural institutions and artifacts and with other people. You will recognize that the diverse and complex cultural positions of makers, audience, and institutions of display influence definitions and the interpretation of art. Understanding this, you can consciously confront the challenge of facilitating the process of the interpretation of your own art. As a visual culture change agent, you can influence the institutions of display that mediate what we value by creating art works that critique, resist, and reject limiting conventions and categories. In so doing you will show us what it means to be an artist who is critically informed and culturally conscious.

Questions for Discussion

1 Describe Klebesadel's tone and approach. How has feminism shaped her ideas on studio art education?

2 How would you characterize Klebesadel's own early art education? Have you or anyone you know ever had a similar experience?

3 How can new museum theory transform the "crit"? If you have taken studio art classes, has this theory been part of your own studio art education? What is the theory's potential? How might it inform other courses as well, across the curriculum?

4 What does it mean to develop agency? What choices are available to artists in the larger world and how should studio arts students evaluate them? How might you position your work within the mediating structures of the museum or gallery, or, if you see yourself working outside the system, how would you create change? What are the politics of cultural institutions in your own community?

5 What kinds of new opportunities are opening up for artists in museums with contemporary art holdings? How has this trend developed? How would you see yourself engaged in collaborative work with museum curators, conservators, and/ or educators?

263

6 How can you best take responsibility for your own education? What do you find most useful from Klebesadel's list of exercises? And how might they empower you in other fields as well? Why does she advocate a collaborative process? What are the merits of virtual versus "real-time" exhibition design in one's education? How can students claim the university gallery as a laboratory for experimentation?

Notes

1 For a foundation in feminist visual culture theory, see A. Jones. (ed.). (2003). *The Feminism and Visual Culture Reader*. London: Routledge.

2 C. Hanisch. (1979). "The Personal is Political." In K. Sarachild, C. Hanisch, F. Levine, B. Leonn, and C. Price. (eds.). *Feminist Revolution: An Abridged Edition with Additional Writings*. New York: Random House, 204–5.

3 C. C. Park. (1996). "Learning from What Women Learn in the Studio Class." In G. Collins and R. Sandell. (eds.). *Gender Issues in Art Education: Context, Content, and Strategies*. Reston, VA: National Art Education Association, 2–8.

4 H. Reckitt. (2001). *Art and Feminism*. New York: Phaidon.

5 H. Foster. (1986). "Subversive Signs." In *RECODING: Art, Spectacle, Cultural Politics*. Seattle: Bay Press, 99–118.

6 N. Broude and M. Garrard. (eds.). (1994). *The Power of Feminist Art*. New York: Harry Abrams; L. Nochlin. (1988). "Why Have There Been No Great Women Artists?" In *Women, Art and Power and Other Essays*. New York: Harper & Row, 147–58; J. Berger. (1972). *Ways of Seeing*. London: BBC and Penguin.

7 E. Hess. (1995). "Guerrilla Girl Power: Why the Art World Needs a Conscience." In N. Felshin. (ed.). *But Is It Art? The Spirit of Art as Activism*. Seattle: Bay Press, 309–31; A. Piper. (1996). *Out of Order, Out of Sight. Vols. I and II*. Cambridge, MA: MIT Press; H. Pindell. (1997). "Commentary and Update of Gallery and Museum Statistics." In L. Sims and H. Pindell. (eds.). *The Heart of the Question: The Writings and Paintings of Howardena Pindell*. New York: Midmarch Arts Press, 3–6, 19–28.

8 L. R. Lippard. (2000). *Mixed Blessings: New Art in a Multicultural America*. Seattle: New Press. (Original work published 1990.)

9 P. Wye. (guest ed.). (1999). "Rethinking Studio Art Education." *Art Journal*, 58: 1, 3–83.

10 R. Greenberg, B. Ferguson, and S. Nairne. (eds.). (1996). *Thinking About Exhibitions*. London and New York: Routledge.

11 P. Duro. (ed.). (1996). *The Rhetoric of the Frame: Essays on the Boundaries of the Artwork*. Cambridge: Cambridge University Press.

12 B. O'Doherty. (1996). "The Gallery as a Gesture." In Greenberg et al., *Thinking About Exhibitions*, 320–40. (Original essay published 1980.)

13 A. Piper. (1985). "Critical Hegemony and Aesthetic Acculturation." *Nous*, 19: 1, 29–40.

14 T. Gouma-Peterson. (1998). *Dancing in the Louvre, Faith Ringgold's French Collections and Other Quilt Stories*. New York and Berkeley, CA: New Museum of Contemporary Art and University of California Press.

15 J. Putnam. (2001). *Art and Artifact: The Museum as Medium*. New York: Thames and Hudson.

16 S. R. Walker. (2001). *Teaching Meaning in Artmaking*. Worcester. MA: Davis Publications, pp. 33–4.

17 S. Lacy. (ed.). (1995). *Mapping the Terrain: New Genre Public Art*. Seattle: Bay Press.

18 M. J. Jacobs. (1995). "Unfashionable Audience." In Lacy, *Mapping the Terrain*, 30–59.

19 D. Trend. (1988). "Cultural Struggle and Educational Activism." In G. Kester. (ed.). *Art, Activism, and Oppositionality: Essays from Afterimage*. Durham, NC: Duke University Press, 169–81.

20 M. Tamen. (2001). *Friends of Interpretable Objects*. Cambridge, MA, and London: Harvard University Press.

11 | THE UNIVERSITY MUSEUM AND GALLERY: A SITE FOR INSTITUTIONAL CRITIQUE AND A FOCUS OF THE CURRICULUM

Lyndel King and Janet Marstine

Editor's Introduction

Lyndel King has been director and chief curator at the Weisman Art Museum at the University of Minnesota, USA, since 1981. King was instrumental in securing funding and selecting Frank O. Gehry as the architect for a new art museum building which opened in 1993. She has served on the board of trustees at numerous organizations, including the Association of Art Museum Directors and the American Federation of Arts. Janet Marstine is assistant professor at Seton Hall University, USA, and is the editor of this volume.

Together, we show in this chapter how the university gallery that foregrounds new museum theory can provide students with powerful experiences in critical thinking and new models of interdisciplinary learning. Through case studies of the Weisman Art Museum, University of Minnesota, and the Tang Teaching Museum and Art Gallery, Skidmore College, the chapter highlights the catalytic role of contemporary artists, such as Mark Dion and Fred Wilson, who critique the museum. It discusses the special properties of the university gallery that make it an ideal site for radical thinking. And it examines the metaphorical processes of "mining" and "digging" that artists use to reveal the largely unspoken value systems of museums and universities. The chapter asserts that individual projects like Dion's "Cabinet of Curiosities" at the Weisman can provoke students to challenge the disciplinary parameters of the museum and the university. It argues that the campus-wide embrace of critical museum theory, as at Skidmore, leads to systemic pedagogical change, particularly with an insightful facilitator such as Wilson.

A hodge-podge of objects fills the gallery, from early modernist paintings to coins and medals to eyeglasses and personal photographs. Accompanying wall texts quote from old letters, internal memos, transcriptions of conversations, and other seemingly obscure documents in the museum's archives. Close scrutiny exposes the secretive and often exploitative behavior of museum administrators courting potential donors. It also reveals evidence of the complex and contradictory revaluation that occurs when objects move from the domestic sphere to public collections. This 1992 exhibition "Aren't They Lovely?" was the result of an intervention by artist Andrea Fraser at the University Art Museum, University of California (UC), Berkeley. Curators there invited Fraser to create an installation with objects from the permanent collection. She chose to focus on one specific bequest, that of alumna Thérèse Bonney. Fraser's primary interest was not, however, Bonney and her collection but the methods by which museums legitimize culture. Thus, alongside excerpts from documents relevant to the bequest, Fraser exhibited all the objects from the bequest; these included pieces that curators had deemed worthy – and had accessioned (or officially acquired for the permanent collection) – and those that curators had judged unworthy – and had not accessioned – and which had been permanently stored in the basement.[1]

How did the acquisitions process reduce Bonney's life to the value of the objects the museum acquired? What does the intervention tell us about the value of art and the value systems of museums? How does classification impose meaning? And how does the classification of objects create and reinforce social hierarchies? Moreover, what kind of learning opportunities does such an intervention offer to university students? And why is the university art museum an ideal site for institutional critique?

University museums are perfectly situated to embrace conflicting ideas about museums and to confront these ideas for didactic purposes. Because of their history, museums and galleries of art on university campuses in the United States have the potential to engage students in direct experiences of museum practices and in critical thinking about museums. Natural history, science, technology, and anthropology museums usually came into existence on campuses to maintain collections. From the beginning, they bore the weighty responsibility of preserving vast specimen collections and providing research opportunities for scientists. University art galleries and museums, conversely, were often established without a collection. Some important college galleries were, of course, based on collections and sometimes art collections followed quickly after a college gallery was founded. But most campus art museums originated differently. Frequently, they began as adjuncts for art departments to show the work of faculty and students in the visual arts. In other cases, they started off as informal learning resources intended to provide access to art for students across disciplines. The founding purpose of most university art museums gave them an all-university educational mission and a penchant for experimentation. This resulted in a focus distinct from that of college natural history museums.

Certainly, some university natural history museums engage students from many disciplines, but they less easily initiate the kind of unconventional collaborations that university art museums can foster. Because art museums are the most common kind on university campuses, they are the sites most likely to be involved in institutional critique. University galleries promote self-critique by commissioning artists who make the museum the subject of their work to create projects with students and faculty from across the curriculum.

Curators at diverse museums today, from powerhouses like the British Museum to smaller venues such as the Maryland Historical Society, are commissioning artists to engage in projects that recontextualize their institutions. Motivated by a need to see their collections freshly, to attract new audiences, and to become more culturally sensitive, curators look to artists to discover alternative approaches. University art museums are important participants in this trend. And, in fact, they can become places for critical inquiry perhaps more comfortably than other kinds of museums, because they operate in an academic climate where the questioning of authority is encouraged. University museums have a teaching mission and experts to choose from in almost any subject imaginable, including museums themselves. They are ideal environments for exploring the value systems of display institutions.

Since the early twentieth century, artists have been critiquing the museum as mediator.[2] Marcel Duchamp's "Readymades," his introduction of slightly altered ordinary consumer products into the exhibition space, poke fun at the concept of "aura" that museums claim for their collections. Joseph Cornell's worlds in a box reject the taxonomies of the modern museum. Such irreverent works were commonly shown at university galleries. The first incidence of a museum commissioning an artist to act as guest curator occurred at the Rhode Island School of Design ("Raid the Icebox," 1969–70). RISD asked Andy Warhol to curate an exhibition of works from its holdings that were long neglected and out of public view. Warhol chose to exhibit, instead of individual objects, whole collections – including shoes – as they were arranged in storage. The project revealed the fetishistic process of accumulation in which museums engage.

In the late 1960s and the 1970s, a larger body of artists, among them Marcel Broodthaers, Daniel Buren, Hans Haacke, and Joseph Kosuth, made institutional critique the mainstay of their work (see chapter 10). The social and political unrest of the 1960s and the theoretical treatises that fueled it led artists to question institutional values, including those of the museum. They challenged modernist claims of the autonomy of the artist, arguing that the institution is a framing device that imposes meaning. Artists looked to expose the ideological viewpoints that museum narratives encode, sometimes through making "museums" of their own. Minimalism offered artists a means to reject the veneration of the object. Conceptual Art, with its focus on language, encouraged artists to voice their critique directly to the viewer. Installation Art held possibilities for site-specific critique. Although many of the artists involved created their watershed works for large public museums, they impacted on university galleries, too, through lectures, essays, and smaller-scale projects.

By the mid-1980s, institutional critique had become a significant trend in postmodern artistic practice. Informed by feminist theory, Louise Lawler, Barbara Kruger, Sophie Calle, and others challenged gendered formulas of representation, including the concept of originality, the use of authoritative wall texts, the belief in universality, and the production of spectacle. Many of these artists have lectured and exhibited widely at university museums.

In the late 1980s and early 1990s, artists began to "take over" the gallery space itself, appropriating the roles of curator, educator, exhibit designer, and even registrar. They saw museum work as performance – examining, classifying, indexing, teaching – a process more illuminating than the finished product of the museum display. Spurred, in part, by the first publications on new museum theory, curators invited artists to create work that examined their institutions in new ways. In these projects, artists considered what institutions concealed as much as what they revealed. Many artists drew from postcolonial theory to focus on and contextualize cultures marginalized by the museum. Archives and storage areas became prime resources in the search for new cultural narratives. "Mining" and "digging" were metaphors that these artists used to describe their work.

When artists were welcomed to produce their projects *in situ*, they had opportunities to witness, collaborate with, and intervene in the day-to-day operations of the institution. Most artists were not overtly against the museum but strove to promote awareness of the systems of power within cultural institutions. Artists such as Andrea Fraser, Fred Wilson, and Mark Dion looked from the inside out to provide a pivotal model for learning about museums. And in the university gallery they often found a partner willing to assume risks in order to gain insight. The university gallery has often been in the forefront of institutional self-criticism and reform.

Andrea Fraser set a precedent for museum critique with her performance piece *Museum Highlights: A Gallery Talk* (Philadelphia Museum of Art, 1989). Assuming the persona of a docent or guide, she quoted from a pastiche of archival sources about both the museum and the poorhouse to parody the shallow, status-oriented "museum-speak" that tour guides often spout.[3] This piece and her UC Berkeley exhibition are part of her larger commitment to appropriating the language of museum founders, trustees, curators, educators, and corporate sponsors to reveal the class structures and archaisms that museums promulgate, even as they commission artists like her to reveal them.

Fred Wilson was catapulted to national prominence when, in 1992, the Maryland Historical Society asked him to curate and reinstall its collections in a provocative new way. He reclaimed objects long hidden in storage because of the explosive racial history they represent and juxtaposed them with celebrated pieces. In so doing, he replaced the quaint, nostalgic atmosphere with one that probes a deeper, more complex past. Wilson adopted traditional museum exhibit categories based on medium. In a case labeled "Metalwork, 1723–1880," he juxtaposed silver goblets produced for wealthy Maryland households with iron shackles made for the slaves that such householders owned. For another display, with the standard museum title "Cabinet-Making, 1820–1960," Wilson added a crude wooden whipping post to a grouping of elegant antique chairs.[4] Though this project was not his first artistic critique of museum practice, it caught the imagination of museum curators eager to expand their audiences and enliven their collection displays. Wilson has created projects with similar aims at university galleries and has lectured widely about his work.

Wilson's installations question curatorial judgment at museums, focusing not only on what museums choose to display but also on what they choose not to display and the racially biased motivations behind both decisions. He is a master at unexpected juxtapositions and at using collections to reveal attitudes long hidden, even to those with long experience with the institution – perhaps most profoundly hidden from those with the longest experience. By recontextualizing collections, Wilson reveals how institutions define themselves and how this self-definition defines history. He describes his process as " a *trompe l'oeil* of curating."[5] Effective *trompe l'oeil* entails close scrutiny of reality.

Artist Interventions in the University Museum:
The Frederick R. Weisman Art Museum

Some artists that critique the museum are drawn to the university gallery because it offers willing and able partners for learning and collaboration; with its focus on academics, the university community has the capability to do the in-depth research needed to support artist-led projects. In turn, some university curators seek out artist-led collaborative pieces because they recognize that many students – and faculty – are turned off by high-polish exhibits in which conclusions have been reached long before a show opens. Together, the artist and the university gallery can establish a learning community of students, faculty, and museum staff in an open-ended process intended to stimulate debate.[6] In fact, some of the most exciting work in museum critique occurs in such learning communities.

The Frederick R. Weisman Art Museum at the University of Minnesota, like many museums since the early to mid-1990s, has worried that its institutional voice is intimidating and authoritarian, not leaving room for other opinions. The Weisman has experimented with wall texts signed by individual curators and wall texts that provide multiple points of view about individual objects. It has worked to validate individual visitors' points of view while continuing to value curatorial expertise. It has commissioned Frank O. Gehry to design a new museum building (1993) with sculptural qualities that spark new perspectives. And it has engaged artists to present subversive viewpoints on the museum. Mark Dion's 2001 project for the Weisman, "Cabinet of Curiosities" (figure 11.1), demonstrates the potential of the university gallery as a laboratory for experimentation.

Dion has long been fascinated by the curiosity cabinet or *Wunderkammer* – those late sixteenth- and seventeenth-century collections of natural and man-made objects assembled by aristocrats, scholars, and wealthy merchants that were the precursors of the modern museum and the modern university. At Minnesota, he created a learning community to challenge systems within the university as well as within the museum.[7] The project involved an elaborate process of culling from university-wide collections to revisit the history of museums, specifically the curiosity cabinet. Dion's art and process reveal museums as unnatural – or artificial – congregations of objects. He and his collaborators give new meaning to collections by recontextualizing them according to the constructs that the group pursues.

Dion is obsessed with museums:

271

FIGURE 11.1   Mark Dion, "Cabinet of Curiosities," installation for the Frederick R. Weisman Art Museum, University of Minnesota, 2001. © Frederick R. Weisman Art Museum

> When I go to a place, the first thing I do is check into the hotel, put my bags down, and go to the museums. I'm a complete museum junkie. These kinds of things and their arrangements interest me, as well as the way that museums always tell the official story. They tell how society would like to see itself represented; what it values, how it deals with its problematic past and its heroic past, how it brags on itself, how it contextualizes its mistakes. All of that is embedded in museums, so they are incredibly rich sources of not only material history but also etiology and politics. Because their function is so didactic, I think they are ideologically very transparent.[8]

With irony, Dion exposes the histories and underlying biases of museums and demonstrates how museums define the world. He understands museums – and academic processes – very well but he remains an artist, slightly an outsider. At the same time, through performance, he seems dangerously close to doing museum work himself. He is drawn to the museum as a clear expression of cultural norms yet, by subverting its systems and procedures, shows its underlying fallaciousness.[9] Dion is a curator-artist, like Fred Wilson. Yet Dion's projects bring natural history and cultural history together in a process that is not quite *trompe l'oeil* but more like Frankenstein's unnatural creation, whose product resembles the model but is by no means a clone. Like David Wilson, who assembled the mind-altering Museum of Jurrasic Technology in Los Angeles, and Rosamund Purcell, who recreated at Tufts University the seventeenth-century *Wunderkammer* of Danish physician, archeologist, and linguist Ole Worms, Dion employs the methods of archeology and of museums to raise basic questions: What is a museum? Why is it a museum? And, similarly to Eric Gable (chapter 4), Dion positions the museum as theater and museum processes as drama. He and his collaborators play the roles of archeologists and museum staff while museum objects serve as props and visitors become the theater audience. Dion and his partners perform the painstaking excavation, classification, and display techniques to show how subjective choices make history. He explains: "To better understand the museum, I have at various times had to become the museum, taking on the duties of collecting, archiving, classifying, arranging, conserving and displaying. Personifying the museum condenses its activities and articulates how the museum's various departments function like vital organs in a living being."[10] By inviting Minnesota students to personify the museum along with him, Dion empowers them to experience the complexities and contradictions of institutions in a visceral way. This is teaching at its most interactive.

In some projects, Dion engages in actual archeological digs – though at sites that professional archeologists would not select. The digs enable him to fuse his interests in the environment and the arts. In other works, archeology is a metaphor that he uses to describe scavenging through archives and storage areas, as he does at the University of Minnesota. In either case, he calls his performative mode a "fieldwork model."[11] He typically assembles the objects that he's collected, cleaned, and classified into a curiosity cabinet.

Through creating such a cabinet, Dion provokes his collaborators and audiences to consider what happens to an object once it is collected – in this case twice, for the university and for the project. He also guides them to examine the relationship between collecting and making art. He makes them aware of the politics of representation – the subjectivity of classification and modes of display. And he leads them to critique the knowledge systems of universities. His goal, he asserts, is to "open up the laboratories and storerooms to reveal art and science as the dynamic processes that they are."[12]

Dion is one of several artist-cum-critics of the modern museum who revisit its antecedents to challenge disciplinary boundaries between art and science and to foreground what the rational museum has marginalized. Theorist Stephen Bann has championed this trend. He writes, "Curiosity has the

273

valuable role of signaling to us that the object on display is invariably a nexus of interrelated meanings – which may be quite discordant – rather than a staging post on a well trodden route through history."[13] Dion asserts, "I must confess a fondness for curiosity cabinets particularly since they most closely resemble the surrealistic quality of the back room of many museums, rather than the exhibition galleries."[14] He sees the process of creating a curiosity cabinet as a means to reveal what museums – and universities – usually conceal. He also embraces it as a means to breathe new life, through idiosyncratic juxtapositions, into the process of viewing objects; unlike the modern museum, in which classification systems render the viewer passive, the curiosity cabinet is not over-interpreted and is an art form in itself, based on the personal vision of the collector. The curiosity cabinet requires the active participation – the curiosity – of the viewer.[15]

What exactly is a curiosity cabinet? It is an encyclopedic collection of *naturalia* – objects created by God – and *artificialia* – objects created by humans. It is a microcosm or world in miniature intended to represent universal knowledge.[16] Collectors amassed hundreds or even thousands of specimens, *naturalia* from the animal, vegetable, and mineral worlds and *artificialia* from an equally wide spectrum, including musical instruments, antiquities, scientific instruments, coins, weapons, and objects associated with indigenous peoples. Rarities, particularly objects considered hybrids and/or deviations from the norm, were most appreciated. By overstepping traditional boundaries, such materials were believed to represent the unifying principles of the macrocosm. For example, coral was prized because, though formed from the skeletons of sea creatures, its deposits look like plants. Petrified wood, seashells, snake skins, mammoth bones, fossils, ostrich eggs, antlers, wax portraits, stuffed animals, dried flowers, mummified body parts, and mechanized automatons were popular because they seem to hover between life and death. Some of these materials were crafted to transform nature into art; animals were cast in silver, shells were ornately carved. Some special objects in the curiosity cabinet were of dubious authenticity; for instance, many collectors boasted of unicorn horns (actually narwhals' tusks). Objects that played on the viewer's expectations of scale were celebrated, such as giants' footsteps and minutely carved nut and cherrystone miniatures. Materials thought to have occult powers were treasured, including bezoars (stony concretions that form in the stomachs of camels and other animals), which, when hollowed into a cup and drunk from, were thought to be an antidote to poison. A Mannerist sensibility shaped taste to the extreme, sometimes to the point of the grotesque.

There was great variation among curiosity cabinets. The Italian form of the *studiolo* (for example, that of Francesco I de'Medici) was a hermetic, fully planned space. The *Wunderkammer* of northern Europe (for instance, that of Duke Albrecht V of Bavaria) was usually more open and haphazard. All, however, were private spaces; knowledge was power and, thus, curiosity cabinets were the sole preserve of the collector, his advisers, and distinguished visitors and scholars.[17] Cabinets were organized according to the collector's whims; knowledge was never compartmentalized into distinct disciplines as it is in the modern museum. Collectors organized their cabinets by material (e.g. silver, wood, ivory), aesthetics, a philosophical statement or one of the universalizing rubrics of the period (e.g. the four seasons, the four elements, the four cardinal directions, the seven virtues, the seven planets). The associative process of connecting objects to iconographic schemes could be either direct, as through appearance, or obscure, as through myth. Categories were unstable and overlapping; collectors embraced this quality, as it highlighted anomalies. The fluidity of organizational programs reflects the concept of an infinite and variable nature created by God. Cabinets were intended to generate multiple readings. The aim of the cabinet was not only to collect the world in miniature but to suggest correspondences among objects.

The cabinet itself – the cupboard, case, drawer, shelf, and/or panel – in which the collection was housed provided a structure through which to suggest multiple connections and complex ancient wisdom. Though these structural elements were filled to overflowing, suggesting the diversity and infiniteness of creation, symmetry and other regular patterns imposed visual correspondences.

Curiosity cabinets served to represent the collectors, symbolizing their status, wealth, and education. More importantly, they positioned the collector as having the divine gift of creativity; no longer a mere witness to God's work, the collector was now an active participant, able to comprehend and reproduce wisdom from the natural world and even, through the collection's allusions to metamorphosis, to suspend time, to bring the dead to life and life to death. As collectors animated the curiosity cabinet through asserting interlocking relationships, they metaphorically controlled the world.

Not all curiosity cabinets were owned by private individuals; some were associated with universities, including the University of Pisa, Leiden University, and Copenhagen University. These cabinets, primarily botanical, medical, natural history, and antiquities collections, were used in teaching and research. Curiosity cabinets shaped the university in profound ways, stoking

275

its aspirations to universality. The university curiosity cabinet also impacted on the university museum; in fact, the first university museum, the Ashmolean at Oxford University, which opened in 1683, was formed from the contents of a curiosity cabinet.[18]

In his archeological persona, Dion uses the device of the curiosity cabinet to unearth the past and present of the museum and the university. He states, "In going back to the seventeenth century, I'm trying to imagine how things could have been different, to follow branches on the tree of knowledge that died of dry rot."[19] Dion believes that, by making a contemporary curiosity cabinet, students can better understand the production of knowledge and use of authority at the university and the museum. With such insight, students can critique educational systems and advocate change. Through the artistic process and through merging art and science, "Cabinet of Curiosities" challenged the ordering systems of the museum and the university that structure our memory and our world views. What does it mean to possess and, thus, control through collecting and classifying? And how can the contemporary artistic process, shaped by pre-Enlightenment methods, free us from the constraints of classification systems?

At the Weisman, Dion collaborated with the museum's director of education and a class of undergraduate and graduate students from several disciplines to research and present an exhibition of hundreds of objects from diverse collections at the university. Through the device of the curiosity cabinet, the people involved pulled together and recontextualized objects separated by discipline and by location to establish new relationships and to show the instability of classification systems. Universities collect – like most social institutions, businesses, and government agencies – to structure identity and create the illusion of continuity against an uncertain future.[20] As a major research institution, Minnesota has huge holdings across the disciplines in more than 50 collections. Its herbarium alone contains 800,000 specimens; its entomology collection holds 2.9 million specimens.

University collections claim universality, just like their predecessor, the curiosity cabinet. Yet those items not displayed at university museums and galleries are virtually invisible to anyone except the specialist. They are dispersed in hallways, classrooms, laboratories, administrative offices, quads, libraries, archives, closets, and warehouses. They comprise teaching and research collections, such as models, specimens, plaster casts, photographs, scientific illustrations, maps, mechanical devices, archeological and anthropological materials, books, letters, commemorative objects, and portraits. Many of these resources, though outdated for research, are critical to studying disciplinary and educational history; most are now being neglected, due to lack of funding and the prioritizing of digital sources over material culture.[21]

Dion's class operated at several levels over about a year and a half. During the first semester, a student who received university credit for an independent study project scouted the field for good sites – in archeological terms. In documenting the university's collections, she found that several had distinct identities in the special collections area of the university library, such as the Givens collection of African-American literature, the Northwest architectural archives, the Kerlan collection of children's literature, and the Jean-Nicholas Tretter collection in gay, lesbian, and trans-gender studies. Others were contained within departments, for instance, the rocks and minerals collection at the Department of Geology and Geophysics, within institutes, including the Jane Goodall Institute for Primate Study, or within centers, for example, the Center for Holocaust and Genocide Studies. Some were in more formally organized museums, like the university's Bell Museum of Natural History, the Goldstein Museum of Design, the Minnesota Historical Veterinary Museum, and the Weisman Art Museum. The project was explained to curators and faculty in charge of collections during this initial research. They were thrilled with the possibility that their specialized and sometimes obscure collections might be exhibited to the public in a meaningful way.

In the second semester, Dion and the museum's education director led a seminar-style research class. Dion was in residence one week of every month. Six graduate students and two seniors participated, including majors in art history, studio art, library science, liberal studies, and anthropology. The class was cross-listed in museum studies (an interdisciplinary minor at the university), art history, and American studies. Perhaps because the class was being offered at the art museum and listed primarily for liberal arts credit, most of the students were liberal arts majors. For the project to be totally successful, however, in terms of Dion's theories, students in the history of science, biology, geology, and other sciences would also be involved.

In the seminar, students investigated the university's collections as they read about and discussed the work of Dion, the history of museums, and the history of the cabinets of curiosity as forerunners to museums. Dion explained his vision and set parameters for the project. The cabinets were to be based on the organization of the world during the sixteenth century, when these forerunners of museums had originally been assembled. Under Dion's supervision, students in the seminar determined the cabinet themes – those superficial ways of categorizing objects and their meanings that are the very basis of museums' collections and operations. These chose: the underworld; the sea; the air; the terrestrial realm; humankind; the library or archive; vision; sound and time; and history. Each student picked a theme and cabinet for which he or she was responsible and adopted several collections to investigate. They scavenged collections in what Dion calls a "scatter-gun" approach, selecting random objects that caught their interest, particularly anomalies.[22]

In the third semester, students prepared the exhibit, after instruction in professional practice such as safe handling and registration methods (figures 11.2 and 11.3). Several students received internship or independent study credit for their contribution, and some students who didn't need credits worked as volunteers. No one dropped out. Students made final selections and, under Dion's direction, determined the arrangement of the exhibit. Seven hundred and one objects were displayed in nine wooden, period-style cabinets made to Dion's specifications.[23] In addition, on a wall adjacent to the cabinets, 53 objects that did not fit well into any of the thematic sections were hung salon style, floor to ceiling. Dion was in residence for the final two weeks of the project and for its opening.

Students developed approaches to the display of objects appropriate to the general themes. For example, in the cabinet on the allegory of history, each shelf was devoted to a different way of thinking about history. One shelf represented history as explained by religion. Another shelf defined history as the record of the everyday life of ordinary people, while a third reflected on history as a record of important events and people. Objects on the shelf for history as explained by religion included a nineteenth-century Christian Bible, a wood statue of the Egyptian goddess Isis from 350 BC, a bronze Ming Dynasty Buddha, and a porcelain eighteenth-century figure of Apollo. A dragon figurine, a Pinocchio marionette, and a grouping of Paul Bunyan memorabilia, including a giant ring with his initials, rounded out the shelf. The shelf dedicated to history as a record of important events and people held the University Circus 1903 first prize trophy for "Best Side Show," vice-president Hubert H. Humphrey's hat, a tear-gas grenade from anti-Vietnam war demonstrations on campus, a World War II Red Cross nurse's hat, early computers, a basketball championship cup, and ribbons from immigrant fraternal organizations.

Categorizing diverse objects and creating structures to establish relationships that make sense are part of the fundamental work of museums. Yet Dion's cabinets of curiosity are as eccentric as those of the late sixteenth

FIGURE 11.2   A student transports a zebra head for Mark Dion's "Cabinet of Curiosities," Weisman Art Museum, University of Minnesota, 2001. © Frederick R. Weisman Art Museum

century. At the Weisman, students grouped together a dinosaur bone, a Chinese burial vase from 2500 BC, a dried bat, a nineteenth-century mourning hat, a stuffed raven, a mastodon tooth fossil, and pieces of malachite and rose quartz in the Cabinet of the Underworld. In the Cabinet of Humankind, they juxtaposed Chinese silk foot-binding shoes, a Nazi photo album, a skull-measuring device, a silver cigarette case, a glass baby bottle with a metal nipple, a corset, birthing forceps, a 1914 cubist sculpture by Jacques Lipchitz, and a black strapless bra.

The result was seductive in both its anthropological specificity and its aesthetic beauty. The cabinets, set on plinths, functioned as a framing device,

FIGURE 11.3 A student places a model of an eyeball in the Allegory of Vision Cabinet for Mark Dion's "Cabinet of Curiosities," Weisman Art Museum, University of Minnesota, 2001. © Frederick R. Weisman Art Museum

suggesting protection, veneration, and the suspension of time. Compartments seemed at first glance to impose a rational ordering system; yet the installation, like its Mannerist predecessors, proved impossible to contain. Objects overlapped and projected out from the overstuffed shelves; some stood on top of the cabinets while others lay on the floor. Closed drawers made the viewer imagine an infinite number of additional items inside. The lack of glass on the cabinets beckoned the viewer to get a closer glimpse of individual objects, but the plinths served as a distancing mechanism that forced audiences to acknowledge the chaotic whole. The experience was decentering. It implied that culture cannot be contained by classification systems.

The project was, in a certain way, straightforward and built on tasks that are familiar parts of the academic experience – reading, critical discussion, and writing; however, these research activities were, unlike those of most seminars, not abstract. They had concrete consequences. The making of a museum (it seemed more than a mere exhibit) from a group of seemingly disparate objects communicates in a direct way what museums and universities are and how they operate. "Cabinet of Curiosities" was a particularly effective teaching tool because it privileged process over product. Dion and the students performed self-consciously the roles of the museum worker, noting the subjective choices involved. Students were co-curators as each created a museum from a group of objects, bringing to it his or her own experience and prejudices as well as scientific research. They were educators who offered guided tours of the exhibit and published booklets on its meaning. One, called "The Keys to the Cabinet," was a book of drawings by students depicting the scheme of their cases; the other contained student essays explaining their selection of objects. The students were also registrars and preparators engaged in the more laborious tasks of museum work – arranging loan agreements, handling and packing objects for transport, writing condition reports, and preparing mounts.

Dion and the students acted out their drama with playful exaggeration so that the viewer could understand their deconstructive stance. As Dion described his general approach, "We're always telling the tall tale with a wink to the audience so that they know they are always let in on the joke. We're never really deceiving them in a way that they would be entirely excluded or that they would ever mistake this for fact."[24] Through mimicry, he and the students demonstrated to the viewer that protocols and procedures make meaning. As they meticulously attempted to construct systems and hierarchies in their microcosm, the absurdity and impossibility of producing unity became clear. Their theater – including the tours and publications – made visible the contradictions that museum narratives try hard to suppress. "Cabinet of Curiosities" offered no resolution. It was an open-ended dialogue among disparate objects that challenged the modern tendency to see categories as naturally determined. The randomness of the performers' choices provoked the viewer to ask how and why an object was selected and classified and to consider what was absent as well as what was present. The seeming arbitrary quality of the juxtapositions elucidated the power of display.

By blurring the traditional boundaries between the university and its museums, Dion's project demonstrates the potential for learning that the campus gallery possesses. Students left the project questioning the premise that all objects – or ideas – that meet an evaluator's criteria must be more similar than they are different. They learned to question assumptions about systems, to recognize both their value and their fallacies. The title of the opening-day panel discussion, "Constructing the Cabinets/Reconstructing a University of Knowledge," reflects the participants' view that reclaiming the antecedents of the rational museum leads to new insights into institutions of display and of education. As an artist invested in environmental issues, Dion sees the current lack of cross-disciplinary work as a barrier to understanding.[25] He and his collaborators used the curiosity cabinet to critique the discipline-bound discourse of the museum and of the university. "Cabinet of Curiosities" championed an associative process of acquiring knowledge, based on fostering relationships among fields. In so doing, it empowered students to critique their university education and to take responsibility for promoting change.

The Role of Museums at the University: The Frances Young Tang Teaching Museum and Art Gallery

With projects like Dion's, the university gallery can become a learning community in which students, curators, and faculty come together to explore the challenging questions of new museum theory. These artist-led initiatives serve as models for in-house museum critiques and interventions. The Weisman has spurred several such projects. For some institutions, though, the artist-led critique is merely a superficial exercise, a symbolic gesture to declare that the university gallery is engaged in contemporary discourse; the curator commissions an outsider to create a finite project and then go away. The gallery guards against larger systemic change by fashioning an environment in which faculty, staff, and students remain aloof.

On the other hand, progressive institutions are using their galleries to infuse the curriculum with new museum theory. Skidmore College is in the forefront of this movement. In October of 2000, with the opening of its Frances Young Tang Teaching Museum and Art Gallery, the college launched an ambitious and radical plan to make new museum theory a linchpin of arts, humanities, and science education. A small, private college in Saratoga Springs, New York, Skidmore has the resources and the leadership to set an example of this new kind of learning. It is likely that, with student and faculty lobbying, a wider range of colleges and universities will emulate its innovative strategies in the future.

As the title of the museum indicates, the Tang focuses on teaching first and collections second. Skidmore's goal is to use objects to help students become critical thinkers. The Tang defines its mission as being "to foster interdisciplinary thinking and studying, to invite active and collaborative learning and to awaken the community to the richness and diversity of the human experience through the medium of art."[26] It does so by involving the whole campus in developing a new model of the museum, in which, theoretically, every decision is transparent and every project is a cross-disciplinary collaboration. Skidmore is a college-wide learning community that has no museum studies program but instead embraces new museum theory by doing it. The Tang demonstrates the premises of new museum theory; students and faculty learn theory through practice, through their participation in museum projects.

Because the Tang, like Experience Music Project (chapter 5), is a new museum without the elitist baggage of older institutions, its creators could envision a revolutionary game plan. But where EMP is still bound by income from the gate, the Tang, as a university gallery, is governed by academic freedom; it is in the privileged position of making exhibitions that are provocative rather than popular. Moreover, as an institution with only 4,000 objects and a modest endowment, the Tang recognizes that, to flourish, it has to position itself through ideas, rather than collections. Students and faculty from across the curriculum generate the ideas. Upon winning a major grant for exhibition development, Skidmore president Jamienne S. Studley declared, "Our goal is to build on the Tang's reputation for intense and experimental interdisciplinary activity so that the museum becomes as central to academic inquiry as the library, the laboratory, the seminar room, and the studio." Susan Bender, associate dean of the faculty, added, "No one else is doing this. We're redesigning the concept of interdisciplinary education in the context of the Tang Museum."[27]

Museum staff empower the campus community to claim ownership of the institution by inviting its members to use the tone and language most comfortable to them. As curator Ian Berry explains, museum theory is what guides the Tang but ideas are expressed in numerous ways to meet diverse needs. He asserts:

> We are an idea-based institution. We start with ideas – rather than collections. And we welcome the diverse languages of disciplines across campus and of audiences across the community. Exclusively speaking the language of art history can alienate many potential constituencies. Here, geographers, mathematicians and poets, for example, have the freedom to express ideas in language appropriate to their disciplines.[28]

With ideas at its core, the Tang has the ability to change and adapt more than most other institutions; in fact, the Tang is defined by change. Its dynamism attracts a wide following. Holland Cotter of the *New York Times* calls it a "young, very on-the-ball museum."[29]

To follow through on its mission statement, the Tang solicits ideas from students, faculty, and visiting artists. Most exhibitions are co-curated by a Tang staff member and one or more faculty. Participants have come from fields as diverse as English, anthropology, dance, sociology, psychology, exercise science, chemistry, and biology. Berry calls himself the "producer" for team-based planning.[30] Curators and other Tang staff are committed to learning from their faculty partners. In a Tang exhibition review, anthropologist Nancy Mithro reports "a willingness to discover new vistas of interpretation that diverge from the static merry-go-round of established exhibit practices."[31]

Often, a team will conceive a whole project at once, from related course syllabuses to educational programming. This helps create a seamless unity between exhibitions and classroom experience. The team works to envision new possibilities for interaction and to accommodate diverse learning styles. Berry describes the working process:

> We start with an idea and we get the group to talk about it without preconceived notions about the "right kind" of objects and experiences. We want our viewers to engage like we have. And we try to be transparent. We offer a lot of entry points to create active users. Our labels contain questions, suggestions and problems to solve. Our catalogues are not just records of shows but alternative ways to address an idea. These strategies are not necessarily new by themselves but the way we combine them into our core mission is.[32]

The Tang's architecture, by Antoine Predock, clearly articulates the institution's mission through its focus on making connections and on meeting students' intellectual needs. He sited the building at a crossroads between the campus and the town. The building's three main wings and two monumental staircases reach out in all directions, suggesting another crossroads – a metaphorical one of ideas and objects, students and faculty, museum and campus. The design features numerous areas for groups to gather in, including classrooms, a storage area, a print room, a rooftop terrace, and an auditorium. It contains two expansive, irregularly shaped galleries that can be easily configured to meet diverse needs. It has no grand facade but instead offers three alternative entry-ways. Predock was inspired by Howard Gardiner's *Frames of Mind: The Theories of Multiple Intelligences*, a seminal study for museum educators, in designing spaces for many kinds of learning – from visual to bodily, musical to mathematical. Glass walls enclose many of the areas, including storage, suggesting transparency in policy and in design. Predock asserts, "Traditional hierarchical and programmatic separations merge as spaces visually eavesdrop and the distinction between display and archive, subject and object dissolve. The building invites one to pause, reflect, perform and explore."[33]

Exhibitions are interdisciplinary, appealing to a wide cross-section on campus. For example, a 2001 exhibition on mapping juxtaposed geographical maps, maps of the human body, and contemporary art that explores mapping. Students often play a central role. In a 2002 performance in conjunction with a Paul Henry Ramirez exhibition, "Elevatious Transcendsualistic," student dancers moved through the galleries on exercise balls to become part of his biomorphic paintings that, themselves, spill out over the floors and walls (figure 11.4).[34] Exhibitions are designed to be theatrical, to entice new audiences to the Tang. For its inaugural exhibition, former director Charles A. Stainback decided literally to make a "big bang" with an exhibition of sound, "S.O.S.: Scenes of Sounds." Critic Lawrence Biemiller noted, "When S. O. S. is in full voice – drawers playing, telephones ringing, installations knocking and shouting and whispering – the main gallery is so noisy that you seem to lose yourself in sound." Stainback explained, "We knew it was going to be noisy. But that's part of taking on the building."[35] Still, displays don't prize spectacle over substance; in fact, shows are anti-gloss, prioritizing the exhibitionary process over a finished product. Reviewer Holland Cotter remarked that a show on Pop art, which juxtaposed work from the 1960s with contemporary art, "doesn't have the heft and polish of a masterpiece presentation. Instead, it feels personal, happenstantial, like history in the making, almost anti-masterpiece."[36]

New museum theory informs decision-making, as in the 2002 exhibition "Staging the Indian: The Politics of Representation." As anthropologist Mithlo writes, the curators were "self-reflective of exhibit practices" even though the project "does not appear to have been a relatively safe or easy endeavor." For instance, in writing labels for the show, curators were unsure whether to identify the contemporary Native American artists by tribal affiliation or simply by name. The curators wished to respect the artists' freedom to be individuals, yet also did not want to make the mistake of asserting western values that privilege individual over group achievement. One of the artists responded by stating, "Be true to your audience." He explained matter-of-factly, "You chose me because I'm native." Mithlo argues that the Tang handled such situations with the cultural sensitivity and willingness to share power that new museum theory advocates:

These undoubtedly uncomfortable moments serve to define a new exhibits era that may perhaps best be termed "postcollaborative" in nature. Although

FIGURE 11.4 "Balls," performance view, in the Paul Henry Ramirez exhibition "Elevatious Transcendsualistic," Tang Teaching Museum, Skidmore College, Saratoga Springs, New York, 2002. Courtesy of the Frances Young Tang Teaching Museum and Art Gallery at Skidmore College. Photograph by Jerry L. Thompson

the parameters of the exhibit method are tried and tested (the historic-contemporary juxtaposition), the process of implementation is overt. It is my opinion that only within the context of a strong educational mission can an institution survive such a challenge to its own authority. The Tang Teaching Museum and Art Gallery has this capacity.[37]

Other Tang exhibitions claim museum theory as their subject. A 2003 exhibit, "Living with Duchamp," displayed works by this first artist to engage in museum critique along with pieces by contemporary artists shaped by him. The innovative exhibit design referred back to Duchamp's own exhibition design. A 2002 retrospective of Fred Wilson demonstrated that museum critique can bring new insight to the study of institutions and the framing of culture.

Wilson's influence has continued in his current role as Luce Distinguished Visiting Fellow in Skidmore's new Program of Object Exhibition and Knowledge. He serves as liaison between the Tang and academic life to "develop a culture of museum-based inquiry."[38] Wilson is in residence every other semester from spring 2004 through fall 2007. He is teaching seminars for students and faculty, doing advising, overseeing interns, leading campus-wide discussions, giving gallery tours, and organizing a national symposium on the role of the museum in a liberal arts education. He's pushing the boundaries of discipline-based study and finding new ways to communicate the theoretical principles that shape his work. He's thinking about museum exhibitions as catalysts for curricular innovation. He's trying to create a larger cultural shift at Skidmore.

Despite Skidmore's worthy efforts, frustrations remain. Some faculty members are resistant to changing their way of teaching; the Tang relies often on a core group of "regulars" for ideas and support. Students still play relatively conventional roles, doing internships, occasionally organizing exhibits, and serving as the primary audience, although their opinions are often solicited. Their work is shown at the Tang only once a year within the annual thesis major exhibition. Otherwise, it is shown at the Schick Art Gallery in the Art Department or the student-run Case College Center Gallery. In addition, many Tang visitors continue to rely on traditional ways of using museums. Further, the Tang has no active acquisitions program but instead relies on donations and bequests from collectors to expand its permanent collection of teaching objects.

The Tang is clearly a work in progress but that makes it also a place of possibilities, especially with Fred Wilson in a position of leadership. Berry says that the key to long-term success is to ensure that programming continues to fulfill the mission of the museum and that the mission of the museum continues to meet the needs of the college. The Tang is already sparking what curator Berry calls "those magical transformative moments" for students, faculty, Tang staff, and even guest artists who often remark that they've experienced at the Tang a discourse not occurring at other institutions.[39]

Conclusion

Campus initiatives shaped by museum theory impact on the way that curators, faculty, and students think about the politics of display. When guest residencies are not treated as guerrilla acts but as long-term committed collaboration, these residencies institute substantive change. The Weisman and the Tang are not alone. The Henry at the University of Washington, the University Art Museum at the University of California, Berkeley, the Grey Gallery at New York University, and the Wexner Center at Ohio State University show the results of such initiatives, as curators mix up the collections, conduct institutional archeology, become more transparent in their decision-making processes, and sometimes even perform their work in public. Such examples demonstrate that one of the most important roles of the artist is to lead scholars to new conceptual paradigms. By embracing new museum theory as Dion and Fred Wilson have introduced it, learning communities at Minnesota, Skidmore, and elsewhere testify that the university gallery has the power to transform education as we know it.

Questions for Discussion

1 What is unique about the university gallery? How is it conducive to institutional critique?
2 What is institutional critique? How is it informed by new museum theory? Why are metaphors of digging and mining so apt? Why are museums welcoming such work?
3 What is a curiosity cabinet? Why does Dion find it a useful tool? Compare the curiosity cabinet to the modern museum. What does the phrase "the politics of representation" mean? Discuss the relationships among the curiosity cabinet, the university, and the university museum.
4 Describe the roles of students in "Cabinet of Curiosities." How is the piece a performance? And how is such a performance a teaching tool? What is a learning community?
5 How does Dion want to change university education? How does "Cabinet of Curiosities" articulate his views?
6 Compare and contrast the learning opportunities of the Weisman and the Tang. How do they both give new voice to students? How do the museums echo Klebesadel's call to rethink arts education (chapter 10)?
7 How can the experiments at the Weisman and the Tang help students to rethink the student exhibition?

8   How does the Tang promote critical museum theory without formally teaching it in the classroom? Contrast the educational possibilities of the Tang with those of your university gallery.

9   How do you think Fred Wilson will contribute to the Tang? What is the future of initiatives such as Skidmore's?

Notes

1   A. Fraser. (2003). "'Aren't They Lovely?' 1992." In Y. Dziewior. (ed.). *Andrea Fraser: Works 1984–2003*. (ex. cat. Kunstverein in Hamburg), 134–6.

2   On the history of artists critiquing the museum, see J. Putnam. (2001). *Art and Artifact: The Museum as Medium*. New York: Thames and Hudson; K. McShine. (ed.). (1999). *The Museum as Muse: Artists Reflect*. (ex. cat. Museum of Modern Art, New York); B. Wallis. (2003). "Institutional Critique as Countermemory: Some Current Approaches to the Museum." Conference paper presented at *"La Generazione delle immagini*: Facts and Fiction," Milan.
    http://www.undo.net/cgi-bin/openframe.pl?x=/Pinto/gene4/wallis_eng.htm

3   See A. Fraser. (2003). "'Museum Highlights: A Gallery Talk' 1989." In Dziewior, *Andrea Fraser*, 244–53; S. Rodrigues. (2002). "Institutional Critique versus Institutionalized Critique: The Politics of Andrea Fraser's Performances." *thirdspace*, 1: 2. www.thirdspace.ca/articles/rodrigue.htm.

4   On Wilson, see L. G. Corrin. (ed.). (1994). *Mining the Museum: An Installation by Fred Wilson*. Baltimore and New York: Contemporary and New Press; M. Berger. (ed.). (2001). *Fred Wilson: Objects and Installations, 1979–2000*. (ex. cat. Center for Art and Visual Culture, University of Maryland, Baltimore County); F. Wilson. (2003). *Fred Wilson: Speak of Me As I Am*. (ex. cat. MIT List Visual Arts Center, Cambridge, MA).

5   Quoted from the website of the Tang Teaching Museum and Art Gallery at Skidmore College. www.skidmore.edu/tang/releases/wilson.htm (accessed February 9, 2003).

6   On creating such an environment for studio art students, see L. Weintraub. (1999). "The Studio Potential of the University Gallery." *Art Journal*, 58: 1, 36–41.

7   This concept was originally created by Dion in 1997 for the Wexner Center for the Arts at Ohio State University.

8   Quoted in D. Herman. (2001). "The Dave Herman Laboratories Interview: Mark Dion." *National Forum*, 81: 3, 36–7.

9   Studies on Dion include J. Leslie. (ed.). (1997). *Natural History and Other Fictions: An Exhibition by Mark Dion*. Birmingham: Ikon Gallery; A. Coles and M. Dion. (eds.). (1999). *Mark Dion: Archaeology*. Greenville, SC: Black Dog; L. G. Corrin, M. Kwon, and N. Bryson. (eds.). (1997). *Mark Dion*. London; Phaidon Press.

10 Quoted in McShine, *Museum as Muse*, p. 98.

11 Quoted in M. Kwon. (1997). "Miwon Kwon in Conversation with Mark Dion." In Corrin et al., *Mark Dion*, p. 19.

12 Kwon, "Conversation with Mark Dion," p. 19.

13 For more on contemporary curiosity cabinets, see P. Mauriès. (2002). *Cabinets of Curiosities*. London: Thames and Hudson, pp. 224–35; S. Bann. (2003). "The Return to Curiosity: Shifting Paradigms in Contemporary Museum Display." In A. McClellan. (ed.). *Art and its Publics: Museum Studies at the Millennium*. Malden, MA, and Oxford: Blackwell, 126–9.

14 M. Dion. (1997). "The Natural History Box: Preservation, Categorization and Display." In Corrin et al., *Mark Dion*, 128–39, p. 135 (from a lecture of 1995).

15 Bann, "Return to Curiosity," p. 120.

16 For more on the history of the curiosity cabinet, see O. Impey and A. MacGregor. (eds.). (1985). *The Origins of Museums: The Cabinet of Curiosities in Sixteenth- and Seventeenth-Century Europe*. Oxford: Clarendon Press; Mauriès, *Cabinets of Curiosities*, pp. 12–184; P. H. Smith and P. Findlen. (eds.). (2002). *Merchants and Marvels: Commerce, Science, and Art in Early Modern Europe*. New York and London: Routledge; and the website for the 1995 University of California, Santa Barbara exhibition by B. Robertson and M. Meadow, "Microcosms: Objects of Knowledge (A University Collects)." http://microcosms.ihc.ucsb.edu/index.html.

17 On etymology, see P. Findlen. (1989). "The Museum: Its Classical Etymology and Renaissance Genealogy." *Journal of the History of Collections*, 1: 1, 59–78.

18 S. W. G. de Clercq and M. C. Lourenço. (2003). "A Globe is Just Another Tool: Understanding the Role of Objects in University Collections." ICOM Study Series 11, *University Museums and Collections*, 4–6.

19 Quoted in Kwon, "Conversation with Mark Dion," p. 33.

20 M. Winzen. (1998). "Collecting – So Normal, So Paradoxical." In I. Schaffner and M. Winzen. (eds.). (1998). *Deep Storage: Collecting, Storing, and Archiving in Art*. A. Böger. (trans.). Munich and New York: Prestel, 22–4.

21 On university collections see P. J. Boylan. "European Cooperation in the Protection and Promotion of the University Heritage." ICOM Study Series 11, *University Museums and Collections*, 30–2. See also the monumental study led by Bruce Robertson and Mark Meadow on of the University of California's collections: B. Robertson and M. Meadow. (2002). "Microcosms: Objects of Knowledge." *AI and Society*, 14, 223–9; and the associated website http://microcosms.ihc.ucsb.edu/index.html.

22 Quoted in R. Williams. (1999). "Disjecta Reliquiae: The Tate Thames Dig." In Coles and Dion, *Mark Dion: Archaeology*, 72–101, p. 79.

23 The cabinets had been made for the earlier Wexner Arts Center exhibition.

24 Quoted in Herman, "Dave Herman Laboratories Interview: Mark Dion," p. 35.

25 Putnam, *Art and Artifact*, pp. 74–5.

26 Quoted from the Tang's website. www.skidmore.edu/tang/mission/index.htm.

27 Quotes from a Skidmore College news release on its website. http://apollo.skidmore.edu/news/news.release.detail_show?p_news_id=137.

28 Quote from Ian Berry, curator of the Frances Young Tang Teaching Museum and Art Gallery. Interview by J. Marstine, December 17, 2003. Much of the background information on the Tang in this chapter comes from the interview and from the Tang's website. http://tang.skidmore.edu.

29 H. Cotter. (2002). "Collectors with a Weakness for the Ornery." *New York Times*, August 30, section E, 28.

30 N. M. Mithlo. (2003). "Staging the Indian: The Politics of Representation [exhibition review]." *American Anthropologist*, 105: 1, 156–61, p. 159.

31 Mithlo, "Staging the Indian," p. 159.

32 Quote from Berry interview by Marstine, December 17, 2003.

33 Quoted on the Skidmore College website. www.skidmore.edu/tang/news_and_information/tang_opens.htm. For more on the building, see J. E. Czarnecki. (2001). "Antoine Predock Creates an Energetic Home for the Arts in the Tang Teaching Museum and Art Gallery." *Architectural Record*, 189: 5, 224–31.

34 D. Fernandez. (2002). "Balls." In *Paul Henry Ramirez: Elevatious Transcendsualistic* (ex. cat. Frances Young Tang Teaching Museum and Art Gallery), 46–51.

35 Quoted in L. Biemiller. (2002). "Notes from Academe: Art that Pricks Up Your Ears." *Chronicle of Higher Education*, 47: 12, 88.

36 Cotter, "Collectors with a Weakness," p. 28.

37 All quotes from Mithlo, "Staging the Indian," pp. 157, 158.

38 Quote from S. Bender in a Skidmore news release. http://apollo.skidmore.edu/news/news.release.detail_show?p_news_id=137.

39 Quote from Berry interview by Marstine, December 17, 2003.

12 | MUSEUM ARCHIVES AS RESOURCES FOR SCHOLARLY RESEARCH AND INSTITUTIONAL IDENTITY

Lois Marie Fink

Editor's Introduction

Lois Marie Fink is research curator emerita at the Smithsonian American Art Museum, USA, and author of *American Art at the Nineteenth-Century Paris Salons*. She is currently writing a history of the Smithsonian American Art Museum.

In her chapter, Fink demystifies the often-secret world of the museum archives. Through wide-ranging examples, many from her own experience, she surveys the wealth of materials in museum archives as she demonstrates the importance of the archives to institutional policy and civic identity. She asserts that archives fill the basic human need to make decisions based on knowledge and acceptance of the past. Fink puts into context the idiosyncrasies of museum archives, charting effective strategies for research. And while she holds that accessing physical documents in real-world archives is invaluable, she acknowledges that digitization of archival materials will have a profound impact. The chapter makes clear that archival work is a key component of critical museum theory. Secondary sources provide insight into collections and exhibitions, those most public of museum activities, but archival materials can elucidate the more controversial, and thus hidden, aspects of museum operations, such as financial matters, donor relations, trustee influence, and conservation policy. Moreover, using museum archives confirms that museums are not monoliths but are diverse organizations run by individuals, each shaped by political and social considerations. Fink shows the power of an archive to reveal the complexities and contradictions of museums. She wants to see museum archives become more accessible and readers become more informed about their usefulness.

The use of archival materials for research involves a sense of adventure that rarely accompanies the obligatory reading of secondary sources. You never know what you will find in sifting through personal letters and diaries, spying on meetings, learning about plans that never saw the light of day, finding personal opinions that contradict public statements. Such documents turn the past into the present, where ideas and actions can be observed as they develop with all of the doubts and hopes that accompany an unknown conclusion. Delving into layers of papers for significant discoveries is akin to the unearthing process of archeologists as they dig even deeper into a promising site, and, indeed, "archives" and "archeology" share an ancient word root that signifies origins and beginnings. In both fields documents or objects are sought not as dusty curios of a bygone age, but for their value in bringing new understanding from the past to life in the present.

As resources for research, museum archives hold a wealth of materials in all areas of history, science, technology, and art. They also serve an essential purpose for the museums themselves, for holdings of self-generated records of the founding, policies, and problems of the past form the basis of an institution's identity.

The intent of this chapter is to encourage readers to utilize the archives of museums for two basic purposes: research on topics in the subject fields of archival collections, and studies of museum practices on the basis of institutional records. I will consider the content and purposes of archival collections and their specialized organization as compared with library resources. I will also offer some practical suggestions for use. Emphasis will lean toward my own field of art history. A sketch of the need for archives introduces the subject.

Why Archives were Formed

Record keeping had its beginning in a distant past when information beyond the brevity of human memory became essential to the welfare of individuals and communities. In the western world archival practices can be traced to ancient Greece and Rome, where the complexities of those societies required recourse to former plans and actions. Important materials kept by the Athenians in a temple on the public square continue to inform our cultural life today: in addition to the laws and treaties of the state, they also preserved manuscripts of plays by Aeschylus, Sophocles, and Euripides, and the defense written by Socrates upon his condemnation. During the medieval era types of records and methods of organizing them developed in response to the different needs of churches and the Vatican. Through centuries of authoritative political rule in Europe, government archives were closed to the public, dispossessing ordinary citizens of the ability to turn to the decisions of the past on questions of justice or property disputes. One of the significant innovations of individual liberty sparked by the French Revolution was the insistence that archival records be open to the citizenry. The French also initiated a national central depository for the papers of the state and authored certain modern principles of archival storage and retrieval.[1]

Art in France is inextricable from government policies – which made it necessary for me to do research at the Archives Nationales for my studies on American art in Paris. I marveled at the continuity of those records during the turbulent years of French history in the nineteenth century. Throughout political changes of empires, monarchies, and republics, in spite of revolutions and foreign wars, civil servants continued to preserve and organize the papers of each succeeding administration. Scores of art historians have written about French art and art institutions – not least because the records exist and are accessible. This is not universally true in Europe, where archives have sometimes been restricted or even destroyed for political reasons. For example, in Italy (in at least one locality), when officials of the new regime took over, they threw out the records of the old regime. The continuity and accessibility of archival records are essential for the conception of a national cultural heritage and its promotion among citizens and the global community.[2] No nation in the world has done a better job of PR for its own culture than has France.

In the United States, almost as soon as independence was won, government and private officials began sporadic efforts to preserve historical documents. However, while a number of the states succeeded early in their history in founding an archive, national officials would not create a central repository for more than 150 years. In the meantime, each agency kept its own records – or trashed them, as managers saw fit. Generating the documents of a nation that was decidedly future-oriented, the federal government did not make serious efforts to preserve and organize papers that marked its past. A more specific reason affecting the delay was turf rivalry between the State Department and other agencies. Before the National Archives was created in Washington in 1934, "the records of the government of the United States were in worse condition, were less accessible, and were less used than those of any comparable nation in the Western world," historian O. Lawrence Burnette lamented.[3]

From the middle of the twentieth century Americans have become aware of the essential role played in national life by the preservation of records. Native American tribes have established their entitlements and privileges by referring to state and federal archives; access to the Nixon tapes contributed to the downfall of a presidency; release of materials relating to the Cuban missile crisis and the Vietnam war enabled historians to reassess those events by filling in missing information, and stimulated efforts to extract lessons for current policies. The knowledge and interpretation of past events inevitably affect policy decisions and public trust.

Among its vast holdings the National Archives in Washington contains the original manuscripts of the Declaration of Independence and the Constitution. Many files pertaining to American cultural history are also located there and at the auxiliary repositories of the presidential libraries. In addition, some kind of record will be found in the National Archives whenever the life of an individual or an institution intersects with federal regulations or actions (which happens more frequently than you might suppose). Merl M. Moore, research collaborator at the Smithsonian American Art Museum (SAAM), has extracted information from passports at the archives that made possible the identification of individuals in nineteenth-century paintings and the tracing of Americans in their treks through European countries. He has used ship manifests to pinpoint the time artists went abroad or arrived in the United States, and census records to determine the locations of their residencies and the identity of family members.[4] I used the records of the Fine Arts Commission at the National Archives to spy on a discussion about the controversial Saarinen 1939 architectural design for a Smithsonian art gallery. Though commission members said little in public about the proposed building, in private their tongues were loosened. Aghast at the simplicity of beauty in the architect's modern approach, they railed at the lack of columns and pediments as found in the traditional classical mode of official Washington. Expressing their revulsion among themselves, they found the Saarinen plan equivalent to "the chaos of the Nazi art of today."[5]

The Content and Purposes of Museum Archives

The archives of museums are, of course, more focused than the broad sweep of materials found in government files. Museum holdings center on collections, exhibitions, and administrative policies – records of great interest to scholars, but preserved mainly for the needs of the institution. As complex organizations that deal with a diverse audience, private and public funding, and the responsibility for valuable collections, museums require substantial evidence of past performance in all these areas. Recourse to the archives provides staff members with information relating to specific problems and to the more general sense of the museum's continuity through decades of change.

In regard to particular questions, for example, curators and architects at the Smithsonian were asked to restore the Arts and Industries Building on the mall to its original appearance in preparation for the bicentennial of the nation in 1976. A century of changes to the structure would have made that task daunting, if it had not been for the original drawings and plans which researchers retrieved from the Smithsonian Institution Archives. Closely following those documents as guides, staff members produced an historically accurate and impressive renovation.

Archival research has provided SAAM with a sense of identity in spite of its history of disruptions in location, four different names, and a variety of approaches to collections policy. In the early years after the founding of the Smithsonian in 1846, acquisitions were mostly casts and engravings; European and Asian art objects as well as American were gathered in the late nineteenth and early twentieth centuries; and finally, deaccessioning procedures were put into place in the 1980s. Throughout all of these changes, evidence from the archives reveals that a primary focus on American art persisted as the underlying continuity of the museum's collection and exhibitions.[6] Knowledge of this background has helped staff members to define current programs and move toward plans for the future.

Without an understanding of their institution's history – as found in the archival records – administrators and their staffs cannot confidently define the museum to their current patrons and boards, to the public – or even to themselves. Awareness of the founding mission, of early policies, and of institutional strengths and weaknesses form a background for sound decisions and actions in the present. This is not to say that policies should never be changed – times and situations bring new opportunities and problems – but the constructive development of an institution (as of an individual) requires knowledge and acceptance of the past as the basis of identity.

The records staff members and outside scholars most frequently use are those that pertain to the collections, that part of a museum which accounts for the most significant expenditures in money, time, and expertise. Collections serve as the public face of the institution: prospective donors are courted; new acquisitions are heralded; stellar pieces provide opportunities for pride of possession and a competitive edge over other institutions. Files kept in the offices of curators and the registrar include accession details of each object along with photographs, news-clippings, articles from periodicals, and relevant correspondence. Archival documentation of a particular object may include invaluable information about the work or the artist that is unavailable elsewhere. "In my opinion, I never did anything finer," wrote Gari Melchers of his painting *The Bride* (1903), in a letter in the SAAM curatorial records. Changes in the title of a piece can be verified: *The South Ledges, Appledore* (1913) by Childe Hassam while in private collections was known as *Summer Sea: Isle of Shoals* and *Sunny Blue Sea*. At the SAAM the artist's original title was restored. Curatorial archives are active files as curators continue to add relevant letters, exhibition and conservation records, and other pertinent information.

Curatorial records of a painting can also include contextual material. Papers in the SAAM collection on a painting by Bernardino Luini contain information about the unscrupulous practices of art dealers in New York City at the turn of the century. When acquired in 1906 as part of the bequest of Harriet Lane Johnston, this Renaissance panel depicted a full-length Madonna reaching toward the Christ Child, who appeared to be running away from her. Connoisseur Bernard Berenson had titled the work *Madonna and Child in the Act of Running*. News-clippings, however, reveal that the panel originally belonged to a larger scene that included St Elizabeth with the infant St John – and a lamb, which the Christ Child was trying to mount. A dealer had painted out the lamb and cut the panel into three pieces, which he then sold as separate works. When conservators in the 1930s removed the added cover of paint, the lamb reappeared. The entire drama is part of the Luini file.

The use of primary sources as found in archival records conveys an intimacy of acquaintance with the past, humanizing studies of persons or institutions that might otherwise seem to be only bloodless abstractions. Diaries such as that of Jervis McEntee offer glimpses of thought and feeling across the years. In his journal about the 1877 exhibition of the National Academy of Design in New York, McEntee wrote that he watched as fellow artist William Sonntag searched for his painting on the gallery walls. When at last Sonntag found it – hung in a dark corner and barely visible – "his eyes filled with tears."[7] With McEntee we become silent observers of Sonntag's crushed hopes for his work at that event.

In addition to preserving papers generated within the institution, museums also collect materials from outside sources that relate to their collections and programs. This practice provides context for objects in their collections and forms stronger bonds with the communities that constitute their publics. Records of Spanish missions and accounts of early pioneers in California are part of the archives of the Junipero Sera Museum in San Diego. Inventories and account books of craftsmen are in the archives of the Henry Francis du Pont Museum in Winterthur, Delaware. At the Philadelphia Museum of Art, where the collection covers the broad expanse of world history, archival records pertain to the diversity of its holdings and include materials ranging from illuminated medieval European and Asian manuscripts to the letters and notebooks of recent American artists.

The archival program of the Museum of Chinese in the Americas, New York, collects and preserves all kinds of records from the community it serves. Museum staff members work in close cooperation with volunteers to gather papers, photographs, oral history tapes, and films from laundries, factories, restaurants, schools, and tenements, "to rescue and reconstruct a history of Chinese Americans and the community they built in New York's Chinatown."[8] These archives have become an important source for the identity of the Chinese American community in New York City, and a unique repository for scholars of Asian American history from all over the world.

Archives are commonly identified as collections of papers but, as archival collecting for the Chinatown museum archives demonstrates, many types of objects can be included. The ultimate in variety for an archival collection unquestionably belongs to the Andy Warhol Museum in Pittsburgh, where, archivist John Smith explains, a "staggering accumulation of boxes, shopping bags, trunks, and filing cabinets," stuffed with the artist's obsessive collecting of everything from junk mail and dime-store ashtrays to crucifixes and icons, represents "the most extensive and most significant documentation of any American artist's life and times."[9] During his lifetime Warhol and his associates packed over six hundred cardboard boxes labeled "Time Capsules" with objects pertaining to particular events or experiences. These archival materials are so critical to our understanding of Warhol that museum administrators have made the archives and its activities an "exhibit." Warhol Museum visitors can enter the archives, as they do the galleries, and watch, behind glass windows, archivists and researchers at work. Every time archivists go through one of the boxes, the procedure is taped, thus forming a record of specific objects contained in the boxes – and the reaction of those who watch the process. Archivist Matt Wrbican observes that response to the archival materials for many viewers "is stronger than their reaction to the artwork displayed, since the source material has not been seen before."[10] Viewers perceive the archival objects not only as individual units, but also in proximity to each other and in the context of a particular time. Intended to serve as a study center for scholars of Warhol and for the popular culture of the second half of the twentieth century, this peerless gathering serves as a memorable example of how archival collections can exceed the limits of papers and documents.

Organizing Museum Archives

The accumulation of objects in the archives of the Warhol and Chinese history museums – as well as in more traditional archival files in other institutions – contains materials of many different sizes, shapes, and origins. All of these must be gathered into a central location, systematically arranged, and made retrievable if they are to be of use to museum staff and outside scholars. This requires professional expertise, time, and money – commodities that are often in short supply in museums.

As recently as the 1980s, few museums in the United States had accessible archival files. For many, establishing an archives could not compete with pressing day-to-day priorities. At the Smithsonian Institution, for instance. a centralized collection of archival records was not undertaken until 1970, though individual museums had kept their own files for many years.

Professional archival organizations recognized that this general lack of attention to proper record preservation was seriously detrimental to the institutions, their communities, and scholarly research, and from the 1980s these groups have encouraged the founding and maintenance of museum archives. A gathering known as the Belmont Conference, sponsored in 1979 by the Smithsonian's Archives of American Art, gave the initial impetus for this surge of concern. Representatives from institutions in the United States and Canada drafted guidelines on the founding of archives which were distributed to hundreds of museums. A brochure defined the scope of an archival program, suggested criteria for the retention of records, and described points to consider for their systematic arrangement, emphasizing that records should be made accessible to staff and to scholars. Participants at the conference developed a sense of professional community that persists to the present day, in workshops that promote the founding of new archives and encourage the development of established collections.[11]

In addition to serving institutional and community needs, museum archives have been identified as national resources by national archival associations and federal granting agencies. The Society of American Archivists (SAA) has also been instrumental in encouraging the founding and professionalization of museum archives. In 1981 the SAA instituted a task force on museum archives and authorized the publication of an introductory manual addressed not to professional archivists but to museum staff members with little or no archival training.[12] Stressing the significance of museums for American cultural life, the SAA received support from the National Historical and Records Commission to fund start-up programs. In the mid-1980s a survey of 225 accredited museums by Alan Bain of the Smithsonian Institution Archives disclosed that 80 percent of the institutions indicated an interest in the management of their archival records, and 40 percent requested information on the establishment of an archives.[13]

In spite of such noteworthy accomplishments, many museums did not respond to the offers of assistance that began in the 1980s. More than ten years later archivist Bain, who conducted the survey noted above, observed that much still needed to be done. "Unlike other cultural institutions," he remarked, "museums, with a strong history in the collecting of artifacts and objects to document mankind, have shown a dreadful lack of concern in maintaining or developing programs to store documentation about themselves."[14]

I asked Bain if the situation remains the same today. The lack of a recent survey to provide numbers precluded a definitive answer, but he has observed that more professional archivists are attending the museum section at SAA meetings, which indicates progress toward additional archival development. University museums in particular have been responsible in preserving their archives and encouraging use by scholars. Bain believes that funding remains the most restrictive factor, at least for the smaller institutions. Why certain large and well-known art museums have no accessible central archives is a question only they can answer. He points out that, as holders of collections, museums necessarily have to keep records (the accreditation process requires some kind of acceptable system), which in the absence of a central repository usually takes place in individual offices or the institution's library. Procedures aimed at creating and maintaining more effective and accessible records are sometimes initiated by a grant-funded contract to a professional archivist.

Bain also points out that cultural factors affect a perceived need for archives. In the 1970s and early 1980s universities and museums promoted scholarship with a strong emphasis on research based on primary sources. The current trend of museums to function as popular entertainment has diminished the use of institutional archives, while scholarship based entirely on secondary sources has come to be common practice.

Archivists share some aspects of their task with librarians, but the nature of materials in their care as unique objects requires different kinds of responsibilities. Each book in a library is catalogued and retrievable as an individual item according to author, title, and subject matter within a universal system found in every library (with certain exceptions). The manner in which museum archives are assembled can differ from one institution to another because the principles of organization reflect particular qualities of each museum. The history of a museum, its mission statement, and its administrative configuration determine the kinds of archival materials that are generated and the interest areas of additional collections. These basic components answer questions of who created the records, for what purpose, and the bureaucratic role of the offices in charge. Together, they suggest how archival materials fit into the larger historical picture of the museum.

For example, a research reference in the Smithsonian Institution Archives reads "National Collection of Fine Arts, Office of the Director, Records 1895–1975, Record Unit 311, Box 21." The identification begins with the largest gathering of materials – those relating to an entire museum or bureau of the Smithsonian, the National Collection of Fine Arts. It then sequentially narrows to smaller groups of papers or objects: first, a particular office within the National Collection (that of the director), which is the source of the papers, with an indication of the span of years included in this series, followed by the number of a record unit within those broad limits, and finally one of the boxes of papers in that particular unit. A researcher seeking this piece of information would have approached it from the opposite direction, starting with knowledge of a particular event about which documentation is sought – in this case, a meeting of the museum's commission members in April, 1937. Locating this paper would begin with reference to a summary guide to Smithsonian archival records, where contents for broad categories, such as "the National Collection of Fine Arts," are indicated according to series numbers and record units. An additional guide to record units serves to focus the search toward the appropriate box. Within the box one of the labeled folders will be found to contain the desired record, minutes of a particular meeting.

The principle for this organization of materials is based on their provenance. That is, they are organized according to the originating source, and within that category, as a general rule, the arrangement respects the original order imposed on the papers as they were generated – which in many cases is chronological.

In the above example, a specific piece of information was the object of research; it began with the known fact that a meeting took place at a particular time. Archival research can also be undertaken for more general information and insights; a topic relating to the museum's history in the decade of the 1930s could be enriched by reading through the minutes of the commission meetings during those years. A researcher can focus on a specific topic, such as the documentation of an event or an individual, or seek a better understanding of particular aspects of a museum's history, questions about the museum's patronage, changes initiated in educational practices through the years, and so on. In order to make the most efficient use of time spent in the archives, it is helpful to have some knowledge of the administrative organization of the museum and a basic outline of its history.

Organizing archival materials is one of the primary tasks of archivists and, in the real world, the diversity and volume of archival materials require more sophistication for the creation of orderly files than the basic principles noted above. In addition, professional archivists must also describe the content of major groups and subgroups of materials in written or electronic guides so that items of interest can be identified and retrieved. These descriptions are sometimes fairly detailed and may include a brief history of an administrative office or curatorial department represented in a major group, along with its most significant activities and events. However, a relentless increase in the volume of documents and papers being generated in our own time (the "paperless" age!) has necessitated a trend in some institutions to forgo such elaboration in favor of more summary identification.

In an effort to avoid being overwhelmed by paper and machine-readable records, archivists must also appraise potential archival materials to determine what is worthwhile to keep and what is sheer dross to be discarded – perhaps their most controversial task. In some instances, administrators make such decisions before materials get to the central archives. Irretrievable actions, such as the destruction of papers or objects, may later be regretted. Art museums are especially vulnerable to such actions with regard to their archives and their collections, for the fugitive nature of taste can mislead a sense of lasting significance. Like all interpreters of historical records, curators and archivists are subject to some extent to the values of their own time – and that limitation can determine what is preserved in a particular archival collection as well as what is not. A scholar researching the Renaissance era, Leonard Barkan, recognized the possibility as he delved into archival files. "I was learning a different set of meanings for *archive*, seeing it not as the sum total of events and things that had been recorded but as the system that governed what could be recorded."[15]

The Archives of American Art (AAA) of the Smithsonian Institution gathers many types of materials: the diaries, correspondence, and photographs of artists and collectors, and microfilm copies of the archival files of museums nationwide. These collections have made possible the enormous expansion of scholarship in American art that has taken place since the mid-1950s, when the AAA was founded. Throughout the latter decades of the twentieth century, the bureau added to its acquisitions program new categories that correspond to developing interests in the art world; one such area, for example, is Latino art.

The curator of manuscripts at the archives, Elizabeth S. Kirwin, points out that although the collecting policy to a degree is determined by reacting to scholarly pursuits, it also operates dynamically by anticipating future needs. In the 1960s the AAA gathered many papers relating to art during the New Deal era – which subsequently helped to spawn a host of dissertations on subjects in this field in the 1970s and 1980s. Thus the AAA tries to respond to current interests, but also anticipates the future by opening new areas. At the present time the AAA is actively pursuing records in the crafts field, even though currently there is little request for such resources. This initiative was due to Lynda R. Hartigan, formerly chief curator at the Smithsonian American Art Museum, whose own research and drive have led to extending resources at the AAA in the fields of crafts and folk art. From the standpoint of collectors, archival papers are easier to acquire when the need is low. Kirwin quotes as the basis of her collection philosophy: "If you build it, they will come!"

Like other record-keeping professions, museum archivists for some years have applied techniques using electronic media to various aspects of their work. Some institutions have placed guides to their archival files online, where they can be conveniently accessed by researchers. Michigan State University, for example, cites online the contents of its repository of Archives and Historical Collections, offering an inventory, collection summary, and identification of individual files with the name of the creator, dates, and quantity of information received therein. Combining traditional archival principles with new technical practices opens possibilities for reaching more researchers, nationally and internationally, "for the representation of knowledge and the management of information relating to the world's cultural heritage," according to *Archives and Museum Informatics*, a periodical that supports digitization.[16]

The ultimate project of online archival practice is to make the entire contents of a collection available in a digital version. Such is the recent achievement of the AAA: all of its 167 reels of the Downtown Gallery records can now be accessed on the website of the archives, comprising "nearly 200,000 digital images of correspondence, artists' files, business records, printed material and photographs documenting the gallery's role in contemporary American art."[17] Requiring three years to complete and the support of a grant from the Henry Luce Foundation, Inc., the Downtown Gallery online project is the first of its kind for the AAA.

Using Museum Archives

We are privileged to have throughout the United States public libraries that are open to all. Visitors from around the world marvel at the Library of Congress in Washington, where anyone can walk in, apply for an identification card, and use the incredible treasures of resources. Archival holdings of unique items that may be of great historical or monetary value, however, necessarily require procedures more complex than the familiar ease of retrieving books in a library. The security of the collections and their preservation determine that rules be followed regarding their access and use.

Scholars should consider a couple of caveats before planning to research in a specific institution. Some museum archives are not open to researchers outside the museum. The reason may be that institutional records have not been centrally gathered and properly arranged to make them accessible (as noted above, not an uncommon situation), or there may be no staff person to assist in locating materials. Some private institutions put their archives off-limits to scholars for their own reasons; they are not required to permit research within their documents. In addition, even where archives are open to outsiders, restrictions may exist regarding access to certain papers or files – perhaps for legal reasons, to honor the request of a donor, or to protect the privacy of a living person. To avoid disappointment and wasted time, scholars should determine – before making long-distance trips or defining a research project dependent upon particular archival sources – if, indeed, the materials they want to consult are readily available.

Researchers requesting to use archival records are customarily asked to identify themselves, their institution, and their project. Personal belongings such as purses, briefcases, and coats must be stowed in checkrooms because only paper and pencils (not pens), laptops, and pertinent research notes are permitted in the study area. In some archives pencils and paper are provided by the institution to further limit the introduction of excessive materials on research tables. Obviously, such measures are meant to prevent theft or accidental damage. A private institution, such as the New York Historical Society, may require the payment of a fee to use its archives.

Preservation of materials, especially fragile and old items, requires that readers take special care in perusal so that all items studied will remain intact for others in the future. Only one file folder at a time should be open, and the order of papers should be maintained as found. When handling delicate papers or photographs, researchers may be asked to wear white cotton gloves, which are provided.

Scholars should feel free to ask questions and to explain the nature of their projects to the archivists, for it is not always possible to tell from written descriptions of the collections where certain papers may be located. As part of their professional responsibilities, archivists are equipped to help researchers; they can be invaluable allies in making fruitful use of time. Because archival materials are relatively unpredictable in terms of what they may include, scholars had best not proceed with foregone conclusions but, instead, keep an open mind in order to use creatively documentary items that may reshape a project.

As is true of all research but especially in archival studies, it is important to keep an accurate record of all materials used. Note the complete location in terms of the archival group, series, box number, and folder number, if that is provided. When afterwards doing the obligatory checking of quotations to be used in a publication, it is much more trouble to retrace steps in archival papers than is the case for quotations from published sources.

After the research and writing of an article or book manuscript is completed and publication is assured, scholars must request permission to use quoted sources. The complete archival location of each reference (which was carefully noted) must be supplied. In some cases, it may be necessary to ask the permission of the owner or writer of certain papers, or the writer's estate. It is prudent to be aware of any such restrictions while researching. Generally speaking, the use of public archives, such as the National Archives in Washington and the presidential libraries, does not require permission.

Going back to original sources endows a research paper with an authenticity that can come in no other way. Results are well worth the time and effort that are required. And the special reward for you as an archival researcher will be the sense of presence that comes from holding in your hands the original documents that represent history in the making.

Questions for Discussion

1   What is an archive? How do archives aid in decision-making processes, from rehangs of the permanent collection to cataloguing and beyond? How do they guide institutional identity? What is the relationship between archives and civic identity?
2   Compare the different attitudes toward archives in France and the United States. Why do some museums still not make their archives accessible? What can be done to change this? What are the repercussions of inaccessibility for institutions, for scholars, and for visitors?
3   How and why is a museum archive different from a library? How are the two organized? What kinds of materials can be found in museum archives? Why is it helpful to know some of the background of a museum before using its archives? How can an archivist help users in their research?
4   Write a job description for an archivist. What qualities should she or he possess? What kind of influence might she or he have in the museum?
5   Why did the Andy Warhol Museum make an exhibit of its archives? Why do some visitors have a stronger reaction to these archives than to the displays of visual art? How might this precedent change the way we conceptualize archives in general?
6   How is archival research important to new museum theory? If you were to spend a month in the archives of Monticello (chapter 4), EMP (chapter 5), the SANG (chapter 7), or the Heard (chapter 8), what questions would you ask and what materials would you seek out? What information might be buried there that would further illuminate the institution?

Notes

1   For further historical background, see E. Posner. (1984). "The European Tradition." In M. F. Daniels and T. Walch. (eds.). *A Modern Archives Reader: Basic Readings on Archival Theory and Practice*. Washington, DC: National Archives and Record Service, 1–14. See also R. Berner. (1983). *Archival Theory and Practice in the United States: A Historical Analysis*. Seattle and London: University of Washington Press.
2   For information about the Archives Nationales and other repositories in Paris with materials that relate to American art, see S. Grant. (1997). *Paris: A Guide to Archival Sources for American Art History*. Washington, DC: Archives of American Art, Smithsonian Institution.
3   O. L. Burnette, Jr. (1969). *Beneath the Footnote*. Madison: Madison State Historical Society of Wisconsin, p. 7. The author relates the development of early federal archives and the founding of the National Archives, pp. 3–20.
4   Moore's files pertaining to these data and other useful materials are accessible in the American Art/Portrait Gallery Library of the Smithsonian Institution.

5   Minutes of the Meeting of the Commission of Fine Arts, September 15, 1939. Fine Arts Commission. microfilm roll no. 7, National Archives, Washington, DC.

6   L. M. Fink. (1983). "An Introduction to the Collection and Research Resources of the National Museum of American Art." In *Descriptive Catalogue of Painting and Sculpture in the National Museum of American Art*. Boston: G. K. Hall, ix–xii.

7   McEntee diary, April 2, 1877. Archives of American Art, Smithsonian Institution.

8   A. Cooper and M.-L. Liu. (1991). "Salvaging the Past." *Museum News*, 50–2, p. 50.

9   J. Smith. (1996). "The Andy Warhol Museum." *Museum Archivist*, 10: 2, 7–8. (Reprinted from *Carnegie Magazine*, January/February, 1996, 63: 1.)

10 S. Vowell. (1993). "Reading a Poker Face: Books on Andy Warhol. The Andy Warhol Museum Archives." *Archives of American Art Journal*, 33: 4, 24–32, p. 32.

11 *Draft Guidelines for Museum Archives*. (1979). Washington, DC: Archives of American Art, Smithsonian Institution. Kathleen Hartt discusses the importance of the events. See K. Hart. (1988). "An Agenda for Museum Archives: The Belmont Conference and Beyond." *Museum Archivist, Newsletter of the Museum Archives Roundtable*, 2: 2, 1–3, p. 2.

12 W. A. Deiss. (1984). *Museum Archives: An Introduction*. Chicago: Society of American Archivists.

13 National Historical and Records Commission. (1988). *Federal Funding for Museum Archives Development Programs*. Washington, DC: National Archives and Records Administration, p. 8.

14 A. Bain. (1992). "Documenting Museums as Institutions and as Purveyors of Culture: Records, Papers, and Special Collections." *Museum Archivist*, 6: 2, 14–21, p. 15.

15 L. Barkan. (1999). *Unearthing the Past: Archaeology and Aesthetics in the Making of Renaissance Culture*. New Haven, CT, and London: Yale University Press, p. xxiii.

16 *Archives and Museum Informatics: Cultural Heritage Informatics Quarterly*, from the periodical's mission statement, which first appeared in (1997) 11: 1, n.p. See also K. Barata. (comp.). (1997). "Bibliography of Electronic Records Research to May of 1997." *Cultural Heritage Informatics Quarterly*, 11: 1, 323–46.

17 *Primary Source, The Newsletter of the Archives of American Art, Smithsonian Institution*. (2002). n.p. These records are available at www.aaa.si.edu/findaids/downgall/downgall.html.

BIBLIOGRAPHY

Abt, Jeffrey. (2001). *A Museum on the Verge: A Socioeconomic History of the Detroit Institute of the Arts*. Detroit: Wayne State University Press.

Adorno, Theodor W. (1967). "Valéry, Proust, Museum." In *Prisms*. Samuel and Shierry Weber. (trans.). Cambridge, MA: MIT Press, 173–86.

Alexander, Victoria D. (1996). *Museums and Money: The Impact of Funding on Exhibitions, Scholarship, and Management*. Bloomington: Indiana University Press.

Altshuler, Bruce. (1994). *The Avant-Garde in Exhibitions: New Art in the 20th Century*. New York: Harry N. Abrams.

"America's Museums." (1999). Special issue of *Daedalus*, 128: 3.

Ames, Kenneth, Barbara Franco, and L. Thomas Frye. (eds.). (1997). *Ideas and Images: Developing Interpretive History Exhibits*. Walnut Creek, CA, London, and New Delhi: Altamira Press.

Ames, Michael M. (1986). *Museums, the Public, and Anthropology: A Study in the Anthropology of Anthropology*. Vancouver: University of British Columbia Press.

—— (1992). *Cannibal Tours and Glass Boxes: The Anthropology of Museums*. Vancouver: University of British Columbia Press.

Anderson, Gail. (2004). *Reinventing the Museum: Historical and Contemporary Perspectives on the Paradigm Shift*. Walnut Creek, CA, London, and New Delhi: Altamira Press.

Ardouin, Claude Daniel. (ed.). (1997). *Museums and Archaeology in West Africa*. Washington, DC, and Oxford: Smithsonian Institution Press.

Arnold, John, Kate Davies, and Simon Ditchfield. (eds.). (1998). *History and Heritage: Consuming the Past in Contemporary Culture*. Dorset: Donhead.

Asma, Stephen P. (2001). *Stuffed Animals and Pickled Heads: The Culture and Evolution of Natural History Museums*. Oxford and New York: Oxford University Press.

Ault, Julie. (ed.). (2002). *Alternative Art New York, 1965–1985*. Minneapolis and London: University of Minnesota Press in association with the Drawing Center, New York. A Cultural Politics Book for the Social Text Collective.

Bal, Mieke. (1992). "Telling, Showing, Showing off." *Critical Inquiry*, 18, 556–94.

—— (1996). *Double Exposures: The Subject of Cultural Analysis*. London and New York: Routledge.

Bann, Stephen. (1984). *The Clothing of Clio: A Study of the Representation of History in Nineteenth-Century Britain and France*. Cambridge: Cambridge University Press.

—— (1998). "Art History and Museums." In Mark Cheetham, Michael Ann Holly, and Keith Moxey. (eds.). *The Subjects of Art History: Historical Objects in Contemporary Perspective*. Cambridge and New York: Cambridge University Press, 230–49.

Banner-Haley, Charles Pete. (1999). "The Necessity of Remembrance: A Review of the Museum of African American History." *American Quarterly*, 51: 2, 420–5.

Barker, Emma. (ed.). (1999). *Contemporary Cultures of Display*. New Haven, CT, and London: Yale University Press and Open University. Art and its Histories series.

Barkan, Elazar and Ronald Bush. (eds.). (2002). *Claiming the Stones/Naming the Bones: Cultural Property and the Negotiation of National and Ethnic Identity*. Los Angeles: Getty Research Institute. Issues and Debates series.

Barringer, Tim and Tom Flynn. (eds.). (1998). *Colonization and the Object: Empire, Material Culture, and the Museum*. London and New York: Routledge. Museum Meanings series.

Baudrillard, Jean. (1983). *Simulations*. New York: Semiotext.

Bazin, Germain. (1967). *The Museum Age*. Jane van Nuis Cahill. (trans.). New York: Universe Books.

Bearman, David and Jennifer Trant. (eds.). (1997). *Museums and the Web 97: Selected Papers*. Pittsburgh, PA: Archives and Museum Informatics.

—— (2001). *Museums and the Web 2001: Selected Papers from an International Conference*. Pittsburgh, PA: Archives and Museum Informatics.

Becker, Carol, James Clifford, Henry Louis Gates, Jr, et al. (1992). *Different Voices: A Social, Cultural, and Historical Framework for Change in the American Art Museum*. Marcia Tucker. (ed.). New York: Association of Art Museum Directors.

Belk, Russell. (1995). *Collecting in a Consumer Society*. London and New York: Routledge.

Benjamin, Walter. (1968). *Illuminations*. Harry Zohn. (trans.). Hannah Arendt. (ed.). New York: Schocken Books.

—— (1982). "Edward Fuchs: Collector and Historian." In Andrew Arato and Eike Gebhardt. (eds.). *The Essential Frankfurt School Reader*. New York: Continuum, 225–53, 356–62.

Bennett, Tony. (1995). *The Birth of the Museum: History, Theory, Politics*. London and New York: Routledge.

—— (1998). *Culture: A Reformer's Science*. London and Thousand Oaks, CA: Sage.

Berger, John. (1972). *Ways of Seeing*. London: BBC and Penguin.

Berger, Maurice. (ed.). (2001). *Fred Wilson: Objects and Installations, 1979–2000* (ex. cat. Center for Art and Visual Culture, University of Maryland, Baltimore County).

Berlo, Janet. (ed.). (1992). *The Early Years of Native American Art History: The Politics of Scholarship and Collecting*. Seattle: University of Washington Press; Vancouver: University of British Columbia Press.

——, Ruth B. Phillips, Carol Duncan, et al. (1995). "The Problematics of Collecting and Display." *Art Bulletin*, 77: 1 and 2, 6–24, 166–85.

Black, Barbara J. (2000). *On Exhibit: Victorians and their Museums*. Charlottesville, VA: University of Virginia Press.

Blake, Nayland, Lawrence Rinder, and Amy Scholder. (eds.). (1995). *In a Different Light: Visual Culture, Sexual Identity, Queer Practice*. San Francisco: City Lights.

309

Blatti, Jo. (ed.). (1987). *Past Meets Present: Essays about Historic Interpretation and Public Audiences*. Washington, DC, and London: Smithsonian Institution Press.

Boswell, David and Jessica Evans. (eds.). (1999). *Representing the Nation, A Reader: Histories, Heritage, and Museums*. London and New York: Routledge in association with the Open University.

Bourdieu, Pierre and Alain Darbel. (1991). *The Love of Art: European Art Museums and their Public*. Caroline Beattie and Nick Merriman. (trans.). Cambridge: Polity.

Boylan, Patrick J. (ed.). (1992). *Museums 2000: Politics, People, Professionals and Profit*. London: Heritage-Care-Preservation-Management Programme, Museums Association, in association with Routledge.

Bray, Tamara L. and Thomas W. Killion. (1994). *Reckoning with the Dead: The Larson Bay Repatriation and the Smithsonian Institution*. Washington, DC: Smithsonian Institution Press.

Brenson, Michael. (1998). "The Curator's Moment." *Art Journal*, 57: 4, 16–27.

Brigham, David. (1995). *Public Culture in the Early Republic: Peale's Museum and its Audience*. Washington, DC, and London: Smithsonian Institution Press.

Brydon, Anne. (1998). "Out of Step: Toronto's Bata Shoe Museum." *American Quarterly*, 50: 4, 809–30.

Cameron, Duncan. (1972). "The Museum: A Temple or the Forum." *Journal of World History*, 14: 1, 189–202.

Carbonell, Bettina Messias. (ed.). (2004). *Museum Studies: An Anthology of Contexts*. Malden, MA, and Oxford: Blackwell.

Carrier, David. (2001). "Art Museums, Old Paintings, and Our Knowledge of the Past." *History and Theory*, 40, 170–89.

Childs, Elizabeth. (ed.). (1997). *Suspended License: Censorship and the Visual Arts*. Seattle: University of Washington Press.

Clarke-Hazlett, Christopher. (1999). "Of the People." *American Quarterly*, 51: 2, 426–36.

Clavir, Miriam. (2002). *Preserving What is Valued: Museums and First Nations*. Vancouver: University of British Columbia Press.

Clifford, James. (1988). *The Predicament of Culture: Twentieth-Century Ethnography, Literature, and Art*. Cambridge, MA: Harvard University Press.

Conn, Steve. (1998). *Museums and American Intellectual Life, 1876–1926*. Chicago and London: University of Chicago Press.

Cooke, Lynne and Peter Wollen. (eds.). (1995). *Visual Display: Culture Beyond Appearances*. New York: New Press. Dia Center for the Arts Discussions in Contemporary Culture series.

Coombes, Annie E. (1994). *Reinventing Africa: Museums, Material Culture, and Popular Imagination in Late Victorian and Edwardian England*. New Haven, CT, and London: Yale University Press.

—— (1998). "Museums and the Formation of National and Cultural Identities." *Oxford Art Journal*, 11, 57–68.

Corrin, Lisa G. (ed.). (1994). *Mining the Museum: An Installation by Fred Wilson* (ex. cat. Contemporary, Baltimore and Maryland Historical Society in association with New Press).

Corson, Miguel Angel. (ed.). (1999). *Mortality Immortality? The Legacy of 20th-Century Art*. Los Angeles: Getty Conservation Institute.

Coxall, Helen. (1999). "Re-Presenting Marginalized Groups in Museums: The Computer's 'Second Nature?'" In Cutting Edge: The Women's Research Group (ed.). *Desire by Design: Body, Territories and New Technologies*. London and New York: I. B. Taurus, 123–38.

Crane, Susan A. (ed.). (2000). *Museums and Memory*. Stanford, CA: Stanford University Press.

Crimp, Douglas. (1993). *On the Museum's Ruins*. Cambridge, MA, and London: MIT Press.

Crow, Thomas E. (1985). *Painters and Public Life in Eighteenth-Century Paris*. New Haven, CT, and London: Yale University Press.

Cuno, James. (ed.). (2004). *Whose Muse? Art Museums and the Public Trust*. Princeton, NJ, and Oxford: Princeton University Press in association with Harvard University Art Museums.

——, Michael Fitzgerald, Michael R. Leaman, et al. (1997). "Money, Power, and the History of Art." *Art Bulletin*, 79: 1, 6–27.

Dana, John Cotton. (1999). *The New Museum: Selected Writings of John Cotton Dana*. Newark and Washington: Newark Museum and American Association of Museums.

Davalos, Karen Mary. (2001). *Exhibiting Mestizaje: Mexican (American) Museums in the Diaspora*. Albuquerque: University of New Mexico Press.

Davis, Douglas. (1990). *The Museum Transformed: Design and Culture in the Post-Pompidou Age*. New York: Abbeville Press.

Davis, Peter. (1999). *Ecomuseums: A Sense of Place*. London and New York: Leicester University Press.

Debord, Guy. (1994). *The Society of the Spectacle*. Donald Nicholson-Smith. (trans.). New York: Zone Books.

Deepwell, Katy. (1995). *New Feminist Art Criticism: Critical Strategies*. Manchester: Manchester University Press.

Delson, Susan. (2002). "Wiring into a Changing Climate: Museums and Digital Art." *Museum News*, 81: 2, 51–5, 63–4.

Di Leonardo, Michaela. (2000). *Exotics at Home: Anthropologies, Others, American Modernity*. Chicago and London: University of Chicago Press.

Dillworth, Leah. (ed.). (2003). *Acts of Possession: Collecting in America*. New Brunswick, NJ, and London: Rutgers University Press.

Dubin, Margaret. (2002). *Native America Collected: The Culture of an Art World*. Albuquerque: University of New Mexico Press

Dubin, Steven C. (1999). *Displays of Power: Memory and Amnesia in the American Museum*. New York and London: New York University Press.

Duncan, Carol. (1995). *Civilizing Rituals: Inside Public Art Museums*. London and New York: Routledge.

—— and Alan Wallach. (1980). "The Universal Survey Museum." *Art History*, 3: 4, 448–69.

Duro, Paul. (ed.). (1996). *The Rhetoric of the Frame: Essays on the Boundaries of the Artwork*. Cambridge: Cambridge University Press.

Düttman, Alexander García, Werner Hamacher, John G. Hanhardt, et al. (1995). *The End(s) of the Museum* (ex. cat. Fundació Antoni Tàpies, Barcelona).

Dziewior, Yilmaz. (ed.). (2003). *Andrea Fraser Works: 1984 to 2003* (ex. cat. Kunstverein in Hamburg).

Edson, Gary. (ed.). (1997). *Museum Ethics*. London: Routledge.

Eichstedt, Jennifer L. and Stephen Small. (2002). *Representations of Slavery, Race and Ideology in Southern Plantation Museums*. Washington, DC, and London: Smithsonian Institution Press, 2002.

Einreinhofer, Nancy. (1997). *The American Art Museum: Elitism and Democracy*. London: Leicester University Press. Contemporary Issues in Museum Culture series.

Elderfield, John. (ed.). (1998). *Imagining the Future of the Museum of Modern Art* (ex. cat. Museum of Modern Art, New York).

Elsner, John and Roger Cardinal. (eds.). (1994). *The Cultures of Collecting*. Cambridge, MA: Harvard University Press.

Erikson, Patricia Pierce. (2002). *Voices of a Thousand People: The Makah Cultural and Research Center*. Lincoln, NE: University of Nebraska Press.

Erwitt, Elliott. (1999). *Museum Watching*. London: Phaidon.

Falk, John and Lynn D. Dierking. (2000). *Learning from Museums: Visitor Experiences and the Making of Meaning*. Walnut Creek, CA: Alta Mira Press.

Fienup-Riordan, Ann. (ed.). (2005). *Akluit, Ciuliamta Things of our Ancestors: Yup'ik Elders Explore the Jaconsen Collection at the Ethnologisches Museum Berlin*. Marie Meade. (trans.). Seattle and London: University of Washington Press in association with Calista Elders Council, Bethel, Alaska.

Findlen, Paula. (1994). *Possessing Nature: Museums, Collecting, and Scientific Culture in Early Modern Italy*. Berkeley, CA: University of California Press.

Fisher, Philip. (1991). *Making and Effacing Art: Modern American Art in a Culture of Museums*. New York: Oxford University Press.

Flood, Finbarr Barry. (2002). "Between Cult and Culture: Bamiyan, Islamic Iconoclasm, and the Museum." *Art Bulletin*, 84: 4, 641–59.

Foucault, Michel. (1970). *The Order of Things: An Archaeology of the Human Sciences*. New York: Pantheon.

—— (1972). *The Archaeology of Knowledge and the Discourse on Language*. A. M. Sheridan-Smith. (trans.). New York: Pantheon.

—— (1973). *The Birth of the Clinic: An Archaeology of Medical Perception*. A. M. Sheridan-Smith. (trans.). New York: Pantheon.

—— (1977). *Discipline and Punish: The Birth of the Prison*. Alan Sheridan. (trans.). New York: Pantheon

Fusco, Coco. (1994). "The Other History of Intercultural Performance." *Drama Review*, 38: 1, 143–67.

Gardiner, Howard. (1985). *Frames of Mind: The Theories of Multiple Intelligences*. London: Paladin.

Gaskell, Ivan. (2000). *Vermeer's Wager: Speculations on Art History, Theory and Art Museums*. London: Reaktion.

Giebelhausen, Michaela. (ed.). (2003). *The Architecture of the Museum: Symbolic Structures, Urban Contexts*. Manchester and New York: Manchester University Press. Critical Perspectives in Art History series.

Glaser, Jane and Artemis A. Zenetou. (eds.). (1994). *Gender Perspectives: Essays on Women in Museums*. Washington, DC, and London: Smithsonian Institution Press.

Gombrich, Ernst. (1979). "The Museum: Past, Present and Future." In *Ideals and Idols: Essays on Values in History and in Art*. Oxford: Phaidon, 189–204.

Goodman, Nelson. (1983). "The End of the Museum?" *New Criterion*, 2: 2, 9–14.

Gosden, Chris and Chantal Knowles. (2001). *Collecting Colonialism: Material Culture and Colonial Change*. Oxford and New York: Berg.

Grasscamp, Walter, Molly Nesbit, and Jon Bird. (2004). *Hans Haacke*. London and New York: Phaidon.

Greenberg, Reesa, Bruce W. Ferguson, and Sandy Nairne. (eds.). (1996). *Thinking About Exhibitions*. London and New York: Routledge.

Greenfield, Jeanette. (1996). *The Return of Cultural Treasures*. Cambridge and New York: Cambridge University Press.

Grewal, Inderpal. (1999). "Constructing National Subjects: The British Museum and its Guidebooks." In Lisa Bloom (ed.). *With Other Eyes: Looking at Race and Gender in Visual Culture*. Minneapolis and London: University of Minnesota Press, 44–57.

Hallam, Elizabeth and Brian V. Street. (eds.). (2000). *Cultural Encounters: Representing Otherness*. London and New York: Routledge. Sussex Studies in Culture and Communication series.

Handler, Richard and Eric Gable. (1997). *The New History in an Old Museum: Creating the Past at Colonial Williamsburg*. Durham, NC, and London: Duke University Press.

Harris, Neil. (1990). *Cultural Excursions: Marketing Appetites and Cultural Tastes in Modern America*. Chicago and London: University of Chicago Press.

——, Wim De Wit, James Gilbert, and Robert Rydell. (1993). *Grand Illusions: Chicago's World's Fair of 1893* (ex. cat. Chicago Historical Society).

Haxthausen, Charles. (ed.). (1999). *The Two Art Histories: The Museum and the University*. Williamstown, MA: Sterling and Francine Clark Art Institute; New Haven, CT: Yale University Press.

Heffernan, Ildiko. (1987). "The Campus Museum Today." *Museum News* (June), 26–35.

Hein, George E. (1998). *Learning in the Museum*. Routledge: London and New York. Museum Meanings series.

Hein, Hilde S. (2000). *The Museum in Transition: A Philosophical Perspective*. Washington, DC, and London: Smithsonian Institution Press.

Henderson, Amy and Adrienne Kaeppler. (eds.). (1997). *Exhibiting Dilemmas: Issues of Representation at the Smithsonian*. Washington, DC, and London: Smithsonian Institution Press.

Henderson, Justin. (1998). *Museum Architecture*. Gloucester, MA: Rockport.

Hirsch, Joanne S. and Lois H. Silverman. (eds.). (2000). *Transforming Practice: Selections from the "Journal of Museum Education" 1992–1999*. Washington, DC: Museum Education Roundtable.

Holo, Selma. (1999). *Beyond the Prado: Museums and Identity in Democratic Spain*. Washington, DC, and London: Smithsonian Institution Press.

Holt, Elizabeth Gilmore. (1979). *The Triumph of Art for the Public, 1785–1848: The Emerging Role of Exhibitions and Critics*. Princeton, NJ: Princeton University Press.

Hooper-Greenhill, Eilean. (1992). *Museums and the Shaping of Knowledge*. London and New York: Routledge.

—— (ed.). (1994a). *The Educational Role of the Museum*. London and New York: Routledge. Leicester Readers in Museum Studies series.

—— (1994b). *Museums and their Visitors*. London and New York: Routledge.

—— (ed.). (1995). *Museum, Media, Message*. London and New York. Routledge. New Visions, New Approaches series.

—— (ed.). (1997). *Cultural Diversity: Developing Museum Audiences in Britain*. London: Leicester University Press. Contemporary Issues in Museum Culture series.

—— (2001). *Museums and the Interpretation of Visual Culture*. London and New York: Routledge. Museum Meanings series.

Hornstein, Shelly and Florence Jacobowitz. (eds.). (2003). *Image and Remembrance: Representation and the Holocaust*. Bloomington and Indianapolis: Indiana University Press.

Hoving, Thomas. (1975). *The Chase, the Capture: Collecting at the Metropolitan*. New York: Metropolitan Museum of Art.

—— (1994). *Making the Mummies Dance: Inside the Metropolitan Museum of Art*. New York: Touchstone.

Hung, Wu. (2001). "Reinventing Exhibition Spaces in China." *Museum International*, 53: 3, 19–25.

Hutchens, James W. and Marianne Stevens Suggs. (eds.). (1997). *Art Education: Content and Practice in a Postmodern Era*. Renton, VA: National Art Education Association.

Huyssen, Andreas. (1995). *Twilight Memories: Marking Time in a Culture of Amnesia*. London and New York: Routledge.

Hyde, Sarah. (1997). *Exhibiting Gender*. Manchester: Manchester University Press.

Impey, Oliver R. and Arthur MacGregor. (eds.). (1985). *The Origin of Museums: The Cabinet of Curiosities in Sixteenth- and Seventeenth-Century Europe*. Oxford: Clarendon Press.

Jacknis, Ira. (2002). *The Storage Box of Tradition: Kwakiutl Art, Anthropologists, and Museums, 1881–1981*. Washington, DC: Smithsonian Institution Press.

Jones, Mark. (ed.). (1992). *Why Fakes Matter: Essays on Problems of Authenticity*. London: British Museum Press.

Jones-Garmil, Katherine. (ed.). (1997). *The Wired Museum: Emerging Technology and Changing Paradigms*. Washington, DC: American Association of Museums.

Kammen, Michael G. (1991). *Mystic Chords of Memory: The Transformation of Tradition in American Culture*. New York: Knopf.

Kaplan, Flora E. S. (ed.). (1994). *Museums and the Making of "Ourselves": The Role of Objects in National Identity*. London: Leicester University Press.

Karp, Ivan and Steven D. Lavine. (eds.). (1991). *Exhibiting Cultures: The Poetics and Politics of Museum Displays*. Washington, DC: Smithsonian Institution Press.

Karp, Ivan, Christine Mullen Kreamer, and Steven D. Lavine. (eds.). (1992). *Museums and Communities: The Politics of Public Culture*. Washington, DC: Smithsonian Institution Press.

Kingery, David. (ed.). (1996). *Learning from Things: Method and Theory of Material Culture Studies*. Washington, DC, and London: Smithsonian Institution Press.

Kirshenblatt-Gimblett, Barbara. (1998). *Destination Culture: Tourism, Museums, and Heritage*. Berkeley, CA: University of California Press.

Kleeblatt, Norman L. (ed.). (2002). *Mirroring Evil: Nazi Imagery/Recent Art* (ex. cat. Jewish Museum, New York, in association with Rutgers University Press).

Knell, Simon J. (2004). *Museums and the Future of Collecting*. Aldershot and Brookfield, VT: Ashgate.

Köb, Edelbert. (2000). *Museum Architecture: Texts and Projects by Artists*. Cologne: Walter König.

Krech III, Shepard and Barbara A. Hail. (eds.). (1999). *Collecting Native America, 1870–1960*. Washington, DC: Smithsonian Institution Press.

Kreps, Christina F. (2003). *Liberating Culture: Cross-Cultural Perspectives on Museums, Curation and Heritage Preservation*. London and New York: Routledge. Museum Meanings series.

Kurin, Richard. (1997). *Reflections of a Culture Broker: A View from the Smithsonian*. Washington, DC, and London: Smithsonian Institution Press.

Lafranchi, Guy and Daniel Egger. (2001). *Prisoners of Museum*. Vienna and New York: Springer. RIEAeuropa Concept series.

Layton, Robert, Peter Stone, and Julian Thomas. (eds.). (2001). *Destruction and Conservation of Cultural Property*. London and New York: Routledge.

Leinhardt, Gaea and Karen Knutson. (2004). *Listening in on Museum Conversations*. Walnut Creek, CA, London, and New Delhi: Altamira Press.

Linenthal, Edward T. (2001). *Preserving Memory: The Struggle to Create America's Holocaust Museum*. New York: Columbia University Press.

—— and Tom Engelhardt. (1996). *History Wars: The Enola Gay and Other Battles for the American Past*. New York: Henry Holt.

Lowenthal, David. (1985). *The Past is a Foreign Country*. Cambridge and New York: Cambridge University Press.

—— (1998). *Possessed by the Past: The Heritage Crusade and the Spoils of History*. Cambridge and New York: Cambridge University Press.

Lubar, Steven and W. David Kingery. (eds.). (1993). *History from Things: Essays on Material Culture*. Washington, DC: Smithsonian Institution Press.

Luke, Timothy. (1992). *Shows of Force: Power, Politics, and Ideology in Art Exhibitions*. Durham, NC, and London: Duke University Press.

—— (2002). *Museum Politics: Power Plays at the Exhibition*. Minneapolis and London: University of Minnesota Press.

Lumley, Robert. (ed.). (1988). *The Museum Time Machine: Putting Cultures on Display*. London and New York: Routledge.

MacClancy, Jeremy. (ed.). (1997). *Contesting Art: Art, Politics and Identity in the Modern World*. Oxford and New York: Berg.

Macdonald, Sharon. (ed.). (1998). *The Politics of Display: Museums, Science, Culture*. London and New York: Routledge.

—— and Gordon Fyfe. (eds.). (1996). *Theorizing Museums: Representing Identity and Diversity in a Changing World*. Oxford and Cambridge, MA: Blackwell.

—— and Roger Silverstone. (1990). "Rewriting the Museum's Fictions: Taxonomies, Stories and Readers." *Cultural Studies*, 4: 2, 176–91.

Mack, Gerhard. (1999). *Art Museums into the 21st Century*. Basel: Birkhäuser.

MacLean, Margaret. (ed.). (1993). *Cultural Heritage in Asia and the Pacific*. Los Angeles: Getty Conservation Institute.

Maleuvre, Didier. (1999). *Museum Memories: History, Technology, Art*. Stanford, CA: Stanford University Press.

Malreux, André. (1967). *Museum Without Walls*. Stuart Gilbert and Francis Price. (trans.). Garden City, NY: Doubleday.

Mansfield, Elizabeth. (ed.). (2002). *Art History and its Institutions: Foundations of a Discipline*. London and New York: Routledge.

Martin, Paul. (1999). *Popular Collecting and the Everyday Self: The Reinvention of Museums?* London and New York: Leicester University Press.

Martinez, Katharine and Kenneth L. Ames. (eds.). (1997). *The Material Culture of Gender, the Gender of Material Culture*. Winterthur, DE: Henry Francis du Pont Winterthur Museum; Hanover, NH: University Press of New England.

Malt, Carol. (2004). *Women's Voices in Middle-East Museums: Case Studies in Jordan*. Syracuse, NY: Syracuse University Press. Gender, Culture and Politics in the Middle East series.

Mauriès, Patrick. (2002). *Cabinets of Curiosities*. London: Thames and Hudson.

Maxwell, Anne. (1999). *Colonial Photography and Exhibitions: Representations of the "Native" and the Making of European Identities*. London: Leicester University Press.

McAlister, Melani. (1996). "'The Common Heritage of Mankind': Race, Nation, and Masculinity in the King Tut Exhibit." *Representations*, 54, 80–103.

McClellan, Andrew. (1999). *Inventing the Louvre: Art, Politics and the Origins of the Modern Museum in Eighteenth-Century Paris*. Cambridge: Cambridge University Press.

—— (ed.). (2003). *Art and its Publics: Museum Studies at the Millennium*. Malden, MA, and Oxford: Blackwell.

McClusky, Pamela. (2002). *Art from Africa: Long Steps Never Broke a Back* (ex. cat. Seattle Art Museum in association with Princeton University Press).

McLean, Fiona. (1997). *Marketing the Museum*. London and New York: Routledge.

McShine, Kynaston. (ed.). (1999). *The Museum as Muse: Artists Reflect* (ex. cat. Museum of Modern Art, New York).

McTavish, Lianne. (1998). "Shopping in the Museum? Consumer Spaces and the Redefinition of the Louvre." *Cultural Studies*, 12: 2, 168–92.

Melosh, Barbara. (1989). "Speaking of Women: Museums' Representations of Women's History." In Warren Leon and Roy Rosenzweig. (eds.). *History Museums in the United States: A Critical Assessment*. Champaign, IL: University of Illinois Press, 183–214.

Merriman, Nick. (1991). *Beyond the Glass Case: The Past, the Heritage, and the Public in Britain*. Leicester: Leicester University Press.

Messenger, Phyllis Mauch. (ed.). (1999). *The Ethics of Collecting Cultural Property: Whose Culture? Whose Property?* Albuquerque: University of New Mexico Press.

Mihesuah, Devon A. (ed.). (2000). *Repatriation Reader: Who Owns American Indian Remains?* Lincoln, NE: University of Nebraska Press.

Miles, Roger and Lauro Zavala. (eds.). (1994). *Towards the Museum of the Future: New European Perspectives*. London and New York: Routledge. New Visions, New Approaches series.

Mirzoeff, Nicholas. (ed.). (1998). *The Visual Culture Reader*. New York and London: Routledge.

Mithlo, Nancy Marie. (2003). "Staging the Indian: The Politics of Representation [exhibition review]." *American Anthropologist*, 105: 1, 156–61.

Mitter, Rana. (2000). "Behind the Scenes at the Museum: Nationalism, History and Memory in the Beijing War of Resistance Museum, 1987." *China Quarterly* 161: 1, 279–94.

Montaner, Josep Maria. (1995). *Museums for the New Century*. Barcelona: Editorial Gustavo Gili.

Moore, Kevin. (1997). *Museums and Popular Culture*. London and Washington, DC: Cassell. Contemporary Issues in Museum Culture series.

Muensterberger, Werner. (1993). *Collecting: An Unruly Passion, Psychological Perspectives*. Princeton, NJ: Princeton University Press.

Müller, Klaus. (2002a). "Going Global: Reaching out for the Online Visitor." *Museum News*, 81: 5, 47–53.

—— (2002b). "Museums and Virtuality." *Curator: The Museum Journal*, 45: 1, 21–33.

Nelson, Robert S. (2000). "The Slide Lecture, or the Work of Art History in the Age of Mechanical Reproduction." *Critical Inquiry*, 26: 3, 414–34.

Newhouse, Victoria. (1998). *Towards a New Museum*. New York: Monacelli Press.

O'Doherty, Brian. (1972). *Museums in Crisis*. New York: G. Brazillier.

—— (1976). *Inside the White Cube: The Ideology of the Gallery Space*. Santa Monica: Lapis Press.

Ostrower, Francie. (2002). *Trustees of Culture: Power, Wealth and Status on Elite Art Boards*. Chicago and London: University of Chicago Press.

Patin, Thomas. (1999). *Discipline and Varnish: Rhetoric, Subjectivity, and Counter-Memory in the Museum*. New York and Bern: Peter Lang.

Pearce, Susan M. (ed.). (1991). *Museum Studies in Material Culture*. Leicester: Leicester University Press; Washington, DC: Smithsonian Institution Press.

—— (1992). *Museums, Objects, and Collections: A Cultural Study*. Washington, DC: Smithsonian Institution Press.

—— (ed.). (1994a). *Interpreting Objects and Collections*. London and New York: Routledge. Leicester Readers in Museum Studies series.

—— (ed.). (1994b). *Museums and the Appropriation of Culture*. London and Atlantic Highlands, NJ: Athlone Press.

—— (ed.). (1995a). *Art in Museums*. London and Atlantic Highlands, NJ: Athlone Press.

—— (1995b). *On Collecting: An Investigation into Collecting in the European Tradition*. London and New York: Routledge.

—— (ed.). (1997). *Experiencing Material Culture in the Western World*. London: Leicester University Press. Contemporary Issues in Museum Cultures series.

—— (1998). *Collecting in Contemporary Practice*. London and New Delhi: Sage; Walnut Creek, CA: Alta Mira Press.

—— (ed.). (1999). *Museums and their Development: The European Tradition, 1700–1900*. London: Routledge in association with Thoemmes Press.

—— and Alexandra Bounia. (eds.). (2002). *The Collector's Voice: Critical Readings in the Practice of Collecting*. 4 vols. Aldershot and Burlington, VT: Ashgate.

Peers, Laura and Alison K. Brown. (eds.). (2003). *Museums and Source Communities: A Routledge Reader*. London and New York: Routledge.

Perry, Gill and Colin Cunningham. (eds.). (1999). *Academies, Museums and Canons of Art*. New Haven, CT, and London: Yale University Press and Open University. Art and its Histories series.

Phillips, David. (1997). *Exhibiting Authenticity*. Manchester and New York: Manchester University Press.

Phillips, Ruth and Christopher B. Steiner. (eds.). (1999). *Unpacking Culture: Art and Commodity in Colonial and Postcolonial Worlds*. Berkeley, CA, Los Angeles, and London: University of California Press.

Pointon, Marcia. (ed.). (1994). *Art Apart: Art Institutions and Ideology Across England and North America*. Manchester and New York: Manchester University Press.

Pomian, Krzysztof. (1990). *Collectors and Curiosities: Paris and Venice, 1500–1800*. Cambridge: Polity.

Porter, Gaby. (1990). "Gender Bias: Representations of Work in History Museums." *Continuum*, 3: 1, 70–83.

Preziosi, Donald. (1996). "Collecting/Museums." In Robert S. Nelson and Richard Shiff. (eds.). *Critical Terms for Art History*. Chicago and London: University of Chicago Press, 281–91.

—— (2003). *Brain of the Earth's Body: Art, Museums, and the Phantasms of Modernity*. Minneapolis and London: University of Minnesota Press.

—— and Claire Farago. (eds.). (2004). *Grasping the World: The Idea of the Museum*. Aldershot and Burlington, VT: Ashgate.

Price, Nicholas Stanley, M. Kirby Talley, Jr, and Alessandra Melucco Vaccaro. (eds.). (1999). *Historical and Philosophical Issues in the Conservation of Cultural Heritage*. Los Angeles: Getty Conservation Institute.

Price, Sally. (2001). *Primitive Art in Civilized Places*. Chicago: University of Chicago Press.

Prior, Nick. (2002). *Museums and Modernity: Art Galleries and the Making of Modern Culture*. Oxford: Berg.

Putnam, James. (2001). *Art and Artifact: The Museum as Medium*. New York: Thames and Hudson.

Rectanus, Mark W. (2002). *Culture Incorporated: Museums, Artists, and Corporate Sponsorship*. Minneapolis and London: University of Minnesota Press.

Roberts, Lisa C. (1997). *From Knowledge to Narrative: Educators and the Changing Museum*. Washington, DC, and London: Smithsonian Institution Press.

Roberts, Mary Nooter, Susan Vogel, and Chris Müller. (1994). *Exhibition-ism: Museums and African Art* (ex. cat. Museum for African Art, New York).

Robertson, Bruce and Mark Meadow. (2002). "Microcosms: Objects of Knowledge." *AI and Society*, 14, 223–9.

Robison, Olin, Robert Freeman, and Charles A. Riley II. (eds.). (1994). *The Arts in the World Economy: Public Policy and Private Philanthropy for a Global Cultural Community*. Hanover, NH, and London: University Press of New England. Salzburg Seminar.

Rosenzweig, Roy and David Thelen. (1998). *The Presence of the Past: Popular Uses of History in American Life*. New York: Columbia University Press.

Roth, Michael S. and Charles G. Salas. (eds.). (2001). *Disturbing Remains: Memory, History, and Crisis in the Twentieth Century.* Los Angeles: Getty Research Institute. Issues and Debates series.

Rothfield, Lawrence. (ed.). (2001). *Unsettling "Sensation": Arts-Policy Lessons from the Brooklyn Museum of Art Controversy.* New Brunswick, NJ, and London: Rutgers University Press.

Ryback, Timothy. (1993). "A Reporter at Large: Evidence of Evil." *New Yorker*, 69: 38, 68–81.

Rydell, Robert. (1984). *All the World's a Fair: Visions of Empire at American International Exhibitions, 1876–1916.* Chicago: University of Chicago Press.

——, John E. Findling, and Kimberly D. Pelle. (eds.). (2000). *Fair America: World's Fairs in the United States.* Washington, DC: Smithsonian Institution Press.

Sandberg, Mark B. (2003). *Living Pictures/Missing Persons: Mannequins, Museums, and Modernity.* Princeton, NJ, and Oxford: Princeton University Press.

Sandell, Richard. (ed.). (2002). *Museums, Society, Inequality.* London and New York: Routledge. Museum Meanings series.

Sax, Joseph L. (2001). *Playing Darts with Rembrandt: Public and Private Rights in Cultural Treasures.* Ann Arbor: University Michigan Press.

Schaffner, Ingrid and Matthias Winzen. (eds.). (1998). *Deep Storage: Collecting, Storing and Archiving in Art.* A. Böger. (trans.). Munich and New York: Prestel.

Schneider, Andrea Kupfer. (1998). *Creating the Musée d'Orsay: The Politics of Culture in France.* University Park, PA: Pennsylvania State University Press.

Searing, Helen. (1982). *New American Art Museums* (ex. cat. Whitney Museum of American Art, New York).

Shaw, Wendy M. K. (2003). *Possessors and Possessed: Museums, Archaeology, and the Visualization of History in the Late Ottoman Empire.* Berkeley, CA, and Los Angeles: University of California Press.

Sheehan, James J. (2000). *Museums in the German Art World: From the End of the Old Regime to the Rise of Modernism.* Oxford: Oxford University Press.

Sherman, Daniel J. (1989). *Worthy Monuments: Art Museums and the Politics of Culture in Nineteenth-Century France.* Cambridge, MA, and London: Harvard University Press.

—— and Irit Rogoff. (eds.). (1994). *Museum Culture: Histories, Discourses, Spectacles.* Minneapolis: University of Minnesota Press. Media and Society series 6.

Siegel, Jonah. (2001). *Desire and Excess: The Nineteenth-Century Culture of Art.* Princeton, NJ, and Oxford: Princeton University Press.

Simpson, Elizabeth. (ed.). (1997). *The Spoils of War: The Loss, Reappearance, and Recovery of Cultural Property.* New York: Harry N. Abrams in association with the Bard Graduate Center for Studies in the Decorative Arts.

Simpson, Moira G. (2001). *Making Representations: Museums in the Post-Colonial Era.* London and New York: Routledge.

Singerman, Howard. (1999). *Art Subjects: Making Artists in the American University.* Berkeley, CA, Los Angeles, and London: University of California Press.

Spalding, Julian. (2002). *The Poetic Museum: Reviving Historic Collections.* Munich, London, and New York: Prestel.

319

Staniszewski, Mary Anne. (1998). *The Power of Display: A History of Exhibition Installations at the Museum of Modern Art*. Cambridge, MA, and London: MIT Press.

Steiner, Christopher B. (1994). *African Art in Transit*. Cambridge: Cambridge University Press.

Stewart, Susan. (1984). *On Longing: Narratives of the Miniature, the Gigantic, the Souvenir, the Collection*. Baltimore, MD: Johns Hopkins University Press.

Stocking Jr, George W. (ed.). (1985). *Objects and Others: Essays on Museums and Material Culture*. Madison: University of Wisconsin Press.

Stone, Peter G. and Brian L. Molyneaux. (eds.). (1994). *The Presented Past: Heritage, Museums and Education*. London and New York: Routledge.

Suchy, Sherene. (2004). *Leading with Passion: Change Management in the Twenty-First Century Museum*. Walnut Creek, CA, London, and New Delhi: Altamira Press.

Tamen, Miguel. (2001). *Friends of Interpretable Objects*. Cambridge, MA, and London: Harvard University Press.

Taylor, Brandon. (1999). *Art for the Nation: Exhibitions and the London Public: 1747–2001*. New Brunswick, NJ: Rutgers University Press.

Teather, J. Lynne. (1991). "Museum Studies: Reflecting on Reflective Practice." *Museum Management and Curatorship*, 10: 4, 403–17.

Thomas, Nicholas. (1991). *Entangled Objects: Exchange, Material Culture, and Colonialism in the Pacific*. Cambridge, MA, and London: Harvard University Press.

—— (1999). *Possessions: Indigenous Art/Colonial Culture*. London: Thames and Hudson.

Thomas, Catherine. (ed.). (2002). *The Edge of Everything: Reflections on Curatorial Practice*. Banff: Banff Centre Press.

Thomas, Selma and Ann Mintz. (eds.). (1998). *The Virtual and the Real: Media in the Museum*. Washington, DC: American Association of Museums.

Torgovnick, Marianna. (1990). *Gone Primitive: Savage Intellects, Modern Lives*. Chicago: University of Chicago Press.

Townsend, Melanie Adaire. (ed.). (2003). *Beyond the Box: Diverging Curatorial Practices*. Banff: Banff Centre Press.

Trent, John Whittier. (1997). "The Enola Gay on Display: Hiroshima and American Memory." *Positions: East Asian Cultures Critique*, 5: 3, 863–78.

Vergo, Peter. (1989). *The New Museology*. London: Reaktion.

Vogel, Susan, Arthur Danto, R. M. Gramly, Mary Lou Hultgren, Enid Schildkrout, and Jeanne Zeidler. (1988). *ART/Artifact: African Art in Anthropology Collections* (ex. cat. Center for African Art, New York).

Wallace, Mike. (1996). *Mickey Mouse History and Other Essays on American Memory*. Philadelphia: Temple University Press.

Wallach, Alan. (1998). *Exhibiting Contradiction: Essays on the Art Museum in the United States*. Amhurst: University of Massachusetts Press.

Walsh, Kevin. (1992). *The Representation of the Past: Museums and Heritage in the Postmodern World*. London and New York: Routledge.

Watson, Katharine, Kenneth E. Carpenter, Linda J. Docherty, et al. (1994). *The Legacy of James Bowdoin III*. Brunswick, ME: Bowdoin College Museum of Art.

Weil, Stephen E. (1990). *Rethinking the Museum and other Meditations*. Washington, DC: Smithsonian Institution Press.

—— (1995). *A Cabinet of Curiosities: Inquiries into Museums and their Prospects*. Washington, DC, and London: Smithsonian Institution Press.

—— (1997). *Museums for the New Millennium*. Washington, DC, and London: American Association of Museums and the Center for Museum Studies, Smithsonian Institution.

—— (2000). *Making Museums Matter*. London and Washington, DC: Smithsonian Institution Press.

West, Patricia. (1999). *Domesticating History: The Political Origins of America's House Museums*. Washington, DC, and London: Smithsonian Institution Press.

West, W. Richard, Evan M. Maurer, James D. Nason, et al. (2000). *The Changing Presentation of the American Indian*. Washington, DC, and New York: National Museum of the American Indian, Smithsonian Institution, in association with University of Washington Press.

White, Peter. (ed.). (1996). *Naming a Practice: Curatorial Strategies for the Future*. Banff: Banff Centre Press.

Wilson, Fred. (2003). *Fred Wilson: Speak of Me As I Am* (ex. cat. MIT List Visual Arts Center, Cambridge, MA).

Witcomb, Andrea. (2003). *Re-Imagining the Museum: Beyond the Mausoleum*. London and New York: Routledge. Museum Meanings series.

Wright, Gwendolyn. (ed.). (1996). *The Formation of National Collections of Art and Archaeology*. Washington, DC: National Gallery of Art.

Wu, Chin-tao. (2002). *Privatising Culture: Corporate Art Intervention since the 1980s*. London and New York: Verso.

Wu, Hung. (2000). *Exhibiting Experimental Art in China*. Chicago: David and Alfred Smart Museum of Art, University of Chicago.

Yanni, Carla. (2000). *Nature's Museums: Victorian Science and the Architecture of Display*. Baltimore, MD, and London: Johns Hopkins University Press.

Yoo, David. (1996). "Captivating Memories: Museology, Concentration Camps, and Japanese American History." *American Quarterly*, 48: 4, 80–99.

Young, James E. (2000). *At Memory's Edge: After-Images of the Holocaust in Contemporary Art and Architecture*. New Haven, CT: Yale University Press.

Zolberg, Vera L. (1986). "Tensions of Mission in American Museum Education." In Paul J. Dimaggio. (ed.). *Non-Profit Enterprise in the Arts: Studies in Mission and Constraint*. New York and Oxford: Oxford University Press.

INDEX

Note: References to illustrations are in italic. There may also be textual references on the same page.